Freeway

Allgemeine Ausgabe
Englisch für berufliche Schulen

von
Catherine Küpper
Susanne Neyer
Wolfgang Rosenkranz (Hrsg.)
Graham Tucker

Ernst Klett Verlag
Stuttgart · Leipzig

Freeway Allgemeine Ausgabe

Englisch für berufliche Schulen

Herausgeber: Wolfgang Rosenkranz

Autoren: Catherine Küpper, Susanne Neyer, Wolfgang Rosenkranz, Graham Tucker

Berater: Veit Kibele, Christian Rode, Dagmar Wagner

Werkübersicht:
Schülerbuch, 978-3-12-800041-1
Lehrerhandbuch, mit Lehrer-Service-DVD-ROM und 2 Audio-CDs, 978-3-12-800042-8
Workbook mit 1 Audio-CD, 978-3-12-800043-5
Vokabellernheft, 978-3-12-800044-2
Schülerpaket: Workbook und Vokabellernheft, 978-3-12-800048-0
Freeway Online-Ergänzungen unter www.klett.de/online

1. Auflage 1 8 7 6 5 4 | 20 19 18 17 16

Redaktion: Helen Smyth
Herstellung: Angelika Lindner

Gestaltung: B2 Büro für Gestaltung, Andreas Staiger, Stuttgart
Umschlaggestaltung: ya:design, Roman Triebelhorn, Stuttgart
Illustrationen: Jeonsook Lee, Köln; Andreas Staiger, Susanne Kunz, Stuttgart
Satz: B2 Büro für Gestaltung, Andreas Staiger, Susanne Kunz, Stuttgart
Reproduktion: Meyle + Müller Medien-Management, Pforzheim
Druck: Druckhaus Götz GmbH, Ludwigsburg

Printed in Germany
ISBN 978-3-12-800041-1

9 783128 000411

Vorwort

Das neue *Freeway* deckt die neuesten Lehrpläne und die neuen Prüfungsformate aller Bundesländer ab und führt zielsicher zur Fachhochschulreife-Prüfung an Fach- und Berufsoberschulen, Höheren Berufsfachschulen und Fachschulen. Es orientiert sich an den fremdsprachlichen Kompetenzen des Europäischen Referenzrahmens (Niveau B1/B2).

Die wichtigsten Neuerungen auf einen Blick:
- durchgehend neue Texte und neue Aufgaben
- erweiterter „Practice"-Teil mit interaktiven und produktiven Aufgaben
- durchgehend verstärkte Förderung der kommunikativen Kompetenzen – auch in den Übungen zur Grammatik
- systematische Schulung der verschiedenen Kompetenzen von der ersten Unit an („Training skills – How to ...")
- Einbindung abwechslungsreicher Mediationsaufgaben
- Förderung des eigenverantwortlichen Lernens durch ausführliche deutschsprachige Anleitungen und Übersichten zur Schulung der Kompetenzen im Anhang („Skills files") mit durchgehenden Verweisen im Lehrbuch
- verstärktes interkulturelles Lernen sowie Einbindung der Berufswelt am Beispiel eines Auslandspraktikums
- „Video lounge" u. a. mit Filmen der **BBC Motion Gallery** zur Förderung des Seh-Hör-Verstehens

Bewährtes bleibt erhalten:
- systematischer Aufbau der Units nach dem bewährten Doppelseitenprinzip

Unitteil	Überschrift	Inhalte
A	Getting started	nach einem bildgesteuerten Einstieg erste inhaltliche Auseinandersetzung mit dem Thema
B	Language	systematische Übung der Grammatikschwerpunkte – im *Basic course* die Wiederholung der grundlegenden *tenses*, im *Advanced course* komplexere Formen wie z. B. *passive voice*, *conditional* oder *reported speech*
C	Reading	intensive Textarbeit zur gezielten Vorbereitung auf die schriftliche Abschlussprüfung
D	Practice	handlungsorierentierte interaktive und produktive Aufgaben (u. a. Rollenspiele); Förderung des Hörverständnisses

- flexible Handhabung: Einzelne Unitteile (z. B. „Language") können entfallen oder in die individuelle (häusliche) Arbeit verlagert werden.
- klare grammatikalische Strukturierung und bewährte Grammatik-Progression
- benutzerfreundliche Grammatikübersicht im Anhang
- systematische und intensive Prüfungsvorbereitung durch „Training skills" und eine große Anzahl von „Exam preparation units"

Weitere Bestandteile des Lehrwerks:

Workbook mit Audio-CD und Prüfungsvorbereitung: Übungen zur Grammatik, zur Förderung der Arbeitstechniken *(skills)* und des Hörverstehens (alle Audios des Schülerbuchs sind auf der Audio-CD im Workbook) und zusätzliche Units zur Prüfungsvorbereitung

Vocabulary notebook: abwechslungsreiche Übungen zum thematischen Aufbauwortschatz trainieren alle Vokabeln, die zum erfolgreichen Bestehen der Prüfung notwendig sind.

Lehrerhandbuch mit den Audio-CDs und einem Lehrer-Service-DVD-ROM: u. a. mit Hinweisen zur Differenzierung

Wir wünschen Ihnen viel Spaß und Erfolg bei der Arbeit mit *Freeway – Allgemeine Ausgabe*.

Basic course

Advanced course

Cross-cultural communication

Exam preparation

Anhang

Online-Links unter www.klett.de

800041-0030: der alphabetische Wortschatz zum Schülerbuch (deutsch-englisch) einschließlich Grundwortschatz

800041-0040: die berufsspezifischen Vokabeln zu den Bereichen Wirtschaft, Technik und Sozialwesen

Der jeweilige **Unit Online-Link**: die thematischen Wortfelder im MP3-Format

Verwendete Symbole

A1.1	Hörtexte auf der Schüler-CD im Workbook und den Lehrer-Audio-CDs, inkl. Tracknummer
‹R›	Verweis auf eine Kompetenz, die in der Aufgabe besonders geübt wird: P = Produktion; R = Rezeption; I = Interaktion; M = Mediation.
	Wortschatz-Aufgabe
	Partnerarbeit
	Gruppenarbeit
	weiterführende Aufgabe im Internet bzw. Verweis auf nützliche Stichwörter für eine Internetrecherche
► SF 9	Verweis auf die entsprechenden Fertigkeiten im Anhang; SF = Skills file
► GF 3	Verweis auf die entsprechende Grammatik-Information im Anhang; GF = Grammar file
Video lounge 1	Videos u. a. der **BBC Motion Gallery** auf der Lehrer-Service-DVD-ROM; Aufgaben zur Video lounge im Anhang
Online-Link 800041-0001	Unter www.klett.de/online stehen Zusatzmaterialien zum Download bereit.
Training skills	Lern- und Arbeitstechniken
Facts	Hintergrundinformationen
Language	nützliche Redewendungen
Grammar	kurze Zusammenfassung der wichtigsten Grammatik-Themen

Textquellenverzeichnis **S. 32** people-press.org, Dezember 2008, © (Where do you get most of your national and international news, December 2008) by The Pew Research Center For the People & the Press; **S. 41** Two Caravans by Marina Lewycka, London: Penguin/Fig Tree, 2007, page 242; **S. 41** Slam by Nick Hornby, London: Penguin, 2008, page 92; Bend it like Beckham by Narinder Dhami, Stuttgart: Ernst Klett Verlag, 2003, page 25; **S. 52** www.climatechoices.org.uk; **S. 60**: Cloning Miranda © 1999 by Carol Matas; **S. 63**: Greenpeace Nachrichten 2/09, page 2, "Gen-Soja für Markenmilch", adapted; **S. 70** www.statistik.at, Statistik Austria: Urlaubs- und Geschäftsreisen, Erstellt am 12.2.2009; **S. 107** www.wko.at, EU Commission, EUROSTAT, OECD, Februar 2010; **S. 111** www.marketingcharts.com, © 2010 Experian Information Solutions, Inc. All rights reserved; **S. 115** www.espad.org/unitedkingdom; **S. 123** www.presseanzeiger.de, November 2008, Gamesindustry.com (Newzoo BV); **S. 127** www.guardian.co.uk, Joseph Rowntree Foundation.

Online-Link
800041-0001

Unit 1
Young people in Europe

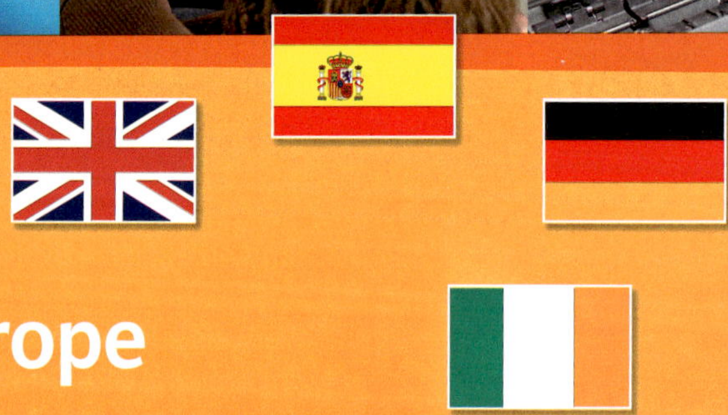

A Getting started: www.thisisme.uk

‹P› Before reading

a) Look at the photos above. What is your first impression of the young people? What do you think they are interested in?

‹R› Understanding the text

b) Read the personal blogs of these young people on page 9. Then match the photos to the blogs.

c) Which of the following statements about the young people are true and which are false? Correct the false statements.

1. The young people are all college students.
2. Sharon's hobby is snowboarding.
3. Sharon earns money at a fitness centre to pay for her own flat.
4. Antonio is studying Information Technology.
5. Antonio often meets his friends.
6. Patrick is currently living in Ireland.
7. Patrick has a part-time job.
8. Isabelle belongs to an environmental organization.
9. Isabelle is a school teacher and teaches social care.

d) Copy the table below into your exercise book. Write down what the young people usually do and what they are currently doing.

What he/she usually does	What he/she is currently doing
Example: Sharon usually …	She is currently …
…	…

http://www.thisisme.uk

A1.1

A Hello! I'm Sharon from Newcastle in England. I'm 17 years old and I live at home with my mum and my younger brother. At the moment I'm doing a National Diploma in sport at Newcastle College. In my free time I love to go snowboarding. That's what I enjoy doing the most. When I'm not studying at college I have a part-time job in a fitness centre. I work there twice a week to help finance my expensive hobby.

B Hello there! I'm Antonio. I'm 18 years old and I live in a small flat in Barcelona in Spain. I want to become a computer technician. That's why I'm attending an IT course at Barcelona College at the moment. It's a two-year course. I have a really interesting part-time job in a computer store just a few minutes from where I live. I work there every day after college so I don't have much time to see my friends.

C Hi there! My name is Patrick from Dublin in Ireland. I'm 19 and I'm currently living and working full-time in Paris, France, where I hope to achieve my dream and become a professional musician. I'm a guy who likes to have fun. I like to go to parties and clubs and just generally chill out with my friends. I'm interested in all styles of music but my favourite type of music is hip-hop.

D Hi! I'm Isabelle. I'm 19 and I'm from Cologne in Germany. I go to college. At the moment I'm studying social care there. I'm also a member of WWF and I do a lot of campaigning work for them. I often visit primary schools and do environmental projects with the children. By the way I have three pet chickens.

(290 words)

‹M› **e)** Sie haben im Internet Isabelles Blog gelesen und erzählen Ihrer Freundin auf Deutsch, was Sie über Isabelle wissen.
► SF 22 Mediation/translation

f) Match the words from the texts above with their definitions.

1. twice (line 8)
2. course (line 13)
3. part-time job (line 14)
4. store (line 14)
5. currently (line 18)
6. achieve (line 19)
7. club (line 21)
8. environmental (line 29)

a) a plan of study which usually ends with an exam
b) work which you do for only some of the day or the week
c) a large shop where you can buy many different types of goods
d) at the present time, at the moment, now
e) two times
f) concerning the air, water and land in or on which people, animals and plants live
g) reach an aim, especially after a lot of work
h) people meet there to dance and talk

‹I›
After reading

g) Interview a partner. Find out the information below about him/her and write it down. Then present your partner to your class. You can use the expressions in the language box for the presentation.

Interview

• name • age • family • home town • interests • likes and dislikes • personality • favourite music • future plans

Language

- I would like to introduce …
- He/She is …
- He/She has …
- He/She comes from …
- He/She lives in …
- In his/her free time …
- He/She likes/enjoys/loves/can't stand …
- He/She plans to …

‹P› **h)** Write your own personal blog for the social networking website, www.thisisme.uk.

B Language

1 College and work ►GF16 Present simple

http://www.newcastle-college.uk/international

Newcastle College

Home | School leavers | Adults and Part-time | International

What you must study on the International Diploma Course:

1. English
2. second language (French or German)
3. History or Geography
4. Science (Biology and Physics)
5. Mathematics
6. Information technology

How we test you: four projects, class presentations, essays (at the end of term), work placements (office, hospital or factory), tests (every 3 months) and six final examinations (at the end of the second year).

After the course: go to university, start a job training programme, get a good job – anywhere in Europe

a) Work in pairs. One of you is a student at Newcastle College who is on the International Diploma Course. The other person uses the prompts below to ask questions. The answers are given in the website.

Example: Which second language – learn?
Student A: Which second language do you learn on the course?
Student B: I learn French on the course.

1. Which science subjects – study?
2. How many projects – carry out?
3. How often – take – tests?
4. When – hand in – essays?
5. Where – do – your work placement?
6. When – sit – final exams?
7. How many exams – do?
8. What – plan to do after the course?
9. What kind of job – want to have later?

b) Now find another partner. He/she uses the prompts in exercise a) to ask questions about the student from Newcastle.

Grammar

Present simple
Example: Polly goes to college by bus.
Bei regelmäßigen oder wiederholten Handlungen

Present continuous
Example: Now Polly is talking to her teacher.
Bei Handlungen, die im Augenblick oder vorübergehend stattfinden

►GF16 Present simple
►GF17 Present continuous

2 In the college

■ Describe what the students are doing in the photos.
►GF17 Present continuous

Example: Tom is reading a newspaper.

Tom

Sue and Dave

Alice and Karen

Sarah

Lisa

3 A work placement

■ Wayne is a student at Newcastle College. At the moment he is doing a work placement at Carrick's, a local factory.

Compare Wayne's normal day at college with what he is doing today. Make complete sentences and use as many of the tense markers in the box below as possible.

Example: Wayne usually goes to college by bus, but today he's driving his mum's car to work.

A normal day at college	Today
1. go to college by bus	– drive his mum's car to work
2. start college at half past nine	– begin work in the factory
3. have English till half past eleven	– work on a machine
4. have an hour's break at lunchtime	– have half an hour for his lunch
5. eat lunch in college with his classmates	– have lunch with the other workers
6. work in the library till three o'clock	– help one worker with a project
7. have a Mathematics course till five o'clock	– clean a machine for another worker
8. go home by bus	– drive home
9. do homework at eight o'clock	– go to bed early

Tense markers

Present simple		Present continuous	
usually normally every morning	every day in the evenings every afternoon	at the moment this morning currently	this evening right now today

‹M/I› 4 A phone call

■ Work in pairs. ► SF 22 Mediation/translation

Sie interessieren sich für einen International Diploma Course und wollen mehr über die Praktika wissen, die man dabei ableisten muss. Sie telefonieren mit einer englischen Studentin und stellen ihr Fragen zum Praktikum.

Sie wollen wissen:
1. wo sie das Praktikum jetzt durchführt
2. wie viele Stunden sie normalerweise pro Woche arbeitet
3. was sie in ihrem Praktikum im Augenblick macht
4. wie viel Geld sie normalerweise bekommt
5. ob sie dieses Praktikum genießt.

‹P› 5 An e-mail to a friend

■ You are a student at Newcastle College and are currently doing an International Diploma Course. You want to tell an English-speaking friend about it. Write an e-mail to him/her in about 100 words.
► SF 25 Personal letters and e-mails

‹R› C Reading: Why we are here

A1.2

http://www.thisisme.uk

HOME PHOTOS

"For me life in England is wonderful because you meet so many people of different nationalities here. Where I come from it is completely different. My home town in Germany is very small and it certainly doesn't have a cosmopolitan atmosphere like London. I go to a college of art and design here in London where I am currently doing a course in fashion design. At the moment I am working in a clothes shop as part of my course. At the weekends I have a stand at a market. I sell clothes that I design myself. It's a very good way to meet many different and interesting people. My English is much better now, so I can communicate more easily. In my free time I also like to go out with my English friends and practise my English. I don't really know what to do after the course at college. After my exams maybe I can start a job training programme in Germany."

Britta, 20, from Germany, lives in London.

http://www.thisisme.uk

HOME PHOTOS

"I come from a village near Warsaw but currently I am living and working in Glasgow in Scotland. It is a big change for me. I like the multicultural feeling of Glasgow and I have friends from many different countries. But I want to save as much money as I can during my stay here in Britain and so I have two jobs. I work as a waiter in a restaurant at lunchtime and in the evening, and as a cleaner in an office block early in the morning. This gives me enough money to live on and to save, but it also means I am at work all of the time. I have a nice boss at the restaurant and the chef there makes very good meals. The rest of the staff is friendly, too, but I don't have much time to socialize. I think after about two years here in Glasgow I want to go home. I think it is hard to settle here in Scotland. Although my English is much better now than at the beginning I still find it difficult to understand the Scots. I want to start a better life in Poland. Maybe I can train to be a chef."

(383 words)

Jarek, 19, from Poland, lives in Glasgow.

Understanding the text

a) Find the most suitable option. Only one option is true.
► **SF12 Multiple choice exercises**

1. Both of the young people come from …
   a) Eastern Europe.
   b) small towns in Europe.
   c) large towns in Europe.
   d) European capital cities.

2. They both like to live in Britain because they …
   a) can go to a good college there.
   b) are with people from their own countries.
   c) meet people from all over the world.
   d) like English food.

3. To earn money they both …
   a) have two part-time jobs.
   b) have more than one job.
   c) work on Sundays.
   d) work in shops.

4. They both want to go back to their home countries because they …
   a) don't like the people in Britain.
   b) don't speak English well enough.
   c) want to start job training courses.
   d) want to study at university there.

b) Answer the following questions in complete sentences.

1. What is Britta studying at the moment?
2. How does she get to meet interesting people?
3. How is Jarek's English?
4. Why doesn't he have much time to socialize?

After reading

c) Explain the jobs in the box using the words on the right.

Example: A fashion designer is a person who creates new clothes.

1. **fashion designer**
2. chef
3. web designer
4. salesperson
5. social worker
6. motor mechanic
7. office worker
8. nursery school teacher
9. computer technician
10. architect
11. street worker

create · repair · meals in a restaurant · design · firms in creating their own home page · read · buildings · people in need · stories to little children · help · sell · new clothes · type · cook · programs · goods in a shop · cars · install · give · advice to teenagers in trouble · support · letters to customers

‹I› **d)** A British college's online magazine wants to do an article about young Europeans who live in Britain. The magazine sends its student journalists to interview some young people who have come to Britain.

Work in pairs. Prepare the interview and then act it out.
Student A is a student journalist. Use role card A to find out about the young European.
Student B is a young European who answers the journalist's questions. See role card B on page 132.

Role card A

A student journalist

Find out about the young European.

his/her name • country of origin • reasons for coming to Britain • workplace • free time • plans for the future

‹P› **e)** Write an article about young Europeans in Britain for the online magazine in about 100 words.

D Practice

Training skills – How to describe pictures

‹R› **1 A part-time job** ►SF26 Describing illustrations and photographs

a) Look at photo number 1 and choose the most suitable option. Only one option is true.

1. What type of picture is it?
   a) cartoon
   b) black-and-white photo
   c) colour photo
2. What kind of situation can you see?
   a) serving a customer
   b) sales talk
   c) interview
3. What is the location?
   a) supermarket
   b) restaurant
   c) kitchen
4. Who do you see in the picture?
   a) a young woman, wearing a white T-shirt and blue jeans
   b) a young woman, wearing a red shirt and white trousers
   c) a young woman, wearing a blue top and a black skirt
5. What is the person doing?
   a) watching TV
   b) serving salad
   c) talking to a friend
6. Where exactly is the person in the picture?
   a) on the right-hand side in the background
   b) on the left-hand side in the background
   c) on the left-hand side in the foreground
7. How can you describe the atmosphere in the picture?
   a) awful
   b) friendly
   c) quiet
8. Why does it have this kind of atmosphere?
   a) because the people are smiling
   b) because the people are screaming
   c) because the people are watching TV

1

2

b) Describe the first photo using the answers from exercise a).

c) Describe the second photo on your own.

‹R› While listening

A1.3 **d)** Listen to Sarah Smith. She is talking about her part-time job. Then give short answers to the following questions. ►SF14 Short answer questions

1. Where does Sarah work?
2. How much money does she earn?
3. What does she like best about the part-time job?

e) Listen to the CD again and complete the following sentences.

1. Sarah works on Fridays, Saturdays and …
2. Sarah has a part-time job because she wants to finance …
3. Sarah's work clothes consist of …
4. Most guests arrive at …
5. Sarah's favourite bands play …
6. Sarah does not like …

‹P› 2 Youth subcultures

a) Look at the photos. Match them with the youth subcultures below. Two subcultures do not match. ► SF 13 Multiple matching exercises

Youth subcultures

• emo • punk rocker • grunge • rapper • surfer • skater
• rocker • raver

b) Choose one of the youth subcultures and describe the corresponding photo in detail.

c) Find out more about a youth culture that interests you on the Internet.

‹P› d) Create a poster about the youth subculture that you have chosen. Present it to your class. ► SF 34 Creating a poster

Facts

Teenagers have different lifestyles and interests to their parents to the point where a youth subculture develops. Each youth subculture has its own fashion styles, music, interests, behaviour, activities and political attitudes. Some people call a youth subculture a 'scene' when there is a strong identity within a group in a particular place.

Key Words

• punk rocker • casual • emo
• biker • skater • gothic • surfer
• grungies • hip-hopper • mod
• metalhead • rocker • raver
• preppy

Unit 2
Getting a job

A Getting started

1 MTC – A successful company

Before reading

a) Match the people in the photos with the statements below.

A Hi. I'm Suzy Wong. I'm in the Sales Department at MTC.

B Hello. My name's Peter Turner. I work in the IT Department.

C I'm Jack O'Toole. I'm head of the Personnel Department.

D Hello, I'm Debbie, Debbie King. I'm in Manufacturing at MTC.

E I'm Ray Austen. I work in Research and Development.

b) Match the activities with the statements. Two activities do not match.

1. look after the computer systems
2. operate machines
3. buy raw materials
4. manage the staff
5. manage the money that the company makes
6. find and test recipes for new products
7. sell the company's products

Understanding the text

‹R› **c)** Put the following events in the order they appear in the text on page 17.

1. find a successful recipe
2. sell drinks in cans
3. produce ready-to-eat meals
4. open their first factory
5. begin with the production of pet food
6. earn a million pounds for the first time
7. go to the USA
8. make cakes and sweets at home

‹P› **d)** Use the phrases in c) to give a summary of the development of MTC.

http://www.mtc.com/our_story

A1.4 NEWS | BRANDS | CAREERS | **OUR STORY** | CONTACT

A MTC is one of the largest family-owned companies producing food, drinks, sweets and pet food in the world with more than 100 manufacturing units. Its headquarters is in England but it operates in about 120 countries.

B It all started in 1905 when Martha Trick sold her home-made cakes and sweets in York, England. She was so successful that her husband George and all the family had to help her. A few years later Martha developed the recipe for 'Trix', a new brand of sweets.

George and Martha Trick (1905)

This was a huge success and Martha and George soon opened their first factory, which still exists today. Many other products followed.

C In the 1920s they made their first million and the company, MTC (short for Martha Trick's Confectionery) has been growing ever since. In 1935 Martha's son Terence bought the Caddogg pet food company and started to sell pet food in cans. A year later Martha's other son Woody went to America with £50,000 in his pocket and opened a factory in Chicago.

D After World War II MTC began to produce canned drinks and frozen food. In the last few years new MTC boss and Martha's great-granddaughter, Sally Trick, has developed other business fields: MTC is now one of the biggest producers of convenience food worldwide. (215 words)

After reading

e) Which of the words below are used with 'make', which are used with 'do'?

Example: to make millions

- millions • products • business • money • test • a difference
- a choice • a job • friends • a favour • good • a speech
- a mistake • wrong

f) Make meaningful sentences with the expressions from exercise e).

Example: MTC has made millions by selling food and drinks.

Training skills – How to describe statistics

2 The development at MTC

‹P›

a) Complete the description of chart 1 using the words below.
► SF 28 Describing diagrams

- sharply • slowly • rose
- fell • remained

b) Describe the development of profits at MTC (see chart 2) in the same way.

Chart 1 shows the changes in the number of employees at MTC from 1905 until 2010. In the beginning the number of employees was very small. It grew [1] but steadily until 1926. In the following years the number [2] at about the same level. However, from 1947 to 1989 the number of employees [3] [4] to about 20,000. From 1989 to 2010 the number [5] slowly for the first time.

Chart 1: MTC employees (1905–2010)

Number of employees

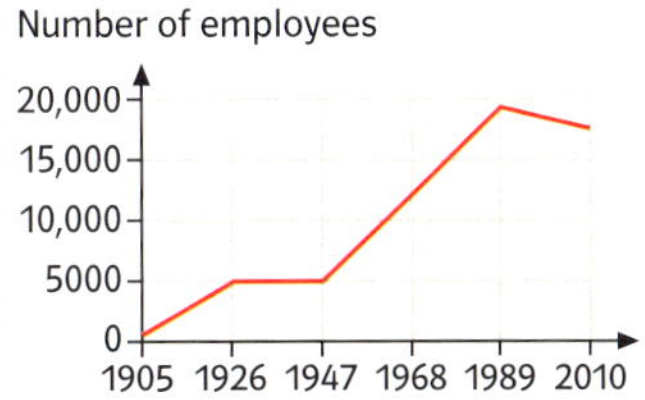

Chart 2: Profits at MTC (1905–2010)

Profits in millions of pounds

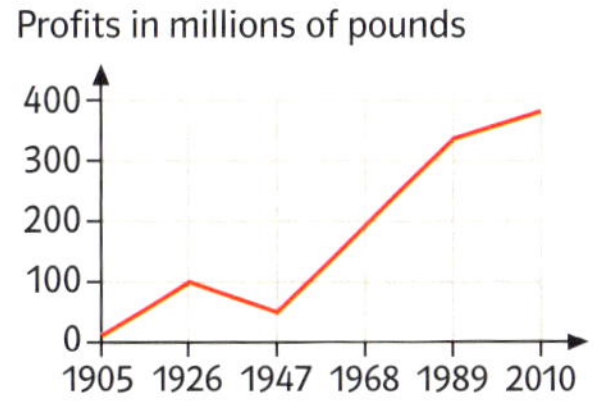

B Language

1 The rise of Britain's biggest supermarket

a) Complete the information about Tesco using the past tense.

In 1919 Jack Cohen started to sell food at a market in the East End of London. He made a profit of £1 on his first day! The name Tesco [**1. come**] to life five years later when Mr Cohen [**2. buy**] tea from Mr T. E. Stockwell and Mr Cohen [**3. use**] the first letters of their names. In 1929 he [**4. open**] the first store in North London. More and more stores [**5. follow**]. The company [**6. continue**] to grow in the 1930s when Mr Cohen [**7. build**] large office buildings and a warehouse. In the 1950s Tesco [**8. expand**] quickly by buying other stores, and selling more and more products. Tesco Leicester [**9. go**] into the *Guinness Book of Records* in 1961 as the largest store in Europe. Seven years later Tesco [**10. develop**] its first 'superstore'. At that time supermarkets [**11. change**] the way in which people [**12. shop**]. In 1974 Tesco [**13. begin**] to sell petrol and [**14. become**] the UK's largest independent petrol dealer. In 1995 the company [**15. manage**] to become the largest food retailer in the UK. A year later Tesco [**16. introduce**] its first 24-hour store. In 2000 Tesco.com [**17. enter**] the online shopping market.

b) Complete the following information about Tesco in the same way as in the example. Use negative forms.

Example: On his first day Mr Cohen made a small profit. He did not make a big profit.

1. Mr Cohen bought tea from Mr Stockwell. He did not …
2. He used the first letters of their names. He …
3. In 1929 Mr Cohen opened his first store in North London.
4. Tesco built large office buildings in the 1930s.
5. In the 1950s the company expanded quickly.
6. In 1961 Tesco Leicester became the largest store in Europe.
7. In 1995 the company was the largest food retailer in the UK.

Grammar

Past simple
Example: Sue lived in Glasgow from 2002 to 2008.
Bei Handlungen zu einem bestimmten Zeitpunkt oder in einem abgeschlossenen Zeitraum in der Vergangenheit

Present perfect simple
Example: Sue has lived in Leeds since 2008.
Mit einem Zeitraum, der noch andauert, und mit bestimmten Zeitbestimmungen und Adverbien

► GF 18 Past simple
► GF 20 Present perfect simple

‹I› **c)** Make up questions about the words below. Ask a classmate to answer them. The answers are in the text in a).

Example:
Student A: How much profit did Jack Cohen make on his first day?
Student B: He made a profit of £1.

• £1 • tea • North London • in 1961 • the first 'superstore' • petrol • in 2000

2 Big supermarkets, small supermarkets

■ Describe what has happened to Tesco and Royce & Sons in the last few years. ► GF 20 Present perfect simple

Example: Tesco has been in North London for many years. Royce & Sons have been in North London since 2005.

	Tesco	Royce & Sons
1. be in North London	for many years	since 2005
2. open	a lot of supermarkets up to now	only two little shops so far
3. make a profit	always	only once
4. start business in the USA	just	not yet
5. break a record	already	never

‹I› 3 A job for you?

a) Linda Smith has applied for a job in a big supermarket. In an interview she has to talk about her life and career. In pairs, take her role, using the card on page 132, and the role of the interviewer and prepare the interview.

Role card A

Interviewer

1. When / born?
   Example: When were you born, Ms Smith?
2. When / live / in Exeter?
3. How long / live / in London?
4. When / go to college?
5. What / do / then?
6. How long / be / a shop assistant at Morrisey's?
7. What / do / in your free time / when / young?
8. When / start / learning German?
9. How long / be interested / working with people?
10. When / hear / about the job advertisement?

b) Work in pairs and prepare a talk about yourselves. Work with a classmate and ask and answer questions about the following:

- date of birth • school • college • exams • address
- trips abroad • fluency in English • work experience • hobbies

‹I› 4 How long or how many?

Work in pairs. Use the verbs in brackets to ask and answer questions.
► GF 21 Present perfect continuous

1. Daniel Jones got a job with a big supermarket chain a year ago. His job has been to work on two projects so far. [**work**]
   Example:
   Questions: How long has Daniel been working for the supermarket?
   – How many projects has he worked on?
   Answers: He has been working for the supermarket for a year.
   – He has worked on two projects.
2. Daniel's secretary Jane began to type letters an hour ago. Six letters are complete now. [**type**]
3. At the moment Larry, one of the shop assistants, is serving his 45th customer. He started work three hours ago. [**serve**]
4. Trudy's job is to look after the customers' children. Today she started at eight o'clock in the morning. She has just said hello to the 20th child. [**look after**]
5. The baker in the supermarket began work eight hours ago. Now there are five hundred fresh loaves of bread. [**make**]
6. Lucy is just finishing the third and last page of her homework. She sat down at her desk two hours ago. [**do**]

Grammar

Present perfect simple
Example: John has repaired the car.
Bei Handlungen in der Vergangenheit ohne Zeitangabe, das Ergebnis ist wichtig

Present perfect continuous
Example: Alex has been repairing his car for two hours.
Bei Handlungen, die in der Vergangenheit begonnen haben und noch andauern

► GF 20 Present perfect simple
► GF 21 Present perfect continuous

‹P› 5 The story of ???

a) Find information about the development of an interesting company or organization on the Internet. Take notes. Use your notes to write about the company in about 100 words.

b) Read the text to the class but do not mention the name of the company or organization. The rest of the class have to find out the name.

Key Words

- company • development
- history • organization

Or just use the name of the company that you are interested in.

C Reading: Applications

Before reading

a) You need three things for a written job application. Find their names using the following words.

• application • certificates • copies • curriculum • letter • of • of • vitae

Understanding the text

b) Match the terms *job advertisement*, *curriculum vitae* and *letter of application* to the texts A, B and C.

c) Complete the sentences using the most suitable option according to the texts. Only one option is true.

1. The hotel is looking for somebody who …
   a) likes to be with people.
   b) likes to work alone.
   c) wants to work there permanently.
   d) likes to work with computers.

2. One essential qualification is to …
   a) be able to deal with other people.
   b) speak Russian fluently.
   c) be a quick worker.
   d) be a smoker.

3. Julia wants to study in …
   a) New Zealand.
   b) Mexico.
   c) Japan.
   d) Australia.

4. Julia is …
   a) a tolerant person.
   b) an ignorant person.
   c) an arrogant person.
   d) a difficult person.

5. Julia likes to play …
   a) football.
   b) table tennis.
   c) tennis.
   d) golf.

6. Julia already has some experience …
   a) working in another country.
   b) leading people.
   c) working in a bar.
   d) working in England.

‹P› ## After reading

d) Would you invite Julia for an interview? Why or why not?

e) Would you apply for the placement as hotel assistant? Why or why not?

f) Describe your present and future qualifications, and say what kind of job or work placement you would like to apply for.

A1.5

A

Looking for a WORK PLACEMENT as a hotel assistant?

You like working with people from different countries? You speak different languages? Then we look forward to getting your application. As a hotel assistant you will work in different parts of the hotel such as the restaurant, the bar, the reception as well as the housekeeping department.

Essential requirements:
– You need to speak English and German fluently.
– You must be able to work in a team.
– You must have basic computer skills.

We offer work placements for one year. If you are interested, please send your letter of application and CV to:
Grange City Hotel, Mr Joseph Wildbloom, 8-14 Cooper's Row, London EC3N 2BQ

(116 words)

B

Mönckebergstr. 41
74081 Heilbronn
Germany
Mobile: +49 171 23 45 67 89
julia.meyer@mynewjob.de

20 September 20…

Grange City Hotel
Mr Joseph Wildbloom
8–14 Cooper's Row
London EC3N 2BQ
Great Britain

Dear Mr Wildbloom

With reference to the online advert on your homepage, I would like to apply for a work placement as a hotel assistant. I am German and 18 years old.

I am an open-minded person and I am very interested in working in new areas. I have already got some experience in working in a hotel: I had a part-time job at the Madison Hotel in Hamburg last year. I worked in the reception and in housekeeping.

My present aim is to get to know as much as possible about hotel work as my long-term aim is to become a hotel manager. In order to achieve this aim I want to study at the Australian International Hotel School (AIHS) in Canberra.

Your hotel is my first choice because of its size and its high-class facilities. I believe the work placement would be a very interesting and rewarding experience for me.

I enclose my CV and copies of certificates.

I look forward to hearing from you.

Yours sincerely

Julia Meyer

Encls.

(199 words)

C

Julia Meyer
Mönckebergstr. 41
74081 Heilbronn
Germany
Mobile: +49 171 23 45 67 89
julia.meyer@mynewjob.de

Personal Statement

I am a student at a college of further education who is looking for a work placement in a hotel with a good reputation. I enjoy working with people and I am interested in getting experience of hotel work. I am also looking for a challenge where I can use and improve my skills.

EDUCATION

2008–2011
Berufliche Schule City Nord (college of further education)
Fachhochschulreife (A levels) in 2011
Business studies A
Mathematics B
Social studies A

2003–2008
Heinrich-Wolgast-Schule (intermediate secondary school)
GCSE in 2008

WORK EXPERIENCE

Part-time job at Madison Hotel GmbH
Reception desk and housekeeping

INTERESTS

Sports: I am an active volleyball and tennis player, and I also enjoy watching football.
Leadership: I train a 9–12-year-old volleyball team at a sports club.

SKILLS

Language: I speak English and German fluently. I have a good working knowledge of French and Spanish.
Computing: I have good computer skills, especially in Word, Excel, Access, and PowerPoint.
Driving: driving licence

(178 words)

D Practice

1 Finding the right candidate

Before listening

a) Look at the photos and match the interview candidates with suitable jobs in the list below.

• chef • salesperson • motor mechanic • nursery school teacher
• nurse • computer technician • bank clerk • electrician

b) Give reasons why their clothes suit these jobs.

‹R›
While listening

A1.6 **c)** Listen to the two interviews and find out the following information about each interview.

1. the name of the manager
2. the kind of job or work placement on offer
3. the applicant's name
4. the applicant's skills

After listening

d) Which applicant would you give the work placement to? Give reasons for your choice.

2 Word web: Applying for a job

► SF 21 Word webs

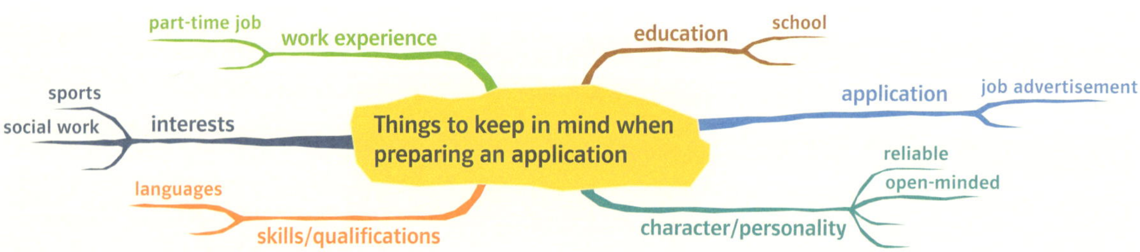

a) Copy the word web into your exercise book and write down words from Unit 2 and other words that you know. If necessary use a dictionary.
► SF 11 Using a dictionary

b) Work with a partner. Compare your word webs and then add more words to them.

‹P› 3 Writing an application

► SF 23 Formal letters and e-mails

Sports Works

We are a leading British sports equipment manufacturer. We are looking for young reliable students from Europe to do work placements in our plants in Hamburg, Rome and Budapest. We need people for our:

- Manufacturing departments
- Sales offices
- Nursery schools for our employees' children

If you are interested in one of these areas and you are aged 16–25, then send a letter of application and a full CV to our personnel manager, Mr Jack Jones. Please note that our company language is English.

Sports Works
Attn Mr Jack Jones
430 Bath Road
Bristol BS4 3HQ
England
http://www.sportsworks.co.uk

a) The above advertisement appeared in the German magazine *Sporty* last week. Choose the work placement you would like to apply for.

b) Use the word web on page 22 to make notes for your application.

c) Write your letter of application and CV.

‹I› 4 Role play: Having an interview

Video lounge 1

a) You have been invited for an interview for one of the work placements in the advertisement above.
Work in groups. Get together with students who have chosen to apply for the same work placement as you. Half of your group play the applicants (see role card A "applicant" on the right) and the other half play the employers (see role card B "employer" on page 132).
Prepare the interview and act it out.

b) Decide in class which applicants you would give the work placement to.

Role card A

Applicant

Think about:
- education
- work experience
- skills and qualifications
- personality and character
- interests and hobbies
- possible questions.

Online Link
800041-0003

1

2

3

Unit 3
The youth market

A Getting started

‹P› **1 Buy it!** ► SF 26 Describing illustrations and photographs

a) Describe the photos and say what products you could advertise with them.

b) Who could the target groups of these adverts be?

‹R› **2 Young people as consumers**

Before reading

a) Read the heading of the text on page 25. What do you think it is about?

‹R› ### Understanding the text

b) Complete the sentences with words or expressions from the text.

1. Andy did not know anybody on the first days in the ... ...
2. Like the other students Andy was interested in ... and ...
3. Andy's answers to the other students' questions were not ...
4. The group noticed that Andy did not have the right ...
5. Andy saw that the group's clothes had well-known ... on them.

c) What do you think? What did Andy do after he had met the group?

After reading

‹P› **d)** Write an ending to Andy's story in about 50 words.

A1.7

You're nothing – without the right brands

by Cilla Brown

After Andy Burns had moved to a new town with his family he felt quite lonely. On his first day at college he decided to go to the cafeteria. He hoped to meet some new people there. While he was eating his lunch he saw a group of students from one of his classes at the next table. They were talking about music and sport so Andy decided to join them. While they were getting to know each other one boy asked Andy: "Do you support Manchester United?" A girl asked him: "Do you like Justin Timberlake?" Another boy in the group wanted to know if he had the new "Mega Racer" computer game. Andy answered "yes" to all the questions although the truthful answers were "no".

Things seemed to be going fine until one of the students saw his trainers. At once the student started to laugh: "Where did you get those shoes from?" Andy had not thought much about them before. They were just blue sport shoes that his parents had bought him for Christmas.

Looking at the group Andy noticed that they all had similar logos on their trainers – ticks and stripes like the ones on footballers' boots on television. And it was not only their shoes: their T-shirts all had similar logos, and everyone in the group seemed to have the same college bag with a puma in silver on the side.

Andy was very confused but from that day on he decided to be like the rest of the group.

(261 words)

‹P› 3 Are you a well-informed consumer?

► SF 32 Giving a talk or presentation

- Think about the following questions and prepare a short presentation to give in class.

1. What is the best thing you have bought in the last few months?
2. Is it a branded or a no-name product?
3. Who made it?
4. Where did they produce it?
5. What is it made of?
6. What type of packaging did it come in?

‹I› 4 Consumer goods – what do we really need?

a) Make a list of the three consumer goods and services that are most important to you. You can use the items below and/or your own ideas. Put the most important thing first, etc.

• television • mobile phone • MP3 player • car • pen and paper
• bicycle • books • telephone • PC • cosmetics • digital camera
• CDs • computer games • DVDs • running shoes • Internet

b) Work in pairs. Tell your partner what your three most important things are, and why. Then try to agree on a common order of the three most important things.

B Language

1 Manchester Shopping Centre ►GF18 Past simple

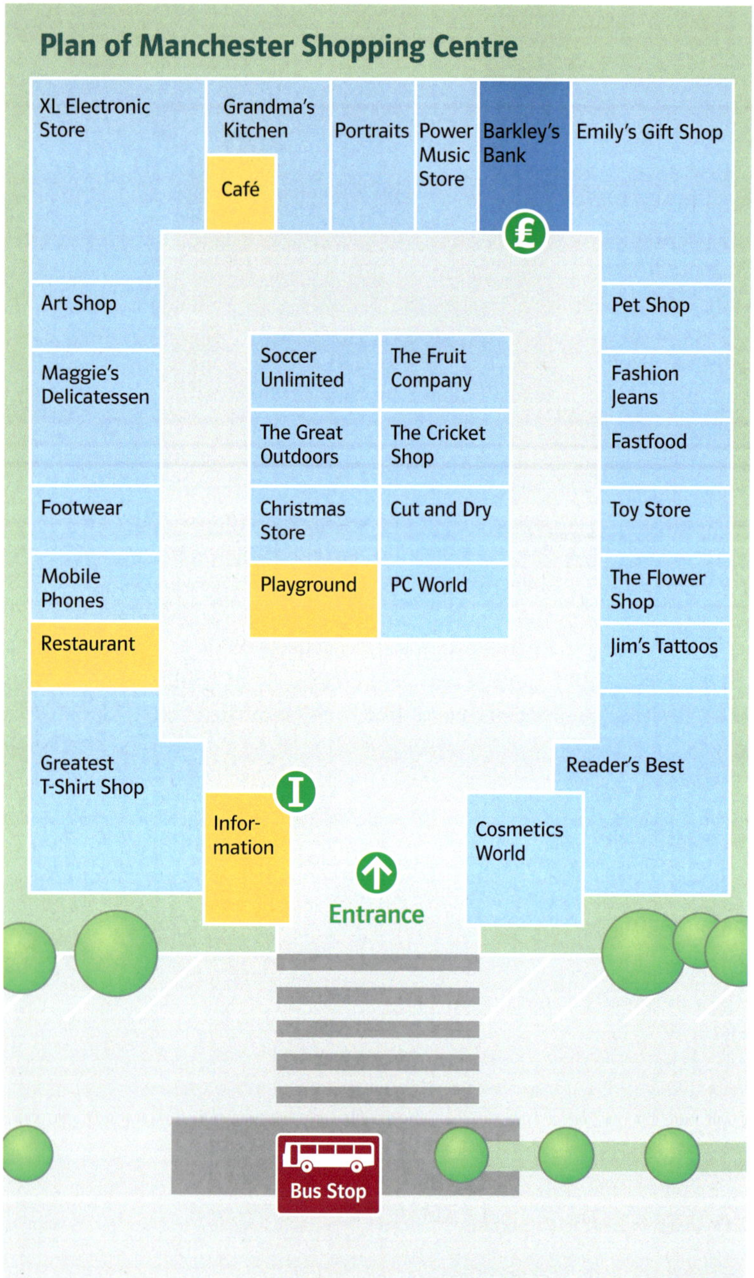

Grammar

Past simple
Example: Sue lived in Glasgow from 2002 to 2008.
Bei Handlungen zu einem bestimmten Zeitpunkt oder in einem abgeschlossenen Zeitraum in der Vergangenheit

Past perfect simple
Example: After Sam had bought a CD he went home.
Für Handlungen oder Zustände, die vor einem Zeitpunkt in der Vergangenheit abgeschlossen waren

Past continuous
Example: While Sam was waiting at the bus stop it started to rain.
Bei Handlungen, die in der Vergangenheit schon im Gange waren, als eine neue Handlung eintrat

►GF18 Past simple
►GF22 Past perfect simple
►GF19 Past continuous

a) Last Sunday Andy went shopping at Manchester Shopping Centre with his new girlfriend, Mary. Look at the list of what they had to do and find out where they did the different things on the plan of the centre.
Example: Andy tested the new Manchester United football at Soccer Unlimited.

b) Andy and Mary wanted to do their shopping as quickly as possible. Find the shortest way through the shopping centre and put the list on the right in the correct order. They started at the bus stop.

c) Now describe Andy and Mary's shopping trip in the following way:
Example: After Andy and Mary had arrived at the shopping centre Mary exchanged the red T-shirt for a smaller size. After Mary had exchanged the red T-shirt …

‹I› 2 What did you do after…?

a) Read the dialogue below in pairs. Replace the underlined parts and act out the new dialogue.

Student A: What did you do last weekend (yesterday / last week / last Friday…)?
Student B: I went shopping.
Student A: What did you do after you had been shopping?
Student B: After I had been shopping I drank a coffee at the coffee bar.

b) Find another partner and act out a similar dialogue.

3 A bad day for shopping ► GF19 Past continuous

■ While Andy and Mary were going home they met one of Andy's new classmates, Mark. He had been shopping, too. But some things had gone wrong. Say what happened to him.

1. get dressed / telephone – ring
   Example: While Mark was getting dressed the telephone rang.
2. run to – bus stop / bus – leave
3. walk to – shopping centre / start – to rain
4. listen to – new CD / meet – his ex-girlfriend
5. look at – book / mobile phone – ring
6. drink – cup of coffee / drop – cup
7. test – MP3 player on offer / somebody – buy last one
8. try on – new pair of jeans / fire-alarm – go off
9. sit on – bus / bus – break down

4 Back from the shopping trip

■ Put the verbs in brackets into the correct form of the past tense (past simple, past perfect or past continuous).

After Andy and Mary [**1. arrive**] at Andy's house they [**2. unpack**] all the things they [**3. buy**]. After they [**4. put**] the things away, they [**5. turn on**] the TV. While they [**6. watch**] a commercial about tennis shoes, Andy [**7. notice**] that he [**8. buy**] the wrong shoes. After they [**9. discuss**] going back to the shop to change the tennis shoes, they [**10. decide**] to get the new shoes on their next shopping trip.

‹P› 5 Your last shopping trip ► SF25 Personal letters and e-mails

■ You have a friend in the USA. Write him/her an e-mail. Describe your last shopping trip in about 100 words. Use each of the words 'after' and 'while' at least twice in your e-mail.

C Reading

‹R› 1 Protecting young consumers

Before reading

a) What does the photo on the right show us?

b) Have you ever bought something on the Internet or by phone? Talk about your experiences.

Every day we see adverts and commercials that say "buy this", "try it" or "do this". The advertisers try to tell us how to behave and what to buy. Young people in particular are at risk when shopping, especially on the Internet because they often believe more easily what the advertisers tell them.
Cheshire County Council in north-west England has created a page on its website that gives young people tips about shopping on the Internet and on the phone. You can read an extract from it below.

A1.8

http://www.shopping-advice/

Home > Business > Young Consumer > **Shopping Advice** | **Cheshire County Council**

Shopping Advice for Young People

A Do you use the Internet to buy CDs, DVDs, and clothes? When you do this you have the same rights as when you buy in a shop, but the trader must give you some additional information. This must include details about the goods or services and confirmation of the sale. If you change your mind and want to cancel your order, the consumer protection regulations give you a cooling-off period of fourteen days after the day on which you receive the goods. In this period you can cancel your order. For services, this period is the same after the day you agreed to go ahead with the service.

B Have you ever bought or sold anything on eBay or on any other auction platform? These sites are very popular and you can buy anything from toys, books, clothes, DVDs, to concert tickets. But there are a few things to remember when buying things from Internet auctions:

- Check out the sellers. Can you trust them? Have they sold goods before? Is there any feedback on them? Can you get your money back if there is a problem with the goods? Where are the sellers based?
- Compare prices before you place a bid.
- Check to see how much postage you have to pay.
- Check how you have to pay and if your payment is safe.

C Do you use your mobile phone to read about goods or services? If you have a mobile phone you must be careful about scams. Sometimes you may receive a text message which says that you have won a cash prize. When you ring the number it is a premium rate number and the cost of the call can be very high. It is best to delete such messages immediately. Other messages offer ringtones, wallpapers or news alerts. Such services are generally expensive because you receive them at a premium rate. Such a text message can cost you as much as £2 per message. If you want to stop these expensive texts, all you must do is send the word "STOP" to the short code.

(351 words)

Understanding the text

c) Match the following headings with a suitable paragraph in the text. Two of the headings do not fit.

1. Dangers when using your mobile phone
2. Consumer protection
3. Shopping at home
4. Internet auctions
5. Buying a mobile phone

d) Answer the following questions about the text in complete sentences.

1. What can you do if you order something on the Internet and then you change your mind?
2. What other rights do you have as a buyer on the Internet?
3. What information can you find about a seller on the Internet?
4. What kind of messages is it best to delete on your mobile phone?
5. Why is it best to do this?

e) Use words and expressions from the text to complete the summary.

However, there are certain dangers when you buy [**1**] on the Internet. It is very important to know that you as a consumer have certain [**2**]. The [**3**] must give you detailed information about the product he/she is selling. Moreover, after you have bought something you can always [**4**] your order. You have fourteen days to do this. This is called the [**5**]. When buying something from an Internet [**6**] such as eBay you should also be careful before placing a [**7**]. Check out all the relevant details such as the cost of [**8**] you have to pay. When you use a mobile phone be careful of [**9**], for example, when you read a [**10**] telling you that you have won something. This can often be very [**11**] for you. You should [**12**] such messages right away.

f) Find words in the text which have the same meaning as the following words and phrases and give line numbers.

1. purchase
2. further
3. products
4. to say 'yes' to
5. information about someone's experiences
6. cost of stamps and packaging
7. right away
8. money

‹M› **After reading** ► SF 22 Mediation/translation

g) You work for your local council and your head of department, who doesn't understand a lot of English, has asked you to give him a summary of section B of the Cheshire County's "Shopping Advice for Young People" in German. Complete this task.

‹P› **h)** Write some tips for young consumers about shopping in town. Use about 150 words.

Training skills – How to do a role play

‹I› ## 2 A sales talk

a) Work in pairs. Choose a product. Possible products for sale: a mobile phone plus contract; the latest designer jeans; the latest MP3 player

b) Choose a role. Student A is a salesperson in a German department store. See role card A "salesperson". Student B is an English-speaking customer. See role card B "customer" on page 132.

c) Prepare the role play and act it out.

Role card A

Salesperson

You have a part-time job in a German department store. Your job is to persuade customers to buy.

Think about the advantages of the product, how it compares with other products on the market, its price, etc.

Language

- Excuse me…
- Can you tell me…?
- Would you be interested in…?
- May I give you some information about…?
- That sounds interesting.
- I'm (not) interested in…
- What about…?

D Practice

1 Radio commercials

1

2

3

4

5

‹R› Before listening ► SF 26 Describing illustrations and photographs

a) Describe the photos.

A1.9 While listening

‹R› **b)** Listen to the radio commercials and match them with the photos. Two of the pictures do not match.

c) Copy the chart below into your exercise book. Then listen to the commercials again and answer the questions.

	Commercial 1	Commercial 2	Commercial 3
1. Who are the advertisers?	...	...	...
2. What are they advertising?	...	...	...
3. What are the slogans?	...	...	...

After listening

d) Outline the message of each commercial.

e) Describe the target groups. Think about age, gender and interests.

‹M› **f)** Fassen Sie die Argumentation der „Friends of the Planet"-Radiowerbung auf Deutsch zusammen. ► SF 22 Mediation/translation

‹P› **g)** Create a flyer which will get people to support the "No Car Day" campaign.

‹P› 2 Creating a TV commercial

a) You have applied for a job at the advertising agency "Mad for Marketing". The agency wants to test you. Work in teams. Decide on a product or service and plan a TV commercial. Think about the following:

- name for the product/service • company • price • target group
- slogan • jingle • storyline • roles • sound • location • script
- logo

b) Act out your TV commercial and then present it to the other teams.

c) Write a short text for the agency in which you describe and explain the decisions that you made. Also give other ways to market your product.

Facts

The four important keywords of marketing are product, pricing, promotion, placement.

Product: The company needs to think about the quality of the product, its uniqueness, its packaging and the branding.

Pricing: The company needs to set a price for the product, including a discount.

Promotion: The company needs to think of various forms of advertising, e.g. newspaper advertisements, billboard, merchandising, sponsoring, online advertising.

Placement: The company needs to think about the distribution of the product, e.g. retailing.

3 An advertisement for a non-profit organization

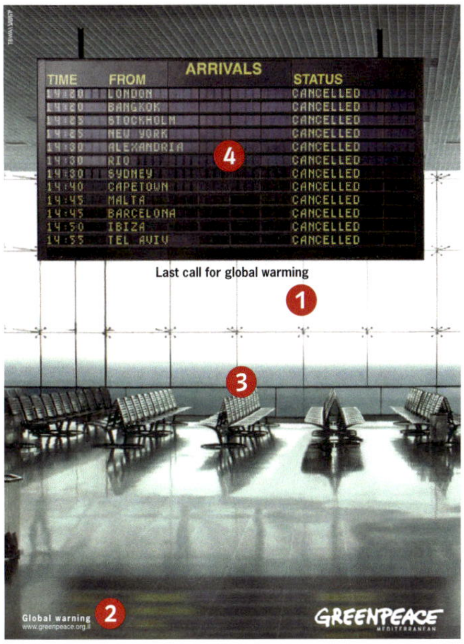

Facts

The AIDA formula is a theory used in marketing. It describes how to sell products to possible target groups and it gets people to buy products.

Attention	Interest	Desire	Action
attract the target group	make the target group look more closely	convince the target group that they want the product or service	make the target group do something

a) Describe what you can see in the advertisement.
► SF 26 Describing illustrations and photographs

‹R› b) Match the parts of the AIDA formula in the Facts box with the numbers in the above advertisement.

c) What is the advert for?

d) Who do you think the target group is?

e) What effect does the advert have on you?

f) Do you think the advert is successful? Why? Why not?

‹P› g) Find an advert on the Internet and analyze it. Present it to the class.

Key Words
- advertisement
- commercial

‹I› 4 Should advertising be banned?

‹I› a) Discuss the topic below. Work in groups.

Topic: "Advertising should be banned from magazines and TV programmes for young people."

Group A: Take the position of a college student. See role card A.
Group B: Take the position of a company representative. See role card B "company representative" on page 132.
Group C: Take the position of a parent. See role card C "parent" on page 132.

b) Choose one person in your team to take part in the discussion. This person introduces himself/herself and states his/her position.
► SF 3 Having a discussion

c) Discuss the pros and cons of the ban. The other students take notes.
► SF 33 Taking notes

d) After the discussion the other students vote for or against the ban.

Role card A

Student

You are not sure about the ban.
Possible arguments:
- information
- entertainment
- waste of time
- spend too much money

Unit 4
Media in our lives

A Getting started

1 Who needs newspapers?

‹P› **a)** Describe the cartoon. ► **SF 27 Describing cartoons**

b) In your opinion, what is the message of the cartoon?

c) Describe how the numbers of people in the US getting news online, on TV and in the newspaper has changed. ► **SF 28 Describing diagrams**

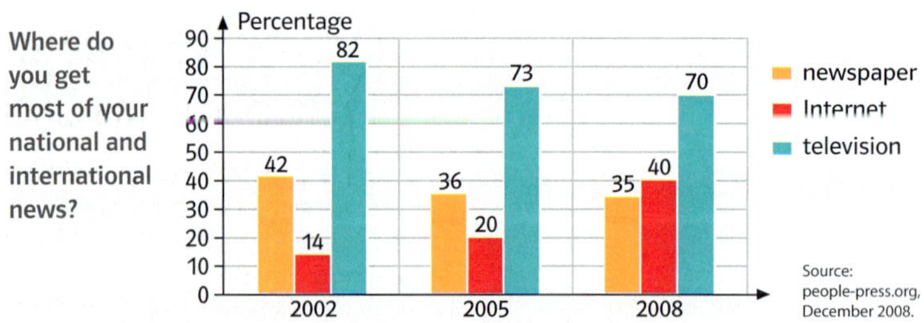

d) Analyse the bar chart and think of reasons for the changes.

e) Explain the link between the cartoon and the bar chart.

‹I› **f)** Work in groups. Do a survey to find out how many hours you and the other members of your group watch TV, do work or play games on the computer, and read newspapers or magazines during one week.

g) Produce a bar chart showing the results of your survey. Present your chart to the class and compare your results with the other groups.

2 Watching TV

‹R› Before reading

a) Look at the headline of the article. What do you think it is about?

A1.10

Do you know what your children are doing right now?

by Jessy Clarkson

A Today more and more parents tend to use a screen – either a TV screen or a computer monitor – as an electronic babysitter. However, the reasons which parents often give for their decision are surprising. Firstly, they think watching TV and using the computer is educational. Secondly, they think that their children relax better in front of the screen.

B If you look at surveys you can see that the number of hours children spend sitting in front of the TV screen is constantly rising. Very young children already spend an average of two hours a day in front of the screen. Scientists say, however, that children of that age shouldn't watch any TV, because their brains are not able to understand so much information, and it can confuse them. Children aged between 2 and 8 years spend an average of 3 hours a day in front of the TV screen. By the age of 8 they can spend as much as 4 hours in front of the TV and an additional 2 hours in front of the computer.

C What effect does this have on children? Long-term surveys have found that children are more likely to be overweight and aggressive. They also have serious problems paying attention for a longer period of time and they often become slow learners at school. This means that their chances of going on to higher education fall dramatically.

D Another aspect is that because more and more commercials are shown on TV children can watch up to 40,000 commercials each year. The problem is that children between 6 and 8 are not able to understand that the aim of commercials is to sell products.

E The conclusion that scientists come to is that children should spend less time in front of the screen and spend more time reading books, or they should do more sport and meet friends.

(320 words)

Understanding the text

b) Now that you have read the text, summarize the writer's main ideas.

c) Answer the following questions about the text.

1. Why do parents let their children watch so much TV?
2. Why shouldn't children under the age of two watch TV?
3. Watching too much TV can have serious consequences for young children. What can happen?
4. Why shouldn't children watch so many commercials?
5. What should children do instead of watching TV?

After reading

‹P› **d)** Copy the chart on the right into your exercise book. Find further reasons in the text why children sit in front of the TV and the ways it affects them.

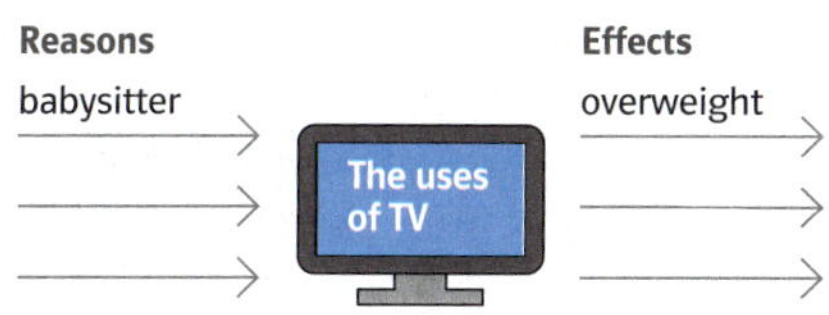

e) Add ideas of your own to the chart.

f) Prepare a talk about the uses of TV using the ideas in your chart.
► SF 32 Giving a talk or presentation

B Language

1 The media in the future ► GF 24 Will-future

‹I› a) Ask your classmates the following questions about the use of media in the future. The words in the language box below can help them to answer the questions.

1. people / use / Internet more often
   Example:
   Student A: What do you expect? Will people use the Internet more often in the future?
   Student B: I suppose people will use the Internet more often in the future.
2. people / write / more e-mails
3. young people / watch / less TV
4. we / buy / more newspapers
5. students / use / laptops in class
6. use of mobile phones / increase
7. the media / influence people / more

Language

probably • I expect • I suppose

Grammar

Will-future
Bei unsicheren Vorhersagen
Example: I think the mobile phone will help us in many ways.

Bei Entscheidungen, die im Moment des Sprechens getroffen werden
Example: Just a minute, I'll help you!

Future with 'going to'
Bei Absichten und geplanten Vorhaben
Example: I am going to stay in New York for a week.

► GF 23 Future with 'going to'
► GF 24 Will-future

b) Now answer the questions using the short form and give reasons.

Example:
Student A: What do you expect? Will people use the Internet more often in the future?
Student B: Yes, they will because you can easily find important information on the Internet.

2 Doing homework on a laptop ► GF 23 Future with 'going to'

■ Make sentences using 'going to' as shown in the example.

1. Jason is sitting in front of his laptop and has turned it on.
   Example: Jason is going to do some work on his laptop.
2. Jason cannot remember what homework he has to do. He opens his ICQ messaging service to talk to a classmate.
3. The homework is to find some information on the Internet. Jason starts his browser.
4. Jason has opened his e-mail program and clicks on the "Create mail" icon.
5. Jason has finished his homework and wants to relax. He clicks on his favourite game on the desktop.
6. It is seven o'clock in the evening. Jason's parents have prepared dinner.
7. Jason is tired. He switches off the laptop.

3 The development of a telecommunications company

- Put the verbs in brackets into the correct future form.

Jim Dawson is managing director of a telecommunications company. He is talking to his staff about the future development of the company.

"Ladies and gentlemen, I would like to talk to you about the future development of our company. Management has already decided to go ahead with plans for the new office building. We **are going to open** it next March. We hope that it **will secure** the success of our company in the future.

We all expect that Internet use [**1. increase**] in the next few years and that we [**2. have**] thousands of new customers. Management has plans to invest more in Internet technology, especially in the mobile web. That is why we [**3. buy**] new servers and we [**4. update**] our network. Since mobile phones have become more important and the number of users of the mobile web has also increased, the mobile web [**5. grow**] in the future. This [**6. probably help**] us to be more profitable. We have also had good news from our bank: They [**7. lend**] us £1 million. We expect that this [**8. make**] it easier for us to make innovations in a difficult market."

4 Comparing different kinds of media

► GF7 Adjective and adverb

- Complete the text with the suitable form of the words in brackets.

It is **easy** to find information on the Internet. You just press a button and a new page opens **quickly**. Usually the Internet works [**1. good**] and you can download your files [**2. accurate**], but sometimes it breaks down.
What about newspapers? They show [**3. interesting**] news and are [**4. educational**]. What are the [**5. real**] advantages of reading a newspaper or magazine compared to using the [**6. fast**] Internet? First of all, you can read a newspaper wherever you go. You do not need electricity or a wireless connection. If your newspaper is stolen, you can replace it [**7. easy**], because it is [**8. cheap**]. Another advantage is that a newspaper is [**9. good**] for the environment because it is [**10. recyclable**] and it is not made of [**11. harmful**] toxic material. In addition, if a newspaper prints something which is not correct, you can read the correction the following day. Finding out that something is wrong on the Internet is [**12. complicated**], if not [**13. impossible**]. Moreover, you can [**14. quick**] find the latest news in a newspaper, whereas on the Internet you have to look for the publishing date, which you cannot always find so [**15. easy**].

5 Managing situations – A new PC

► SF 22 Mediation/translation

‹M› - Sie chatten mit einem englischen Freund und berichten ihm von Ihrem neuen PC. Übertragen Sie die folgenden Sätze sinngemäß ins Englische.

1. Sie haben Geld gespart und werden einen neuen PC kaufen.
2. Sie werden wahrscheinlich einen neuen PC mit einem großen Bildschirm kaufen.
3. Sie nehmen an, dass der neue Computer einen Blu-ray-Player haben wird.
4. Ihr Lehrer hat Ihnen die Aufgabe gegeben, im Internet Informationen zu suchen. Sie werden das heute Abend tun.
5. Sie können im Augenblick Podcasts nicht schnell herunterladen.
6. Sie erwarten, dass auf Ihrem neuen, schnellen PC alle Programme besser laufen werden.

‹R› C Reading: Lost in a virtual world

Before reading

a) Look at the pictures that go with the articles on page 37. What do you think the articles are about?

Understanding the text

b) Match the four articles on the opposite page with suitable headings. Two headings do not match.

1 **Net piracy may send parents to prison**

2 **The Internet stops your children reading**

3 **The history of the World Wide Web**

4 **Governments want to ban dangerous video games**

5 **The Internet saves the world**

6 **Beware of the wolf**

c) Match the verbs in box A with the words in box B according to the text.

A	B
a) to download	1. games
b) to book	2. ideas
c) to exchange	3. music
d) to invent	4. instant messaging
e) to play	5. the law
f) to do	6. a programming language
g) to join	7. the Internet
h) to break	8. a trip
i) to use	9. a social networking site

Training skills – How to write a composition/comment

‹P› **d)** Find advantages and dangers of computers and the Internet in the texts on page 37. Make two lists.

Advantages of computers and the Internet	Dangers of computers and the Internet
...	...

e) Work in pairs. Add your own ideas to the list of advantages and dangers.

f) Comment on this statement: "Teenagers should not have their own computers because it is too dangerous." Write at least three arguments for and three against this statement using complete sentences.
► SF16 Writing a composition/comment

‹M› **g)** In Ihrem Politikunterricht sprechen Sie über die Chancen und Gefahren des Internets. Sie erhalten die Aufgabe, ein kurzes Referat über die Risiken des Internets auf Deutsch zu halten. Bereiten Sie dieses Referat mit Hilfe der Zeitungsartikel auf Seite 37 vor.
► SF22 Mediation/translation

A1.11 **A**

Where would we be without it? We could not sell our old CDs on eBay, download music or book a cheap holiday trip to Majorca. All of these things are made possible by the World Wide Web and most of us cannot imagine life without it.

The Internet started as a service for the American Army which needed its own communication network. Soon universities found that they could use the Internet to exchange ideas over long distances. Then computer expert Tim Berners-Lee invented the new programming language HTML and in 1991 he put his software onto the Internet and people could use it for free. Two years later anyone could use the Web and suddenly, businesses and people worldwide could communicate with one another.

Now we can say that the Internet has really changed our lives!

(135 words)

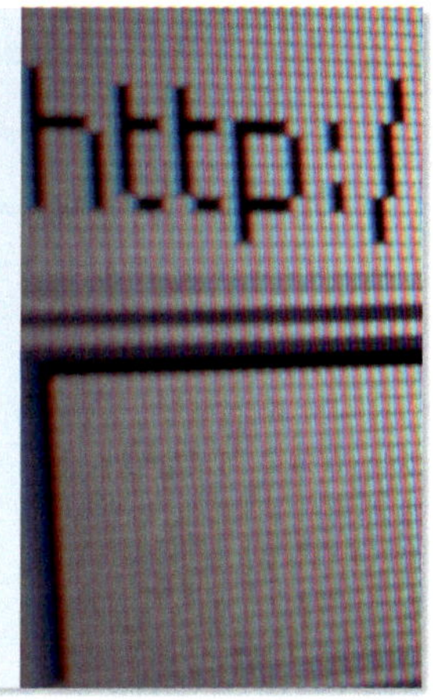

B

Your children spend hours in front of their computers or games consoles every day, but do you know what games they play?

At the moment only about 10% of computer games have age limits. Many governments have proposed a classification system for games in order to keep children from playing games which are not suitable for them. Soon it will be illegal for shops to sell games to a child below the recommended age.

However, governments expect parents to act, too. They advise parents to keep computers and games consoles out of children's bedrooms. Parents should ask their children to play games in the living room so that they can see what their children are doing.

(116 words)

C

Jessica is a normal teenage girl who loves the Internet. Last year she joined a social networking site and has done a lot of instant messaging with friends and also with people she does not really know. Two months ago she started to chat with "Lucy" who persuaded Jessica to tell her the name of the town where she lives, the name of her school and her phone number. Jessica did all this. She even sent a photo of herself to "Lucy". The problem was that "Lucy" was a man. It all ended when "Lucy" turned up at Jessica's school and at her home. Jessica was so frightened that she told her parents. Luckily the police put an end to this story.

"Social networking sites such as Facebook attract young people," says expert Simon Watson, "and home-made videos can be great fun – but on the Internet you can find video clips of children and teenagers which would give their parents many sleepless nights! We still have a lot of educational work to do."

(173 words)

D

Many parents do not know that their children download music and films illegally from the Internet. About 6.5 million Britons – most of them teenagers – downloaded music illegally last year. This costs the music industry alone £200 million a year.

Britain's biggest providers have now agreed on measures to stop Internet piracy. They will send thousands of letters to homes in the UK where they have found illegal downloading. In this way they want to inform parents that their children are breaking the law and warn them to keep an eye on their children. If this does not help, these cases may go to court and parents may end up in prison.

After all – parents are responsible for their children!

(119 words)

D Practice

‹R› 1 It's all in the news

Before listening

a) Choose two of the following items which you are especially interested in when you listen to the news on the radio. Give reasons.

- weather • politics • local news • crimes • sports • accidents
- television • traffic news • famous people

A1.12 While listening

b) Listen to the news reports. Find out which items in the box above are mentioned and in which order.

c) Match the news reports with the following places. Two places do not match.

- Exeter • Delhi • Liverpool
- Chicago • London • California

d) Listen to the reports again. Find the most suitable options according to the news reports. More than one answer can be true.

Report 1
1. A small passenger plane crashed.
2. The plane went up in flames.
3. Fourteen children were killed.
4. A couple saw the crash.

Report 2
1. Children watch thousands of killings on TV.
2. When they are 16, children watch 16,000 murders.
3. Children who watch too much TV can get fat.
4. Children should not have televisions and computers in their bedrooms.

Report 3
1. The weather report announces the weather for Monday and Tuesday.
2. In the afternoon there will be some showers and thunderstorms in London.
3. The temperature will go up to nearly 20 degrees Celsius on Monday.
4. The weather will be bright and sunny on Monday.

Report 4
1. Steven McNeill reports on motorway No. 26.
2. A lane on the motorway near Exeter is closed.
3. The radio station asks its listeners to report details.
4. Steven McNeill will come on air again within the next half an hour.

‹P› After listening

e) You are a reporter for a local radio station. Prepare a short piece of news and present it in class.

Training skills – How to describe a cartoon

‹P› ### 2 Someone to watch over you …

► SF 27 Describing cartoons

a) Describe and analyze cartoon 1. Use the following phrases:

Description:
"The illustration shows …"

Analysis:
"The cartoonist wants to point out that …"

Your opinion:
"I think this cartoon is …"

- desert island • palm tree
- surveillance camera • to observe

b) Describe cartoon 2 in a similar way.

1

2

‹I› ### 3 Big Brother at school?

Many schools in Britain have installed cameras in the yards and corridors to protect the children and the teachers. Now there is a discussion going on if schools should also introduce CCTV (closed circuit television) cameras in classrooms. Head teachers believe that this will help to stop students breaking the rules. Students, however, …

- Next week a discussion is going to take place in your college about the introduction of CCTV.

  Student A is a student at the college. You are going to speak for the students. You can find your role card A on this page.
  Student B is a head teacher. Student C is a teacher. Student D is a police officer. You can find your role cards on page 133.
  Introduce yourselves and present your arguments. Discuss the pros and cons of the introduction of CCTV into the college and try to reach an agreement.

Role card A

Student

You and your classmates do not like the idea of cameras in the classroom. Try to find arguments against this idea and suggest other ways of making students behave better.

Online Link
800041-0005

Unit 5
Social change

A Getting started: Times change

‹P› **Before reading**

a) Describe the above photos.
► SF 26 Describing illustrations and photographs

b) Describe how society in western countries has changed over the past 100 years. Refer to the photos in your answer.

c) How is your lifestyle different to that of your parents and grandparents when they were your age?

‹R› **Understanding the texts**

d) You are in the English section of a German bookshop. You read the comments on the backs of three books as well as an extract from each one. Match the comments (1–3) with the extracts (A–C) on page 41.

Comments on the backs of the books

1 He is sixteen and a skater. Life is going on nicely – he is thinking about college and he has met a nice girl. Then a little accident happens.

2 She lives in Southall, London, a part of the city where many families of Indian origin live. Her parents want her to be a nice conventional Indian girl. But she has other plans.

3 An idyll of the English countryside: a beautiful evening in a field, and a group of workers are having a birthday party. But who picks the strawberries these days?

Book extracts

A Yaketa said, "my […] job pays only the minimum wage, not a proper nurse's salary. Then they make deductions. Tax. Food. Accommodation. Uniform. Training fee. Agency fee. At the end of the week I have nothing left."

"I know about these deductions," I said. "We are strawberry pickers. Accommodation, food, transport; everything comes out of our wages. You know I had not expected such meanness in England."

From *Two Caravans* by Marina Lewycka, London: Penguin/Fig Tree, 2007, page 242.

B There was a little chemist's next door to the Starbucks, so we went in there, but we got out quick* when Alicia saw a friend of her mum's in there. She saw us, too, this woman, and you could tell she thought we'd gone in to buy condoms. Ha! Condoms! We were way beyond condoms, missus! Anyway, we realized that we could never go into a chemist's that size – not just because we might have been spotted, but because neither of us would be able to ask for what we wanted. Condoms were bad enough, but pregnancy tests were in a different class of trouble and embarrassment. We walked on to the Superdrug around the corner.

From *Slam* by Nick Hornby, London: Penguin, 2008, page 92.

* colloquial form of quickly

C I was sitting on the sofa, still wearing my Harriers kit. "You're not a young girl anymore, Jesminder […] now your sister's engaged, it's different," said Dad. He was at the bar in the corner, getting himself a whisky. I didn't drink, but right now I could have done with one myself. "You know how our people talk."

"She's the one getting married, not me!" I said resentfully.

"I was married at your age," Mum snapped. "You don't even want to learn how to cook Indian food!" I didn't see what that had to do with it.

"Anyway I'm not playing with boys any more." Maybe that would shut them up.

"Good." Mum headed off towards the kitchen.

"I'm joining a girls' team," I went on. "They want me to play in proper matches."

From *Bend it like Beckham* by Narinder Dhami, Stuttgart: Ernst Klett Verlag, 2003, page 25.

(317 words)

e) Choose the correct options. More than one answer can be true.

1. Alicia and her boyfriend go into a shop to buy …
   a) cosmetics.
   b) superdrugs.
   c) condoms.
   d) a pregnancy test.
2. They go to a drugstore because …
   a) they want to talk to the manager.
   b) it's cheaper than the chemist's.
   c) nobody knows them there.
   d) they couldn't get what they wanted.
3. In Yaketa's job she …
   a) gets free accommodation.
   b) receives a poor wage.
   c) has to buy her own food and uniform.
   d) earns a lot of money each week.
4. The strawberry pickers in England …
   a) are satisfied with their jobs.
   b) expected this treatment in England.
   c) don't have to pay for transport.
   d) are unhappy with their pay.
5. Jesminder is not happy because …
   a) her father drinks.
   b) she doesn't want to get married.
   c) she doesn't want to play football with girls.
   d) her parents don't really understand her.
6. Her mother isn't happy with Jesminder because …
   a) she is a typical Indian girl.
   b) she isn't interested in cooking Indian food.
   c) she doesn't want to eat Indian food.
   d) she isn't good enough for a football team.

f) Find the words in the above texts that match the definitions.

1. money which working people have to pay to the government
2. person who cares for ill people, especially in hospital
3. room or building in which you stay or live
4. amount of money which is paid regularly to a worker
5. shop in which you can buy medicine or cosmetics
6. a lot of problems
7. become part of a group

B Language

1 Guessing game ►GF14 Defining relative clauses

a) Explain the following words using 'who' or 'which'.
Example: A feminist is a person who fights for women's rights.

1. feminist	tool	(accommodate) ill people
2. drugstore	place	(explain) words
3. dictionary	film	(fight) women's rights
4. hospitals	shop	(hand out) credit cards
5. drill	person	(sell) beauty products
6. island	worker	(give) information about a special topic
7. documentaries	book	(lie) in the sea
8. bank clerk	building	(make) holes in walls

‹I› **b)** Now describe other people/things in the same way but don't mention their names. The rest of the class has to say who/what they are.
Example: It is a shop which sells food. Answer: It's a supermarket.

2 Women then and now ►GF15 Non-defining relative clauses

a) Complete the following text. Fill in 'who' or 'which' to make non-defining relative clauses.

Mary Wollstonecraft, [**1**] was born in London in 1759, was a British writer and feminist. One of her books, [**2**] is about the rights of women, became very important in the women's rights movement in Europe (see Facts). Wollstonecraft, [**3**] had various love affairs, got a bad name because of her lifestyle. One day she helped her sister Eliza, [**4**] wanted to leave her husband and her child for a better life. But social norms, [**5**] existed at that time, forced her sister to live in poverty, because she wasn't allowed to marry again. Wollstonecraft, [**6**] found out that women could not have a career, started to write. At about the same time she met William Godwin, [**7**] later became her husband. Godwin and Wollstonecraft, [**8**] married in 1797, had a daughter, [**9**] was also called Mary. She later became Mary Shelley and wrote the book "Frankenstein", [**10**] is very popular even today.

Mary Wollstonecraft

Grammar

Defining relative clauses
Example: The man who/that is getting on the bus is on his way home.
Bei Personen werden die Relativpronomen who *oder* that *verwendet.*
Example: The bus which/that is at the bus stop is going to Bristol.
Bei Sachen werden which *oder* that *verwendet.*
Example: The man (–) I saw was a good football player.
Ist das Relativpronomen Objekt des Satzes, kann es weggelassen werden.

Non-defining relative clauses
Example: His wife, who is 26, works in an office.
Nicht notwendige Relativsätze werden in Kommas eingeschlossen.
Example: The bus, which was a double-decker, was waiting.
That *wird hier nicht verwendet.*
Example: Henry, who I saw yesterday, is going to hospital next week.
Ist das Relativpronomen Objekt des Relativsatzes, darf es nicht weggelassen werden.

Modal auxiliaries
Example: Cars must/have to stop at red lights.
Für modale Hilfsverben können auch entsprechende Ersatzformen verwendet werden.
Examples: He was not allowed to park his car there.
You will have to leave at 8 o'clock.
Die Ersatzformen werden insbesondere für die Vergangenheit und die Zukunft eingesetzt.

►GF14 Defining relative clauses
►GF15 Non-defining relative clauses
►GF13 Modal auxiliaries

Facts

The women's rights movement refers to the fight for freedom and equality for women, e.g. the right to vote and to equal pay. The movement started in Europe in the late 18th century. Today the women's rights movement is called 'feminism'.

b) Complete the text about British comedian, Shazia Mirza, using the information about her life. Decide if a relative clause is necessary or not, and if you can leave out the relative pronoun.

Shazia Mirza [**1**], **who was born in England in 1975**, is a woman [**2**] **nearly everybody in Britain knows**. Shazia is the first British Muslim [**3**] **who has her own comedy show**. When she started doing her first comedy shows her parents [**4**] did not know about the new profession [**5**]. They thought that their daughter [**6**] was a teacher at a comprehensive school [**7**]. Shazia was so successful with her shows [**8**] that she gave up her job as a teacher. In her shows she makes fun of topics [**9**]. Her favourite topics are Muslim traditions and the new roles [**10**]. Shazia also writes articles for a current affairs magazine in Britain and in 2008 she won the Columnist of the Year Award [**11**].

Some information about Shazia Mirza's life

a) She had studied science at university.
b) The Columnist of the Year Award is one of the most important awards for British journalists.
c) She has her own comedy show.
d) The comprehensive school is in Tower Hamlets, London.
e) She was born in England in 1975.
f) Her parents are very religious Muslims.
g) Shazia had taken up a new profession.
h) Her shows were even broadcast on TV.
i) Her topics are of public interest.
j) Nearly everybody in Britain knows her.
k) Women have new roles in society.

3 Women's roles have changed

a) Talk about women's roles today. Make sentences using the verbs in brackets. ► GF13 Modal auxiliaries

1. take part in government [**can**]
   Example: Today women can take part in government.
2. go to school [**must**]
3. study at university [**can**]
4. wear what they like [**can**]
5. ask their husbands for their okay when they want to go out with friends [**needn't**]
6. marry the man their parents choose [**needn't**]
7. read [**can**]
8. give up their new roles [**needn't**]

b) Talk about women's roles in the past. Make sentences as in the example.

1. vote in elections [**not be allowed to**]
   Example: 200 years ago women were not allowed to vote in political elections.
2. work at home and in the fields [**have to**]
3. attend university [**not be allowed to**]
4. stay at home [**have to**]
5. marry the man their parents chose [**have to**]
6. wear trousers [**not be allowed to**]
7. read in most cases [**not be able to**]
8. take on new roles [**not be allowed to**]

c) Now compare women's roles today with women's roles 200 years ago.
Example: Today women can take part in government but 200 years ago they were not allowed to vote in elections.

4 Men's roles have changed, too

‹P› ▪ Compare men's roles 200 years ago, today and in the future. Use modal auxiliaries and their substitutes.

Example: 200 years ago boys had to go to work when they were 14. Today they must go to school until they are 16. I suppose that in 200 years' time they will have to go to school until they are 18.

C Reading: New ways of helping people

Training skills – How to anticipate, skim and scan

‹P› **Before reading** ► SF 9 Anticipating, skimming, scanning

a) Where does the text "Special school for blind children in Scotland" on page 45 come from?

b) Describe the photos that go with the text and guess what the text is about. ► SF 26 Describing illustrations and photographs

‹R› **c)** Skim through the text without reading it in detail, that means run your eye over the heading and subheadings quickly. Say in one or two sentences what the text is about.

Understanding the text

d) Read all of the text and match the key points below with the headings in the text.

1. Youth in Action programme – Dundee
   Example: These key points match the heading: The European Youth in Action Programme
2. open-minded, responsible, tolerant and interested in people
3. training in social and language skills – interaction with blind children
4. spent a year working in Scotland – helped blind children with daily activities
5. organization of free time activities – creative ideas for games and projects
6. blind people between 2 and 24 years of age – school campus

e) Answer the following questions in your own words. Your results from exercise d) can help you.

1. What facilities are there for blind children on the campus?
2. What do the volunteers learn during their year at the school?
3. What are the volunteers' special tasks at the school?
4. What should people who work in the school be like?
5. What did Stefan do last year?

f) Find the noun(s) that correspond to the adjectives from the text. You can use a dictionary.

1. young (line 3)
2. unpaid (line 5)
3. voluntary (line 6)
4. foreign (line 6)
5. handicapped (line 11)
6. disabled (line 26)
7. creative (line 36)
8. interested (line 40)
9. responsible (line 42)
10. tolerant (line 42)

After reading

‹I› **g)** Work with a partner. One of you covers his/her eyes with a scarf. Walk through your school building with your partner to help and guide you. Switch roles after five minutes. When you are back in class talk about your experiences, your feelings, any problems you had, etc.

‹P› **h)** Apply for a voluntary year at the Special school for blind children in Dundee. Write a detailed letter in which you give your reasons for applying. ► SF 23 Formal letters and e-mails http://www.specialschool-dundee.com

A1.13

Special school for blind children in Scotland

A The European Youth in Action Programme

The Youth in Action Programme, founded by the European Commission, offers young Europeans, aged eighteen to thirty, the chance to express their personal commitment through unpaid and full-time voluntary activities in foreign countries. The volunteers get board, accommodation and insurance.

One of the organizations involved in the Youth in Action programme is the Scottish Special School for blind and visually handicapped children and young adults in Dundee, a city in the east of Scotland.

B Profile of the organization

Our Special school has a school house, two home buildings, flats for staff members and volunteers as well as an outdoor area with a new garden of the senses, which is also open to people from the community. We accept children from the age of 2 years and, if necessary, they can learn and live here up to the age of 24.

C Learning opportunities for volunteers

When doing their voluntary service at our school, volunteers not only get key qualifications in the areas of social skills and organizational structures, they also learn to deal with young disabled people. Additionally, volunteers can do a language course which enables them to manage typical communicative situations of daily life with special focus on child care.

D Tasks

Volunteers can also take part in our leisure time programme. Abilities like computer skills, mechanical skills and musical talent are very useful, and volunteers can also develop ideas for new games, activities or projects. Creative ideas are always welcome!

E Essential requirements

The volunteer should be open-minded about working with disabled people as well as interested in new experiences. It is also essential to be responsible and to be tolerant towards people from foreign cultures.

Volunteers should be able to get along with staff members as well as with the handicapped people.

A working knowledge of the English language would be helpful.

Candidates should explain why they are interested in voluntary service in a detailed letter. Social background, gender, language skills and level of education are important but your motivation is more important.

F Stefan, 19: "A rewarding experience"

"Hi! My name is Stefan, I am 19 years old and from Stuttgart in Germany. Last year I took part in the European Voluntary Service. I spent one year in Dundee and worked with children who are blind. My daily routine was to help the children be more independent in tasks like getting dressed, preparing food, cleaning up or using money. In the evenings I read stories to the children or we played musical instruments. All in all I'd say that my voluntary service at the Special school in Dundee has taught me lots of things that I could not have learned at college."

(460 words)

D Practice

1 Young and female

‹P› Before listening ► SF 27 Describing cartoons

a) Describe the cartoon.

b) After looking at the cartoon, what do you think the person who you are going to hear is talking about?

‹R› While listening

A1.14 **c)** Listen to the young woman and answer these questions.

1. What is the woman's name?
2. Where does she work?
3. Why is life sometimes difficult for her?
4. Who helps her?

d) Listen to the young woman again. Then correct these statements if necessary.

1. Her grandmother was a teacher for people with special needs.
2. Treatment in a hospital today is different from what her grandmother experienced.
3. In her job the speaker works on her own.
4. She works part-time and does not do any night shifts because she is a single parent.
5. Her job is the most important thing in her life so it has to come first.

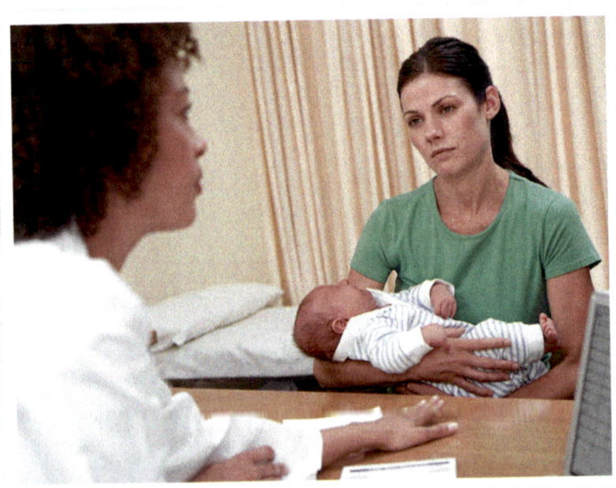

‹P› After listening

e) In Britain, as in many other countries, single parents often have problems combining work and family life. Make a list of the problems they might have to face. Then find a solution to each problem.

f) Imagine you are a single parent and you have a full-time job. Describe your daily routine.

2 Community school centres

‹R› Understanding the text

a) Scan the text "A new concept for community schools" to find all of the facilities a community school centre offers and make notes.

Example: a canteen

A1.15

A new concept for community schools

by Richard Atkins

In the near future community school centres with a completely new concept will open their doors to the public in different cities and towns in Britain. Each centre will not only be home to a secondary school but also to a nursery school, a primary school, a college and a school for students with special needs. The different schools will all be located around one courtyard and they will share common facilities, for example a canteen, a two-storey library, a multi-media conference room, a dance and fitness studio, and a gym. All corridors and rooms will have wheelchair access.

The nursery school is a very important part of the new centre. It will offer full-time care for the children of young mothers and fathers so that they can attend various college classes to learn computer skills or how to look after their children in a responsible way. And the young parents will be able to do their courses, knowing that their children are in the safe environment of the nursery school across the courtyard. Moreover, the college will offer adult learning courses which will help people who left school early to get better qualifications and then to get better jobs.

The new centre will also have a wide range of health services, such as a clinic, which offers contraception advice and personal advice relating to health. In addition, the centre will have facilities for parents and students where social workers advise them on personal problems.

(251 words)

‹M› **b)** A college in your twin town in Britain has invited your class on a visit next year. You know that the town will soon open a new commmunity school centre and you think it would be interesting to visit it. At the next meeting about the visit you explain in German what you have read about the new centre. Use the notes that you made in exercise a).
► SF 22 Mediation/translation

‹P› **c)** Draw a plan of this new community school centre. Use your imagination in designing the centre and its facilities.
Present your drawing and ideas to the class. Explain the functions of the different buildings and how they interact.

‹I› After reading

d) Work in pairs.

Student A: You are a college student in a new community centre in Britain. Read the information on your role card, introduce yourself and play your role. Present your problems and explain why you like the new community school centre.

Student B: You are a single parent. You can find your role card on page 133.

Role card A

Student

Ryan(na) Ferris
- student at the college
- little money for books and college equipment
- in a wheelchair
- lives alone
- rather lonely
- often needs medical treatment.

1

2

3 "And this little warning light flashes when the outside air becomes too polluted to breathe."

Unit 6
Ecology

A Getting started

1 Our beautiful planet? Video lounge 2

‹P› **Before reading** ► SF 27 Describing cartoons

a) Describe the above cartoons and explain their messages.

b) What do the cartoons have to do with the topic of ecology?
Match the cartoons with the following headings (1–6). Three headings do not match.

1. environmental education
2. air pollution
3. recycling waste
4. healthy food
5. vandalism
6. global warming

Understanding the text ► SF 9 Anticipating, skimming, scanning

‹R› **c)** Match the following headings (1–4) with the paragraphs (A–D) on page 49 and with the key points (i–iv).

Headings	**Key points**
1. tasks of the Environment Bureau	i. air pollution – water pollution
2. environmental worries	ii. burning fossil fuels – greater rainfall
3. climate change	iii. planning improvements
4. looking after the local environment	iv. responsible use of resources – recycling – transport

A1.16

A BETTER ENVIRONMENT FOR US ALL

A Concerns about the environment are growing day by day. According to a recent survey people in the UK are becoming increasingly worried about environmental issues and global warming. Air pollution is top of the list, but aspects such as waste management and the pollution of our seas, lakes and rivers follow closely.

B However, perhaps the most important issue affecting our environment is climate change. The burning of fossil fuels in cars, power stations and industry emits gases such as carbon dioxide (CO_2) into the atmosphere. According to experts these gases contribute to long-term climate change. In the UK these changes can affect us in a complex way. Winters are likely to become wetter and summers drier.

C Solving global and national environmental problems means taking action locally. So, helping to look after your local environment is very important. You can do this in different ways. We can all use fewer resources at home and work. We can all recycle waste and reduce the number of trips we make in the car by walking, cycling or taking public transport instead.

D The Environment Bureau has a wide range of duties and powers relating to the improvement of our environment. Part of our responsibility is to encourage the conservation of natural resources, animals and plants. We at the Environment Bureau encourage local governments and communities to identify their local environmental problems so that they can then try to solve them. Problems range from the use of natural resources such as oil, to pollution control and the improvement in the quality of life in our communities. We at the Environment Bureau can give your community a service. We aim to provide you with the latest information on the state of the local environment so that we can then help you in planning any environmental improvements. You can get more information on the Internet.

(314 words)

d) Find the most suitable options according to the text. More than one answer can be true.

1. People are especially worried about …
   a) climate change.
   b) pollution.
   c) animals and plants.
   d) the conservation of natural resources.
2. The main cause of climate change is …
   a) fewer resources.
   b) gases from burning fossil fuels.
   c) rainfall.
   d) waste.
3. People can be more environmentally friendly by …
   a) not using their cars so often.
   b) using a bike.
   c) recycling rubbish.
   d) saving water.
4. The Environment Bureau helps people by …
   a) building new power stations.
   b) cleaning the rivers.
   c) giving them information.
   d) recycling waste.

‹P› After reading ► SF31 Internet research

e) Check the web to find out more about environmental organizations in Britain. Present your results to your class.

2 Do people care about the environment?

‹P› ■ Give your opinion on the statements using the phrases in the box.

1. Michael is of the opinion that they should punish people who damage the environment much harder.
2. Lena believes that people should buy more organically grown food.
3. Carol sometimes does not know what to do with the different types of rubbish.
4. In Ben and Tara's view we have to use less water and then more people in the world will be able to survive.

Language

- I think that …
- I believe that …
- I'm of the opinion that … because …
- In my view …
- As far as I am concerned …

B Language

1 Water for life

▪ Dr Emma Roberts, a voluntary worker with Water for Life, gave an interview on Radio Bristol last month. This is part of the interview. Report what she said using the reporting verbs in the language box.

1. "Every 17 seconds a child in the developing world dies from water-related diseases."
   Example: In the interview Dr Roberts said that every 17 seconds a child in the developing world died from water-related diseases.
2. "Every day people in the world's poorest countries face this problem."
3. "They can drink dirty water that can kill them or die of thirst."
4. "It is a gamble that often carries a high price."
5. "It is heartbreaking to see children who are dying."
6. "For £2 a month everyone here in Bristol can help."
7. "Whole communities can benefit from this help."
8. "It doesn't really matter how much a person gives."
9. "Every gift helps someone to get clean water to survive."

Language

She …
- said that …
- went on to say that …
- told us that …
- informed us that …
- stated that …
- added that …
- concluded that …

Grammar

Reported speech

Example: She said, "I want to help children in Africa." *wird zu:* She said that she wanted to help children in Africa.

In der indirekten Rede ändern sich die Zeitformen wie folgt:
present → past
past → past perfect
present perfect → past perfect
will → would

Auch Pronomina, Orts- und Zeitbestimmungen werden angepasst.

► GF 26 Reported speech

2 How you can help

▪ This is what some people said after reading the Water for Life advert. Report what they told you.

1. Ron: "I saw this advert in the newspaper, too."
   Example: Ron said/told me that he had seen that advert in the newspaper, too.
2. Julie: "My friend gave me the advert."
3. Sam: "I decided to give £2."
4. Tom and Mark: "We donated the money online."
5. Nick: "I filled in the form immediately."
6. Jack: "I didn't know much about this problem."
7. Lisa and Sarah: "We have made the decision to give £5 a month."
8. Jenny: "I haven't checked out this website yet."
9. Dan: "My friend has just read the advert, too."
10. Sandy and Darren: "We didn't realize how important it was to help."

3 A world without seafood

▪ After some people had seen this photo in a magazine, they started to talk about this environmental topic. Report what they said.

1. Sally: "Restaurants will soon have no fish on the menu."
   Example: Sally said that restaurants **would** soon **have** no fish on the menu.
2. Christian: "As I understand it, I will have to pay more for my fish and chips in the future."
3. Helen: "I like tuna, but as I see it I won't be able to get it so easily in the supermarket."
4. Alex and Jane: "We won't be able to buy so much seafood so cheaply."
5. Owen: "In my opinion, I won't have any fish protein to eat apart from algae."
6. Sharon: "As I see it, governments will have to act quickly to avoid a disaster."
7. Bill and Ben: "After reading the article that went with the photo we are sure the catastrophe will happen in our lifetime."
8. Donna: "I won't eat so much fish after reading this article."

4 World Nature Fund

‹I› ▪ Sally Neville belongs to the World Nature Fund. Below you can find some questions that people have asked her.
Work in pairs. One student reports the questions. The other student reports what Sally said.

1. "What do you do in the organization to protect the environment?" [**organize all kinds of activities**]
   Example:
   Student A: People often asked Sally what she did in the organization to protect the environment.
   Student B: Sally said that she organized all kinds of local activities.
2. "Where is the nearest branch of the organization?" [**have branches in all major cities**]
3. "How much do you have to pay to join the organization?" [**donate £10 a year**]
4. "Where can I get a membership form?" [**download online**]
5. "Have you sent leaflets about the organization to our college?" [**send some brochures some months ago**]
6. "When will you come to our college to give us more information?" [**come soon**]
7. "How long has the organization existed?" [**begin in 1961**]
8. "When did you join the organization?" [**become a member in 2007**]
9. "Why did you become a member of WNF?" [**read an interesting article about WNF's activities**]

5 "Water, water, everywhere, but not a drop to drink"

‹I› **a)** Work in groups of four. Discuss the problems relating to water in our world today. Use the role card on the right and the cards on page 133, and make meaningful statements. Make notes during the discussion.

‹P› **b)** Use your notes to write a report about what the members of your group said.

Example: Patrick thought that people had to …

Role card A

Talk about the following things:
- must help poor countries
- environmental organizations
- time is running out

C Reading

1 You are what you eat

‹P› Before reading

a) Describe the pie charts and the photos. ► SF 26 Describing illustrations and photographs
► SF 28 Describing diagrams

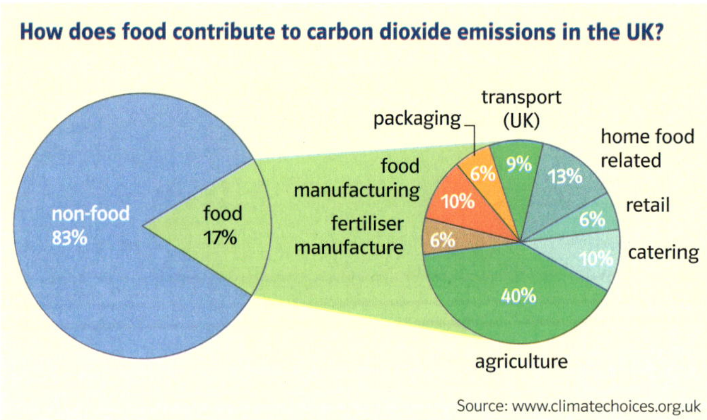

b) Look at the headline of the following article and guess what it is about.

A1.17

How many air miles are there in your hamburger?

by Mary Brayshaw

A Have you ever asked yourself where the food you buy comes from? South African apples, Argentinian beef, Spanish strawberries, Brazilian pineapples, Indonesian king prawns, Indian bananas – they are all common on our supermarket shelves today.

B According to the latest research the average British basket of food has travelled over 50,000 miles from producer to consumer. Food miles, the transportation of food from the farm to your home, use enormous amounts of fossil fuels, which contribute to air pollution and global warming. For this reason food miles harm our environment.
This is why more than thirty food companies in Britain have signed a promise to reduce their food transport miles. They promise to reduce pollution by using rail and shipping instead of road and air transportation. Big food stores in Britain have promised to label products which come by air. These labels will have a logo of an aeroplane on them.

C But researchers have also found that agriculture and manufacturing processes and packaging in the food industry have even greater negative effects on our environment than the so-called food miles. They say that the transport energy for hamburgers is only 20 per cent of the total energy needed in their production.

D In order to encourage its citizens to be more environmentally friendly, the City of Manchester has started an eco-food challenge. They picked out six families to take part in the six-month challenge. The families must cut their energy and water consumption as well as their waste, and they must pay attention to the food they buy. Rather than counting their food's calories they should try to calculate its environmental impact instead. When shopping they should choose organic food which has been grown locally. Also they should only buy fruit and vegetables which have been produced in season, for example strawberries in early summer. A "green advisor" helps the families. As a prize the winners will receive solar equipment for their house. (330 words)

‹R› Understanding the text ► SF 9 Anticipating, skimming, scanning

c) Without reading the text in detail skim through it and say what it is about in a few sentences.

Training skills – How to work with a dictionary

d) The following words are taken from the text. Identify them as nouns, verbs or adjectives in the context of the text. ► SF11 Using a dictionary

1. average (l. 6)	3. harm (l. 12)	5. label (l. 17)
2. contribute (l. 10)	4. promise (l. 14)	6. challenge (l. 28)

e) Find the meaning of the above words using the following parts of an English-English dictionary. Words often have more than one meaning so make sure you find the meaning of the word in the text.

average (n.) – **1.** An **average** is what you get by adding two or more numbers and dividing the result by the amount of numbers you added. **2.** An amount or quality that is **average** is the standard or usual amount/quality of a group of things or people.

average (adj.) – **1.** You use **average** to say that a person or thing is typical or normal. **2.** Something that is **average** is ordinary: it is not so good, nor is it so bad.

challenge (n.) – A **challenge** is **1.** something new and difficult and you must make a big effort to do it. **2.** an invitation from a person to compete or argue with them.

challenge (v.) – If you **challenge** a person **1.** you ask them to compete or argue with you. **2.** You want to know whether what they say is true or whether what they do is correct.

contribute (v.) – **1.** If you **contribute** to a thing **1.1.** you try to make it successful. **1.2.** you pay money or you give assistance to something, usually for charitable purposes. **2.** If something **contributes** to a situation, it is one of the reasons for it. **3.** If you **contribute** to a newspaper or magazine, you write articles for them.

harm (v.) – **1.** To **harm** someone means to hurt them and cause them physical pain. **2.** To **harm** something means to damage it or make it less useful.

label (n.) – A **label** is a piece of paper or another material that is placed on an object. It gives information about the object, for example it tells what it is, who owns it, or how you can use it.

label (v.) – **1.** If you **label** something, you put a label on it to mark it. **2.** If you **label** people as something, you describe or think of them in a certain way, even though they do not agree with your opinion.

promise (n.) – **1.** A **promise** is a declaration which you make to a person saying that you will definitely do something or give them something. **2.** If someone or something shows **promise**, it looks as if they will be successful in future.

promise (v.) – **1.** If you **promise** that you will do a thing, you tell a person that you will certainly do it. **2.** If you **promise** someone a thing, you tell them that you will certainly give it to them. **3.** If a situation or event **promises** to have a special quality, you expect it to have that quality.

f) Identify the underlined words as nouns or verbs in the context of the sentences and find a suitable definition in the dictionary above.

1. The bottles got wet and all the labels came off.
2. The employees have long working hours – 50 hours a week is about the average.
3. The governments promise stricter laws on car emissions.
4. The elderly have much to contribute to the community.
5. The football team has challenged and beaten the best teams in the world.

g) Replace the words "average" (l. 6), "contribute" (l. 10), "harm" (l. 12) and "label" (l. 17) in the text on page 52 with words or phrases from the above dictionary.

h) Answer the following questions on the text using your own words.

1. Why are food miles a problem for the environment?
2. What have some companies done to reduce food miles?
3. What has the City of Manchester done to help the environment?
4. What kind of food should the families taking part in the Manchester challenge buy?

‹M› **i)** Als Mitglied einer Umweltorganisation wollen Sie Ihre Gruppe über diesen Zeitungsartikel informieren. Stellen Sie dazu die wichtigsten Aussagen des vorliegenden Textes auf Deutsch zusammen. Formulieren Sie ganze Sätze. ► SF22 Mediation/translation

D Practice

1 Clubbing with Carol

Before listening

a) Read the headlines and guess what the listening text is about.

1 Nightclub generates its own electricity

2 Clubbing without a bad conscience

3 Party till you drop and save the world

4 UK's first eco-disco to open in London

‹R› While listening

A1.18 **b)** Listen to the radio show and find the most suitable options. More than one answer can be true.

1. The show "Clubbing with Carol" is broadcast by …
   a) London Eye Radio on Friday afternoon.
   b) London Air Radio on Friday afternoon.
   c) London Eye Radio on Saturday morning.
   d) London Air Radio on Saturday afternoon.
2. "Clubbing with Carol" informs listeners about …
   a) pubs in London.
   b) nightclubs in London.
   c) places to go dancing in London.
   d) musicals in London.
3. What is special about the Crystal Club in Soho? It uses …
   a) nuclear energy.
   b) solar energy.
   c) fossil energy.
   d) wind energy.
4. How do they want to generate 60% of the energy to run the club? They want to …
   a) use low-flush toilets, waterless urinals and automatic taps.
   b) use a system like that in electric cigarette lighters.
   c) get their energy from London Electricity.
   d) use energy from the dancers' movements.
5. What will happen to the rest of the energy? They will …
   a) sell it to London Electricity.
   b) save it in large batteries.
   c) sell it to their neighbours.
   d) power the houses in the neighbourhood.
6. The Crystal Club has …
   a) a shiny ceiling.
   b) comfortable wheelchairs.
   c) two bars.
   d) two large dance floors.
7. On the opening night they will entertain the clubbers with …
   a) R&B and Funky House music.
   b) DJs Darina and Simon.
   c) a free drink.
   d) Funk and Soul music.
8. What do clubbers get who cycled or travelled by public transport? They will …
   a) save £12.
   b) only have to pay £12.
   c) receive free entry.
   d) receive free entry and get £12.

‹I› After listening

c) Work in pairs. Student A works for a youth magazine. He/she interviews the club manager Kadeem Abasi about the ecological concept of his club. See role card A "Young journalist". Student B is the club manager. See role card B "club manager" on page 133. Act out the interview.

‹P› **d)** Would you go to an eco-disco? Why? Why not?

Role card A

Young journalist

Ask about:
- materials used in the disco
- energy
- drinks
- transport
- waste

2 Sustainable schools

Hi! I'm Daniel and last year my college won the Green Flag because we took part in a world-wide challenge between schools to make them environmentally friendly. The programme is called "Eco-schools" and it is organized by the non-profit "Foundation for Environmental Education". Currently 43 countries around the world are taking part.

How did we win the Green Flag? We concentrated on four environmental topics: waste, school grounds and equipment, energy and healthy living. We used the future workshop to create an environmentally friendly concept.

Now it's your turn. Get involved and win the Green Flag!

‹P› ◘ Read the personal statement above and use the future workshop (see Facts) to create an environmentally friendly concept for your college.

Critique phase I: Think of things that your college does to protect the environment. Structure them in a word web similar to the one below.

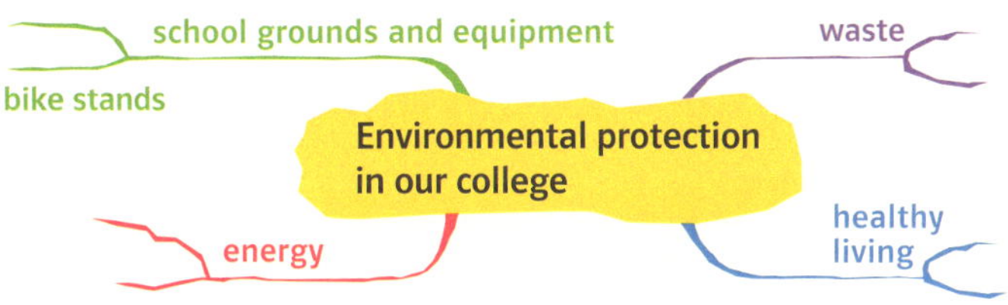

Critique phase II: Now think of things which are harmful to your college environment.

Fantasy phase I: Get together in small groups and collect ideas to turn your school into a sustainable college. Use the Internet for help.
Fantasy phase II: Prepare a presentation with your ideas. Suggestions for your presentation: posters, collages, market stalls, interviews, PowerPoint presentations.
► SF 32 Giving a talk or presentation
Fantasy phase III: Present your concept to your class.

Realisation phase I: Vote for the group that has got the best ideas.
‹M› **Realisation phase II:** Verschriftlichen Sie die besten realisierbaren Ideen, indem Sie einen Brief auf Deutsch verfassen, der an die Schulleitung Ihrer Schule gerichtet ist. ► SF 22 Mediation/translation

Facts

A future workshop helps you to develop creative solutions to a problem. The future workshop has three phases:

1. In the critique phase you speak freely about the positive and negative aspects of your present situation.
2. In the fantasy phase you turn the results from the critique phase into positive ideas, visions and dreams. Be as creative as you can.
3. In the realisation phase you check your ideas regarding their practicability. When you have found a solution, write down an action plan.

Key Words

• eco-schools • environmental school programmes • environmental education • sustainability • sustainable schools

1

2

3

4

Unit 7
Man and technology

A Getting started: Your choice?

‹P› **Before reading** Video lounge 3

a) Look at the four photos above and describe the different ways in which electricity is produced.

‹R› **Understanding the text**

b) Find the most suitable options according to the text on page 57. More than one answer can be true.

1. Ainsworth is a town in …
   a) Nebraska.
   b) Mexico.
   c) Canada.
   d) an area where not much really happens.

2. Today, visitors who go to Ainsworth can see …
   a) a big wind farm.
   b) a viewing platform.
   c) lots of horse thieves.
   d) wind turbines that are more than 100 metres high.

3. The area around Ainsworth is ideal for the installation of wind farms because …
   a) there are favourable winds from the north and south.
   b) there are favourable winds from the east and west.
   c) the winds are very strong.
   d) the winds are not too strong.

4. One of the big disadvantages of wind turbines is that …
   a) they can be seen against the sky.
   b) they are often built far away from the demand for energy.
   c) you can hear the sound of new technology.
   d) they need a lot of empty space.

A1.19

The answer is blowing in the wind

by Rick Martin

A Many people say that Ainsworth, Nebraska lies in the middle of nowhere. The town even has an annual Middle of Nowhere Festival. One of the big advantages of being in the middle of nowhere is the wind. Some years ago officials from the Nebraska Public Power District put up wind monitors at different places around the state. Soon they found out that Ainsworth has wonderful winds flowing down from Canada and up from Mexico. And the winds are just right, not too hard and not too soft.

B About ten years ago Nebraska Public built two small turbines just some miles north of Ainsworth in an area which was not known for its modern technology but for a long history of horse thieves. The first turbines generated power for nearly 400 homes. When you drive out of Ainsworth today, you can't miss the three dozen turbines – up to 350 feet high – in the hills beside grazing cattle. And you can hear the sound of a new era, the sound of energy that is created without burning coal, the sound of the future. Standing beneath the 8.5 ton blades of the turbines you can hear them go whoosh – whoosh – whoosh as they turn …

C "It was like a wonder when we were picked to be the first big wind farm in Nebraska," says the mayor of Ainsworth. When the project was finished, Nebraska Public even created a viewing platform near the main road where visitors can have an impressive view of the big flowers of steel standing out against the wide skies of Nebraska. "Nobody has complained about them," the mayor adds.

D Of course, wind energy can profit from high oil prices and the trend towards putting taxes on carbon dioxide emissions. However, smaller countries are running out of places where they can put wind turbines. Open land is not a problem in the United States however, the main problems are that the wind does not blow all of the time and wind farms are often built far from the big cities where the demand for electricity is the greatest. So wind energy may be a wonder for Ainsworth, Nebraska, but it seems that it is not the answer to all of our energy problems.

(379 words)

‹M› **c)** You are preparing a presentation in German about wind energy in the USA. Find suitable information in the text to complete the chart in German.
► SF 22 Mediation/translation

Vorteile des Standorts	Beschreibung des Windparks	Reaktion der Bevölkerung	Vorteile der Windenergie	Nachteile der Windenergie
…	…	…	…	…

After reading

d) Make sentences about the advantages and disadvantages of wind power.

Example: On the one hand there is enough land for wind farms in the USA but on the other hand …

e) Talk about other ways of producing electricity, and their advantages and disadvantages in the same way. The words in the box may help you.

Forms of electricity production
coal • oil • gas • biofuels • nuclear energy • solar energy • hydro power

Advantages and disadvantages
enough land • relatively cheap • CO_2 • easy to produce • free • expensive technology • environmentally friendly • dangerous • renewable • exhaustible • problems with waste • emissions • dependent • climate changes • environmental problems • food production

B Language

1 The future of energy

■ A lot of suggestions from different groups in society can be read in the newspapers or heard in the news. Complete the following suggestions in the passive voice. 'Must', 'should', 'can' or 'could' must be used at least once.

1. Use oil more carefully!
   Example: Oil should be used more carefully.
2. Save energy!
3. Promote solar power and other renewable forms of energy!
4. Reduce energy consumption!
5. Make nuclear energy safer!
6. Use more biogas!
7. Make wind turbines more efficient!
8. Find new deposits of gas and oil!
9. Make traditional power stations cleaner!

Grammar

Passive voice
Example: New technologies were developed.
Das Passiv wird gebildet mit einer Form von to be *in der jeweiligen Zeit und der 3. Form des Verbs (Partizip Perfekt).*
Example: Coal is transported to power plants by ship.
Der Ausführende kann mit by *angehängt werden.*
Example: Energy consumption must (should, can) be reduced.
Das Passiv kann auch mit Hilfsverben gebildet werden.

► GF 28 Passive voice

2 How electricity is produced

a) Describe how electricity is produced in a coal-fired power station.

1. coal / transport / to the coal-fired power plant / by ship
   Example: Coal is transported to the coal-fired power plant by ship.
2. it / store / near the power plant
3. coal / burn
4. water / heat
5. steam / produce
6. steam / lead / through turbines
7. the blades of the turbines / drive / by the steam
8. magnets inside the generators / move
9. electric energy / produce / in the generators
10. it / send / into power lines
11. steam / cool down
12. water / use again

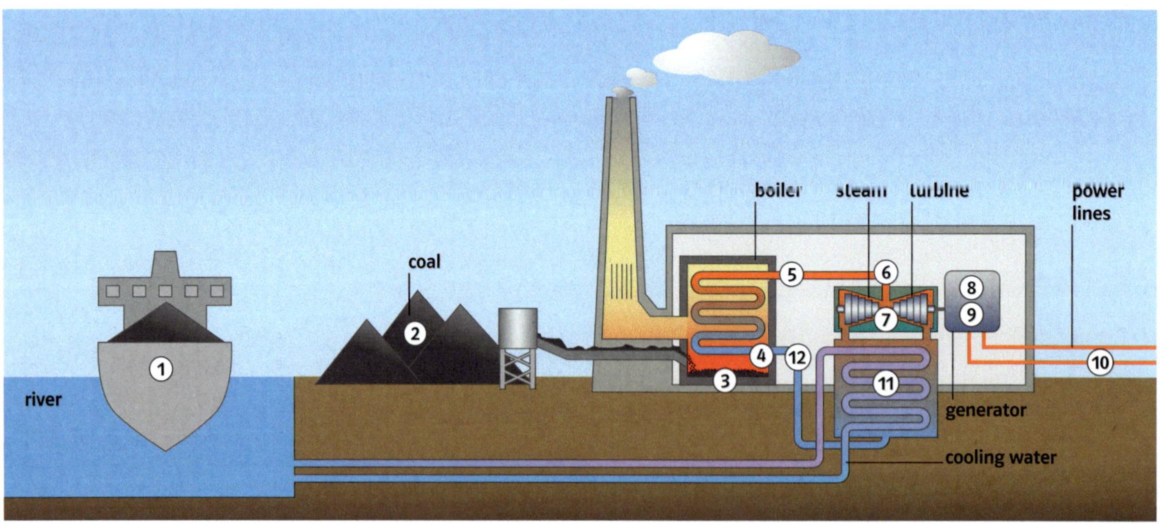

b) Write a description of the process in a complete text. Connect the sentences with words from the box.

Language

then • afterwards • later • finally • and so • in this way • next

‹I› 3 Where were things made?

- Look around your classroom and you will see lots of different products like clothes, shoes and electronic goods. Where were they made? Ask and answer questions about products such as T-shirts, sweaters, caps, school bags, mobile phones, MP3 players, school books, glasses, earrings, pens, drinks, etc.

Example:

Student A: Where were your trainers made?
Student B: My trainers were made in Vietnam. – And where were your glasses produced?
Student A: My glasses were produced in China. Or: I don't know where they were produced. Or: I think they were produced in Asia.

4 Ainsworth wind farm

- Complete the following text about Ainsworth wind farm using the passive voice in the right tense. The first example has been done for you.

Some years ago wind monitors were put up [**1. put up**] in different places around Nebraska. Soon it [**2. find out**] that Ainsworth has wonderful winds. People in Ainsworth were surprised when their area [**3. pick**]. First two small turbines [**4. build**] north of Ainsworth in an area which [**5. know**] for its horse thieves a hundred years ago. Today there is a large wind farm which [**6. cannot, miss**] by visitors. When the project [**7. finish**] a year ago a viewing platform [**8. create**]. Power for nearly all of the homes in Ainsworth [**9. can, generate**] by the wind farm today. The sound of a new era [**10. can, hear**] and this is a sound that [**11. create**] without burning coal. "A disadvantage is that wind farms [**12. often build**] far from big cities in the last few years," says the mayor of Ainsworth. "Of course, not all questions [**13. answer**] by wind energy in the future but it is a big step forward."

‹P› 5 The use of energy in transport/Production processes

- Do one of the following tasks, 1 or 2:

1. Write a short report about the development of the use of energy in transport from the past to the future. Think about steam engines and other inventions, the transport situation today and ideas for the future. Use the passive voice at least five times. The words in the box can help you.
2. Choose an interesting product and describe its production process. Information from the Internet can help you. Use the passive voice at least five times in your description. Connect your sentences using words from the language box in exercise 2b).

Language

engine • steam • diesel • petrol • electric motor • hybrid car • biodiesel • biofuels • solar power • hydrogen

C Reading

1 Cloning Miranda

‹R› Before reading

a) Look at the cover and say what you think the novel is about.

The following text is an extract from the novel "Cloning Miranda" by Carol Matas, page 65.

She starts to talk in a rush, her voice hard, her eyes hard, as if that's the only way she can get the words out. “All right, Miranda, we are going to tell you something now which is bound to upset you. But I think it's better to be upset than to be dead. So, here it is.” She takes a short breath. “That girl is an exact duplicate of you. She was created from DNA taken from you at birth. She's your insurance policy. So many children die in car crashes or of some horrible illness, all because they can't get a replacement organ or some bone marrow or something. We, your father and I, were determined that you would not suffer that fate. We were not going to see you die. So we made a duplicate. She was created here, with the sole purpose of donating to you anything you might need.”

My knees suddenly feel wobbly and I get so shaky I begin to topple over. Dr Mullen puts me in a chair.

“Like a liver,” I say, my voice barely a whisper.

“Yes,” she says, her voice defiant. “Like a liver.”

“So you are going to sacrifice her to save me?”

“It must be done. She's not a real person, Miranda. She's a copy. She's been raised in a lab.”

“But she talks. She feels. She's afraid!”

“Nonsense. This is the moment she's been waiting for.”

I can't speak. I am so shocked, I can't think. A duplicate. A … a … and then the word comes to me and I say it out loud. “A clone.” I start to laugh. “It's a joke, right? It's just a big joke.” They look at me in silence. I stop laughing. “You're not my parents,” I scream. “You're some horrible monsters. This isn't happening. It's not real! It's all a dream. A dream. I want to wake up. I want to wake up!” I'm laughing and crying and screaming. I think I'm losing my mind.

I turn to Dr Mullen. “Give me something so I can sleep,” I demand. “I just can't stand to be awake any longer.”

Dad looks like he is about to cry. Mother just looks mad. I go back to bed and lie down. I want blackness.

(383 words)

From *Cloning Miranda* by Carol Matas, Stuttgart: Ernst Klett Sprachen, 2003, page 65.

‹R› Understanding the text

b) Say if your ideas about the novel in exercise a) were right.

c) Do the following tasks.

1. Name the four people who appear in the extract.
2. Say what fifth person is mentioned.
3. Describe Miranda's reaction to the news about her clone.
4. Explain her parents' motives for cloning their daughter.
5. Mother says, "She was created here." (line 15). Where do you think the characters are at the moment?
6. Why, do you think, is Miranda there right now?
7. Find verbs and expressions in the text that describe how Miranda and her mother use their voices. How do these words express their emotions?
8. Find adjectives in the text that express emotions.

After reading

d) How do you think you would react in Miranda's situation?

‹P› **e)** Miranda needs a liver transplant to save her life. Write an ending to this story.

Training skills – How to write a composition/comment

‹P› 2 Genetic engineering – is it good or bad?

► SF16 Writing a composition/comment

■ What do you think about genetic engineering? Write a composition in about 150 words by following these steps:

1. Write an introduction to the topic.

   Example: Today there is a lot of discussion in the media about genetic engineering. Scientists are developing new methods and they say that they will be able to help millions of people. Many people are worried about the negative effects of these methods …

2. List arguments for and against genetic engineering. The prompts below may help you.

   • chance for childless people • dangerous technology that cannot be controlled • experiments with human beings • new ways of treating deadly diseases • play God • right to decide what happens to one's body • freedom of scientific research • kill human embryos • children as products in a laboratory • no person is harmed

   Example:

For	Against
new ways of treating deadly diseases	…

3. Write complete sentences using connectives from box 1.

   Example: On the one hand scientists hope to find new ways of treating deadly diseases such as …

4. Draw conclusions from the arguments above and state your point of view. The words in box 2 may help you.

   Example: In conclusion I would say that genetic engineering can …

Language 1

firstly • secondly • in addition • moreover • on the one hand • on the other hand • by/in contrast • however • although • next • then • because • therefore • not only… but also • finally

Language 2

in conclusion • as a result • in my opinion • in my view • my opinion is • in short • on the whole • personally I think …

D Practice

1 First child after 55 years

A1.20 **While listening**

a) Say which of the photos could have something to do with the news story.

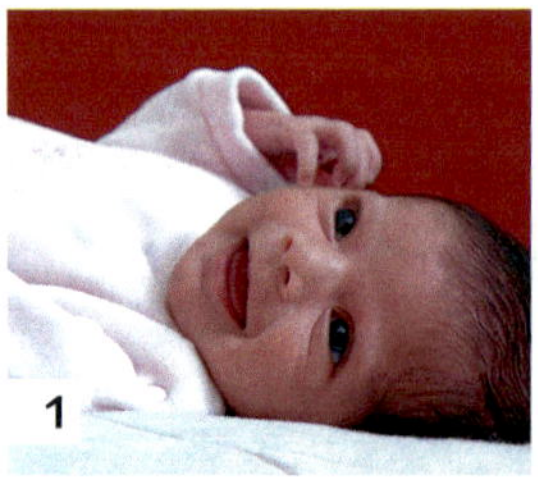
1

2

3

4

5

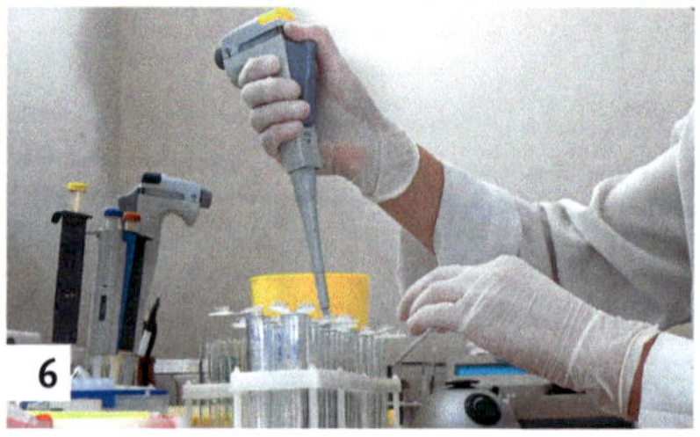
6

7

b) Listen to the story again and find the most suitable options. More than one answer can be true.

1. Mrs Devi is about …
   a) 55. b) 70.
   c) 58. d) 72.
2. Her husband got married …
   a) once.
   b) twice.
   c) three times.
   d) more than three times.
3. Mrs Devi has given birth to …
   a) a daughter. b) a son.
   c) twins. d) her first child.
4. Mrs Devi gave birth …
   a) some weeks ago.
   b) nine months ago.
   c) after in-vitro fertilization.
   d) after ten years of marriage.

‹P› **After listening**

c) Retell the story of Mrs Devi and her husband referring to the photos.

‹P› **2 Is it still in the future?**

1 **Club wants to use gene tests to spot the new Ronaldo. Is this football's future?**

2 **Can biotechnology feed Africa?**

3 **The future of fertility – 100-year-old women giving birth …**

4 **US woman pays $50,000 for cloned puppies**

5 **"I don't want my baby to die!"**

a) Choose one headline and say what the article could be about. Explain how genetic engineering could be used or has been used in that situation.

b) Make up headlines of your own.

‹P› 3 Cloned food

- Describe and analyze the cartoon. ► SF 27 Describing cartoons

‹M› 4 Biotechnology

- Ein englischsprachiger Freund ist interessiert an der Diskussion über Biotechnologie in Deutschland. Fassen Sie den folgenden Kommentar auf Englisch zusammen. Die Stichpunkte im Kästchen können Ihnen dabei helfen.

Language

food • soy(a) • genetically modified • dairy • genetic engineering • genetic material • spray with pesticides • destroy the rainforest

Gen-Soja für Milch?

Kommentar von Hubert Dingelstad

Werber lassen Milchkühe gern unter blauem Himmel auf Bergwiesen grasen. Die Wirklichkeit sieht in der Regel anders aus: Ein Großteil der Tiere lebt in Ställen – und bekommt Futter, das gentechnisch veränderte Pflanzen enthält. Nach Analysen von Greenpeace lassen auch bekannte Molkereien in Deutschland Gen-Soja aus Südamerika verfüttern. Es geht aber auch anders: Die Milchlieferanten eines anderen großen Herstellers ernähren ihre Kühe mit traditionellen Pflanzen, also ohne Soja und ohne Gen-Pflanzen. Die Werbung für Milch und Milchprodukte betont die regionale Herkunft und Naturnähe. Tatsächlich werden dabei die Verbraucher grob getäuscht. Die Nachfrage nach billigem Tierfutter ist verantwortlich für Umweltvernichtung in großem Stil: In Argentinien und Brasilien wurden für den Anbau von Gen-Soja riesige Flächen Urwald gerodet. Zudem wird Gen-Soja stärker mit Pestiziden gespritzt als herkömmliche Pflanzen, was die Arbeitskräfte und das Trinkwasser gefährdet. Grundsätzlich birgt Genmanipulation von Pflanzen ein großes Risiko: Niemand kann vorhersagen, welche Folgen der Eingriff in das Erbgut der Pflanzen langfristig hat.

From *Greenpeace Nachrichten* 2/09, page 2, "Gen-Soja für Markenmilch", adapted.

Online Link
800041-0008

Unit 8
The tourist industry

A Getting started: Holidays and leisure

Before reading

a) Describe the above photos. ► SF 26 Describing illustrations and photographs

b) Where would you like to spend your next holidays? Say why.

A1.21

Trends in tourism

As part of our series of interviews with important members of the tourist industry this week we interviewed Sandra Peters, the manager of World Wide Tours.

Travel Mag Ms Peters, the tourist industry has become one of the most profitable industries in society today. What kind of holiday do most of your customers want when they book with you?

S Peters Well, traditionally, people like to spend their holidays relaxing on the beach or doing some kind of sporting activity. And in the last few years people have increasingly liked to do these things abroad.

Travel Mag But why do a lot of people decide to go abroad for their holidays?

S Peters That is easy to answer. People earn more money and have more days off work than in the past. So they have more time to spend their money and go away on holidays. And they like to go abroad because of the sunshine. Do you remember the terrible summer we had in England last year? I can understand people wanting to get away for their holidays.

Travel Mag And you have quite a lot of inexpensive foreign holidays in your catalogue.

S Peters That's right. Foreign travel is not as expensive as it was and that has made it even more attractive. The new technology in modern planes contributes to cheaper travel. It is also easier to get to places as transport infrastructures are much better. New airports have been built all over the world. Consequently you can often travel directly to your holiday destination. In this way travelling times have been cut and more exotic places have become more accessible to more tourists.

Travel Mag So, mass tourism has arrived in faraway places, too?

S Peters Yes, it has. Last year we had about 1 million bookings for Spain but we also had 300,000 bookings to countries in the Far East.

Travel Mag But not everybody wants to spend their holidays on a beach.

S Peters No, of course not. We offer a whole range of holidays, from adventure travel and cultural trips to ecotourism, extreme sports tourism, safaris, and even space tourism.

Travel Mag So we can say that your business is still growing?

S Peters Yes, the tourist industry in general has expanded over the years and many companies have profited from this development. Just think about the number of new hotels, restaurants, airlines and taxi services that there are today.

(386 words)

‹R› Understanding the text

c) Give examples of what most people do on holiday.

d) List some reasons why British people go abroad on holiday.

e) Give reasons why faraway destinations have become more attractive to tourists.

f) Explain how the service sector has benefited from tourism (see Facts).

‹M› **g)** You tell a friend who wants to open a travel agency about the interview. Summarize the most important aspects in German.
► SF 22 Mediation/translation

Facts

The economy is divided into three sectors.

Primary sector: extraction and production of raw materials.
Examples: agriculture and mining.

Secondary sector: production of goods.
Example: manufacturing of cars.

Tertiary sector (Service sector): services to consumers and businesses.
Examples: insurance companies, banks and shops.

‹P› After reading ► SF 21 Word webs

h) Copy the word web into your exercise book. Write down words from the text and other words that you know. If necessary use a dictionary.

i) Work with a partner. Compare word webs and then add any new words your partner has found to your word web.

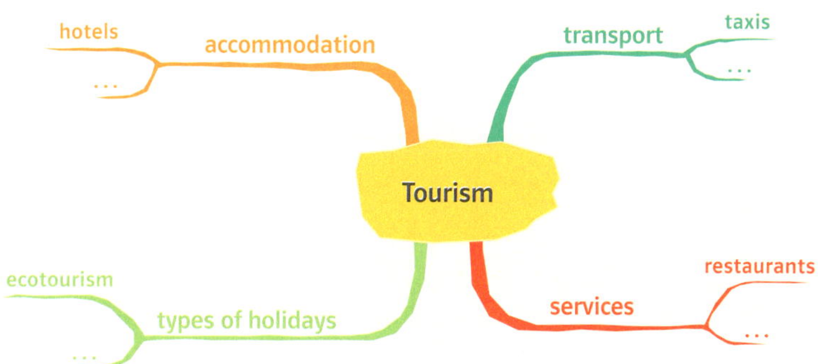

B Language

1 Sightseeing quiz

a) Match the following sights with the correct cities and countries.

Sights	Cities	Countries
Red Square	Paris	USA
Opera House	London	Australia
Ying Sin Koon Temple	Berlin	China
White House	New York City	France
Brandenburg Gate	Washington D.C.	Russia
Statue of Liberty	Sydney	Britain
Eiffel Tower	Moscow	Germany
Tower Bridge	Hong Kong	USA

‹I› **b)** Check if your partner's solutions are correct.

Example:
Student A: What will you see if you go to Paris?
Student B: If I go to Paris in France, I will see the Eiffel Tower.

Grammar

Conditional Type 1
Example: If you travel to New York, you will see the Statue of Liberty.
Present simple *im* if-*Satz* – *Zukunft mit* will *im Hauptsatz*

Conditional Type 2
Example: If I had the money, I would travel around the world.
Past simple *im* if-*Satz* – Conditional *mit* would *im Hauptsatz*

Conditional Type 3
Example: If I had known better, I would have stayed at home.
Past perfect *im* if-*Satz* – Conditional *mit* would have *im Hauptsatz*

► GF 27 Conditionals

2 Planning a trip

‹I› ▪ Jennifer and Carl, two Australians living in Ulm, have decided to get married. They want to get married at home because of their families and friends so they go to a travel agency to get some information about flights. Luckily, the travel agent speaks English, as they don't speak much German.

One student takes the role of Jennifer or Carl, and the other the role of the travel agent. Ask and answer questions.

Examples:
Jennifer/Carl: Which airline will we fly with if we depart at half past five?
Travel agent: If you depart at half past five, you will fly with British Airways.
Jennifer/Carl: Where will we leave from if we fly with Qantas?
Travel agent: If you fly with Qantas, you will leave from Stuttgart Airport.

Airline	Flight number	Departure	Destination	Departure time	Arrival time	Flight time	Price
British Airways	BA 955	Munich International Airport	London Heathrow	Sunday 17:30	Sunday 18:30	23 hours 50 minutes	€782.04
	Layover 3 hours 45 minutes						
	BA 7312	London Heathrow	Sydney Kingsford Smith Apt	Sunday 22:15	Tuesday 06:05		

Airline	Flight number	Departure	Destination	Departure time	Arrival time	Flight time	Price
Qantas	QF 3936	Stuttgart Airport	Frankfurt, International	Sunday 19:51	Sunday 20:30	20 hours 56 minutes	€805.50
	Layover 3 hours 25 minutes						
	QF 6973	Frankfurt, International	Sydney Kingsford Smith Apt	Sunday 23:55	Tuesday 05:10		

3 Tourism and the environment

■ What would happen if …? Complete the suggestions for a better environment using the correct forms of the verbs in brackets.

1. If people [**use**] public transport more, they [**save**] energy.
   Example: If people **used** public transport more, they **would save** energy.
2. If flights [**be**] more expensive, people [**fly**] less.
3. People [**not travel**] so far or so often if they [**think**] more about the environment.
4. If fuel [**be**] more expensive, people [**not use**] their cars so much.
5. Visitors [**do**] sightseeing by bike if cities [**have**] more bikes for hire.
6. If the transport of goods by ship [**be**] faster, more goods [**be delivered**] by ship.
7. If the beaches [**have**] some more bins, the tourists [**not drop**] so much litter.
8. If the guests [**not want**] fresh towels every day, the hotels [**save**] a lot of water.

4 What would you do if …?

‹P› ■ Now use your imagination. Think about things you would do if …

Example: If I had my own plane, I would fly to the States whenever I liked.

1. If I were a travel agent …
2. If my parents owned a house on Hawaii …
3. If my friend asked me to go on holiday to Majorca …
4. If I spoke several languages …
5. If I won the lottery …

5 After the holidays

■ Jennifer and Carl have come back from their honeymoon in Ireland. They had some problems during the trip and now they are having an argument. Complete the dialogue with the highlighted verbs.

Jennifer: Before we can watch TV we must unpack all of our bags and put the washing machine on.

Carl: Well, if you **hadn't taken** so many clothes on holiday, we **wouldn't have needed** so many suitcases.

Jennifer: Oh come on, I needed those pretty dresses, otherwise we wouldn't have got into those trendy discos. If you [**1. not speak**] to that girl in the bar, I [**2. not be**] jealous and then we [**3. not have**] a big argument and we [**4. have**] a perfect trip.

Carl: You always blame me if anything goes wrong. If you [**5. book**] a holiday to Majorca instead of Ireland, we [**6. have**] a wonderful time in the sun and we [**7. relax**] more.

Jennifer: Well, I asked you and you didn't want me to change the flight. But it [**8. be**] more relaxing if you [**9. take**] your driving licence. Then I [**10. not drive**] the car and the accident [**11. not happen**].

Carl: Oh, never mind. If I [**12. not marry**] you, I [**13. not have**] so much fun.

C Reading: Tourism and conservation

A1.22

http://www.ecotourism-foundation.com

About us | Our Initiatives | Learning centre | Support | Ecotourism – Blog

The Ecotourism Foundation

A Local communities and nature need to be preserved. The Ecotourism Foundation has made these two things their top priority. The Foundation is an organization which tries to bring those people living in protected areas into the business of ecotourism. In this way the Foundation believes that nature can be preserved and at the same time the economic situation of the people in such areas can be improved. So what the Foundation does is to help these people by establishing community businesses and providing tourism training and backup assistance.

Farmers at work in the fields, Ecuador

B One perfect example can be found in Belize in Central America: The second largest barrier reef in the world is located in southern Belize. Naturally this area needs to be protected. So the Foundation started a programme to train native fishermen to work as guides for the tourists. They are now able to tell the tourists about the fascinating nature, legends and life in the Caribbean. The positive effect is that the native fishermen no longer need to go fishing. In this way the fish population is protected and the fishermen have a better and less dangerous way of securing their incomes.

Fisherman in Belize

C Another example of ecotourism can be found in Ecuador's Condor Bioreserve. This area has a variety of attractions including thermal springs, forests, interesting animals and a tradition of wood carving. Attractions like these are useful in several ways. Firstly, the money that the tourists spend contributes to the income of the communities in this area. Secondly, interesting traditions stay alive and thirdly, nature is preserved because the communities no longer need to exploit their surroundings in a way that is harmful to the environment.

(279 words)

Facts

Ecotourism (also known as ecological tourism) means to travel to sensitive and untouched areas with the aim of educating the travellers, bringing money to local communities and most important, preserving nature and the different cultures there.

Training skills – How to answer questions on a text

Before reading

a) Look at the photos on page 68 and the heading of the text. What do you think the text is about?

Example: I think the text is about tourism and the pictures show people who could be affected by tourism …

Understanding the text

b) Read the text carefully to get a general impression of it.

c) Summarize the text in a few sentences.

Example: The text is about ecotourism and deals with the functions of the Ecotourism Foundation …

d) Read the questions.

1. What has the Ecotourism Foundation made its top priority?
2. What positive effects does the work of the Foundation have for the people in a protected area?
3. How did the Foundation help people in the protected area in Belize?
4. How can attractions like the ones in Ecuador's Condor Bioreserve be useful?

e) Scan the text and note the lines where you can find the answers.

Example for question 1:
- Lines 1–3

Example for question 2:
- Lines 8–13

f) Look up all of the unknown words which are important for the answer.

Example: community (line 1)
community, n: 1. group of people living in an area of the same race or having the same job, religion or interests; 2. people sharing the same ideas; 3. a group of plants or animals interacting with one another in a place under similar conditions

Example: establish (line 11)
establish, v: 1. get people to believe in something; 2. start something such as a business; 3. show that something is correct

g) Decide which explanation is the most suitable according to the text.

- The first explanation is the most suitable.

- Here the second explanation is the most suitable.

h) Write down key words that you can use in your answers.

Example:
- help natives
- save nature

Example:
- earn money
- start businesses
- get training

i) Answer the questions using your <u>own</u> words.
- You may use the question as an introduction in your answer.
- Give and rephrase the main facts using your key words.
- Always write full sentences.

Example: The Ecotourism Foundation has made nature and the people traditionally living in this area their top priority.

Example: People living in protected areas get help from the Foundation to start …

j) Check your answer.

D Practice

‹R› 1 Sustainable tourism meets mass tourism

Before listening

a) Which photo do you associate with sustainable tourism and which with mass tourism? Say why.

While listening

A1.23 **b)** Listen to Lisa and Matthew who have just come back from their holiday trips. Find the most suitable options according to the statements. More than one answer can be true.

1. What kind of holiday did Matthew go on?
   a) sustainable tourism
   b) mass tourism
   c) safari tourism
   d) medical tourism
2. What sporting activities did Matthew do during the day?
   a) jet-skiing
   b) paragliding
   c) free climbing
   d) swimming
3. How many young adults met in Calella?
   a) about 60 people
   b) about 560 people
   c) about 10 groups with 50 – 60 people per group
   d) about 800 young adults
4. How much did Lisa's hotel cost?
   a) £200
   b) £300 without breakfast
   c) £100
   d) £300 with breakfast
5. What did Lisa do during the day?
   a) hiked to the volcanoes
   b) slept
   c) swam
   d) watched birds and other animals
6. Where might Lisa go next summer?
   a) Costa Rica
   b) Spain
   c) Ireland
   d) Mali

‹P› 2 Reasons for travelling

a) Describe and compare the pie charts. ► SF 28 Describing diagrams

b) Think of reasons for the main differences between the two charts.

c) Which European country could the charts refer to? Give reasons.

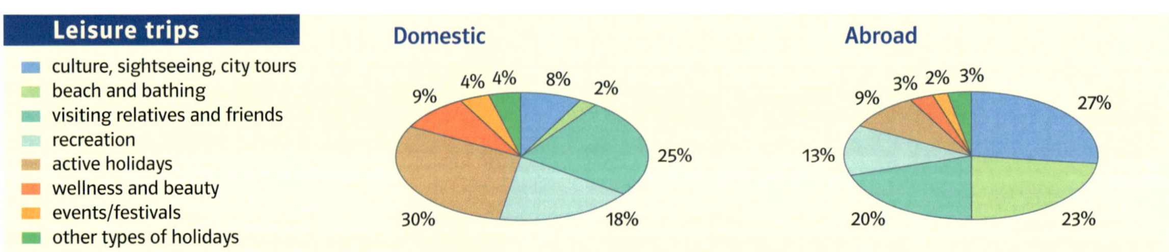

‹P› 3 Designing a brochure

■ Choose a type of holiday that is possible in the area where you live and design a holiday brochure. You can find information on the Internet.

Key Words
- holiday brochure
- holiday
- ecotourism

‹I› 4 Presentation and discussion: Developing an economy

► SF 32 Giving a talk or presentation ► SF 3 Having a discussion

a) The local government of a small area in South Africa (see map below) wants to expand its economy but cannot decide which sector to develop. Investors from different sectors have different ideas about how to use the area: one idea is to mine the gold there, another is to create a manufacturing area, and yet another idea is to develop tourism. The investors meet with the local government to present their ideas. Work in four groups. The first group represents the local government, the second group represents the mining company, the third group represents the manufacturers and the fourth group represents the travel organizations.

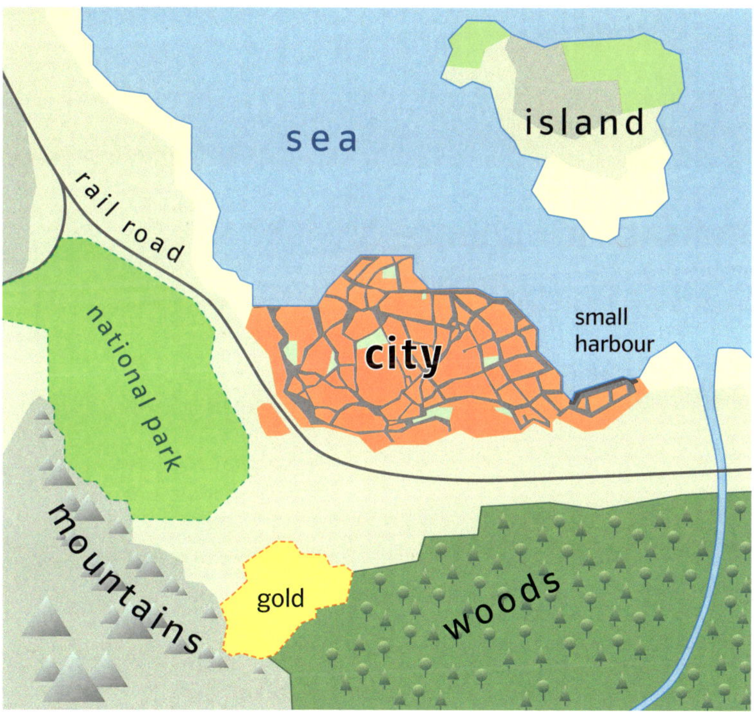

The local government group uses role card A "Local government" on the right. The other groups have to persuade the local government to use the area for their purpose. Prepare and give a presentation. You will find role card B "Mining company", role card C "Manufacturing company" and role card D "Travel organizations" on page 134.

b) After the presentations the government asks questions about the effects of each type of development.

c) All of the groups discuss the pros and cons of the suggestions.

d) Decide in class which ideas are most suitable for the area.

Role card A

Local government
- Before the presentations you should think about the following:
  - what would be best for the area,
  - what would be best for the people living there.
- Ask about the possible effects of each development: jobs, pollution, traffic, tourism, income of people in the area, technical requirements, etc.
- Listen to the three groups carefully. Take notes during the presentation and discussion to help you make a decision later on.

1

2

3

4

Unit 9
Globalisation and multiculturalism

A Getting started: Globalisation – chance or risk?

‹P› Before reading ► SF 26 Describing illustrations and photographs

a) Describe the above photos.

b) Match the photos with the headings on the right. Two headings do not match.

c) Explain what the photos and headings could have to do with globalisation.

- sports
- trade and transport
- communication
- education and training
- labour market
- tourism

‹R› Understanding the text

d) Find the most suitable options according to the text. More than one answer can be true.

1. Bhanu works …
   a) in the cotton fields near Surat.
   b) for very little money.
   c) in a dyeing factory.
   d) in a T-shirt factory.

2. Marlene …
   a) wants to buy American labels.
   b) wants to buy Austrian clothes.
   c) lives a boring life.
   d) thinks American clothes are unfashionable.

3. Matthew can buy …
   a) over 160 different US-branded sneakers all over the world.
   b) US-branded trainers in 160 countries.
   c) fast food only in some countries.
   d) hamburgers all over the world.

4. Nicole's life will change, because …
   a) her company is going to close its factory in Germany.
   b) she must move to the Czech Republic for economic reasons.
   c) she will have to either work for less money in the Czech Republic or risk becoming unemployed.
   d) a manufacturer of MP3 players is moving to the Czech Republic.

A1.24

What's globalisation to them?

A Bhanu, 15, from Surat, India: "Every day my work reminds me of how small the world is. Most of the people in our city work for the textile industry: they either collect cotton in the large cotton fields around Surat or they work in one of the dyeing factories. I'm a dyer and I dye the cotton which is used to make T-shirts that are sold all over the world. The pay is low and the chemicals we use are not good for us. So, some people risk their lives while others make money."

B Marlene, 18, from Vienna, Austria: "Well, what's globalisation to me? I don't know, I'm not very interested in things like that. Maybe it's about being able to buy whatever you like. I love to go shopping with my friends. We really like American labels, especially for T-shirts, jeans and all kinds of accessories. American clothes are so cool! Life would be very boring if we were only able to buy Austrian stuff."

C Matthew, 20, from Chicago, USA: "I'm very interested in other cultures and I love travelling to countries all over the world. Today it is possible to buy cheap flights to any destination. Also, international education standards are great because they help you to get into foreign colleges more easily. The world has changed in many ways, but not every change is for the better. You find the same coffee shops, fast food chains and clothing brands no matter where you go. I can eat a hamburger in more than 100 countries or buy US-branded trainers in 160 countries. So many cities are losing their identities."

D Nicole, 21, from Frankfurt, Germany: "Unfortunately globalisation is going to make life difficult for me in the future. I'm in the second year of my apprenticeship at a leading manufacturer of mobile phones and the company is going to move its factory to the Czech Republic for economic reasons. Should I go with them and make less money and leave my family and friends or should I stay and risk unemployment? Either way globalisation will change my life in a negative way."

(362 words)

e) Answer the following questions in complete sentences.

1. What does globalisation mean to the people in Surat?
2. What is Marlene interested in?
3. In which ways have many cities changed?
4. What kind of problem is Nicole facing?

‹I› **f)** Write down the pros and cons of globalisation according to the texts and discuss them in class. ► SF 3 Having a discussion

After reading

‹P› **g)** "The world is getting smaller." Use the information in the texts and your own ideas to write a comment of about 250 words.
► SF16 Writing a composition/comment

B Language: Welcome to Ohio!

a) Sam, a student in New Zealand, is spending a year in Ohio in the United States of America as part of his course. His tutor gives him a list of things to do before he leaves. Report what the tutor wants Sam to do as in the example. The verbs in the box may help you.

Example: Sam's tutor told him / advised him to send an e-mail to Mr Wilkins in Ohio.

Sam

Checklist
1. **e-mail to Mr Wilkins, your tutor in Ohio**
2. letter to your host family
3. courses at the college
4. flights to Ohio
5. company where students do their work placements in Ohio
6. more about the American way of life

read
find out
write
send
check
contact

Grammar

Infinitive with 'to'
Example: He told her to send an e-mail.
nach bestimmten Verben (ask, tell, advise, expect, etc.)

Infinitive without 'to'
Example: Please let me go.
als Objekt nach make *und* let

Gerund
Example: Julie loves reading.
nach bestimmten Verben (enjoy, like, dislike, hate, prefer etc.)
Example: Julie is interested in reading love stories.
nach Verben, Adjektiven, Substantiven mit Präpositionen

► GF 29 Infinitive
► GF 30 Gerund

b) Sam has received an e-mail back from Ohio. Complete the e-mail using the correct form of the verbs below.

• let • **expect** • make • want • ask • expect

From: studentadvice@ohiouni.us
To: sam_80@wellingtoninstitute.nz
Subject: Student visit

Dear Sam,

We want to give you an idea of what we [1] **expect** you to do during your stay. Your tutors have [2] us to develop a work plan for you. They [3] you to do a work placement in a company two days a week.

You will spend the rest of the week at college. The college [4] you to give a presentation about life in New Zealand and how it differs from the American way of life. So you see, it's not a holiday! We [5] you work hard. But we will [6] you go early on Fridays so that you can see as much of Ohio as possible.

We look forward to meeting you soon.

Regards,
Cathy Jackson
Student Advisor Ohio University

‹I› **c)** Sam has arrived in Ohio and has already made two new friends, Julie and Marvin. You can see below what they like and don't like doing.

1. Work in pairs. Play the roles of Julie and Marvin. Tell each other about your likes and dislikes. Use the words in the box on the right.
   Example: Julie: I enjoy reading love stories.
2. What do they prefer doing?
   Example: Julie prefers reading love stories to fantasy novels.

⊕○○ like	⊖○○ dislike
⊕⊕○ enjoy	⊖⊖○ not enjoy
⊕⊕⊕ love	⊖⊖⊖ hate

Julie

likes	doesn't like
⊕⊕○ love stories	⊖⊖○ sport on TV
⊕○○ disco	⊖○○ fantasy novels
⊕⊕⊕ restaurant	⊖⊖⊖ tennis

Marvin

likes	doesn't like
⊕⊕⊕ baseball	⊖⊖○ ice hockey
⊕○○ cinema	⊖⊖⊖ fast food
⊕⊕○ pop music	⊖○○ TV

‹P› **d)** Match each phrase with the correct preposition. Then make sentences.
Example: I'm interested in playing … / in listening to … / in reading …

1. be **interested**	**in**
2. be good	to
3. be tired	in
4. be afraid	of
5. look forward	for
6. succeed	of
7. apologize	at

e) Sam's work placement is at a logistics company. When he arrives there, he is given a list of guidelines for new employees. Use the words below to complete the guidelines.

• persuade • have • ask • make • **help** • work • discuss • speak

- We are good at [**1**] **helping** customers with their logistic problems. A lot of our work is done on the phone, so remember to be polite. You must also be interested in [**2**] customers about their specific problems.
- Very often our phone lines are busy, so, first you should apologize to callers for [**3**] to wait before [**4**] to you.
- Remember we have to succeed in [**5**] them that we can solve their logistic problems. So, you have to be good at [**6**] their problems.
- At first the work can be difficult, but don't be afraid of [**7**] small mistakes. In this way you will learn. We look forward to [**8**] with you.

C Reading: Multicultural Britain in the global world

‹P› Before reading ►SF 26 Describing illustrations and photographs Video lounge 4

a) Describe the photos.

b) Skim the text to find out what aspects of it the photos refer to.

A1.25

Bradford – A global town

A Consumer habits have become more global: You can buy the same products in New York and New Delhi, and if you want an authentic Indian curry in Bradford, England, you only need to go as far as the next takeaway. Companies are thinking more globally, too: In order to keep costs low, production is often moved from industrialized countries in the West to countries where labour is cheaper such as India, Pakistan and the Far East. As a result those jeans you can buy in the high street, for example, are really cheap but they are produced thousands of miles away rather than in local factories. Finally, employees are forced to think globally: they must move to where the work opportunities are. Such movements of companies and people can change the faces of cities radically and Bradford in the north of England is a good example of this.

B Bradford has a long history of immigration and change. In the nineteenth century the city was a major producer of textiles in Europe. German merchants settled there and built warehouses to store their goods – Bradford's textiles – before selling them. We can still see many of these buildings today in an area of Bradford known as "Little Germany". The German immigrants were soon followed by Italians and Eastern Europeans.

C In the 1950s the next wave of immigrants started to come from India and Pakistan. Most of these immigrants came originally to work in the textile factories. Nowadays, most of the second and third generations work in other sectors. The reason is simple: nearly all of Bradford's textile factories have now closed. Ironically, much of the textile production has moved to the immigrants' home countries. Nevertheless, Bradford still has a large Asian population and you can find a large range of Asian markets and stores which sell both modern and traditional Asian textiles. And so Bradford's long history of the textile trade carries on into the 21st century.

D Bradford has become even more racially diverse following a more recent wave of immigration. Migrant workers from Eastern Europe have come to Britain to escape the poor economic situation in their own countries. If you visit one of Bradford's markets, you will hear a variety of languages, from Polish to Latvian to Russian. However, unlike the Asian immigrants, this group of migrant workers will probably move on as soon as the economic situation changes.

(402 words)

Training skills – How to do multiple choice exercises

Understanding the text ►SF12 Multiple choice exercise

c) 1. Skim the text to get a general impression of it. Names, countries or places, numbers and dates can all be important key words.
Example: Bradford, North of England, Germans, Italians, Eastern Europeans.

2. Read the options in the following exercise carefully.
Example: Many Europeans came to Bradford in the 19th century because …
a) it was a centre for Germans.
b) it had become ethnically diverse.
c) it offered work in the textile industry.
d) it had become one of the leading textile centres in Europe.

3. Scan the text for the relevant information.
Example: 19th century – German merchants – Italians and Eastern Europeans soon followed the German immigrants to the textile centre (see lines 26–27).

4. Read the statements again and eliminate false statements. Is this information mentioned in the text? Is the opposite true?
Example: Eliminate options a and b.

5. Decide which statement is true. Sometimes more than one option is correct.
Example: This leads you to the options c and d.

6. To check your answer, find a reason or reasons why the statements are true.
Example: Options c and d are true because it says in the text that Bradford was a major producer of textiles in Europe (lines 20–21).

7. If you are not sure, do not guess. You may lose credits if your answer is not correct.

d) Do the multiple choice exercise in the same way. Find the most suitable options according to the text. More than one answer can be true.

1. Many firms produce goods abroad because …
a) the workers have left for other countries.
b) they do not have to pay high wages there.
c) they want to sell them to tourists.
d) they can then sell their products more cheaply.

2. The Pakistanis who first came to Bradford worked …
a) in shops.
b) in the textile mills.
c) in engineering plants.
d) in the digital media sector.

3. Almost all of the textile factories in Bradford have closed because …
a) all of the immigrants have left Bradford.
b) the immigrants sold them to companies in the Far East.
c) textiles are now produced more cheaply in Asian countries.
d) the second-generation immigrants do not want to work in Bradford.

4. You can say that Bradford is still very "Asian" because it has …
a) many Thai restaurants.
b) many Asian businesses.
c) a lot of Chinese people.
d) a lot of Asians who have remained there.

5. Bradford is truly multicultural because it has …
a) people from all over the world.
b) cheap markets.
c) a mixture of people from Europe and Asia.
d) textiles from all over the world.

6. The latest wave of migrants to Bradford has come from …
a) India.
b) Pakistan.
c) Eastern Europe.
d) China.

D Practice

1 People on the move

a) Describe the cartoon. ►SF 27 Describing cartoons

b) Explain the message of the cartoon.

2 Keeping trade fair

Before listening

a) Describe the photos. What aspects of global trade would you associate with them? ►SF 26 Describing illustrations and photographs

A1.26 While listening

b) Listen to the podcast and note down the names of the people in the studio.

c) Match the photos on page 78 with the two people being interviewed.

d) Listen to the podcast again and find the most suitable options. More than one answer can be true.

1. The first studio guest has returned from …
   a) Dubai.
   b) India.
   c) Vietnam.
   d) the Far East.
2. He describes …
   a) the living conditions in Asia.
   b) the working conditions in some Vietnamese factories.
   c) some sights in Vietnam.
   d) some products which are made in Asia.
3. He tells us that many Vietnamese people are …
   a) working in Europe.
   b) working in India.
   c) unemployed.
   d) tourists abroad.
4. He works as a …
   a) teacher.
   b) journalist.
   c) disc jockey.
   d) foreign aid worker.
5. The second studio guest has just come back from …
   a) South East Asia.
   b) a Third World country.
   c) West Africa.
   d) abroad.
6. She tells us that Technoserve is an organization which …
   a) gives poor people food.
   b) produces machines.
   c) trains people to become politicians.
   d) helps to train people to run businesses.
7. She works for …
   a) Technoserve.
   b) Fairtrade.
   c) a local newspaper.
   d) an African restaurant in Bradford.
8. She describes how …
   a) the farmers in Ghana work.
   b) the aid workers help people.
   c) Fairtrade works.
   d) the newspaper works.
9. She wants the radio listeners to buy …
   a) the Bradford newspaper.
   b) Fairtrade products.
   c) some chocolate.
   d) the Fairtrade logo.

After listening

e) Describe what you can see in the photos.

1

2

3

f) Choose one of the products shown above. Find out the problems which producers of this product face. Then sum up the support that Fairtrade can offer producers.

Key Words

Check the Fairtrade website in the UK.

1

2

3

Unit 10
International politics

A Getting started: The United Nations and the situation in Africa

Before reading

a) The photos show some of the tasks of the United Nations. Match the photos with the tasks. Two tasks do not fit.

Tasks
- economic development • humanitarian help
- peacekeeping • international law • human rights

‹P› **b)** Have a closer look at one of the photos. Say what the story behind it could be. Think about 'who', 'where', 'when', 'what' and 'why'.

Understanding the text

c) Do the following tasks in complete sentences.

1. Describe the situation of many people in Zimbabwe.
2. Give three reasons for the difficulties in Zimbabwe.
3. Describe the activities of the organizations which give aid in Zimbabwe.
4. Explain how not having enough to eat affects people who are infected with HIV.
5. Describe the effect the high rate of infections has on families and on children in particular.

Facts

The United Nations

Membership: 192 member states
Established: 24 October 1945
Staff: about 40,000
Peacekeeping operations: 16
Budget: USD 4.1 billion (excluding peacekeeping operations)
Official languages: Arabic, Chinese, English, French, Russian, Spanish

A1.27

Help! by Jeremy Dalton | *The Southern Sunday Magazine*

A Thabita Moyo will probably die although she has got the drugs that can save her life. Each month her medicine arrives together with a delivery of Red Cross food aid. Thabita lives in a small village in Masvingo, Zimbabwe and her family's food always runs out after a week or two. After that, Thabita and her children have a small meal only once a day made from wild vegetables or maize that they get from their neighbours.

B Thabita suffers from an HIV infection and the pills help to prevent AIDS from breaking out. But she is not able to take the pills on an empty stomach because the pain is terrible. In this way her body is getting weaker and weaker, so at some point she will have AIDS.

C Thabita is not the only one who does not have enough to eat. As well as several non-governmental organizations, the United Nations' World Food Programme feeds about seven million people in Zimbabwe, more than two-thirds of the population. However, the rations only contain about 600 calories a day, which is less than a person needs to survive. That is why many Zimbabweans have fled across the border to South Africa in order to find work and food.

D Political problems, high inflation and bad harvests have caused the situation in Zimbabwe. Matt Coburn, a UN official, explains, "The soil looks healthy but the problem is that there are not enough quality seeds and no fertilizers." The lack of food has led to an increase in cholera infections, which have already killed more than 3,000 people, and the number is rising. Moreover, one in four Zimbabweans is infected with HIV. AIDS has changed the traditional family model by killing thousands of fathers and mothers. Many children are now in the care of their grandparents or of older brothers and sisters. The number of adults in the working population is decreasing. 60-year-old Sylvia Nyakura had 13 children. Five have already died and they left her with twelve grandchildren who live with her. "There are days when we do not eat," she says. "There's nothing left."

E Furthermore there is no money for books or pens and as a result the children do not go to school. "I don't think I can send the children to school any more," says Shenghi Olomo, who looks after her own children and several grandchildren. "I've sold everything I have to keep them alive. I'm not so worried about school. I'm only worried about food."

(419 words)

Facts

Zimbabwe

Capital:	Harare
Official language:	English
Area:	390,757 km²
Population:	about 12.5 million
Drives:	on the left
Internet TLD:	.zw

d) Match the conditions in which a person can be with their needs.

Conditions
hungry • thirsty • ill • tired • illiterate • desperate • naked • homeless • cold • poor • barefoot • jobless • persecuted

Needs
medicine • hope • drink • food • sleep • clothes • refuge • place to live • heating • work • shoes • money • education

e) Compare your results in d) by making sentences as in the example.
Example: A person who is hungry needs food.

‹M› **f)** Sie wollen auf der Grundlage dieses Artikels an Ihrer Schule zu einer Hilfsaktion für die Menschen in Simbabwe aufrufen. Übernehmen Sie dazu die wesentlichen Argumente aus dem Text.

g) Find out what the following abbreviations stand for and describe their main tasks: UNHCR, UNICEF, WFP, UNCTAD, UNDP.

h) Find out what NGO stands for and give examples of different NGOs.

B Language

1 A report about Senegal

■ Replace the highlighted words with a present participle (ing-form) or past participle (third form of the verb).

Examples:
I belong to an ethnic group [1] called the Wolof.
A lot of the people [2] living in Senegal are very poor.

Hi, my name is Senghor Escale. I come from Senegal, but now I live in Britain. I belong to an ethnic group [**1. which is called**] the Wolof. A lot of the people [**2. who live**] in Senegal are very poor. Most of the people [**3. who leave**] my country come from the eastern part of Senegal. In these areas farmers [**4. who are trying**] to grow food fail to do so as conditions are too hot and dry, and rainfall is very low. For example, the rice [**5. which is grown**] there only amounts to 25% of all the rice [**6. which is needed**] to feed the people.

During the 17th and 18th centuries slaves and gold were the main items [**7. which were traded**] by the French and British. Nowadays the Senegalese want to organize the economy on their own and are trying to increase all kinds of industrial production [**8. which includes**] the production of chemicals and clothes. I hope the situation in my home country will improve in the next few years. Maybe I will return there one day.

Grammar

Gerund
Example: After speaking to the President she left New York.
zur Verkürzung von Sätzen nach after *und* before.

Present participle
Example: Wanting to help children she founded a new organization.
zur Verkürzung von Sätzen mit because, as, while, when.
Example: Every day you can see lots of people visiting the UN buildings *statt* … who are visiting the UN buildings.
zur Verkürzung von Relativsätzen im Aktiv

Past participle
Example: There are lots of restaurants built for tourists *statt* … which were built for tourists.
zur Verkürzung von Relativsätzen im Passiv

► GF 30 Gerund
► GF 31 Participle

2 UNICEF

■ Rewrite the statements about UNICEF, a well-known aid organization for children, using participles and gerunds as in the examples.

1. Because the UN wanted to help children in need following World War II they founded UNICEF.
   Example: Wanting to help children in need following World War II the UN founded UNICEF.
2. After the UN had established the United Nations International Children's Emergency Fund in 1949 they could give food and clothes to children in need.
   Example: After establishing the United Nations International Children's Emergency Fund in 1949 the UN could give food and clothes to children in need.
3. Before UNICEF helped children with long-term projects they had only carried out short-term projects, like giving them clothes and food.
4. Because UNICEF wanted to help children to a better life they tried to improve their chances of a good education.
5. After they had organized projects to educate the children UNICEF then started to train the teachers.
6. Because the Nobel Prize committee knew that UNICEF had carried out so many successful projects to help children all over the world, they gave UNICEF the Nobel Peace Prize in 1965.
7. As UNICEF saw that many children in developing countries were dying they increased the aid given to them in the 1970s.
8. Because many children live in war zones nowadays they need help from organizations like UNICEF.

3 Food aid for Belarus

‹I› ■ Work in pairs and complete the interview using the infinitive or -ing form of the verb in brackets. The first examples have been done for you.

Radio Livestation has created a series called "About your neighbour". Radio presenter Carla Cardoso is interviewing Luke Swanson.

Carla: Hello and welcome to our radio show "About your neighbour". Today we are going to talk about helping [**1. help**] our neighbours and for that reason I have invited Luke Swanson, who has organized an aid project called "Food aid for Belarus".

Luke: Thank you for inviting [**2. invite**] me. I really want to tell [**3. tell**] your listeners about our successful aid project for Belarus and I would like to say [**4. say**] thanks for the money we were able to collect [**5. collect**].

Carla: Before [**6. tell**] us about your trip I would first like [**7. know**] how you got the idea of [**8. help**] people in Belarus of all places?

Luke: Well, one of my friends comes from Belarus and some of her relatives still live there. One day while [**9. have**] lunch she told me about them and how the government has failed [**10. help**] them. So I decided [**11. collect**] money. I have always enjoyed [**12. help**] people.

Carla: How did you arrange [**13. get**] the food to Belarus?

Luke: After [**14. hear**] that it is very difficult to take food over the border we wanted [**15. avoid, drive**] there. So we decided [**16. take**] money there instead and [**17. buy**] the food in Belarus.

Carla: You made over £5,000. How did you succeed in [**18. get**] so much money?

Luke: Instead of just [**19. tell**] people about the project I also showed them photos of smiling children who had received food aid. That worked really well. And I hope [**20. be able, do**] this project again next year.

Carla: Thank you for [**21. tell**] us about your project, Luke, and good luck with it next year.

C Reading: The political system of the USA

Before reading

Video lounge 5

1

2

3

‹P› **a)** Describe the photos.

b) Match the photos with the headings in the text. Two headings do not match.

A2.1

How the system works

A The federal government of the USA

The government of the United States of America is called a presidential federal government. That means both parliament and the president are elected by citizens. A parliamentary federal government, as in Germany for example, works differently. Here the citizens vote for a parliamentary majority which makes up the government. The USA has a system of "separation of powers" with three branches: legislative, executive and judicial. Each branch works independently of the others. A system of "checks and balances" prevents a concentration of power in only one branch.

B The legislative branch – Congress

The legislative branch is represented by Congress. The primary task of Congress is to write, discuss and pass bills, which must be supported by the President. Other congressional tasks are to control the judiciary and the executive branch. Congress can impeach and get rid of the President. Congress can also reverse the President's veto by a two-thirds majority, pass laws, and approve appointments made by the President. Congress can impeach and remove federal judges from office, and it establishes courts.

C The executive branch – The President

The President is Head of State, Head of the Executive and Commander-in-Chief of the armed forces. As Head of State the President meets the leaders of other countries and makes treaties with them if the treaty has been permitted by Congress. As the official head of the US military the President can declare war, although he needs the permission of Congress to do so. The President also influences legislation although his power is limited here. The President passes bills, introduced by Congress, into laws, but he can also veto bills put forward by Congress. Another presidential task is to nominate federal judges with the permission of Congress.

D The judicial branch – The Supreme Court

The Supreme Court was established by the Constitution of the United States of America as the highest court in the country. One of its most important duties is to decide whether cases are constitutional or not. The Supreme Court can declare presidential and congressional actions or laws unconstitutional.

E Elections and voters

There are direct and indirect elections in the USA. Every two years the voters elect the members of Congress by direct vote. The President of the United States of America is elected by indirect vote. Every four years voters elect 538 delegates, who then elect the President. Voters in the USA must be at least 18 years old, they must hold American citizenship, they must have a registered residence and they must be registered in the register of voters.

(429 words)

Training skills – How to do mediation exercises

Understanding the text

‹M› **c)** Als Experte des politischen Systems der USA werden Sie gebeten, für das Schulportal „Schulen im Internet" eine tabellarische Darstellung des amerikanischen Regierungssystems auf Deutsch zu entwerfen. Übernehmen Sie dazu die folgenden Stichwörter in Form einer Tabelle in Ihr Heft und vervollständigen Sie diese mit den Informationen aus dem Text. (Siehe Hilfestellung unten.) ► SF22 Mediation

- Regierungsform • Verhinderung von Machtkonzentration
- Legislative • Hauptaufgabe der Legislative • Exekutive
- Funktionen des Präsidenten • Judikative
- Hauptaufgabe der Judikative • Wahlverfahren • Wahlrecht

1. Read the text to get a general impression.
   ► SF9 Anticipating, skimming and scanning
2. Read the task carefully and find out the text type you are supposed to produce and which language you must use.
   Example: Text type: chart Language: German
3. Read the text again and either mark or note down the information you need to do the exercise.
   ► SF9 Anticipating, skimming and scanning
   Examples: "Regierungsform" only matches the headline of paragraph A, "The federal government of the USA".
4. Now scan paragraph A for words that are similar to or describe "Regierungsform". Select only the relevant points.
   Example: "Regierungsform": Do not describe the kind of "Regierungsform" but only name it – "presidential federal government".
5. A mediation exercise is not a translation! Do not translate words or sentences literally. If you do not know the exact German term, try to paraphrase the English expression.
   Example: "Presidential federal government" = bundesstaatliche Regierungsform mit starker Stellung des Präsidenten

‹M› **d)** Das Schulportal „Schulen im Internet" bittet Sie nun zusätzlich, ein Schaubild auf Deutsch zu beschreiben, in dem das System der Gewaltenteilung in den USA deutlich wird. Übernehmen Sie hierzu die Informationen aus dem Text.

Gewaltenteilung in den USA

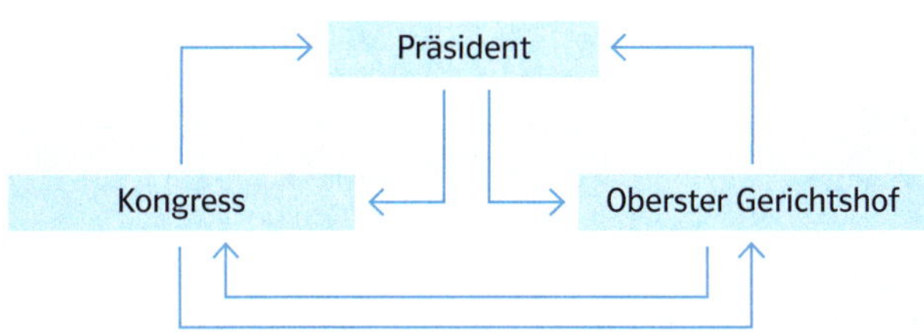

D Practice

1 The future of the European Union

Before listening

‹P› **a)** Decide which of the countries belong to the EU.

- Italy • Slovenia • Norway • Latvia • Russia • Germany
- the Netherlands • Bulgaria • Luxembourg • Turkey • Belarus
- Spain • Greece • Switzerland

A2.2 While listening

‹R› **b)** Listen to four European college students who took part in a discussion in Brussels about "Europe's future". Find out which of the above countries they come from.

c) Listen again and find the most suitable options according to the text. More than one answer can be true.

1. Marika strongly identifies with Europe because …
   a) she has learned a lot about Europe on her travels.
   b) she wants to compete internationally.
   c) she is studying Irish literature.
   d) she has already lived in some European countries and speaks five languages.
2. When asked about the enlargement of the EU, Sanne says that …
   a) every country should be allowed to enter the EU.
   b) too many member states will cause problems.
   c) it is not easy to decide which countries can join.
   d) it will not stay a "union" because the European continent does not have borders.
3. Marko hopes to see …
   a) more competition between EU member states.
   b) good job opportunities in the EU.
   c) a stable economy in the EU.
   d) German workers losing their jobs.
4. Ilana's country still has big problems as …
   a) EU standards make her countrymen reduce production costs.
   b) EU regulations and laws have not come into effect yet.
   c) there is much corruption and people break laws.
   d) small farmers are going bankrupt.

‹P› After listening

d) Get into five groups and pick one potential candidate for EU membership. Find at least five arguments for the accession of "your" country.

e) Have a discussion in class. At least one member of each group must take part. The rest of the students should support their group member and take notes. Then decide in class which country should be allowed access to the EU.

Key Words

- EU enlargement • Copenhagen criteria • future enlargement of the EU
- potential EU candidates

2 Britain's role in the European Union

‹P› **a)** Describe the cartoon on the right.

b) Explain the attitude towards the EU expressed in the cartoon.

"He says we have to change our name to 'The Kilo Shop'."

‹M› **c)** Während Sie ein Praktikum beim Europäischen Parlament (siehe Facts) absolvieren, werden Sie gebeten, für zwei englischsprachige Mitarbeiter den folgenden Kommentar zur EU zusammenzufassen. Schreiben Sie ganze Sätze in englischer Sprache, übersetzen Sie dabei nicht Wort für Wort. ► SF 22 Mediation/translation

Language

European Economic Community (EEC) • Continentals • hostile • to slow down • the Schengen agreement • Schengen II agreement • European Monetary Union • referendum • opponents • supporters

Kommentar

Wohin steuert Großbritannien?

Peer Hanken, Norddeutsche Post

Lange bevor die Briten der damaligen Europäischen Wirtschaftsgemeinschaft (EWG) beitraten, dachten viele Festland-Europäer, dass die Briten sich zu stark vom Rest der Europäer unterscheiden, um engagierte Mitglieder zu werden. Dennoch trat Großbritannien 1973 der EWG bei. Auch britische Regierungen haben ihren Einfluss immer wieder genutzt, um den Integrationsprozess in die EU zu verlangsamen. So hat Großbritannien beispielsweise weder das Schengener Abkommen (Verzicht auf Personenkontrollen an gemeinsamen Grenzen) noch den Prümer Vertrag (grenzüberschreitender Informationsaustausch zur Verfolgung von Straftaten) unterschrieben.

Eines der zentralsten Projekte der Europäischen Union ist die Währungsunion. Bezüglich des Euros hat Großbritannien jedoch entschieden, die eigene Währung, das Pfund, so lange beizubehalten, bis die Briten sich in einem Referendum für den Euro aussprechen.

Auch heute noch wird in Großbritannien immer wieder diskutiert, ob das Land die Beziehungen zur EU intensivieren soll oder ob die Umsetzung von EU-Richtlinien in einigen Bereichen reduziert werden soll. Die Gegner einer Intensivierung der politischen Beziehungen mit der EU werden in GB „Eurosceptics" genannt, die Befürworter „Europhiles". Wollen wir im Interesse einer starken Europäischen Union hoffen, dass am Ende das Pendel zugunsten der Befürworter ausschlägt. ■

(183 Wörter)

Facts

Important institutions of the EU

- European Commission:
  - consists of as many Commissioners as there are member states;
  - executive branch of the EU;
  - proposes legislation and implements EU decisions
- European Council:
  - consists of the heads of state / government of member states;
  - intergovernmental institution with great influence outside the European Community;
- Council of the European Union:
  - consists of varying representatives of the member states; countries have different voting weights;
  - the main decision-making institution
- European Parliament:
  - consists of 736 members;
  - with the Council of the EU it forms the legislative branch of the EU
- European Court of Justice:
  - one judge per member state;
  - represents the judiciary branch;
  - is the highest court in the EU

The EU's main aims: to provide peace, safety, economic and political stability for its peoples.

Online-Link
800041-0011

Unit 11
Living and working in Britain

1 Finding a work placement

‹P› **Before reading**

a) Describe the photos. ► SF 26 Describing illustrations and photographs

b) A college in Stuttgart is sending some students on job placements. Look at the photos again and guess where they are going to work.

‹M› **Understanding the text** ► SF 22 Mediation/translation

c) The teacher who is organizing the placements has just passed on an e-mail and attachment to his students. Sum up Annie Ferguson's e-mail on page 89 in German.

A2.3

From: ferguson@thistle-hotel-glencoe.co.uk
To: info@partnerschaften_bw.de
Subject: Work placements

Dear German students

As part of our partnership with your college we will be delighted to have you at the Thistle Hotel in Glencoe, Scotland, for your work placements. We would like to introduce ourselves: the Thistle Hotel in Glencoe is an exclusive, four star hotel. Our guests come from all over the world and expect high class service. This is one reason why we have invited you to work with us. We believe that we can learn a lot about different customs from our foreign students. We are sure that you will also learn a lot. You will work in the reception, the kitchen, the restaurant and other service areas.

We advise you to contact either the Belfort Guest House on 01855 30691 or the Scotsman's Hotel on 01855 62275 about accommodation. In the attachment you will find a photo of the staff.

We look forward to meeting you next month.

Yours sincerely
Annie Ferguson, Personnel manager

Attachment: Thistle_Hotel_staff.jpg

After reading

d) The teacher has told the students to write a polite e-mail to Annie Ferguson, thanking her for the chance of working in the hotel. Carsten, one of the students, has just finished a first draft. Complete the e-mail using the words on the right.

- meeting • course • appreciate
- allowing • sincerely • forward
- opportunity • experience

From: carsten@mueller.net.de
To: ferguson@thistle-hotel-glencoe.co.uk
Subject: My work placement

Dear Ms Ferguson

Thank you for your e-mail of 15 October 20 … I would also like to thank you for [1] me to work at your hotel.

I would like to take this [2] to introduce myself. My name is Carsten Müller and I am 18 years old. At present I am doing a [3] in hotel management at a college here in Germany.

I am really looking [4] to working at your hotel. I am sure it will be a rewarding [5] for me. Once again I would like to say that I [6] your offer and I look forward to [7] you soon.

Yours [8]
Carsten Müller

e) Use the words on the right and identify the parts of the e-mails in c) and d).

Example: "Dear German students" and "Dear Ms Ferguson" are both salutations.

- salutation
- reason for the e-mail
- news / information / requests (for help) / apologies, etc.
- reference to attachment(s)
- final comment
- complimentary close

‹P› **f)** One of Carsten's classmates has fallen ill and cannot go on the work experience scheme. Write his/her e-mail, explaining what has happened. Show interest in doing a placement in the future.

2 Finding accommodation – Making phone calls

Video lounge 6

‹R› **While listening**

A2.4 **a)** Carsten phones the Belfort Guest House about accommodation. Listen to the call and put the photos into the order they are mentioned.

1

2

3

4

b) Listen to the call again. Note down what Mrs Fletcher said when …

1. Carsten told her when he was coming to Glencoe.
2. Carsten said "your hotel".
3. Carsten asked her if she did evening meals.
4. Mrs Fletcher made Carsten a special offer.
5. Carsten asked how he could book.
6. Carsten didn't quite understand what she said.

After listening

‹I› **c)** Carsten phones the Scotsman's Hotel to compare it to the guest house. Student A plays Carsten using the role card on the right. Student B plays the role of the receptionist. You can find your role card on page 134. Use the phrases in the box.

► SF 5 Making phone calls

d) Decide where you think Carsten would rather stay. Give reasons.

‹P› **e)** Write an e-mail to the place you chose in d). Mention the following:

• the phone call • the dates and prices • your personal details have been filled in on the reservation form (attachment) • you look forward to meeting the person you are writing to • a formal complimentary close

Role card: Carsten

Phone the Scotsman's Hotel to find out the following information:

- availability of a room from the 2nd to the 30th of next month
- rates
- meals
- distance from the Thistle Hotel
- booking requirements
- payment.

Language

- Excuse me, could you speak more slowly, please.
- I didn't quite catch that. Could you repeat what you just said?
- Could you spell that, please?
- Thanks a lot. I'll be in touch. Bye.

3 Writing an e-mail to a friend

Understanding the text

‹R› **a)** Carsten and Andy met when Andy was in Germany two years ago. Find out why Carsten has written an e-mail to Andy.

From: carsten@mueller.net.de
To: andy-white-gc@googlemail.com
Subject: I'm coming to Scotland!

Hi Andy,

Long time, no see. How are you?

Life here in Germany is the same as always. College is very busy, you know how it is.

Anyway, to be honest, the reason I'm writing is that I've lost your mobile number and I'd like to get in contact again. And guess what! I'm coming over to Scotland next month. I'll be working at the Thistle Hotel in Glencoe as part of my college course. And to cut a long story short, maybe we could meet again. Are you still studying in Edinburgh?

It would be great to see you. Anyway, just give me a buzz on 0049 171 6868251 or send me an e-mail.

By the way, do you remember the great time we had on New Year's Eve in Stuttgart? I think you call it Hogmanay in Scotland. Well, I've attached a photo.

Best wishes

Carsten

Attachment: New_Year_Stuttgart.jpg

New_Year_Stuttgart.jpg

‹R/P› **b)** Find some colloquial expressions in Carsten's e-mail. Then write Andy's mail to Carsten using some of these expressions and giving the following points. ► SF 25 Personal letters and e-mails

- Andy now works in a garage.
- He also has lost Carsten's mobile number.
- He suggests they meet in Perth – not far from Glencoe.
- He remembers Hogmanay, too – good time.
- He wants to know if Carsten remembers Sandy – now his girlfriend.
- He asks Carsten to mail him back – cheaper than phoning.
- He ends the e-mail informally.

After reading

c) Use the Internet to find out more about Scotland and the Scottish.

Key Words

- Hogmanay
- the Edinburgh festival
- Robert the Bruce's spider
- Burn's night

Online-Link
800041-0011

1

2

Unit 12
Meeting people

1 Meeting people for the first time

Before reading

‹P› **a)** Describe the situations in the above photos. ► SF 26 Describing illustrations and photographs

Understanding the text

A2.5 ◘ Carsten has arrived in Glencoe for his work placement. He goes to the Thistle Hotel and is met by personnel manager, Annie Ferguson.

Annie: Hello. My name's Annie Ferguson. Please call me Annie. I hope you had a nice flight.
Carsten: Yes.
Annie: And is your accommodation alright?
Carsten: Yes.
Annie: Well, before I introduce you to some of the people you'll be working with, would you like a tea or coffee?
Carsten: Coffee.
Annie: OK. Yes, most young people seem to prefer coffee to tea – even here in Scotland. How do you like your coffee? Cappuccino, latte macchiato or just black? You see, we've become very "European" in Scotland.
Carsten: Cappuccino.
Annie: Right. Well, let's go to my office. I'll give your new colleagues a ring.

A few minutes later.
Annie: Good morning, Amy, Ian. May I introduce you both to Carsten Müller from Germany? Carsten, this is Amy Andrews from reception and Ian McGregor is our chef.
They all shake hands.
Amy: Nice to meet you, Carsten. As Annie said, I work on reception, so we'll be working together in the next few weeks.
Carsten: Yes, good.
Ian: I'm Ian. Pleased to meet you. When you come to my kitchen, I promise you'll experience Scottish cooking at its very best.
Carsten: Ok.
Annie: Amy, could you show Carsten around? I'll get someone to cover for you on reception.

(213 words)

‹R› **b)** Read the dialogue to find out what Carsten did not do so well.

c) Change Carsten's responses so that they are more polite. Use the expressions in the box.

Language

- That sounds great.
- Yes, please.
- It's fine, thank you.
- I'll look forward to that.
- Thank you.
- I'd like …

2 Showing people around

‹R› While listening

A2.6 **a)** Amy takes Carsten on a tour of the hotel. Listen to the conversation and find out which rooms on the plan they entered.

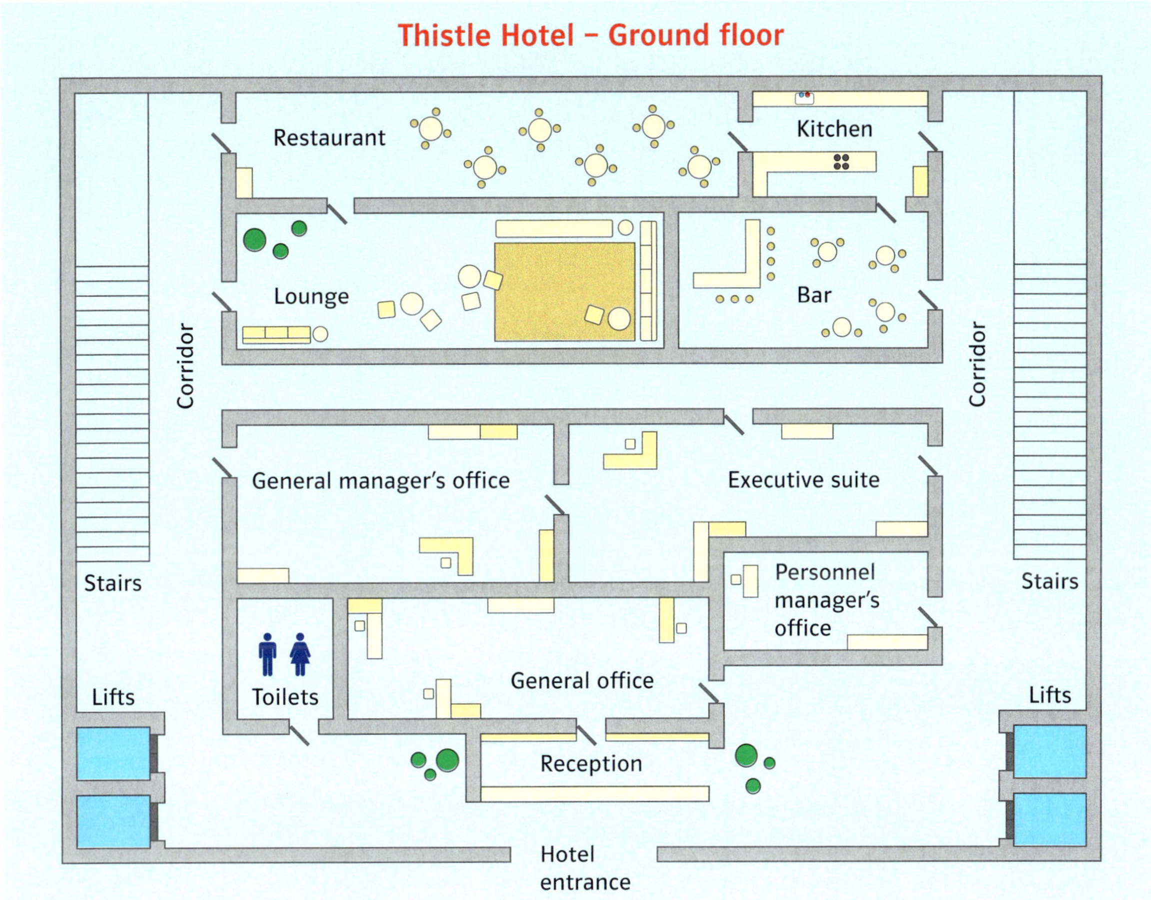

b) Listen to the conversation again and answer the following questions.

1. What is the name of the area in front of reception?
2. Why does Carsten know Joanne?
3. Why can they enter the general manager's office without knocking?
4. What is the executive suite used for?
5. Why is Amy happy when they arrive at the bar?

After listening

‹I› **c)** Work with a partner. Student A is a friend of Ian's, the chef. He/she is at the reception desk and wants to talk to Ian.
Student B is the receptionist on duty and gives Ian's friend directions to the kitchen using the plan in a).

3 Finding the way

■ A guest at the Thistle Hotel wants to get to the following places in town. Explain how to get there using the map below and the phrases in the box.

1. the Glen Theatre
2. the town hall
3. the Highlands Shopping Centre
4. the nearest cash point

Language

- Turn right (into) …
- Turn left (into) …
- Take the first / second street on the right/left.
- Go straight on.
- Cross …
- Go along … until you come to …
- At the traffic lights you turn …

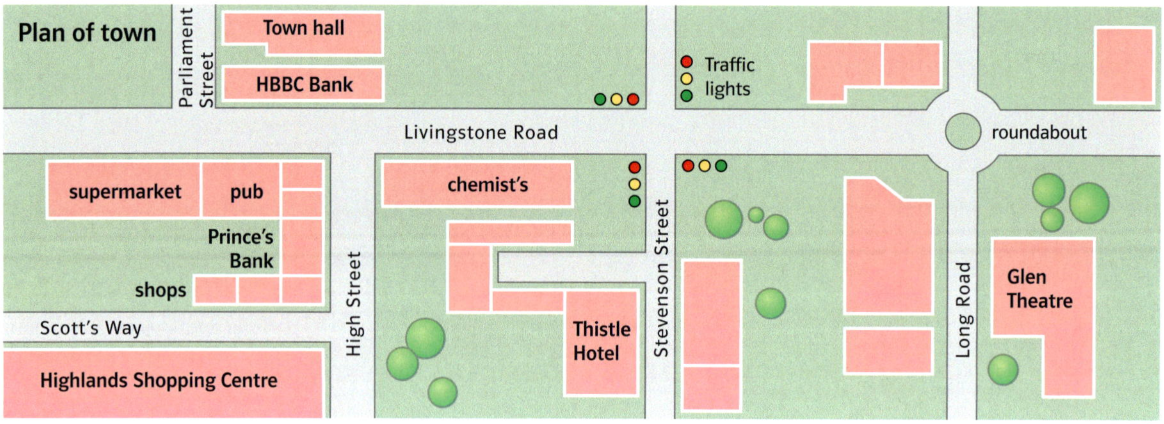

4 Eating out

Before listening

a) It is lunch time. Amy, Annie and Carsten are sitting in the hotel restaurant. The waitress brings the menu. Look at this list of words and match them with the correct definition.

1. chicken tikka	a) a fish often caught in the rivers of Scotland
2. rainbow trout	b) a popular, Scottish soft drink
3. haggis	c) seafood like a shrimp
4. prawn	d) a type of beer, best served cold
5. Irn-Bru	e) an Indian dish, which is spicy but not too hot
6. lager	f) a traditional Scottish dish

‹I› **b)** Carsten cannot understand the menu so Annie tries to explain it. Work in pairs and find out what the food items on the menu are. Explain them in the same way as in the example.

Example:

Carsten: Could you tell me what chicken tikka is, please?

Annie: It's an Indian dish. It's nice and spicy and not too hot.

‹M› **c)** Now design the hotel menu for German guests in German.

► SF 22 Mediation/translation

MENU

Starter
- Tomato soup
- Prawn cocktail
- Country salad

Main course
- Angus beef, chips and peas
- Chicken tikka with fried rice
- Fresh Scottish trout, boiled potatoes and salad
- Haggis and baked potatoes
- Vegetable lasagne

Dessert
- Warm apple pie and custard
- Fruit salad with cream
- Ice cream

Drinks
- Beer (lager or bitter)
- Wine (red, white or rosé)
- Spirits (especially all kinds of whisky)
- Mineral water
- Fruit juices
- Soft drinks (Irn-Bru, lemonade)

‹R› ## While listening

A2.7 **d)** Listen to the dialogue and write down what Annie and Carsten would like to have from the menu.

‹P› ## After listening

e) Place an order for Amy from the menu above.

‹I› **f)** Work in groups of three. Student A and Student B are guests in the restaurant. Student C is the waiter/waitress. Act out a dialogue using the menu on page 94.

5 Making conversation

Before reading

A2.8 **a)** Carsten has made friends with Amy, the receptionist. They arrange to meet in the local pub for a quiet drink. Amy said she'd be there at "half eight". Carsten waits for an hour and then Amy arrives. Why, do you think, has Carsten had to wait so long?

Carsten:	It's nice here. Shall we sit over there?
Amy:	That's fine. Excuse me, are these seats taken?
Guest:	No, you're welcome.
Carsten:	Thanks. What are you having to drink, Amy?
Amy:	Oh, I think I'll have an orange juice. But I'm paying.
Carsten:	No, no. I'll pay.

Carsten waits, and Amy looks at him a little confused.

Amy:	Well, aren't you going to order?
Carsten:	But the waiter hasn't come to our table yet?
Amy:	No, Carsten. In a pub you don't get served. You have to go to the bar and order the drinks there. And you have to pay for them at once.
Carsten:	Oh, I didn't know that. Sorry.

Carsten goes to the bar.

Barkeeper:	Next, please. Yes, sir?
Carsten:	An orange juice and a large glass of beer, please.
Barkeeper:	You probably mean a pint of bitter, don't you?
Carsten:	Yes, I think so.
Barkeeper:	There you go. That'll be 4.10, please.

‹R› ## Understanding the text

b) Explain how the English pub is different to a German pub.

c) Explain the following expressions:

1. Are these seats taken?
2. a pint
3. 4.10
4. Yes, sir?

After reading

‹I› **d)** Amy has invited Carsten to a party where he meets other young hotel trainees from all over the world. Get into groups of five. Student A takes the role of Carsten. You will find the other role cards on page 134. Circulate and start conversations. ► SF 4 Making conversation

Facts

Here are some tips on how to make conversation:
- Never become too emotional or intense.
- Make sure you show interest and are polite.
- Avoid topics like politics, religion, personal problems or illnesses.

Role card: Carsten

Name: Carsten Müller
Home: Stuttgart, Germany
Placement: Thistle Hotel, Glencoe
Journey to Scotland: flight to Glasgow, stopover in Amsterdam
Marital status: single
Interests: Skiing and mountain-biking

1

2

Unit 13
Working in a hotel

1 In the hotel office – a telephone enquiry

Before listening

‹P› **a)** Carsten spends the first week of his placement in the general office of the hotel and at reception. What do you think the people in the photos are doing?

b) What tasks do you think Carsten will do in these areas of the hotel?

‹R› While listening

A2.9 **c)** Listen to an incoming phone call to find out who is talking.

d) Listen to the call again and answer the questions.

1. When will the guest arrive?
2. When will he leave?
3. What kind of room does he want?
4. What else does he want?
5. How much will his stay at the hotel cost?

After listening

‹I› **e)** Work in pairs. Student A plays the role of the receptionist. Student B phones the hotel. Student A asks about the following things and Student B thinks of suitable answers:

- name • address and phone number • type of room required
- meals required • method of payment

2 Making appointments

‹R› **While listening**

A2.10 **a)** Listen to another phone call and find out who is calling and why.

b) Copy Mr McTell's diary into your exercise book. Listen to the call again and fill in his appointments for next week.

	Monday	Tuesday	Wednesday	Thursday	Friday
9.00					

c) Find out when the two businessmen can have their meeting.

d) Explain why they cannot meet earlier in the week.

3 Working in the kitchen

In his second week Carsten is sent to the hotel kitchen to find out more about the work there.

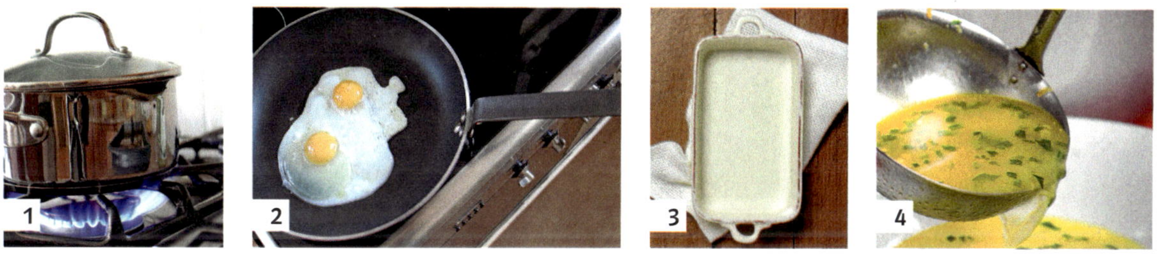

a) Match the kitchen utensils in the photos with the words below.

Kitchen utensils
• serving dish • ladle • saucepan • frying pan

b) Explain what you do with the utensils.

c) The chef, Ian, shows Carsten a recipe for Scottish lamb stew, which is on the menu this week. The recipe is for four people. Carsten has to work out how much or how many of the individual ingredients Ian needs for 35 people.

SCOTTISH LAMB STEW

Ingredients
500g cubed lamb
2 onions – finely chopped
2 leeks – cut into pieces
200g carrots – cut into pieces
25g margarine
200ml red wine
200ml stock
thyme – fresh or dried

Method
- Melt the margarine in a pot and cook the vegetables for about 10 mins.
- Add the lamb to the pot and fry until brown.
- Stir in the red wine and stock.
- Add the salt, pepper and thyme.
- Cook on a low heat for about an hour.
- Serve with crusty bread or boiled potatoes.

‹M› **d)** Carsten writes an e-mail to a German friend about his week in the kitchen. He also describes how to make Scottish Lamb Stew. Write the e-mail in German for Carsten. ► SF 22 Mediation/translation

‹M› **e)** Find a traditional German dish that you could offer to British guests at the hotel. Translate the recipe into English so that Ian could cook it.
► SF 22 Mediation/translation

4 Welcoming guests

In the third and fourth weeks Carsten is on duty at reception.

a) In the box on the right you can find a number of things Carsten may say when a guest arrives. Put the sentences in the correct order.

‹I› **b)** Work in pairs. Make up a short dialogue. Student A wants to check in to the hotel. Student B is the receptionist and uses the phrases in the box in a). Student A thinks of suitable answers.

- One moment, please. I'll check the computer.
- And if there is anything else you need, don't hesitate to ask.
- What's the name, please?
- Good evening.
- Have a nice evening.
- Here's your key.
- The lift is on the right.
- That's on the fourth floor.
- What can I do for you?
- Yes, you are in room number 421.

5 Managing situations: Helping guests

‹I› ■ Some guests have come to reception with their problems. Work in pairs and make up short dialogues. One person is the receptionist. Be polite and try to help them. Use the phrases in the box on the right.

1. Mr O'Shea needs a taxi to go to the airport.
2. Mr Welbeck complains that the heating in his room is not working.
3. Mrs Park wants to go shopping, but doesn't know the area.
4. Mr Hargreaves wants his bill.
5. Ms Valencia wants to change rooms as her present room is too loud.

Language

- Yes, of course.
- I'll see what I can do for you.
- Oh, I'm sorry about that. I'll phone the services department right away.
- It won't take long.
- Here's a map of the town.
- I'll just print it out for you, sir/madam.
- I'm sure that we can arrange something.
- I'll get one for you immediately, sir/madam.
- I'll just check that. One moment, please.

6 Renting a car

‹R› While listening

A2.11 **a)** Before Carsten flies back to Germany, he wants to spend a weekend sightseeing in London. He is planning to drive down by car so he phones a car-hire firm to find out their prices. Listen to the phone call and write down how much it would cost to rent the following vehicles.

‹R› **b)** Listen again to the call and answer the questions.

1. Which seems to be the most suitable car for Carsten? Why?
2. Where can he drop the car in London?
3. Why should he not drive into the centre of London?
4. How can he get into the centre according to John Samson?
5. When will Carsten phone John Samson again?

After listening

‹I› **c)** John Samson has a busy day at the car-hire firm. The Linfords (2 adults and 2 children, aged 10 and 7) are going on holiday in Scotland and they would like to hire a car to travel around the country.

Work in pairs. Student A plays the role of Mr or Mrs Linford and phones John about renting a car for a week. Student B plays the role of John and gives Mr or Mrs Linford information about suitable cars and rates.

7 Saying goodbye

The time has come for Carsten to leave the Thistle Hotel.

Carsten: Well, it's time to say goodbye. It's been so nice here and you have all been so kind to me.

Annie: All good things have to come to an end, Carsten. You've been great and we've really enjoyed having you here. I hope you've learnt a lot, too.

Carsten: Yes, I have. Not only have I learnt a lot about hotel work but I hope my English has improved, too. And I know a lot more about Scotland than I did before. I won't forget the haggis, either. Thanks once again. I really appreciate all the help you gave me. Oh, and give my regards to all the staff who are not in today. Bye.

Annie: Bye, Carsten. Take care.

Understanding the text

‹R› **a)** What do you think the following statements mean?

1. "All good things have to come to an end."
2. "You've been great."
3. "I really appreciate all the help you gave me."
4. "Give my regards to all the staff who are not in today."
5. "Take care."

After reading

‹P› **b)** Carsten is back in Germany and he wants to write a thank-you letter to Annie Ferguson and the staff at the Thistle Hotel. Draft his letter. ► SF 23 Formal letters and e-mails

Online-Link
800041-0011

1

2

3

4

Unit 14
Different countries, different cultures

1 Touring Scotland

Before reading

‹P› **a)** When Carsten got back to Germany he had a look at some of the photos he had taken on his days off.

Look at the photos and describe them.
► SF 26 Describing illustrations and photographs

b) Unfortunately, Carsten is not quite sure which photo is which. Look at the entries in his blog and decide where the photos were taken. Two blog entries do not match.

Example: That looks like … because …

www.carsteninscotland.com

- ► Sat 7th Ben Nevis / highest mountain in Scotland
- ► Tue 10th Loch Ness / didn't see the monster
- ► Sat 14th Glasgow / largest city in Scotland
- ► Wed 18th Oban / whisky distillery
- ► Sun 22nd Aberdeen / North Sea oil
- ► Sat 28th Edinburgh / castle – capital of Scotland

c) Find the places which Carsten visited on the map of Britain on the inside cover.

A2.12

SO YOU WANT TO VISIT SCOTLAND …

As a country for a wonderful holiday, Scotland is hard to beat. We have great hotels to stay in, warm, friendly people, wonderful scenery and a fascinating culture and history.

The kingdom of Scotland was an independent state up until 1707 when it entered into a political union with the Kingdom of England to form the United Kingdom (UK) of Great Britain (GB). However, Scotland has had its own parliament again since 1999: Holyrood is located in Edinburgh, the capital of Scotland.

Scotland is a fascinating country with a number of well-known "brands". One of these brands is tartan, which is instantly recognized all over the world as something that is uniquely Scottish. Originally, only the Highlanders wore tartan. The colour and pattern of the tartan differed depending on which region of the Highlands that the person wearing it came from. Nowadays, tartan is also worn outside Scotland and has become fashionable all over the world.

Alongside tartan, the thistle is one of the most identifiable Scottish symbols. It is used to promote a wide variety of products, services and organizations in Scotland. But why the thistle? Legend says that some sleeping Scottish warriors were about to be attacked by a number of Vikings. The Scots were only saved when one of the Vikings stood on some wild thistles and cried out in pain. The cry woke the Scottish warriors who immediately defended themselves. In the end the Vikings were defeated.

And then there is our national dish, haggis. Traditionally, it is made from the lungs, liver and heart of a sheep. These ingredients are mixed with oatmeal and spices. The mixture is then stuffed into a sheep's stomach. After being boiled for some time, the dish is served. The haggis plays an important role on Burns Night, a Scottish festival celebrating national poet, Robert Burns on January 25. The haggis is brought to the table accompanied by a bagpiper. Guests raise a glass of Scotch whisky and say a prayer for the soul of Robert Burns. However, as you can imagine, not all Scotsmen and women are real fans of haggis.

(359 words)

Understanding the text

‹R› **d)** Carsten's teachers at college back in Germany have asked him to prepare a talk about Scotland and the Scottish.

Read the brochure which Carsten brought back from Scotland and take notes in German.

After reading

‹P› **e)** Use your notes to prepare the talk in German about Scotland and the Scottish. ► SF 22 Mediation/translation

2 What you should know about Britain

Understanding the text

‹M› ▪ The teachers at Carsten's college want Carsten to design a handout for students doing placements in Britain in the future. Read Carsten's tips and summarize them in German. ► SF 22 Mediation/translation

Ten useful tips for German students in Britain

1. Read as much as you can about Britain beforehand.
2. Only shake hands when you meet someone for the first time. After that the British don't like shaking hands.
3. Always try to be polite. Useful words like "please" and "thank you" help a lot! Remember: just answering a question with "yes" or "no" is seen as very impolite by the British. Try not to swear in English – people told me that it sounds unnatural coming from a foreigner!
4. In general, British people don't like close body contact with strangers. Keep a suitable distance.
5. British people often use first names. However, it depends on the rank and standing of the person you are talking to. I would never call the General Manager of the hotel by his first name. Always wait until the person you are talking to suggests using first names.
6. When you are out with British people in a pub, always be prepared to buy 'your round'. You go to the bar to order and you pay straight away.
7. Always remember to form a queue at the bus stop, at the baker's … A true Brit forms a queue of one!
8. Dress code is important. In business a tie is a 'must' for men, and women should be careful not to wear 'showy' clothes. Jeans are a no-no.
9. Don't forget to drive on the left. And always look right before you cross the road. British pedestrians aren't so disciplined as we are in Germany: very often they don't wait for a 'green man' at the traffic lights, they just cross when nothing's coming.
10. Last but not least, smiling is always a good tactic. People seem to like you when you smile!

3 Test your English!

▪ This quiz is designed to find out if you know what to say in special situations. Choose the correct answer. More than one option can be correct.

QUIZ

1. What would you say if you met someone for the first time in a business situation?
   a) Good day.
   b) Pleased to meet you.
   c) Hello there.
   d) Hallo.

2. How may a person in Britain answer an incoming telephone call? By saying …
   a) their name
   b) the phone number
   c) where they are
   d) Hi.

3. How should you ask to see the *Koch* in a restaurant?
   a) Can I see the chief, please?
   b) Is it possible to see the cooker, please?
   c) Where's the chef?
   d) Can I see the chef, please?

4. How would you order a traditional Scottish meal?
   a) Pea soup.
   b) I think I take the lasagne.
   c) I'd like the haggis, please.
   d) For me the fish and chips.

5. How would you ask somebody how you get to a city in Scotland?
   a) Which road do I take to get to Glasgow?
   b) How do I come to Dundee, please?
   c) Am I on the right street to Aberdeen?
   d) Could you tell me how I get to Edinburgh, please?

6. How do you finish a formal letter?
   a) Yours sincerely
   b) Best wishes
   c) Bye
   d) Yours

7. Carsten wants to phone a hotel in London about accommodation. How would he start the phone call?
   a) Hello, this is Carsten.
   b) Carsten here.
   c) Hello, my name's Carsten.
   d) Hello, this is Carsten Müller speaking.

8. How do you ask for the price of a hotel room?
   a) How much do you demand?
   b) How much costs the room?
   c) How much does the room cost?
   d) How much is the room?

4 What about American English?

Before listening

a) After his stay in Scotland Carsten is working in a hotel in Germany again. A lot of the guests come from overseas and this often causes communication problems. Think of situations where this might happen.

‹R› While listening

A2.13 **b)** Listen to Carsten talking to an American guest. As you will hear, Carsten knows his American English. Say in your own words what problems the American hotel guest has.

c) Listen to the conversation again and choose the right option. More than one option can be true.

1. The American has a room on the …
   a) ground floor c) first floor
   b) second floor d) third floor

2. The American has got a message on his …
   a) laptop c) computer
   b) cell phone d) television

3. He pays 220 Euros for his stay at the hotel …
   a) by credit card c) in cash
   b) by check d) in Euro bills

4. The following things are out of order at the hotel …
   a) the telephone in the guest's room
   b) the closet in the guest's room
   c) the computer at reception
   d) the elevator

5. The American guest wants to come back to Germany next year …
   a) on vacation c) for a weekend trip
   b) on business d) for his wedding anniversary

6. The American guest wants to know where he can find …
   a) a cinema c) a bank
   b) a restroom d) a gas station

After listening

d) The guest used the American English words on the right in the conversation with Carsten. Explain in British English what he meant.

Example: The American guest said that the elevator was out of order. In British English an 'elevator' is a 'lift'.

- second floor • cell phone
- closet • bills • elevator
- restroom • vacation
- gas station • freeway
- French fries

e) Decide in which English-speaking countries you could hear the following expressions.

1. Mountie
2. billboard
3. an Aussie
4. Gaelic football
5. a dingo
6. the All Blacks
7. a leprechaun
8. a kiwi

f) Use a dictionary or the Internet to find out what the expressions in exercise e) mean.

Unit 15
Youth unemployment

A2.14

Lost in nowhere land

According to the latest figures the number of school-leavers in Britain who are not in education, employment or training (the so-called Neets) has increased to nearly 1 million. What are the reasons for this development?

Many young people are really worried about the future. They have worked hard to pass their exams. They have written lots of applications and CVs. They have applied to a large number of firms but they have only received rejections. The consequences for young people can be serious. Some experts even speak of the "lost generation" when they talk about the young unemployed. If they do not find an apprenticeship or another way of getting into employment over a longer period, the young people won't get used to working or gain work experience. This may result in a lifetime of unemployment and poverty. Experts also say that this first failure can put people on the road to crime or homelessness.

There seem to be quite a lot of educational, economic and social factors which stop young people finding employment – unhelpful careers advice, poor training and job opportunities in many professions, and a lack of support from families and schools over a long period are just a few examples.

When Terence Parker, 17, from Exeter left school with one GCSE, he completed a BTec in sport. He then thought that he was qualified enough to find a job leading sporting activities for young people but he soon found out that employers wanted job experience, which he did not have. Terence had done some coaching in his holidays, however, that did not seem sufficient.

Of course, it is hard for Terence who feels qualified and is eagerly looking for a job but cannot find one. "You see, I'm still living with my

mum and she helps me in many ways but I feel I should earn my own money and pay her instead of her paying for me."

When Aruna Nun, who is now eighteen, was twelve her mother fell ill and she had to care for her little brothers and sisters. She did not have enough time for school so things went downhill very quickly. She did poorly in her GCSEs and only found a placement for a few months. "My brothers and sisters are a little older now so that I could start a proper job and help at home in the evening. I would like to be a teaching assistant or work in childcare, but of course, there is no chance for me on the job market. That's why I'm thinking about doing a childcare course at college this autumn."

The government is trying to reduce youth unemployment and is aiming to create new jobs by giving employers thousands of pounds for each job which is given to a young person. The government is also appealing to companies to support young people and give them a job, training opportunities or at least a job placement so that they can get work experience. In this way the government hopes to get young people into careers.

Critics say that the government is not doing enough to solve the problem of youth unemployment. They say that there are still too many young people hanging around at home or on the streets instead of doing a proper job. In the long run it is not only these young people who will suffer.

(568 words)

1 Reading comprehension

‹R› **a)** Decide which statements are true. More than one option may be correct. ► **SF12 Multiple choice exercises**

1. Many young people are worried about the future because …
   a) most of their job applications have not been successful.
   b) it is so difficult to get work experience.
   c) a lack of work experience can lead to lifelong unemployment.
   d) they have not managed to pass their exams.

2. Quite a few young people have difficulties finding jobs …
   a) because they do not get enough help from their families.
   b) because there are not enough training facilities in a lot of professions.
   c) because they do not get careers advice.
   d) for a number of different reasons.

3. Terence Parker and Aruna Nun …
   a) did not finish school.
   b) both have little job experience.
   c) do not know what jobs they would like to have.
   d) live at home.

4. The government …
   a) is paying money to companies that employ young people.
   b) is supporting young people by giving them jobs.
   c) wants young people to have the chance to get job experience.
   d) wants to give a job placement to every young person.

5. The author is convinced that …
   a) all young people are not qualified enough to find a job.
   b) the government will solve the problem of youth unemployment in the near future.
   c) there are many different reasons why young people have difficulties finding jobs.
   d) the situation of many young people is not easy and can have negative effects in the future.

b) Do the following tasks on the text "Lost in nowhere land" in complete sentences. Use your own words.

1. Describe the experiences of young school-leavers on the job market.
2. Give reasons for the problems young people have during their job search.
3. Describe Terence's situation.
4. Based on the text, explain how young people can improve their chances of finding a good job.
5. Explain the measures that are taken by the government to change the job situation of young people.

2 Composition

‹P› ◘ Choose either composition 1 or composition 2.
► **SF16 Writing a composition/comment**

1. "Young people today are either too lazy or not qualified enough to get a good job." Discuss.
2. "Life today is a lot more difficult for young people than it used to be." Discuss.

3 Translation

◘ Translate the last two paragraphs (lines 54–69) into good German.
► **SF22 Mediation/translation**

Unit 16
New jobs

1 Reading comprehension

‹R/M› **a)** Sie sollen vor dem Stadtrat eine kurze Einführung zu dem Thema „Verbesserung der Infrastruktur in sozial schwachen Stadtteilen" machen. Bei der Vorbereitung haben Sie den folgenden Artikel entdeckt. Fassen Sie die darin beschriebenen relevanten Punkte zusammen. Formulieren Sie ganze deutsche Sätze. ► SF 22 Mediation/translation

A2.15

Can a new superstore help a rundown area?

When a new superstore opened in a Manchester suburb about a year ago local people hoped that the sun would shine again on their district. The store is one of the so-called 'regeneration partnership stores' which are meant to develop deprived areas, attract further investment and find at least 20% of its staff among local, long-term unemployed or disabled people.

Before the opening of the new store, 80 local people were given an extra training course for eight weeks, which was financed by the local council. About £1,000 of public money was spent on each applicant. "The money is well spent," says one official, "it helps to get long-term unemployed people back to work and it saves the community a lot of money in benefits."

The regeneration partnership model came to Britain from the US where community activists managed to persuade a big American bank to open a branch in Harlem, one of the poorest parts of New York. "It may not always be the answer to an area's problems but the idea is that this kind of new project can be the start of a wider development, attracting further businesses and in this way creating new jobs," the official adds.

"Of course, not all shop owners are happy about the arrival of a big competitor. But I believe we can transform the area and existing businesses can survive if they manage to offer additional services instead of competing in the same fields. We have established a business forum in which businesses and the town council work together. When the long-term unemployed find work, their spending power will increase. The business climate here will also improve, which in turn will attract other shop owners, bars and restaurants."

One year on, not all the wishes have come true. Some retailers are doing quite well while others have been hit hard. The local convenience store has lost a third of its business and has had to dismiss two of its assistants. Local retailers have realized that many shoppers just drive to the big supermarket and then drive home again.

Studies have not clearly shown whether large retail chains really create new jobs or make people lose them. Some groups fear that independent small shops could have disappeared from Britain by 2020. They claim that small businesses create more jobs than the big superstores which only employ one person per £95,000 of turnover – compared to small shops where it is £42,000.

(419 words)

b) Do the following tasks on the text "Can a new superstore ..." in complete sentences. Use your own words.

1. Describe the origin of 'regeneration partnership'.
2. Explain the basic idea behind the project.
3. Give reasons for the council's interest in the new superstore.
4. Describe the benefits of the project for the long-term unemployed.
5. Give reasons for the other shop owners' fear.

2 Composition

‹P› ■ Describe and analyze the following illustrations.

1. ► SF 27 Describing cartoons

'Errrm...I think I'll phone a friend !'

2. ► SF 28 Describing diagrams

Unemployment in per cent

Country	2000	2002	2004	2006	2008	2010
Germany	7.5	8.4	9.8	9.8	7.3	7.5
Spain	11.1	11.1	10.6	8.5	11.3	19.0
Great Britain	5.4	5.1	4.7	5.4	5.6	7.7
EU (27)	8.7	8.9	9.0	8.2	7.0	9.6
Norway	3.4	3.9	4.5	3.4	2.6	3.3
USA	4.0	5.8	5.5	4.6	5.8	9.7

Source: EU Commission, EUROSTAT, OECD, February 2010.

Unit 17
Modern technology

A2.16

Just google it!

It sounds like an American fairy tale. What began in a friend's garage in the middle of the 1990s has since become a billion dollar business and the most powerful media brand in the world.

Google's success story started in 1996 when Larry Page and Sergey Brin were both students at Stanford University in California. They began developing a new kind of search engine that would produce better results than any of the existing ones. At the beginning their search engine was part of the university website but in 1997 the domain name, google.com, was registered.

The word 'Google' seems to be a misspelling of the word 'googol', which represents a number with one hundred zeros. 'Google' has since entered dictionaries and 'to google' now means 'to use the Google search engine to obtain information on the Internet'.

At the beginning Brin and Page were against having advertising in their search engine, but they soon changed their minds. They allowed text ads, but not pop-up advertising. The ads were – and still are – text-based, and users like the clear and simple page design which keeps loading times short. Since 2000 Google has been selling advertisements which are related to the key words that a user enters. In this way advertising is targeted only at users who are interested in a topic. Advertisers pay per click on their links and this ingenious idea has made the company highly profitable. Today, 99% of Google's earnings come from advertising while the big advantage for its users is that all of the services are free.

Google's most popular service is its web search engine, which has a market share of about 60%. Other products include, for example, Google Earth and Google Maps, and the company has also

entered the mobile phone market. In recent years Google's street view service has taken pictures of millions of public and private buildings, which has led to a lot of criticism with regard to people's privacy. The images of city streets are often so detailed that you can see cars or pedestrians clearly. Politicians have even raised doubts about national security because satellite pictures may show targets that are at risk.

The search engine itself is often referred to as "Big Brother" because it records and stores its users' personal searches. Google also scans the e-mails of people who use the company's e-mail-service. This all helps Google to target advertising as exactly as possible. Theoretically, Google would be able to start a file for every user, listing their interests, their appointments, their photos – and even their love affairs.

That is the price users have to pay although experts say that the company cannot afford to assign its data to individuals and sell this to interested third parties. The long-term economic damage to the company would be much greater than any short-term profits. (476 words)

1 Reading comprehension

‹R› **a)** Decide which statements are true. More than one option may be correct. ► SF12 Multiple choice exercises

1. At the beginning the Google search engine …
   a) did not have its own website.
   b) allowed text advertisements.
   c) was developed by a very small team.
   d) did not even have a name.

2. Companies like to advertise on Google's website because …
   a) of the pop-up advertisements.
   b) of the short loading times.
   c) of the connection between the advertisements and the search terms that users enter.
   d) they only have to pay when a Google user visits their website.

3. According to the text Google has …
   a) doubts about national security.
   b) a lot of information about its users.
   c) different services on offer.
   d) taken photos of its users.

4. Many experts believe that …
   a) Google will make a lot of money by selling their users' data to interested companies.
   b) Google could have higher profits in the long run by selling their users' data.
   c) companies are interested in the users' data.
   d) Google is not able to collect users' data and connect the information with individuals.

5. The author points out that …
   a) using Google has its advantages and dangers.
   b) Google is one of the leading media companies in the world.
   c) Google's is a typical American success story.
   d) Google's services have a market share of about 60%.

b) Do the following tasks on the text "Just google it!" in complete sentences. Use your own words.

1. Describe the development of Google in its first years.
2. Outline Google's changing attitude to advertising.
3. Explain the success of the Google search engine according to the text.
4. Give reasons why Google's activities may not always work to the advantage a) of society and b) of its users.

2 Composition

‹P› ■ Choose either composition 1 or composition 2.
► SF16 Writing a composition/comment

1. "Many young people are careless with their personal data on the Internet and especially in social networking websites." Discuss.
2. "The Internet will bring together people of different races and religions, and make the world a more peaceful place." Discuss.

Unit 18
Plastic money for young people

1 Reading comprehension

‹R› **a)** In Ihrer Jugendgruppe werden Sie gebeten, die anderen Jugendlichen über die Verwendung von Prepaid-Kreditkarten zu informieren. Bei der Vorbereitung haben Sie den folgenden Artikel entdeckt. Fassen Sie die darin beschriebenen relevanten Punkte zusammen. Formulieren Sie ganze deutsche Sätze.
► SF 22 Mediation/translation

A2.17

Cash isn't cool anymore

Your children have got pre-paid mobiles. How boring! The new must-have is the pre-paid credit card.

A massive campaign for pre-paid cards is targeting teenagers and children as young as eleven. The cards are expected to replace traditional pocket money in the future. The average age at which children receive their first mobile phone is now just eight and about 20% already use their parents' credit cards to buy goods on the Internet. So it seems to be a logical step forward to give teenagers their own credit cards.

The concept of pre-paid credit cards is similar to that of the cards used in mobile phones – you load money onto a pre-paid card and you can spend it in your favourite stores or shop online. You can also withdraw money from cash machines, pay bills or use the card on journeys abroad. When the card is empty you just top it up again by loading more money onto it. As with any other card you have to sign the back when you receive it and use a PIN (personal identification number) when you want to make transactions.

The big advantage for parents is that the pre-paid card is not a real credit card and children can only spend the money their parents have put onto the card. Therefore, it is impossible to get into debt. This kind of card is considered to be a good way of teaching children how to manage money. It is also safer for children as they do not need to carry cash anymore. The card is protected by a PIN and can be cancelled if it is stolen.

So what are the disadvantages of the card? Well, for credit card companies it is good business. Not only do they reach a lot of new, young customers, they also earn a lot of money. For example, there is an 'issuing fee' of about £10 when you get the card. There may also be an additional monthly fee, a 'reload fee' when you top up your card and a fee of £1 every time you use it.

The difficulty for card companies and internet shops comes when they must check the ages of teenage customers. Cards have already been sent out to 11-year-olds without their parents' knowledge, and one father discovered that his 15-year-old son had bought cigarettes and alcohol on the Internet. His son only had to click the button "I'm over 18" and he could use his pre-paid card to order what he wanted.

Some credit card companies are working on solutions: When they send pre-paid cards directly to children, they have agreed to send notification letters to their parents, too. Moreover, companies are working on the development of a database which can help to check the identity and the age of young customers.

Experts believe that if children are educated, pre-paid cards can be a sensible and safe alternative to cash, and can teach them to handle their money – even in the virtual world of the Internet.

(507 words)

b) Do the following tasks on the text "Cash isn't cool anymore" in complete sentences. Use your own words.

1. Describe the way in which a pre-paid credit card works.
2. Explain the advantages of a pre-paid credit card for young people.
3. Give reasons why parents may be worried about this development.
4. Explain how credit card companies and other firms can profit from the introduction of the pre-paid credit card.

2 Composition

‹P› ◘ Describe and analyze the following illustrations.

1. ► SF 28 Describing diagrams

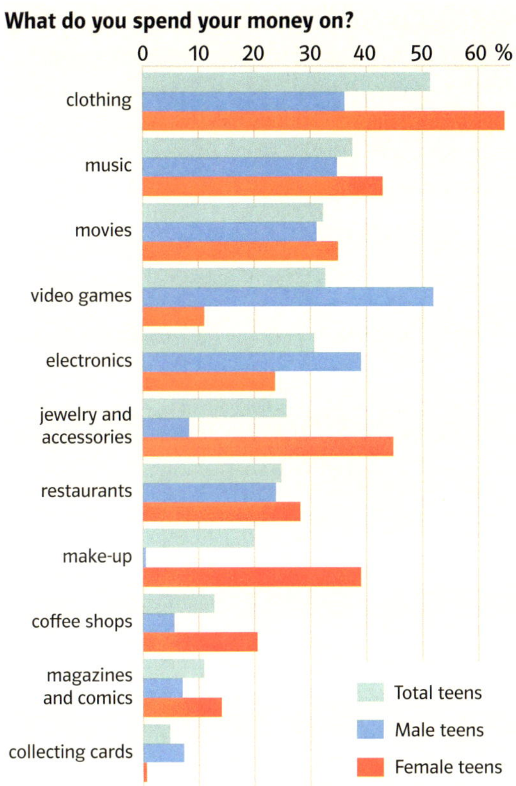

Source: marketingcharts.com

2. ► SF 27 Describing cartoons

"Emily, have you been shopping online during class?"

Unit 19
Young people and society

A2.18

Will we hear the next cry for help?

Barden Road in Leicester, England, is a normal road. Yesterday morning Fiona Pilkington's neighbours were taking advantage of the autumn sunshine, painting garage doors, working in the garden or taking well-dressed children to school past the row of tidy front gardens.

The peacefulness of the scene makes it all the more shocking to find out what happened to Fiona Pilkington and her two handicapped children, who lived in Barden Road. Over the last two years the family had been constantly terrorized by a local youth gang. Last week Fiona became so desperate that she drove, with her mentally handicapped daughter, Frankie, to a location outside the town. While mother and daughter sat in the car, Frankie held her pet rabbit and Fiona set fire to the car. When the fire fighters arrived, the Pilkingtons were already dead.

It will soon be Halloween, a night which was hell for the Pilkingtons. A local youth gang (aged between 12 and 16) terrorized the Pilkingtons and this terror came to a climax on Halloween. Using "trick or treat" as an excuse, the young gang members would put rubbish and fireworks through the Pilkington's letter box and urinate in their front garden.

On other "normal" days, Fiona's son, Anthony, aged 14, who has learning difficulties and who attends a special school for children with mental and physical difficulties, was regularly abused by the gang. It was even worse for Frankie, who was both physically and mentally handicapped. The gang would shout at her every time she left the house, and threw stones and dirt at her. Like her brother, Frankie also attended a special school and she had been very happy there. But, on reaching her 16th birthday, she was going to have to leave the school and neither Frankie nor her mother were prepared for this step. Not having much help or support, and with very little hope for the future, Fiona Pilkington became very depressed. And you know how the story ended!

Some big questions remain. One of them is: "Why did no one sit down with the Pilkingtons and talk about their problems?" A second question is: "Why didn't the neighbours take action?" The third question is, of course: "How can we prevent things like this happening again?" John Evans, the head of social services in Leicester said in an interview: "We have to show parents that it is not OK, for example, for teenagers to wander around the streets until 12 o'clock at night." He went on to say that "society has to teach a lot of parents *how* to bring up their children properly". Moreover, he maintains, parents

have to explain to their children how important it is to live together with different minority groups, such as the Pilkingtons. He believes that cities should offer parents help in the form of special "parent education courses" and he is convinced that if we do not act now, this could be the end of tolerance in our society. From this it is but a short step to a society where the law of the jungle rules. In order to avoid this terrible scenario our towns and cities need to spend a lot more money on the "parent education courses" that John Evans suggests. Without this type of support we will surely see more tragic cases like the Pilkingtons' and wonder – too late – why we didn't do anything to help.

(576 words)

1 Reading comprehension

‹R› **a)** Decide which statements are true. More than one option may be correct. ► SF12 Multiple choice exercises

1. According to the text Mrs Pilkington committed suicide because …
   a) she had lost her husband.
   b) one of her children had died.
   c) she was unhappy because of the bullying.
   d) she was not able to cope with her situation any more.

2. The author of the text claims that Halloween was a bad time for the Pilkingtons because …
   a) they were afraid of ghosts.
   b) groups of teenagers attacked them on the streets.
   c) young people threw things at them.
   d) local youths put nasty things into their letter box.

3. Mrs Pilkington's daughter didn't want to leave school because …
   a) she was unsure about her future.
   b) she couldn't read.
   c) she was contented there.
   d) she didn't like her mother.

4. The head of social services in Leicester is of the opinion that towns should …
   a) spend more money on schools.
   b) finance courses to help parents.
   c) introduce courses for teenagers.
   d) teach minorities.

5. The author of the text wants to show readers the problem of bullying by including …
   a) a report about someone who has been terrorized.
   b) a report by a gang member.
   c) interviews with neighbours.
   d) comments from experts.

b) Do the following tasks on "Will we hear the next cry for help?" in complete sentences. Use your own words.

1. Give the reasons why Mrs Pilkington committed suicide with her daughter according to the text.
2. Outline which questions remain after the death of Fiona and Frankie Pilkington.
3. Explain how the head of social services in Leicester wants to solve the problem of anti-social behaviour among young people.

2 Composition

■ Choose either composition 1 or composition 2.
► SF16 Writing a composition/comment

1. "Young people today do not know the difference between right and wrong." Discuss.
2. "Everybody has the duty to report any form of anti-social behaviour." Discuss.

Unit 20
Young people and alcohol

1 Reading comprehension

‹R› **a)** Sie sollen in Ihrem Jugendzentrum einen Vortrag über die Gefahren von Alkoholkonsum bei Jugendlichen halten. Bei Ihrer Vorbereitung haben Sie den folgenden Artikel entdeckt. Fassen Sie die darin beschriebenen relevanten Punkte zusammen. Formulieren Sie ganze deutsche Sätze.
► SF 22 Mediation/translation

A2.19

Pupils learn lessons in safe drinking

Excessive drinking or binge drinking among young people has become a major concern for parents, doctors, the police and for society in general. There is increasing evidence that irresponsible drinking can have a very serious effect on young people's lives. Moreover, research shows that 15 and 16-year-olds drink double the amount each week that their parents did 20 years ago. Doctors all over the UK report that the number of young people who are taken to hospital with drink-related illnesses or with injuries from drunken violence has risen by a quarter in the last five years. Police reports present a similar picture of excessive drinking among young people, registering an alarming increase in drink-related crime.

In an attempt to halt this trend, several schools have introduced a new course aimed at teaching young people to drink more sensibly. The new "alcohol awareness certificate" concentrates, on the one hand, on the health dangers caused by excessive drinking. For example, lessons warn young people that drinking to excess could make them fat, and also lead to impotence and an inability to enjoy sex. On the other hand, the course deals with the legal side of the problem and focuses on the penalties that people can expect if they are caught buying alcohol for, or selling it to, under-age drinkers.

The ten-hour course also gives young people tips on how they can deal with the problem of excessive drinking. For example, it shows them how to resist group pressure to drink and how to look after a drunken friend. The course also warns young people that alcohol drunk to excess is like seawater: the more they drink, the more dehydrated their bodies become. In some cases, excessive drinking can lead to alcohol poisoning or choking on

vomit, both of which can end fatally.

The course leads to an official qualification and a certificate is worth half a GCSE. In this way, students can get some valuable extra points for their school certificate. Jane Finnmore, the head teacher at an East London secondary school, has found that having a qualification is a great motivation for a lot of her students. Moreover, she is of the opinion that the course is a good way of reaching all teenagers. She says: "The course does not tell them not to drink. It just teaches them about both the positive and negative effects of alcohol."

The students on the course were equally positive about the experience. Alexandra Raphael, 15, said: "It has changed my attitude to alcohol. We learned how it can affect the body, especially when you are pregnant." Paul Rooney, 16, said the course helped to destroy many school playground myths. "It has taught me things that I can now teach others, such as my younger brother," he said.

As with most problems in society, lessons have to be learnt. The alcohol awareness course is just one way of making young people more conscious of the problems related to excessive drinking. With a bit of luck, young people can learn from such measures how to go out for an evening and enjoy being with their friends, without getting blind drunk.

(530 words)

b) Do the following tasks on the text "Pupils learn lessons in safe drinking" in complete sentences.

1. Describe the changes in the drinking habits of young people today.
2. Outline the main points of the alcohol awareness course.
3. Explain the motivation for doing this course.
4. Summarize the reactions to the course as expressed by the people mentioned in the text.

2 Composition

‹P› ◘ Describe and analyze the following illustrations.

1. ► SF 27 Describing cartoons

2. ► SF 28 Describing diagrams

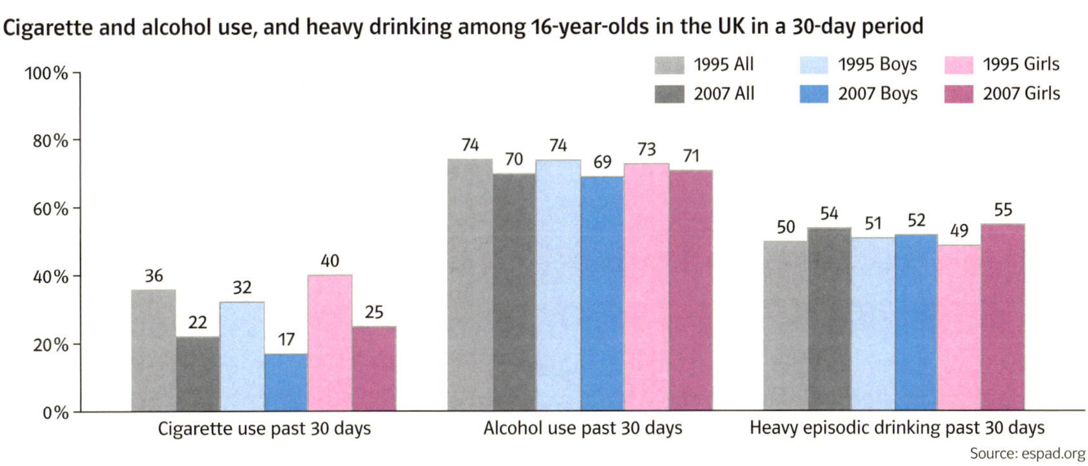

Unit 21
Biotechnology

A2.20

Cloning in a new dimension

In an exciting development scientists have found a new way of cloning cells. Up to now it has only been possible to clone complete animals, which were then capable of growing to adulthood. Chinese scientists have gone one step further and with the development of the new method of cloning, it has now become possible to produce specific body tissues as well.

Most people have heard of Dolly, the sheep. Born in July 1996, Dolly was the first and, without a doubt, the most famous of the cloned animals. Dolly lived until she was six years old before dying of lung cancer. A sheep, such as Dolly, can normally live to the age of eleven or twelve. Some scientists believe, however, that Dolly was already six when she was cloned because the sheep she was cloned from was six years old. As a result, we could, in fact, say that Dolly reached the age of twelve.

After Dolly, a few more animals were successfully cloned. For example, in 2001 a cat called Cc (which stands for copycat) was born in America, in 2003 the first cloned horse was born in Italy and in 2005 a dog called Snuppy (Seoul National University puppy) was cloned in South Korea. Like Dolly, all of these clones were able to produce their own offspring. At this stage of the work with cloning and clones, however, it was still not possible to clone specific body tissues: scientists could either clone a whole animal or nothing at all.

The possibilities that are open to scientists will change with the new era of cloning. Teams in China have worked independently on projects to clone mice and the body parts of mice. A group of scientists in Beijing has cloned 27 mice, which have survived into adulthood. Between their offspring and the offspring's children, the next generations have totalled some 300 mice. Tests with clones have

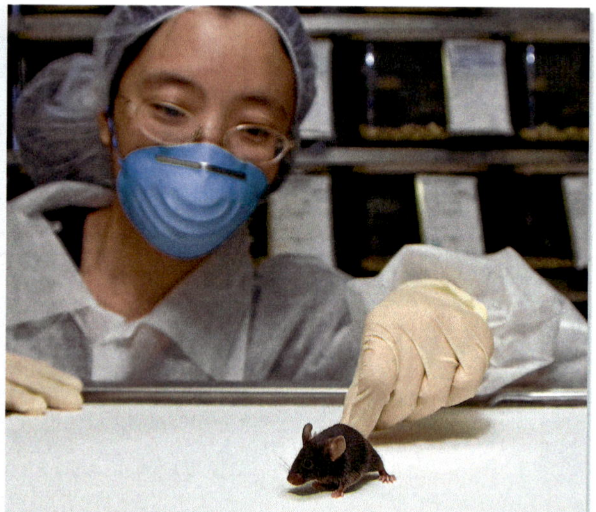

not been done to this extent in any of the previous cases of cloning. And now the scientists have also managed to produce body tissues.

How has this breakthrough been made possible? Scientists have found a way of producing stem cells from skin cells. The skin cells are converted into embryonic-like cells, which are then capable of developing either into body tissues or into complete adult animals.

As a result of these new methods, completely new areas of research are opening up for scientists all over the world. At the moment, the reprogramming methods are not directly applicable to the work with human cells, but in time a similar technique could be transferred to human cells.

Scientifically and technically, many new things are becoming possible, but where does this leave us as far as ethics are concerned? In most European countries at least, scientists are not allowed to use such cloning methods. However, now that we know that such methods are possible, it is probably only a matter of time before we and our scientists use them to produce humans or so-called "designer" babies.

(513 words)

1 Reading comprehension

‹R› **a)** Decide which statements are true. More than one option may be correct. ► SF12 Multiple choice exercises

1. The new cloning technology is unique because …
   a) scientists are now able to clone animals for the first time.
   b) scientists are able to produce body tissues.
   c) humans have been cloned for the first time.
   d) future parents can now choose which colour their baby's eyes will be.
2. The history of cloning includes some success stories: …
   a) a dog called Snuppy was cloned in Seoul in 2005. Two years earlier, a cloned horse was born in Italy and before that, in 2001, Dolly, the sheep was cloned.
   b) Dolly was cloned in 1996, followed five years later by Cc. After two years a cloned horse was born and then Snuppy was produced.
   c) the first cloned animal was Dolly, the sheep, then a cat was cloned, followed by a horse, and a dog was cloned in 2005.
   d) the first clone was a horse called Dolly, then came a dog, a cat called Cc and in 2005 a sheep.
3. The Chinese scientists were able to produce body tissues because …
   a) they took skin cells and changed them into stem cells, which were then used for further transformations.
   b) the cloned mice survived to adulthood.
   c) they were very lucky to get skin cells from mice.
   d) they changed stem cells into embryonic-like cells.
4. Stem cells from a patient's skin …
   a) are useless.
   b) will be used to produce specific parts of the human body one day.
   c) are used to produce a human body.
   d) are changed and then used to produce complete animals.
5. The extraction and application of stem cells …
   a) is not allowed in every country.
   b) is allowed in every country.
   c) will never be used to create humans.
   d) may be used to create humans at some point in the future.
6. The author wants to point out that …
   a) cloning should not be carried out.
   b) cloning may make designer babies possible in the future.
   c) the ethical question of cloning should be taken into consideration.
   d) cloning is not dangerous at all and we need this technology.

b) Do the following tasks on the text "Cloning in a new dimension" in complete sentences. Use your own words.

1. Illustrate the development of cloned animals in the past.
2. Explain the breakthrough that the Chinese scientists have made in cloning research.
3. Outline the possibilities that the new cloning method developed in China has opened up for scientists.
4. Justify the prohibition of the use of stem cells in some European countries.

‹P› 2 Composition

▪ Choose either composition 1 or composition 2.
► SF16 Writing a composition/comment

1. "Cloning stem cells saves lives. Therefore we should support their use in scientific research." Discuss.
2. "Is the power that cloning gives us a blessing or a curse?" Discuss.

Unit 22
Modern transport

1 Reading comprehension

‹R/M› **a)** Sie planen mit Ihrer Familie den nächsten Urlaub und haben den folgenden Artikel entdeckt. Sie wollen Ihre Familie davon überzeugen, mit dem Airbus A380 zu fliegen. Fassen Sie die darin beschriebenen relevanten Punkte zusammen. Formulieren Sie ganze deutsche Sätze.

► SF 22 Mediation/translation

Airbus's superjumbo reduces carbon emissions

Airbus's first flight with the A380 marks a revolution in passenger accommodation. The A380 is able to transport about 850 passengers, which makes it the largest – and if Airbus's claims are true – the greenest aeroplane existing nowadays. In times when frequent travellers are increasingly worried about their carbon footprints, i.e. the amount of carbon dioxide produced during flights, the A380 is a remarkable development.

Airbus is the largest aircraft manufacturer in Europe. The company was founded in 1970 when several European companies joined together under one name. Their aim was to form one European company that could compete with American aircraft manufacturer and market leader Boeing. Airbus's headquarters are located in Toulouse in France. In 2009 Airbus sold and delivered some 498 aircraft, whereas Boeing, on the other hand, was only able to sell and deliver 481.

Now the A380 is said to be another successful strike by Airbus in keeping its lead in the competition with Boeing. The A380 was first built and tested in 2005, and two years later the aircraft was commissioned. Since then 38 aircraft have been taken into service and Airbus has orders for a further 220 planes. Up to now the A380 has brought some 2.5 million passengers to their destinations. With a length of 72.3 metres, a wing span of 79.8 metres and a height of 24.1 metres, the A380 is the largest passenger aircraft in service today. Due to its extraordinary dimensions the A380 is no longer a jumbo-jet but a superjumbo.

During the construction phase, engineers had to face several problems: The biggest was that of getting the maximum number of seats onto the aeroplane. Engineers saw the number of seats as the key to reducing the amount of carbon emissions per passenger. They partly solved the problem by constructing two passenger decks, one on top of the other. For this to be possible the Airbus body had to be elliptical or oval rather than round. The Airbus engineers built a body that is 8.4 metres high and 7.15 metres wide. As a result there is room for three decks, the third being for luggage.

Keeping ecological issues in mind and hoping to further reduce passengers' carbon footprints, engineers turned their attention to uplift. The special shape and angle of the A380's wings cause air currents which pull up the aircraft. According to Airbus, this is one reason why the A380 needs 300kg less fuel per passenger than other aeroplanes. Airbus also claims that this saves 75g in carbon emissions per km and passenger. The low fuel consumption results from being able to transport so many people in just one aeroplane. As a result passengers' carbon footprints are lower when they use the A380 than when they fly with other aeroplanes. Given the fact that a car exhaust produces between 100 and 200g CO_2/km, it comes as a surprise that flying long distances with about 600 others may be more environmentally friendly than sitting alone in your car.

Looking at the A380's amazing dimensions, its seat capacity and its low carbon emissions, it will be interesting to see what future technological developments in air transport will look like. The engineers' inventiveness seems unstoppable and the phrase "the sky's the limit" doesn't seem to hold true any longer. (553 words)

‹R› **b)** Do the following tasks on the text "Airbus's superjumbo reduces carbon emissions" in complete sentences. Use your own words.

1. Outline the development of Airbus.
2. Explain what is meant by the statement, "The A380 is said to be another successful strike by Airbus" (ll. 18–19)?
3. Point out the biggest challenge for Airbus's engineers in developing the A380.
4. Describe how Airbus has been able to reduce its passengers' carbon footprints.

2 Composition

‹P› ■ Describe and analyze the following illustrations.

► SF16 Writing a composition/comment

1. ► SF26 Describing illustrations and photographs

2. ► SF27 Describing cartoons

Unit 23
Sport for health

Getting teenagers back into doing sport

Over the last few years millions of pounds have been spent on sports programmes and facilities for schools by the government. Yet, a report, which came out some months ago, about the fitness levels of British teenagers showed that fewer young people are taking part in sporting activities. The government has now drawn up plans to get young people, and especially the 16 – 20 age group, back to doing sport.

According to the report, obesity among young adults is growing at an alarming rate, and children and teenagers who do not do any kind of sport have more problems with their health than those who do. They are also more likely to have related problems: they often spend a lot of time alone in front of a TV screen or surfing the Internet, which means that they don't have the chance to meet others and develop their social skills. The study also found that teenagers who do not do sport often drop out of college earlier, and become addicted to alcohol and drugs more easily than teenagers who do sport regularly.

In order to tackle these problems the British government is now discussing the idea of introducing parkour into schools after it has been successfully tested in a three-year pilot programme in schools in the Midlands.

"Teenagers like it because it's cool. They see it in movies and on YouTube all the time. Even young adults who were not interested in sport before want to try it out," says John Petersen, who is headmaster at the London College for Social Studies, one of the pilot schools that has been testing parkour.

What is parkour? People doing parkour climb, run, balance and swing across rooftops, parks, stairs, walls, public buildings, almost anywhere, always searching for the most elegant way of getting over obstacles. "Parkour combines running with gymnastics in a kind of freestyle movement. You try to get from A to B as efficiently as possible by running, jumping and moving down a variety of obstacles. It trains your body as well as your mind," says parkour trainer Philip Jason of Parkour World.

Tim Meyers, of the British Department for Children, Schools and Families, disagrees that parkour teaches young adults to be thoughtless and irresponsible. He explains, "In their first year students train in the gym. They learn to manage risks, and to jump and land precisely. When they go outside in their second year, they are strictly supervised by teachers and trainers. I think it's better to learn parkour at college than on the streets without any supervision."

Mary Bath of Parkour Unlimited, one of the companies that trains teachers and runs classes at colleges, says: "Parkour is not about impressing others or doing dangerous jumps. It's about encouraging young people to be active and get fit."

Brian, 17, a student at the London College for Social Studies, maintains that he's not performing parkour to show off. For him, it is a community activity that brings people together. "Parkour encourages children and young adults to become aware of their environment and community. And the best thing about it is that no-one is excluded because all you need is a pair of trainers," he says.

However, the plan to introduce parkour into the school curriculum also has its critics. "There is a very good chance of suffering severe injuries when you do a high jump. A fall from a height can lead to broken bones, head injuries and even death," says Dr Robert Tucker, a health expert at Birmingham University. (601 words)

1 Reading comprehension

‹R› **a)** Decide which statements are true. More than one option may be correct. ► SF12 Multiple choice exercises

1. The report about teenage fitness showed that …
   a) fewer young adults are doing sport because there aren't enough facilities in schools.
   b) more young adults are doing sport as schools offer a lot of sports programmes and facilities.
   c) a smaller number of young adults is doing sport even though there are enough sports programmes and facilities in schools.
   d) a greater number of young adults is doing sport although schools often don't have enough sports programmes and facilities.
2. John Petersen says that …
   a) young adults are attracted to parkour even when they are not normally interested in sport.
   b) young adults who aren't interested in sport are even less likely to do parkour.
   c) teenagers enjoy parkour because they have watched it in films.
   d) teenagers enjoy parkour because they want to be cool.
3. Tim Meyers says that …
   a) you can learn parkour best by swinging across rooftops and running through your city.
   b) it's better to learn how to jump and land precisely first in a gym under the supervision of teachers and trainers.
   c) parkour is a sport you can learn without teachers or training.
   d) after training in a gym for a year you go outside to practise parkour on the streets.
4. According to the text, parkour is …
   a) not suitable for schools because you can only do parkour in the city.
   b) dangerous. When you jump off of high walls, roofs, etc. it can lead to broken bones or worse.
   c) a way of getting teenagers to do sport as well as helping them to deal with problems like alcohol and drug addiction.
   d) a complicated way of getting from A to B.

‹R› **b)** Do the following tasks on the text "Getting teenagers back into doing sport" in complete sentences. Use your own words.

1. Give reasons why the government wants teenagers to do more sporting activities.
2. Explain how someone does parkour.
3. Describe how Brian feels about parkour.
4. Explain the possible advantages and disadvantages of doing parkour as mentioned in the text.

2 Composition

‹P› ■ Choose either composition 1 or composition 2.
► SF16 Writing a composition/comment

1. "Introducing parkour into school curricula is a good way of getting teenagers back to sport." Discuss.
2. "The development of technology is responsible for teenagers' negative attitude towards sport." Discuss.

3 Translation

■ Translate the first paragraph (lines 1–8) into good German.
► SF22 Mediation/translation

Unit 24
Social lives and computers

1 Reading comprehension ►SF 22 Mediation/translation

‹R/M› **a)** Sie haben eine Diskussion mit Ihren Eltern über die Auswirkungen von Computerspielen gehabt. Jetzt haben Ihre Eltern folgenden Artikel im Internet gefunden und bitten Sie, sie genauer über dessen Inhalt zu informieren. Fassen Sie die darin beschriebenen relevanten Punkte zusammen. Formulieren Sie ganze deutsche Sätze.

Do virtual worlds and online gaming affect students' social lives?

At the end of the last century scientists tried to find out if virtual worlds and online gaming really affected students' social lives as many parents, teachers and researchers feared. Several surveys that were done came to one conclusion: virtual worlds and online gaming affect our lives, but not as negatively as many people thought.

Communication is the key to winning quite a few computer games. This is especially true for multiplayer games. Multiplayer games are video games or computer games in which the player takes a role and contributes his/her skills to a social network to win a game or to defeat an enemy, as is the case in warfare games. Other multiplayer games are based on communication between players, simply because this is the aim of the game, to communicate. The player can choose and then play a character in a social network. This sounds strange and even dangerous to some parents, teachers and politicians, and may explain why many people are afraid of the effects these games can have on students.

Some people fear that students can lose all feeling for what is real. And, of course, this can happen if kids are left alone or have problems handling real life. Multiplayer games can indeed be a dangerous pastime for these players. Whenever a relationship in the game gets too difficult, the player can quit the game and start another one, or they can choose a character they always wanted to be and so lose touch with their own personalities. In this way, the player becomes 'unreal' and untouchable for others. Therefore, one can say that online multiplayer games often act as barriers to relationships where real communication is important. This type of behaviour can result in loneliness and isolation.

However, researchers have found out that this isolation is not always the case. The average video game player does not necessarily spend less time than non-video players interacting with parents and friends. Often students end up playing with people they already know. So one can say that although these games do not create large new social networks, they do reinforce existing ones and help to keep relationships going.

There are even a lot of similarities between face-to-face groups and multiplayer communities. Shared values and goals are the basis of understanding and communication in both types of interaction. And, just as in real life, disagreements concerning the acceptance of roles and opinions may lead to conflicts within the multiplayer community. These conflicts can either strengthen or change the community. Long-term interaction lays the foundation for a feeling of community, just as in real life.

Yet, we cannot ignore the negative aspects of multiplayer online games. When someone plays a game that involves interacting online, they leave digital footprints. Operators of online games servers can see who players talked to or played with and what they talked about. In this way, players' relationships and interaction with other players are transparent and this information can then be easily used against the individual player.

Nevertheless, the danger of becoming addicted to these games is still real, and players' social lives can be influenced in a negative way. Therefore, parents should keep an eye on their children, and the length of time they are online or play video games. However, as long as children meet friends face-to-face and interact regularly with teachers and their families, parents needn't be alarmed.

(575 words)

‹R› **b)** Do the following tasks on the text "Do virtual worlds …" in complete sentences. Use your own words.

1. Explain how multiplayer games work.
2. Say why many adults are afraid of the effects of these games on students.
3. Explain in what ways multiplayer games can reinforce relationships.
4. Name some similarities between groups which meet face-to-face and multiplayer communities.
5. Explain what makes online players transparent.

2 Composition

‹P› ▪ Describe and analyze the following illustrations.
► **SF16 Writing a composition/comment**

1. ► **SF28 Describing diagrams**

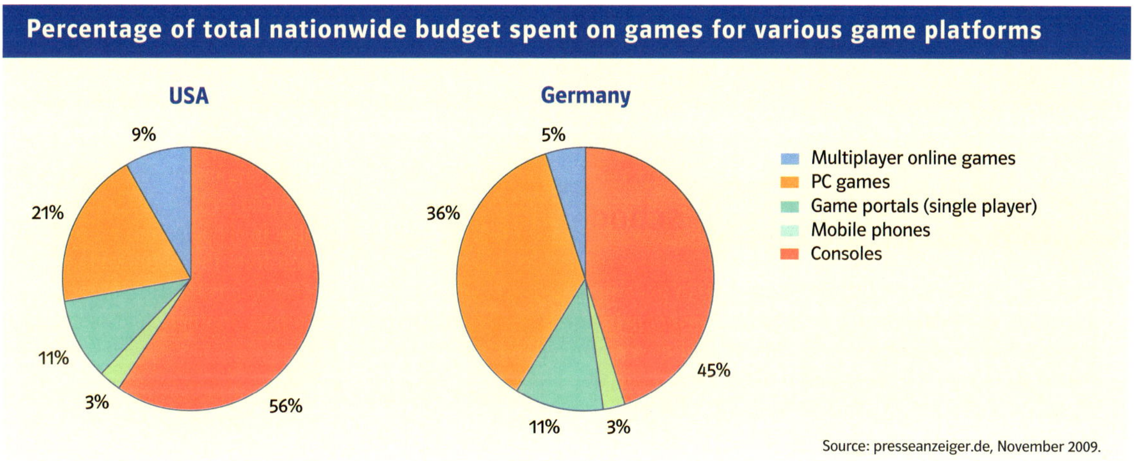

2. ► **SF27 Describing cartoons**

"Do you promise to have and to hold her, longer than the Playstation 3?"

Unit 25
Living in a multicultural society

Banning racism from our schools

Following recent racist incidents the British government has introduced new regulations for nurseries, primary schools and secondary schools. The new rules mean that child carers, teachers and nursery staff have to investigate the reasons for every single quarrel between pupils in the school yard.

As a result of these regulations, every year thousands of children and teenagers in Britain will be labelled 'racists' because not only do teachers have to settle quarrels, they must also record and report all racist confrontations between children to their local authority. Teachers have to explain what the offender did and how they were punished. Even though the new rules have been criticized by the public, local school authorities encourage teachers to report as many racist incidents as possible.

According to a study, examples of racism in schools range from calling one another "chocolate bar", "Paki", "white trash" or "those people" to making fun of children from other cultures because of their clothes or physical appearance. Some children make fun of other children's accents or names, or they may refuse to work, play or sit with children who are from a different culture.

Simon Henley, a teacher at Lady Margaret Secondary School in Leeds, says, "One day, a ten-year-old boy said 'Paki' to an eleven-year-old during an argument in the school yard. Conforming to the new laws I had to contact his parents, suspend him from lessons for that day and report his behaviour to our school authority. Some time later the boy was taken to court to be punished.

Fortunately, the judge thought that we had to find better ways of dealing with incidents like this. Of course, ten-year-old children do understand the term 'Paki' but the boy didn't mean to deliberately harm his friend. The exaggerated talk about racist children is absolutely absurd if you ask me."

But supporters of the reporting method fear that if we don't deal with racist bullying in schools, children will think racism is acceptable in schools and, even worse, in society. Heather Johnston from the Nationwide Children's Bureau thinks, "It's better to record cases of racism where the child didn't mean to hurt another child than not to record them at all."

Teachers and parents report an increasing division between white and black children where none existed before simply because everyday quarrels become so-called 'race problems'. As a result children are actually forced to think in racial categories.

Marvin Meyers, who is a school teacher in Leicester, says, "The responsibility to record every little school yard quarrel wastes my time. Children who grow up in a multicultural society are usually not racist. They're too young to think in such categories. But helping children to see those cultural differences can improve our lives." Of course, there are incidents of deliberate racist bullying in schools that we need to deal with, but aren't there better ways instead of just reporting them to school authorities?

Glasgow, for example, has invested in multicultural community centres in the hopes that projects such as Bollywood aerobics or multi-ethnic teams in local youth football leagues will improve inter-racial relations. Another way of dealing with racist incidents is to tell children that what they have said or done is not right, and to ask them what they meant. Then the teacher can explain to the children why their comments may upset other children.

(563 words)

1 Reading comprehension

‹R› **a)** Decide which statements are true. More than one option may be correct. ► SF12 Multiple choice exercises

1. The British government has introduced new regulations because they want …
   a) to deal with quarrels among teachers.
   b) to do something after the latest cases of racial discrimination.
   c) to do something about indirect racial discrimination in the school yard.
   d) every school yard argument to be examined.

2. Teachers must …
   a) deal with racial arguments between children.
   b) report every case of racial discrimination to the local school authorities.
   c) think of extremely cruel punishments for children who had a racial argument with other children.
   d) report cases where children do not want to work with a child from a different culture.

3. According to the text, racial discrimination includes teasing children from different cultures because …
   a) they can't spell their names properly.
   b) they play different games in the school yard.
   c) they wear different kinds of clothes.
   d) they have a strange accent.

4. Other ways of dealing with the problem of racial discrimination in schools are …
   a) to tell children off for their behaviour.
   b) to suspend them from school.
   c) to explain to children that their behaviour is wrong.
   d) to close multi-cultural community centres.

5. The author of the text wants to show that …
   a) there is an increasing need to deal with racial discrimination in British schools.
   b) the regulation that makes teachers report every single quarrel among children has negative effects.
   c) it is better to talk to a child when he/she bullies another child because of his/her cultural background.
   d) it is good to report every case of racial discrimination so that the offender can be taken to court.

‹R› **b)** Do the following tasks on the text "Banning racism from our schools" in complete sentences. Use your own words.

1. Describe what teachers must do according to the new regulations introduced by the British government.
2. Sum up Simon Henley's attitude to the reporting method.
3. Explain why people continue to support the new regulations even though these regulations are criticized.
4. Give reasons why the new regulations are criticized by teachers and parents, according to the text.

2 Composition

‹P› ◘ Choose either composition 1 or composition 2.
► SF16 Writing a composition/comment

1. "Britain today is a diverse multicultural society, and in the nurseries and schools there are children from many different cultures. This cultural mix has many positive effects on these children." Discuss.
2. "Racial discrimination can negatively affect a child's future chances." Discuss.

Unit 26
Poverty and the welfare state

1 Reading comprehension

‹R/M› **a)** Für ein Schulprojekt informieren Sie sich über Kinderarmut in verschiedenen Ländern. Als Beispiel für Kinderarmut in einem Industrieland haben Sie den folgenden Zeitungskommentar über Großbritannien gefunden. Fassen Sie für einen entsprechenden Bericht die im Kommentar enthaltenen relevanten Punkte zusammen. Formulieren Sie ganze deutsche Sätze.
► SF 22 Mediation/translation

Will we ever end child poverty?

by Jack Meyers

By late on Thursday afternoon, Mary-Jane has £4.70 left to last until Monday morning. Mary-Jane, who is 22 years old, has two small children: Jason aged five months and Joshua, two years old. She is a single mother and because she dropped out of college before finishing, she has no qualifications. Now she lives with her children in a small, one-bedroomed flat since the father of her children left. As she cannot afford beds for her children, they have to sleep together in one large bed, which is quite stressful for the young mother because her two-year-old always wakes up when the baby cries. Apart from the bed, the flat is only furnished with an old washing machine, an oven, a sofa and a TV. They store their belongings in cardboard boxes or just leave them on the stone floor which is not carpeted. Mary-Jane rarely buys fresh fruit or vegetables because they are too expensive. They mostly live on tinned food because it is cheaper.

If you think Mary-Jane lives in a slum in a developing country, like Ethiopia, you are wrong. Mary-Jane lives in Scotland, in the middle of Glasgow, and Jason and Joshua are not the only children in Britain living in poverty. One in five, that is more than two million children, lives in poverty in Britain. It is a tragedy that the number of children living in poverty is still so high in a developed country like Britain. When people think of child poverty, they mostly think of Africa and they ignore the child poverty that exists in developed countries. They say that if children have a home and enough food to eat, as well as access to free healthcare, they need not complain about their situation.

In Britain, people are described as being poor if their income is less than 60% of the average British income. Poverty today means eating cheap, unhealthy food, not being able to afford a hobby or school trips and getting a poor education. Additionally, children in poor families have limited opportunities and come into contact with drugs and crime more easily. Poverty in Britain is not as extreme as in developing countries but we must still tackle it.

What can be done to end child poverty in Britain? Firstly, it is important to get parents into work. The problem here is not only the lack of available jobs in Britain at the moment but it is also difficult to find jobs for people who are poorly educated. So before the government creates new jobs, they must provide better educational standards for poor children. One of the measures the government has promised is to provide free school meals for the children of low-income families.

Secondly, the government must spend more money on childcare and cut childcare costs so that parents are free to find, and go to work.

Thirdly, a minimum wage should be set for low-paid jobs. In this way it would pay off for people living on welfare to get back to work.

In any case, the British government's promise to halve child poverty by 2010 has not been kept. We can only hope that they will keep their second promise, which is to end child poverty forever by 2020.

No matter what happens, Mary-Jane just hopes that her children will have a better life than she has had. She hopes they will get good jobs, live in a pleasant flat and not need to worry about the next shopping trip. (594 words)

‹R› **b)** Do the following tasks on the text "Will we ever end child poverty?" in complete sentences. Use your own words.

1. Sum up the conditions under which Mary-Jane lives.
2. Explain why many people ignore child poverty in Britain.
3. Describe the effects of poverty on children living in Britain.
4. Outline the author's suggestions on how to end child poverty in Britain.

2 Composition

‹P› ◘ Describe and analyze the following illustrations.

1. ► SF 28 Describing diagrams

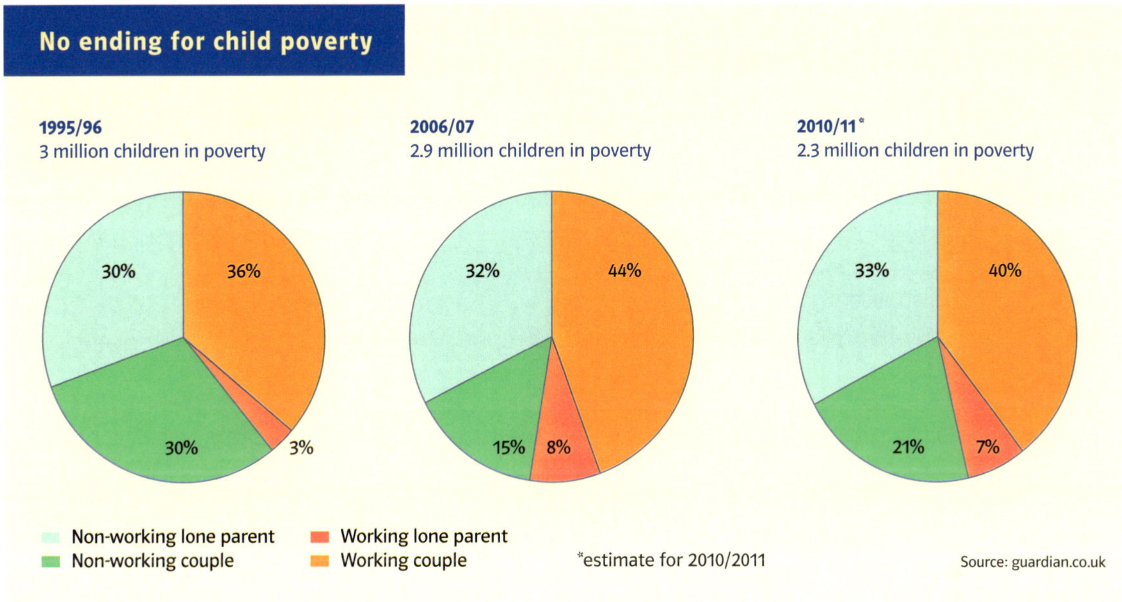

2. ► SF 27 Describing cartoons

Video lounge

1 Applying for a job placement
Unit 2 D4

Before watching

a) Describe the photo.

b) What kind of situation do you think this is?

While watching

c) Watch the film and find out the following:

1. the names of the two people;
2. the type and name of the company.

d) Watch the film again and answer the following questions.

1. Why does the applicant want to work there?
2. What skills must a good employee have?
3. How does the applicant see her future?
4. Which areas will she work in as part of the placement?

After watching

e) Do you think the applicant will get the job placement? Why / why not?

2 Environmental protection
Unit 6 A1

BBC Motion Gallery

Before watching

a) Describe the photo.

b) What do you think the man in the foreground is doing?

c) What could his job be?

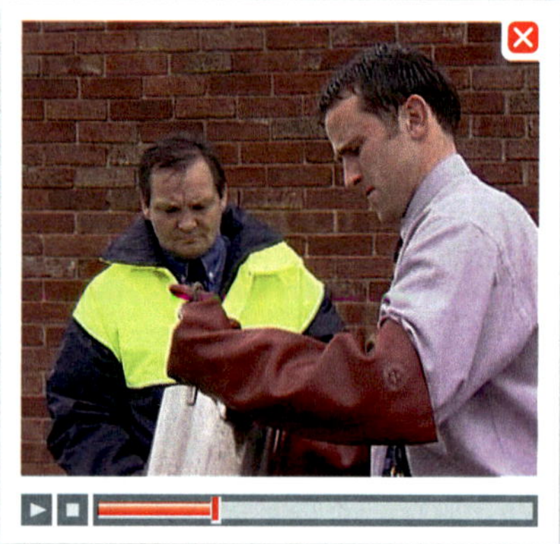

While watching

d) Watch the film and find out if your ideas were right.

e) Watch the film again. Find the most suitable options according to the film. More than one answer may be true.

1. The Environment Agency looks after …
   a) rivers.
   b) farms.
   c) sewage treatment works.
   d) private homes.

2. Anthony Parsons managed to receive his …
   a) A-levels.
   b) driving licence.
   c) Higher National Certificate in Chemistry.
   d) post-graduate diploma in water and environmental management.

3. Anthony Parsons ...
   a) likes working at home.
   b) mostly works in an office.
   c) also works outdoors.
   d) sometimes works underground.
4. This kind of work means that Anthony ...
   a) sometimes feels alone.
   b) has to work at weekends from time to time.
   c) has to get up early.
   d) has to go to his office for meetings with his colleagues.
5. According to Carol Holt environment officers must ...
   a) be good at school.
   b) have a degree in a scientific discipline.
   c) communicate well.
   d) be able to solve problems.

After watching

f) Use your notes from the exercises to give a summary of the work of an environment protection officer.

3 Ecology and/or economy?

Unit 7 A

BBC Motion Gallery

Before watching

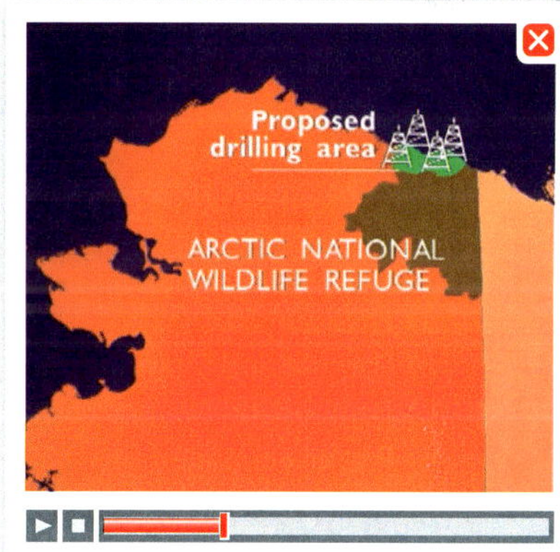

a) Which part of North America is shown in the map?

b) What kind of conflict would you expect in this area?

While watching

c) Watch the first 30 seconds of the film and find out if your answers to a) and b) were right.

d) Watch the complete film. Find out if the following statements are true or false according to the film.

1. Alaska is relatively well developed.
2. The wildlife there is protected by a national refuge.
3. The Arctic National Wildlife Refuge (ANWR) is a haven for wild animals.
4. The people living in the first village shown in the film can make a lot of money from the caribou.
5. Native people think there is no danger to wildlife in that area.
6. There are rich oil fields inside the ANWR.
7. Oil drilling would take place in the caribou area.
8. Oil drilling is already affecting caribou life.
9. Oil is slowly running out on the west coast.
10. All native people of that area are against drilling for oil there.
11. Many things were paid for in the second village by oil companies' taxes.
12. More drilling would bring more money to the area.

After watching

e) "There should be no drilling for oil in national parks." Refer to the film to find arguments for and against this statement. Think of more arguments for and against, and state your personal point of view.

4 Brick Lane – past and present

Unit 9 C

BBC Motion Gallery

Before watching

a) Describe the photo and say what is special about the couple shown.

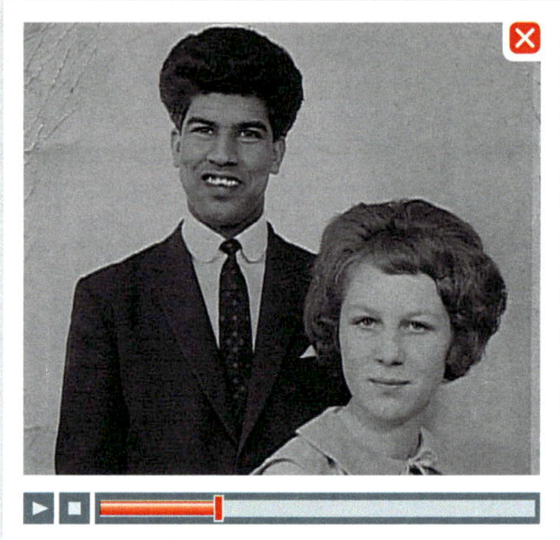

While watching

b) Find the most suitable options according to the film. More than one answer may be true.

1. Pamela …
   a) now lives in another part of London.
   b) was born in 1948.
   c) loved Brick Lane when she was young.
   d) lived in Brick Lane as a young girl.
2. In the fifties and sixties ….
   a) many young men from Asia arrived in Brick Lane.
   b) the face of Brick Lane changed.
   c) the newcomers came to stay in that area.
   d) white girls did not like the Asian newcomers.
3. Shafiq …
   a) thought that England was one of the nicest places before he arrived.
   b) was twenty when he arrived in Brick Lane.
   c) found that his dreams had come true when he arrived.
   d) saw buildings that had been destroyed in World War II.
4. In 1965 …
   a) Pamela and Shafiq got married.
   b) Pamela and Shafiq had known each other for a year.
   c) Pamela changed her religion.
   d) Shafiq changed his religion.
5. Because of their marriage …
   a) Pamela lost all contact with the white community.
   b) Pamela left the East End.
   c) Pamela had difficulties with her mother.
   d) Shafiq had problems with his family.

c) Explain the following text extracts from the film:

1. Pamela: "You can't beat the old Brick Lane."
2. Growing up in the fifties and sixties she witnessed one of the street's most dramatic transformations.
3. He arrived in 1958 when he was 20 dreaming of working for a brighter future in a picture-postcard country.
4. Shafiq: "I was very disappointed."

After watching

d) Couples who belong to different cultures or religions still face the problems Pamela and Shafiq did. Discuss.

5 American immigration

Unit 10 C

BBC Motion Gallery

Before watching

a) Describe the photo.

b) What kind of scene do you think this is?

While watching

c) Watch the film and find out:

1. where the action takes place;
2. what different groups of people are involved;
3. why they do what they do.

d) Watch the film again and answer the following questions.

1. What special kind of "travel industry" is shown in the film?
2. What are the people called who want to cross the border?
3. Why do they take water with them?
4. How many of these people try to cross the border each week?
5. How many get caught trying to cross?
6. What town do they want to reach?
7. How many volunteers work on the border?
8. What percentage of workers in the service industry are migrants?

After watching

e) Explain the following parts of the film commentary.

1. "Meet the people who travel between worlds – the Third and the First."
2. "America can't live without them – but can it live with them?"

6 A job placement at reception

Unit 11 2

Before watching

a) Describe the photo.

b) What kind of scene do you think this is?

While watching

c) Watch the film and find out about the problems the new trainee has.

d) Watch the film again and find out the following information:

1. the departments which the new trainee will get to know;
2. the caller's family name;
3. the date of his arrival;
4. the number of nights he wants to stay at the hotel;
5. the type of room he wants to book;
6. the name of his credit card.

After watching

e) Describe the difficulties that you had when you started a job placement.

Role cards

Unit 1
C Why we are here

d) **Role card B**

Young European

Think up the following information:
- a name
- a country of origin
- reasons for coming to Britain
- a workplace
- free time activities
- plans for the future

Unit 2
B3 A job for you?

a) **Role card B**

Linda Smith

1. Exeter/1990
   Example: I was born in Exeter in 1990.
2. 1990 – 2006
3. since 2006
4. 2006 – 2008
5. customer service at R.S. Reynolds
6. since 2010
7. baby sitting
8. five years ago
9. always
10. last month

Unit 2
D4 Role play: Having an interview

a) **Role card B**

Employer

Prepare questions about:
- education
- work experience
- skills and qualifications
- personality and character
- interests and hobbies.

Be prepared to say something about:
- the work placement
- your company.

Unit 3
C2 A sales talk

b) **Role card B**

Customer

You are a well-informed customer who asks critical questions. You can only speak English.

Think about:
- the disadvantages of the product,
- other better prices and offers,
- the quality of the product, etc.

Unit 3
D4 Should advertising be banned?

a) **Role card B**

Company representative

You sell products to children and teenagers.

Possible arguments:
- information about new products
- children want to have a choice
- new jobs are created

Role card C

Parent

You are against this type of advertising in magazines and on TV.

Possible arguments:
- manipulation
- waste of money
- dangers (ads for alcohol, cigarettes, etc.)

Unit 4
D3 Big brother at school?

■ **Role card B**

Head teacher

You are in favour of CCTV cameras at college because you expect students to behave better then.

On the other hand, you can understand the students' arguments.

Role card C

Teacher

You are not sure if it is a good idea having CCTV cameras in classrooms.

The cameras could help to make life at college easier and safer for everybody but on the other hand you would feel observed every minute of the day.

Role card D

Police spokesperson

You are very much in favour of CCTV cameras.

You give examples of schools where the introduction of cameras has helped to reduce the crime rate.

Unit 5
D2 Community school centres

d) **Role card B**

Single parent

Alex(andra) Foster
- single parent
- has a three-year-old daughter
- wants higher qualifications
- overweight and not very fit
- often needs medical help for his/her daughter
- not enough money to live on

Unit 6
B5 "Water, water, everywhere ..."

a) **Role card B**

Talk about the following things:
- dangers of overfishing
- no need for exotic seafood
- economic help for poor fishermen.

Role card C

Talk about the following things:
- polluted rivers
- environmental problems caused by industry
- governments must act.

Role card D

Talk about the following things:
- clean up your own environment
- local action
- join environmental organizations.

Unit 6
D1 Clubbing with Carol

c) **Role card B**

Club manager

Think about:
- recycling waste
- using environmentally friendly materials, e.g. poly-carbon cups
- generating energy: special dance floor, wind turbine, solar energy system
- organic drinks
- free entry for clubbers who cycle, walk or use public transport.

Unit 8
D4 Developing an economy

◘ **Role card B**

Mining company

- Write down arguments in favour of your project on one card. Think about:
  - ways of using the area that are economically and ecologically correct,
  - the advantages for the people and the local government.
- Write down arguments against the other two projects on another card. Think about the negative things that could happen if the local government decided in favour of one of the other two groups.

Role card C

Manufacturing company

- Write down arguments in favour of your project on one card. Think about:
  - what you want to produce
  - ways of using the area that are economically and ecologically correct
  - the advantages for the people and the local government.
- On another card write down arguments against the other two projects. Think about the negative things that could happen if the local government decided in favour of one of the other two groups.

Role card D

Travel organization

- Write down arguments in favour of your project on one card. Think about:
  - ways of using the area that are economically and ecologically correct,
  - the advantages for the people and the local government.
- On another card write down arguments against the other two projects. Think about the negative things that could happen if the local government decided in favour of one of the other two groups.

Unit 11
2 Finding accommodation – Making phone calls

c) **Role card B**

Receptionist at the Scotsman's Hotel

Name:	Donna McAllister
Hotel number:	Glencoe 62275
Room availability:	10 rooms free for all of next month
Rates:	Full board £60; half board £40
Long stay offer:	15% reduction
Distance to Thistle Hotel:	a ten-minute walk
Booking:	e-mail or online booking form No deposit required

Unit 12
5 Making conversation

d) **Role card B**

Student B

Name:	Frank Flottmann
Home:	Boston, USA
Placement:	Green Hotel, Dundee
Journey to Scotland:	flight to Heathrow – great; train trip to Scotland – terrible
Marital status:	single
Interests:	American football

Role card C

Student C

Name:	Svetlana Bazkova
Home:	St Petersburg, Russia
Placement:	Burns Hotel, Aberdeen
Journey to Scotland:	flight to Glasgow
Marital status:	single
Interests:	computer games

Role card D

Student D

Name:	Min Leh
Home:	Beijing, China
Placement:	Grand Hotel, Edinburgh
Journey to Scotland:	flight to London and drove up
Marital status:	married, 1 child
Interests:	cooking

Role card E

Student E

Name:	Katie O'Neill
Home:	Belfast, Northern Ireland
Placement:	Central Hotel, Glasgow
Journey to Scotland:	ferry from Belfast to Stranraer
Marital status:	single
Interests:	ballroom dancing

Skills files

1 Learning habits
Lerngewohnheiten

Welcher Lerntyp bin ich?

1. Ich bin ein eher visueller Lerntyp, d.h. ich lerne am besten, indem ich Lerninhalte über das Auge aufnehme, z.B. Bilder anschaue, Texte lese.
   D.h. besorgen Sie sich privat häufig englischsprachige Texte, z.B. Comics, Internet, etc. Lesen Sie möglichst viel.

2. Ich bin ein eher auditiver Lerntyp, d.h. ich lerne am besten, indem ich Lerninhalte über das Ohr aufnehme, z.B. Musik höre, Gespräche führe, jemandem zuhöre.
   D.h. versuchen Sie die Liedtexte, die Sie hören, zu verstehen und übersetzen Sie diese ins Deutsche. Schauen Sie Nachrichten im Fernsehen auf Englisch an.
   Es könnte für Sie beispielsweise hilfreich sein, wenn Sie die Lesetexte in diesem Buch anhand der CD im Workbook anhören, um sich neue Vokabeln besser einprägen zu können.

3. Ich bin ein eher kinästhetischer Lerntyp, d.h. ich lerne am besten, indem ich Lerninhalte über meinen Tastsinn aufnehme, z.B. wenn ich mich bewege, experimentiere, Erfahrungen mache, aktiv werden kann.
   D.h. benutzen Sie Selbstlernprogramme (E-Learning) oder versuchen Sie mit englisch- oder amerikanischsprechenden Leuten ins Gespräch zu kommen, z.B. im Irish Pub, in Sportclubs, etc.

Diese drei Lerntypen sind nur die grundlegenden Lerntypen. Studien belegen, dass Menschen besonders schnell und gut lernen, wenn möglichst viele Lernkanäle angesprochen werden, d.h. dass Lernen mit allen Sinnen am effektivsten ist. Nach Möglichkeit sollten neue Lerninhalte demnach durch Lesen, Ansehen, Aktivwerden, Anhören und Sprechen aufgenommen werden. Es könnte für Sie beispielsweise hilfreich sein, wenn Sie die Lesetexte in diesem Buch anhand der CD im Workbook anhören, um sich neue Vokabeln besser einprägen zu können.

Weitere Informationen zu Lerntypen und Online Tests finden Sie im Internet (siehe Stichworte).

Key Words
- Lerntypentest
- Lerntypenbestimmung
- Lerntypentheorien

Tipps für alle Lerntypen, um optimal Sprache zu lernen

Lernen Sie regelmäßig!
Lernen Sie regelmäßig Vokabeln und Grammatik, nicht erst kurz vor Ihrer Klausur. Wenn Sie jeden Tag fünf Vokabeln lernen und diese am Wochenende wiederholen, haben Sie schon 25 neue Vokabeln oder englische Redewendungen in einer Woche gelernt.

Nutzen Sie Songtexte, DVDs, Zeitschriften, Internet!
Die englische Sprache begegnet Ihnen mittlerweile überall: in der Werbung, im Fernsehen, im Radio, in Zeitschriften etc. Also halten Sie Ihre Augen und Ohren offen. Sehen sie sich Ihren Lieblingsfilm auf DVD doch einmal in der englischen Sprache an.

Analysieren Sie Ihre Fehler!
Machen Sie in jeder Klausur immer wieder dieselben Fehler? Versuchen Sie konkret an Ihren Fehlern zu arbeiten. Nehmen Sie sich die zwei Fehler, die Sie in der letzten Klausur am häufigsten gemacht haben, vor und gehen Sie die Erläuterungen in Ihrer Grammatik noch einmal genau durch. Vielleicht können Sie auch noch ein paar Übungen im *Workbook* dazu machen.

Vermeiden Sie lange und komplizierte Sätze!
Gewöhnen Sie sich schnell an, im Unterricht in der englischen Sprache zu kommunizieren. Wenn Sie Ihre Sätze einfach halten, machen Sie auch nicht so viele Fehler und fühlen sich sicherer.

2 Cross-cultural communication
Interkulturelle Kommunikation

Wenn Sie ins Ausland reisen oder in Ihrem Heimatland auf Menschen aus anderen Ländern treffen, sollten Sie sich eventuell auftretender kultureller Unterschiede bewusst sein. Diese Unterschiede können sich auf unterschiedliche Glaubensvorstellungen, Meinungen, Werte und Normen beziehen.

Deshalb sollten Sie folgende Regeln beachten:
- Respektieren Sie alle Menschen.
- Seien Sie gegenüber dem „Anderssein" aufgeschlossen.
- Interpretieren Sie Verhaltensweisen, die Sie nicht verstehen, nicht als unnormal oder falsch.
- Gehen Sie nicht davon aus, dass es nur einen richtigen Weg gibt zu kommunizieren (Ihren!).
- Informieren Sie sich, wenn möglich, vorher über die kulturellen Hintergründe der anderen Person/des anderen Landes.

Informationen zu kulturellen Hintergründen finden Sie im Internet (siehe Stichworte).

Key Words
- kulturelle Unterschiede
- Kulturunterschiede
- Tabus und Regeln + (Name des Landes)

Tipps: Kulturelle Unterschiede

Bekleidung: Wenn Sie ins Ausland reisen, sollten Sie auf Ihre Kleidung achten und sie möglichst den örtlichen Traditionen anpassen. In manchen Ländern gelten kurze Hosen, Miniröcke oder ausgeschnittene Tops als unangemessene Bekleidung in der Öffentlichkeit.

Gestik: Vermeiden Sie ausladende Gestik mit den Händen und Armen. Einige in westlichen Ländern übliche Gesten haben in anderen Ländern keinerlei Bedeutung (z. B. mit den Schultern zucken) oder aber eine gegensätzliche Bedeutung (z. B. bedeutet das Kopfschütteln in Indien „Ja").

Begrüßung: Es gibt verschiedene Begrüßungsarten auf der ganzen Welt (z. B. ist eine Verbeugung die traditionelle Begrüßung in Japan). Um sicher zu gehen, ist es manchmal angebracht, darauf zu warten, wie Ihr Gegenüber die Begrüßung einleitet.

Gesprächsthemen: Seien Sie vorsichtig bei der Wahl der Gesprächsthemen. In den meisten Ländern, so auch in westlichen Industriestaaten, gelten Sexualität, Religion, Politik, Krankheit und Tod als Tabuthemen. Themen, mit denen Sie in den meisten Ländern nicht falsch liegen, sind beispielsweise das Wetter, Sport und Reisen.

Humor: Seien Sie vorsichtig mit Sarkasmus und Humor, da es kulturell bedingt ein unterschiedliches Empfinden darüber gibt, was lustig ist.

Alkohol: In einigen Ländern gilt ein generelles Alkoholverbot und in vielen Ländern ist es verboten, Alkohol in der Öffentlichkeit zu trinken.

Kommunikationsregeln für den Aufenthalt in Amerika

Begrüßung: In der Regel begrüßen Sie sich in den USA, wie in Deutschland, mit einem kurzen Händeschütteln.

Anrede: In der Regel spricht man sich in den USA mit dem Vornamen an. Häufig lassen sich auch Kollegen und Vorgesetzte mit dem Vornamen anreden. Dies ist jedoch kein Zeichen von Freundschaft, Sie sollten trotzdem weiterhin Respekt zeigen.

Höflichkeit: In den USA ist Höflichkeit besonders wichtig und wird sehr ernst genommen. Nach der Begrüßung wird in der Regel gefragt *„How are you?"* In einem Gespräch sollten Sie auch die Worte *will*, *must* oder *want* vermeiden.
Gerne gehört sind dagegen *please*, *might* und *would like to*.

Einladungen: Wenn Sie in den USA eingeladen werden, sollten Sie ein kleines Geschenk mitbringen.

Restaurantbesuch: Im Restaurant warten Sie, bis man Ihnen einen Platz zuweist. Setzten Sie sich nicht einfach an einen freien Tisch.

Warteschlangen: Ob Sie auf den Bus warten, eine öffentliche Toilette aufsuchen möchten, auf dem Postamt sind oder im Supermarkt, es ist immer wichtig, dass Sie sich an das Ende der Reihe stellen und geduldig warten.

Polizeikontrolle: Wenn Sie in den USA von der Polizei angehalten werden sollten, dann legen Sie die Hände auf das Lenkrad und machen so lange nichts, bis Sie zu etwas aufgefordert werden.

Bevor Sie im Ausland arbeiten, sollten Sie sich bei Freunden/Bekannten/Verwandten/Lehrern erkundigen, die bereits in dem Land waren!

3 Having a discussion
An einer Diskussion teilnehmen

Diskussionen dienen dem Austausch von Meinungen und Ideen zu einem bestimmten Thema. Sie können uns auch neue Aspekte liefern, wenn wir uns mit unbekannten Themen beschäftigen.
Ob Sie die Diskussion leiten oder an der Diskussion teilnehmen, Sie sollten sich immer gut vorbereiten und sich an die folgenden Regeln halten.

Regeln und Redemittel für die Diskussionsleitung

- Sorgen Sie für einen geordneten Diskussionsablauf und guten Diskussionsstil, d.h. achten Sie besonders auf die Höflichkeit der Diskussionsteilnehmer.

- Halten Sie Ihre eigene Meinung zurück und bleiben Sie immer neutral.

- Geben Sie eine Einführung in das Diskussionsthema und stellen Sie die Diskussionsteilnehmer vor.

  (As you know,) our discussion today is about …
  On my right/left I have … (name of person or group), who is/are in favour of … / against …

- Bestimmen Sie die Reihenfolge der Wortmeldungen.

  Who would like to open the discussion?
  …, would you like to open the discussion?
  The next person to speak is …, followed by … and then …

- Sorgen Sie dafür, dass alle Teilnehmer die gleichen Chancen haben, zu Wort zu kommen.

  Is there anything you would like to say, …?

- Bringen Sie Vielredner dazu, sich kurz zu fassen.

  I'm sorry to interrupt you, but I'm afraid I have to stop you there.
  Sorry, but I must give the others a chance to put forward their arguments now.

- Sorgen Sie dafür, dass immer nur ein Teilnehmer spricht.

  Please wait your turn. You'll have a chance to speak in a minute!
  If you'd just let … finish, please.

- Notieren Sie sich die wichtigsten Ideen/Argumente und fassen Sie die Diskussion am Ende zusammen.

  Time is running out, so I'd like to sum up what we've been discussing.
  We heard from … that …

- Bedanken Sie sich am Ende der Diskussion bei den Teilnehmern für die Teilnahme an der Diskussion.

  Thank you for taking part in the discussion!

Regeln und Redemittel für Diskussionsteilnehmer

- Stellen Sie zunächst sicher, dass Sie das Diskussionsthema richtig verstanden haben.
- Entscheiden Sie, welche Meinung Sie vertreten.
- Wenn Sie ausreichend Zeit haben, kann es sinnvoll sein, sich mit den Gegenargumenten auseinanderzusetzen. Überlegen Sie sich schon vorher, was Sie den Argumenten der anderen Diskussionsteilnehmer entgegensetzen können.
- Sprechen Sie kurz und bleiben Sie beim Thema.
- Bereiten Sie sich gut auf die Diskussion vor, indem Sie sich vor Beginn der Diskussion Argumente zurechtlegen und diese stichpunktartig aufschreiben. Sie sollten Ihre Argumente immer erläutern und begründen können. Es ist auch hilfreich, wenn Sie sich Beispiele überlegen.

Firstly … secondly … finally …
First I would like to point out …
In addition / Moreover / Besides / Furthermore …
Another significant advantage is …
On the one hand … on the other hand …
Consequently / That is why / Therefore …
However / In contrast to / Nevertheless …
I think / feel / believe / am of the opinion that …
To my mind …
In my opinion …

- Bleiben Sie immer höflich und denken Sie daran, dass es um das Thema geht und nicht um die Personen. Also attackieren Sie nur die Argumente.

I'm sorry, but I (completely) disagree.
That's an interesting point, but …
You've missed the point (entirely).

- Falls Sie etwas nicht richtig verstanden haben und einen Diskussionsteilnehmer unterbrechen möchten, seien Sie höflich.

Sorry to interrupt, but could you please explain/ repeat the point you just made?

- Gehen Sie auf die Meinungen der anderen Diskussionsteilnehmer ein.

You are (quite/absolutely) right.
That's a very good point!
Absolutely!/Exactly!
I agree (with you/Laura).
Andrea made a very valid point when she said that …
I partly agree with Sven. What he didn't mention was …

Weitere Redemittel für Diskussionsteilnehmer

- Vorschläge machen:

I suggest that we …
We would propose that you …
What do you think about …?
If I were you, I would …
Why don't we …

- Auf Vorschläge reagieren:

That's a good idea! / Fine!
OK. / Yes, why not?
OK, if you want, I don't really mind.
I'm not sure that will work.
I think it would be a better idea to talk about …
What about …?

- Nach einer Meinung fragen:

What do you think about …?
How do you feel about …?
What is your view on/about …?
In your opinion what is the best solution?
What would you say?

- Mit Zwischenreden umgehen:

Can I just finish what I was saying, please?
Just a second, I haven't quite finished.
Would you let me / allow me to make my point, please.
I'll just finish what I wanted to say if you don't mind.
You could at least let me finish my sentence!

- Das Thema wechseln:

There is something else I'd like to say …
Have you ever thought of …?
On the other hand …
I'd like to bring up another point.

- Zum eigentlichen Thema zurückkehren:

Let's get back to what we were saying/discussing.
Let's get back to the point.
As I was saying before, …
This discussion is getting away from the original topic.
What we should really be talking about is …

- Nachfragen bei Verständnisschwierigkeiten:

Did I get that right?
Do you really mean that …?
Could you explain what you just said / the point you just made again, please?
Could you give me/us an example, please?

- Missverständnisse aufklären:

I'm sorry, but …
… that's not what I meant to say (at all)!
… you've got me (completely) wrong.
… you've (completely) misunderstood me.
Sorry, I didn't make myself clear. I'll try and explain again.

4 Making conversation
Smalltalk

Als Smalltalk bezeichnet man eine leichte Unterhaltung ohne Tiefgang. Dabei bietet sich eine gute Möglichkeit, Interesse zu zeigen, freundlich zu kommunizieren und Konflikte zu vermeiden. Bei vielen gesellschaftlichen Ereignissen, z. B. Partys, verbringt man die ganze Zeit mit Smalltalk.

Der Smalltalk hat als gesellschaftlicher Brauch eine hohe Bedeutung, indem er besonders dem unverbindlichen Kennenlernen oder der Auflockerung der Atmosphäre dient. Ein geschäftliches Treffen, ein Telefonat, ein Bewerbungsgespräch etc. können Sie immer mit ein paar Minuten Smalltalk einleiten (und beenden).

Bedenken Sie: „*How are you?*" ist keine Frage, auf die Sie mit Ihrem persönlichen Befinden antworten sollten. So ist die Frage nicht gemeint, sondern sie stellt in der Regel nur die Einleitung für den Smalltalk dar.

Beliebte Themen für Smalltalk

- das Wetter (besonders in Großbritannien)
- Anfahrt zu dem Ort des Gesprächs
- der eigene Wohnort / Wohnort des Gesprächspartners.
- die eigene Familie / die Familie des Gesprächspartners (wenn man die Familie kennt!)
- ein aktueller Film oder eine bekannte Fernsehserie
- Auswahl an Sehenswürdigkeiten, Einkaufsmöglichkeiten, Restaurants etc., die eine bestimmte Stadt bietet
- Sport (z. B. aktuelle internationale Sportveranstaltungen)
- Urlaub
- Schule/Universität/Beruf
- Hobbys und Interessen
- ein Thema aus den aktuellen Nachrichten, das nicht kontrovers ist

Ungeeignete Themen für Smalltalk

- Religiöse Themen
- Politische Themen
- Probleme am Arbeitsplatz
- Beziehungs- oder Familienprobleme

Redemittel

- Ein Gespräch beginnen:

Hi!
Hello!
Do you mind if I join you?
Nice to see you (again)!
How are you?
How are you doing? *(informal)*
How are things? *(informal)*

- Ein Thema finden:

Did you see … on TV last night / at the weekend?
Have you seen the new [James Bond] film yet?
Did you read about [that terrible train crash] in the newspaper this morning?
Terrible/Beautiful weather, isn't it?
How was your journey?
Have you ever been here before?
Who do you think is going to win [the football match] this evening?

- Auf den Gesprächspartner eingehen:

Really?
I don't believe it!
Well, I've never heard of anything like that before!
That's the funniest / most interesting / strangest thing I've heard in ages!
I couldn't agree more!

- Füllwörter:

Well, …
Actually, …
Let's see, …
Let me think, …

- Frageanhängsel:

You know …, don't you?
He's …, isn't he?
It hasn't …, has it?

- Das Gespräch beenden:

It was nice talking to you!
Excuse me, I've got to go now.
Hope to see you again soon.
Hope you get home safely.
Give my regards to …
Don't forget to say hello to … for me!
Have you got my mobile number / my e-mail address so that we can stay in contact?

5 Making phone calls
Telefongespräche führen

Im modernen Berufsleben gehören Telefonate in englischer Sprache zum Alltag. Mit etwas Vorbereitung können Ihnen solche Gespräche erheblich leichter fallen.

Vorbereitung auf das Telefongespräch

- Machen Sie sich Stichpunkte in der englischen Sprache oder machen Sie sich eine grobe Skizze über die Punkte, die Sie ansprechen möchten. Das ist besonders wichtig, wenn Sie Geschäftsanrufe tätigen.
- Wenn möglich, finden Sie den Namen und die Durchwahl der Kontaktperson bereits vor dem Telefonat heraus.
- Denken Sie darüber nach, was die Kontaktperson möglicherweise sagen oder fragen wird, und bereiten Sie entsprechende Antworten darauf vor.
- Seien Sie darauf vorbereitet, Wörter zu buchstabieren, insbesondere Namen und Adressen.
- Haben Sie keine Angst, Fehler zu machen.

Während des Telefongesprächs

- Sprechen Sie langsam und deutlich. Stellen Sie Ihre Anfragen eindeutig und sachlich.
- Wenn Sie ein geschäftliches Telefongespräch führen, nennen Sie immer Ihren Vornamen und Ihren Familiennamen und reden Sie die Kontaktperson mit *Mr*, *Mrs* oder *Ms* und ihrem Familiennamen an.
- Wenn Sie ein privates Telefongespräch führen, reicht es, sich mit Ihrem Vornamen zu melden.
- Erwarten Sie nicht, jedes einzelne Wort zu verstehen. Wenn Sie aber meinen, etwas Wichtiges nicht verstanden zu haben, dann fragen Sie nach.

→ **Regeln und Redemittel finden Sie auf der folgenden Seite.**

Regeln und Redemittel

- Wenn die Person wiederholen soll, was sie gesagt hat:

I'm sorry I didn't quite catch what you said.
Could you repeat that, please?

- Wenn die Person etwas noch einmal erklären soll:

I'm sorry, I'm afraid I don't understand what you mean. Could you explain that again, please?
I'm afraid I couldn't quite follow you. Did you mean …?

- Wenn die Person langsamer sprechen soll:

Could you speak a little more slowly, please?

- Seien Sie höflich! Denken Sie daran, „bitte" zu sagen, wenn Sie nach Informationen fragen, und „danke", wenn Ihnen geholfen wurde.

please = bitte
you're welcome / not at all = bitte schön; gern geschehen

- Nennen Sie Telefonnummern immer als einzelne Zahlen. Wenn die gleiche Zahl zweimal hintereinander vorkommt, können Sie *double* sagen (z. B. *44 = double 4*). Für die Ziffer *0* sagt man sowohl im Britischen als auch im Amerikanischen *Oh*. Im Amerikanischen können Sie außerdem auch *zero* sagen.

07145 12206 = Oh (zero) - seven - one - four - five - one - double two - oh (zero) - six

- Wenn Sie Namen nennen, ist es oftmals hilfreich, wenn Sie diese buchstabieren.

Would you like me to spell …?
Would you like me to spell that for you?
It's spelt …
I'll just spell that for you. It's …

- Fordern Sie die Kontaktperson höflich dazu auf, Namen etc. zu buchstabieren, um Verwirrung zu vermeiden.

Could you spell …, please?
Could you spell that for me, please?
Would you mind spelling …?
Would you mind spelling that for me, please?

- Wiederholen Sie die Informationen (Zeiten, Namen, Adressen, Preise etc.), um sicher zu gehen, dass Sie alles richtig verstanden haben.

Let me just check that I've understood all the information you've given me. …
Let me just check that I've understood all the information you're asked for correctly. …
I'll just repeat that back to you to make sure I've got everything down correctly. …
Let me just check that I've spelt your name correctly. …

- Wenn Sie die Kontaktperson nicht richtig hören können, bitten Sie sie, lauter zu sprechen.

I'm sorry, (it's a very bad line,) I didn't quite catch that! Could you speak up a bit, please?
Sorry, it's very loud at my end. Would you mind speaking up a bit?

- Wenn Sie denken, dass Sie sich verwählt haben, fragen Sie nach und entschuldigen Sie sich. Legen Sie nicht einfach auf.

Is that (+ number you want)?
I'm sorry, I think I've dialled the wrong number.

- Wenn Sie vermuten, dass sich ein Anrufer verwählt hat, erklären Sie ihm dies höflich. Legen Sie nicht einfach auf.

I'm sorry, but I think you've got the wrong number. This is (+ number / name / company name).
I'm sorry, there's no one here with that name. This is (+ your number / name / company name).

6 Social calls
Private Telefongespräche

Wenn Sie ein privates Telefongespräch in englischer Sprache führen möchten, können Sie im Wesentlichen den Vorgaben in **Skills File 5** (Telefongespräche führen) folgen. Auch die Formulierungen in **Skills File 4** (Smalltalk) können hilfreich sein.

Redemittel

- Begrüßung:

  Hello!
  Hello, this is …[1]
  Hello …[2]! It's me …[1]

- Ein Gespräch beginnen:

  How are you?
  How are you doing?
  It's great to hear from you!
  I just thought I'd call and find out how you are.
  I just wanted to ring and let you know that …

- Jemand anderen sprechen wollen:

  Could I speak to …[3], please?
  Is …[3] in, please?
  Do you know when …[3] will be back, please?

- Einen Gesprächspartner weiterreichen:

  Just a second, I'll go and find him/her.
  Hold on a minute, I'll see if he/she is in.

- Eine Nachricht weitergeben:

  Could you give …[3] a message, please?

- Eine Nachricht entgegennehmen:

  I'm afraid he/she can't come to the phone right now. Can I take a message?
  I'm sorry, but he/she isn't in at the moment. Would you like me to take a message?

- Zurückrufen:

  Would it be OK to ring back later?
  What time can I ring back?
  I'll ring back in about half an hour, if that's OK.
  Could you give …[3] my number, please, and ask him/her to ring me back?
  You can try ringing again in about [15 minutes] if you want to.
  He/She should be back at about [11 pm].
  Shall I ask him/her to call you back?

- Sich verabschieden:

  Thanks for ringing!
  It was great to hear from you!
  Speak to you again soon, I hope!
  Bye!
  Take care.
  All the best.

1 Ihr Name **2** Name der Person, die am anderen Ende der Leitung ist **3** Name der Person, die Sie sprechen möchten

7 Formal phone calls
Förmliche Telefongespräche

Wenn Sie ein Telefongespräch mit einem Geschäftspartner führen möchten, können Sie im Wesentlichen den Vorgaben in **Skills File 5** (Telefongespräche führen) folgen. Die Grundlage für ein erfolgreiches Geschäftstelefonat wird in den ersten Minuten gelegt. Sorgen Sie deshalb dafür, dass Sie von Beginn an freundlich sind und deutlich sprechen.

Redemittel

- Begrüßung:

Good morning / Good afternoon …[1]!
(This is) …[2] speaking.
Can I help you?
What can I do for you?

- Jemand anderen sprechen wollen:

Could I speak to …[3], please?
Can you put me through to …[3], please?
I'd like to speak to someone in your [sales] department.

- Einen Gesprächspartner weiterverbinden:

Please hold (the line).
One moment please.
I'll connect you with …[3]
I'll connect you with the [sales] department.
I'll put you through to …[3]

- Wenn jemand nicht zu sprechen ist:

I'm sorry, …[3] isn't here.
I'm sorry, …[3] isn't available at the moment / today.

- Nach der richtigen Durchwahl usw. fragen:

Can you give me …[3]'s extension number, please?
I can give you his/her extension number [voice mail number, fax number, e-mail address]. It's …

- Den Grund für den Anruf nennen:

I'd like to receive more information about …
I'm calling about …

- Eine Nachricht weitergeben:

Could you pass on a message, please?

- Eine Nachricht entgegennehmen:

Would you like to leave a message?
Can I take a message?
Would you like me to pass on a message?

- Eine Nachricht auf einem Anrufbeantworter oder einer Mailbox hinterlassen:

Hello, this is …[2] at …[1]. I'm sorry to have missed you.
I'd be grateful if you could ring me back this morning/afternoon.
You can get me on my mobile. The number is …
I'll be in the office all afternoon so you can reach me there.

- Einen Rückruf vereinbaren:

Shall I ask him/her to call you back?
Could you call back later, please?
Could you ask him/her to call me back, please? My number is …[4]
Can I call back later?
I'll call back later if that's OK.
When would be the best time to call back?

- Sich verabschieden:

Thanks for your call!
Thanks for calling!
Thank you very much for your help!
Sorry I couldn't be of more help.
Have a nice day!
Goodbye!

1 Name Ihrer Firma **2** Ihr Name **3** Name der Person, mit der Sie sprechen wollen **4** Ihre Telefonnummer

8 Reading comprehension
Leseverstehen

Die Units in diesem Buch enthalten fiktionale und nicht-fiktionale Texte, die Sie im Unterricht lesen werden. Um über diese Texte sprechen zu können, sollten Sie lernen, möglichst schnell zu lesen. Das Gelesene gleichzeitig auch gut zu verstehen, mag Ihnen schwierig vorkommen, z. B. durch unbekanntes Vokabular oder komplizierte Textstrukturen. Deshalb ist es wichtig, systematisch zu lesen, um die Textinhalte zu erfassen.

Tipps: Schwierige Texte leichter verstehen

Überblick gewinnen
Sie überfliegen den gesamten Text recht zügig und ermitteln, was der Inhalt ist. Es ist manchmal hilfreich, die Gesamtaussage des Textes in einem Satz aufzuschreiben, um sich diese besser einprägen zu können.
Beispiel: *The text is about …*

Textaufgaben lesen
Lesen Sie die Fragen, die an den Text gestellt werden. Falls es keine Aufgaben gibt, stellen Sie selber Fragen an den Text!
Beispiel: *Who?, What?, When?, Where?, Why?, How?*

Detailliertes Lesen
Beim zweiten Lesedurchgang lesen Sie den Text Abschnitt für Abschnitt und markieren die wichtigsten Textaussagen oder Schlüsselbegriffe bzw. notieren sich diese auf einem Blatt.

Tipp: Nutzen Sie die Abschnitte als Lesehilfe, d. h. in der Regel wird in jedem neuen Abschnitt ein neuer, weiterführender Aspekt des Themas genannt.
Beispiel: Fragen Sie nach jedem Abschnitt: „Welche Funktion hat dieser Abschnitt?" oder „Welche neuen Aspekte hat dieser Abschnitt aufgeworfen?"

Nachschlagen
Je nach Schwierigkeitsgrad des Textes wird es einzelne Begriffe oder gar ganze Sätze geben, die unverständlich geblieben sind. Klären Sie Unbekanntes mit einem Wörterbuch.
Wenn Sie ganze Sätze nicht verstehen, bitten Sie zunächst einen Mitschüler um Hilfe.
► SF 10 Surviving without a dictionary
► SF 11 Using a dictionary

Zusammenfassung mit eigenen Worten
Fassen Sie die wichtigsten Aspekte des Textes mit eigenen Worten zusammen. Lösen Sie sich vom Text und finden Sie Ihre eigenen Worte.

9 Anticipating, skimming, scanning
Antizipieren, Skimming, Scanning

Um die Fragen zu einem Text richtig beantworten zu können, benötigen Sie eine Kombination verschiedener Lesestrategien. Die bekanntesten Lesestrategien sind das Antizipieren, das Skimming und das Scanning.

Antizipieren ist die Leseerwartung, die an einen Text gestellt wird. Es bedeutet, dass Sie vorhersagen, worum es in dem Text gehen könnte, ohne den Text gelesen zu haben. Wenn Sie sich bereits vor dem ersten Lesen Gedanken über den Inhalt des Textes gemacht haben und evtl. sogar Ihr Vorwissen zu dem Thema aktiviert haben, wird es Ihnen leichter fallen, auch schwierige Texte zu verstehen.

Skimming bedeutet, einen Text zu überfliegen, um möglichst schnell einen Gesamteindruck vom Inhalt zu erhalten. Danach sollte es Ihnen möglich sein, in einem Satz den Inhalt wiederzugeben.

Scanning bedeutet, einen Text gezielt auf bestimmte Informationen hin zu filtern.

Antizipieren

Bevor Sie den Text lesen, haben Sie bestimmte Erwartungen, die sich beim späteren Lesen bestätigen lassen oder die Sie verwerfen müssen. Versuchen Sie vorherzusagen, worum es in dem Text gehen könnte.

Beim Antizipieren ist es hilfreich folgende Punkte zu beachten:
- Textsorte (Handelt es sich um einen fiktionalen Text, z. B. Romanauszug, Kurzgeschichte, oder handelt es sich um einen nicht-fiktionalen Text, z. B. Zeitungsartikel, Internetseite, Sachtext, Reisebericht?)
- Erscheinungsdatum und Erscheinungsort des Textes (Geben Erscheinungsdatum und -ort einen Hinweis auf das mögliche Thema des Textes, besonders bei Zeitungsartikeln?)
- Layout und Illustrationen (Bilder, Graphiken)

Skimming

Nach dem Antizipieren überfliegen Sie den Text, um sich einen Gesamtüberblick zu verschaffen. Diese Technik kann beispielsweise besonders hilfreich sein, wenn Sie sich in Ihrer Abschlussprüfung zwischen zwei Texten entscheiden können. Skimming heißt auch, dass Sie ungefähr drei- bis viermal schneller lesen als gewöhnlich.

Beim Skimming ist es hilfreich folgende Punkte zu beachten:
- Lesen Sie die Überschrift und die Untertitel, um herauszufinden, worum es in dem Text geht.
- Versuchen Sie, sich ganze Abschnitte anzusehen und nicht Wort für Wort zu lesen.
- Lesen Sie nur den ersten und den letzten Satz jedes Abschnittes.

Scanning

Diese Technik des selektiven Lesens kann besonders hilfreich sein, wenn Sie Fragen zum Text beantworten sollen und nur nach relevanten Informationen suchen.

Beim Scanning ist es hilfreich folgende Punkte zu beachten:
- Lesen Sie die Fragen/Aufgaben zum Text sorgfältig durch.
- Lassen Sie Ihre Augen über den Text fliegen und fokussieren Sie dabei Schlüsselbegriffe. Lesen Sie den Text nicht Wort für Wort.
- Markieren Sie Schlüsselbegriffe oder wichtige Details im Text oder notieren Sie diese.
- Versuchen Sie, anhand Ihrer Notizen die Fragen mit Ihren eigenen Worten zu beantworten.

10 Surviving without a dictionary
Umgang mit Texten ohne Wörterbuch

Auch wenn Ihnen ein Wörterbuch zur Verfügung steht, lesen Sie den Text mindestens einmal vollständig durch, ohne die unbekannten Wörter nachzuschlagen. Versuchen Sie, die Hauptaussage des Textes zu verstehen.

Texterschließung ohne Wörterbuch

- Überlegen Sie, ob der Kontext, in dem das unbekannte Wort auftaucht, Ihnen hilft, das Wort zu verstehen. So können z. B. angrenzende Worte oder Sätze dabei helfen.
- Manche englische Wörter werden gleichermaßen in der deutschen Sprache verwendet.
  Beispiele: *computer, crash, deadline, international, laptop, loyal, tourist …*
- Manche englische Wörter sind der deutschen Bezeichnung sehr ähnlich.
  Beispiele: *cloning, economy, electricity, globalisation, industry, politics, president, technology …*
  Aber achten Sie hier besonders auf „falsche Freunde"!
  Beispiele: *brave* = mutig; *sea* = Meer; *sensible* = vernünftig; *to spend money* = Geld ausgeben
- Manche englische Wörter ähneln Wörtern, die Sie aus anderen Fremdsprachen kennen.
  Beispiele: *announce* (French: annoncer), *organic* (Latin: organicus), *solar* (Latin: solaris)
- Bei zusammengesetzten Wörtern kennen Sie vielleicht zumindest einen der beiden Wortteile.
  Beispiele: *high-class, lifestyle, part-time, salesperson, subculture, work experience*
- Bei manchen Wörtern hilft es, sie laut auszusprechen, weil der Klang des Wortes hilft, die Bedeutung zu finden.
  Beispiele: *bang, clap, crisps, hiss, moo, ouch, ping, whisper*
- Versuchen Sie, die Wortfamilie zu ermitteln (siehe unitbegleitendes Vokabular im SB auf den Seiten 207 bis 251). Ein Teil des Wortes könnte mit einem Ihnen bereits bekannten englischen Wort zusammenhängen. Achten Sie auch auf Vorsilben und Nachsilben.

Vorsilben

- Folgende Vorsilben geben Worten eine negative oder gegensätzliche (≠) Bedeutung:

in-	active ≠ inactive
im-	possible ≠ impossible
il-	literate ≠ illiterate
ir-	relevant ≠ irrelevant
anti-	anti-smoking
counter-	counterrevolution
mis-	to misunderstand
un-	happy ≠ unhappy
de-	to stabilise ≠ to destabilise
dis-	to like ≠ to dislike

- Folgende Vorsilben zeigen einen Anstieg (+) oder eine Abnahme (–) an:

out- (+)	to grow – to outgrow
over- (+)	to heat – to overheat
sub- (–)	standard – substandard
super- (++)	natural – supernatural
under- (–)	to pay – to underpay

- Weitere Vorsilben:

inter-	international	pro-	pro-abortion
post-	post-war	re-	reread
pre-	pre-school	trans-	transatlantic

Nachsilben

- Nachsilben bestimmen den Wortstamm und bilden oft aus Verben und Adjektiven Nomen.

-ation	to nationalize – nationalization	-ing	to begin – beginning	-ness	happy – happiness
-ence	to differ – difference	-y	difficult – difficulty	-or	to act – actor
-er	to teach – teacher	-ment	to improve – improvement		

11 Using a dictionary
Richtiger Umgang mit dem Wörterbuch

Einsprachige Wörterbücher

Das einsprachige Wörterbuch soll bei der Beseitigung von Verständnisproblemen helfen, z. B. wenn Sie einen Text lesen oder einen Text produzieren möchten. Das einsprachige Wörterbuch hilft Ihnen, Wortbedeutungen aus dem Kontext zu entnehmen.

Das Wörterbuch kennenlernen

- Bevor Sie zum ersten Mal mit Ihrem einsprachigen Wörterbuch arbeiten, sollten Sie sich einen Überblick verschaffen, d. h. Sie blättern durch das Wörterbuch und lernen die wichtigsten Hilfen kennen. Nur wenn Sie wissen welche Informationen das Wörterbuch bietet und wo diese stehen, können Sie das Wörterbuch optimal nutzen.
- Achten Sie beispielsweise auf:
  - den Aufbau des Wörterbuchs (Vorspann, Wörterverzeichnis, Nachspann)
  - die Anleitung zur Benutzung
  - das Verzeichnis der Abkürzungen und Symbole
  - verschiedene Listen, z. B. unregelmäßige Verben, Namenslisten
  - Illustrationen und Schaubilder
  - Überblick über die grundlegende Grammatik.
- Nachdem Sie sich einen groben Überblick verschafft haben, schauen Sie sich den Aufbau eines Eintrags genauer an, z. B. das Wort *success*. In einem guten einsprachigen Wörterbuch werden Sie zu dem Eintrag folgende Informationen finden:
  - Schreibung und Worttrennung
  - die verschiedenen Wortarten (Nomen, Verb, Adjektiv, Adverb)
  - Aussprache (anhand von Lautschrift)
  - unregelmäßige Formen
  - die verschiedenen Bedeutungen des Wortes, auch innerhalb einer Wortart
  - Synonyme und Definitionen
  - Beispielsätze zum typischen Gebrauch des Wortes
  - Redewendungen, in denen das Wort verwendet wird.

Mit dem einsprachigen Wörterbuch arbeiten

- Bevor Sie ein Wort nachschlagen, ermitteln Sie die Wortart im Satzzusammenhang, z. B. Nomen, Adjektiv, Verb etc.
- Wenn Sie den Eintrag für das gesuchte Wort gefunden haben, lesen Sie nicht den gesamten Eintrag, sondern beschränken Sie sich auf die Verwendung Ihres Wortes in der gesuchten Wortart.
- Lesen Sie dann alle weiteren Informationen, die Ihnen das Wörterbuch zu dem entsprechenden Stichwort in der gesuchten Wortart gibt, z. B. Beispielsätze oder grammatische Informationen.
- Nehmen Sie sich Zeit zum Lesen des Eintrags und versichern Sie sich, dass Sie die richtige Bedeutung des Wortes gefunden haben. Achten Sie dabei insbesondere auf den Textzusammenhang.

Zweisprachige Wörterbücher

Das zweisprachige Wörterbuch (Englisch-Deutsch, Deutsch-Englisch) soll insbesondere bei der Übertragung von Texten in die andere Sprache helfen, z. B. wenn Sie einen Text übersetzen möchten. Es kann aber auch verwendet werden, um unbekannte Wörter in einem fremdsprachigen Text schnell zu verstehen.

Das Wörterbuch kennenlernen

Bevor Sie zum ersten Mal mit Ihrem zweisprachigen Wörterbuch arbeiten, sollten Sie sich mit dem Wörterbuch vertraut machen. (Siehe Das Wörterbuch kennenlernen auf Seite 150, den ersten Punkt)

- Nachdem Sie sich einen groben Überblick verschafft haben, schauen Sie sich den Aufbau eines Eintrags genauer an, z. B. das Wort *success*. In einem guten zweisprachigen Wörterbuch werden Sie zu dem Eintrag folgende Informationen finden:
  - Schreibung und Worttrennung
  - die verschiedenen Wortarten (Nomen, Verb, Adjektiv, Adverb)
  - Aussprache (anhand von Lautschrift)
  - unregelmäßige Formen
  - die verschiedenen Übersetzungen des Wortes, auch innerhalb einer Wortart
  - Beispielsätze zum typischen Gebrauch des Wortes
  - Redewendungen, in denen das Wort verwendet wird.

Mit dem zweisprachigen Wörterbuch arbeiten

- Bevor Sie ein Wort nachschlagen, ermitteln Sie die Wortart im Satzzusammenhang, z. B. Nomen, Adjektiv, Verb etc.
- Wenn Sie den entsprechenden Eintrag für das Wort gefunden haben, lesen Sie aber nicht den gesamten Eintrag, sondern beschränken Sie sich auf die Verwendung Ihres Wortes in der gesuchten Wortart.
- Lesen Sie zudem alle weiteren Informationen, die Ihnen das Wörterbuch zu dem entsprechenden Stichwort in der gesuchten Wortart gibt, z. B. Beispielsätze.
- Nehmen Sie sich Zeit zum Lesen des Eintrags und versichern Sie sich, dass Sie die richtige Bedeutung des Wortes gefunden haben, ob also die Übersetzung im Textzusammenhang passt.

12 Multiple choice exercises
Multiple Choice Übungen

Multiple Choice Aufgaben unterscheiden sich grundlegend von den Ihnen wahrscheinlich geläufigeren Aufgabentypen, z. B. Fragen zum Text oder dem Schreiben eines Essays.

Bei Multiple Choice Aufgaben wird von Ihnen verlangt, die richtige(n) Antwort(en) aus verschiedenen Antwortmöglichkeiten zu erkennen und nicht eine eigenständige Antwort zu produzieren.

Die meisten von Ihnen werden Multiple Choice Aufgaben als einfachereren Aufgabentyp bezeichnen, weil die richtige Antwort auf jeden Fall dabei ist und Sie zur Not raten können.

Allerdings verlangen Multiple Choice Aufgaben ein detailliertes Textverständnis, z. B. im Hinblick auf die Bedeutung einzelner Wörter oder die Verwendung des richtigen Tempus.

Multiple Choice Aufgaben lösen

- Lesen Sie den Text, um sich einen allgemeinen Überblick zu verschaffen.
- Lesen Sie die Aufgabe gründlich und stellen Sie sicher, dass Sie diese richtig verstanden haben. Es gibt unterschiedliche Aufgabentypen zum Multiple Choice.
  Beispiel 1: *Find the most suitable option according to the text. Only one option is true.* (Es darf nur eine richtige Möglichkeit angekreuzt werden.)
  Beispiel 2: *Write down the correct answers: T (true) or F (false). Only answer if you are sure. Wrong answers will result in a loss of credits.* (Es können mehrere Antworten richtig sein, die Sie ankreuzen müssen. Es kann aber auch sein, dass nur eine Antwortmöglichkeit richtig ist. Es gibt Punktabzüge für falsch gegebene Antworten.)
- Lesen Sie den Text ein zweites Mal und markieren Sie die entsprechenden Abschnitte zu den Aufgaben im Text oder notieren Sie sich diese stichpunktartig auf einem gesonderten Blatt.
- Beantworten Sie die Aufgaben in der angegebenen Reihenfolge. In der Regel beziehen sich die Aufgaben in chronologischer Reihenfolge auf den Text.
- Unterstreichen Sie wichtige Schlüsselbegriffe in der jeweiligen Aufgabe. Das wird Ihnen helfen, sich auf die Informationen zu konzentrieren, die benötigt werden, um die richtige(n) Antwort(en) auszuwählen.
- Lesen Sie alle Antwortmöglichkeiten, bevor Sie eine Antwort auswählen.
- Streichen Sie Antwortmöglichkeiten durch, bei denen Sie sich sicher sind, dass sie falsch sind. Das wird Ihnen helfen, die richtigen Antwortmöglichkeiten einzugrenzen.
- Wenn Sie sich nicht sicher sind, dann versuchen Sie nicht, die richtige Antwort zu erraten. In den Prüfungen bekommen Sie in der Regel Punktabzüge für falsche Antworten.

13 Multiple matching exercises
Zuordnungsaufgaben

Bei der Bearbeitung von Zuordnungsaufgaben wird von Ihnen verlangt, einem Text oder einem Foto etwas zuzuordnen. Die bekannteste Art der Zuordnungsaufgaben ist es, Textabschnitten Überschriften zuzuordnen. Bei dieser Aufgabenart geht es in der Regel darum zu überprüfen, ob Sie die Bedeutung eines Abschnitts verstanden haben.

Zuordnungsaufgaben lösen

- Lesen Sie den Text bzw. sehen Sie sich die Fotos/Schaubilder an, um sich einen allgemeinen Überblick zu verschaffen.
- Lesen Sie die Aufgabe und die Antwortmöglichkeiten und stellen Sie sicher, dass Sie diese richtig verstanden haben. Es gibt unterschiedliche Aufgabentypen zum *multiple matching.*
  Beispiel 1: *Look at the photos. Match them with the words in the box. Two words do not match.* (visuelle Vorlage)
  Beispiel 2: *Listen to the texts and match them with the photos/headings.* (Hörverstehen)
  Beispiel 3: *Match the following headings with the suitable paragraphs in the text. Two of the headings do not fit.* (Leseverstehen)
  Beispiel 4: *Read the text in detail and match the key points with the headings in the text.* (Leseverstehen)
- Lesen Sie den Text ein zweites Mal und markieren Sie die entsprechenden Hinweise zu den Antwortmöglichkeiten im Text oder notieren Sie sich diese stichpunktartig.
- Wenn Sie die Antwortmöglichkeiten zugeordnet haben, dann überprüfen Sie Ihre Wahl, indem Sie den Text noch einmal lesen.
- Es gibt häufig mehr Auswahlmöglichkeiten als für die Aufgabe notwendig. Streichen Sie dann zuerst die Antwortmöglichkeiten, die offensichtlich nicht passen bzw. nicht zugeordnet werden können. Das wird Ihnen helfen, die richtigen Antwortmöglichkeiten einzugrenzen.

14 Short answer questions
Kurzantworten geben

Bei dieser Aufgabe handelt es sich ausdrücklich um eine Textverstehensaufgabe und nicht um Textproduktion. Deshalb sollen Sie hier nicht in eigenen Worten antworten, sondern nur zeigen, dass Sie den richtigen Abschnitt im Text gefunden haben und die entsprechenden Wörter oder Ausdrücke übernehmen können.

Bei dieser Aufgabenart kann es sich handeln um:
- Fragen, die Sie mit Hilfe von Wörtern oder Phrasen aus dem vorliegenden Text beantworten sollen. Sie müssen nur diese Kurzantwort geben und keine eigenen Formulierungen benutzen.
  Beispielfrage: *When did he leave the restaurant?* – **Beispiellösung: at noon**
- unvollständige Sätze, die Sie anhand von Wörtern oder Formulierungen aus dem Text vervollständigen sollen.
  Beispielaufgabe: *Listen to the CD again and complete the following sentences.*
  Sarah works on Fridays, Saturdays and … – **Beispiellösung: Tuesdays**
- unbekannte Wörter, die aus dem Kontext erschlossen werden sollen.
  Beispielaufgabe: *Find a word in the text that has the same meaning as …*
- Pronomina, die einem Substantiv zugeordnet werden sollen.
  Beispielaufgabe: *What does the word 'it' (line 21) refer to?*

15 Gapped summary
Zusammenfassung anhand eines Lückentexts

Gapped summary ist eine Aufgabe zur Überprüfung des Textverständnisses. Dabei verlangt die Aufgabenstellung das Vergleichen eines (längeren) Textes mit einem zweiten kürzeren Text, in dem die wichtigsten Textinformationen des ersten Textes zusammengefasst sind, bei dem jedoch die Schlüsselwörter entfernt worden sind. Sie sind nun aufgefordert, diese Schlüsselwörter im ersten Text zu finden und in die Lücken im zweiten Text einzusetzen. Dabei sollen Sie sich keine eigenen Wörter ausdenken, sondern nur Wörter aus dem ersten Text übernehmen.

Beispiel für einen Lesetext:

Yamasaki, who died in 1986, would have been horrified by the deconstruction of the World Trade Center on September 11, 2001, when two planes flown by terrorists crashed into the twin towers of the WTC.

Beispiel eines gapped summary:
The author points out how [**1.** ...] the architect would have been if he had lived to experience the catastrophe caused by terrorists.

Lösung: 1. **horrified**

16 Writing a composition/comment
Eine Stellungnahme schreiben

Eine Stellungnahme dient der argumentativen Auseinandersetzung mit einem bestimmten Thema. Es handelt sich hierbei um einen klar strukturierten Aufsatz, in dem verschiedene Aspekte zu einem Thema näher beleuchtet werden. Am Ende steht immer Ihre persönliche Meinung, die Sie anhand von Argumenten begründen müssen. Ein argumentativer Aufsatz wird im Präsens (Gegenwart) geschrieben.

Formulierung der Aufgabenstellung

- Erläutern Sie einen vorgegebenen Sachverhalt und beurteilen Sie diesen kritisch, indem Sie zuerst verschiedene Aspekte anführen und anschließend Begründungen/Beispiele einbringen, die Ihre Sichtweise unterstützen.
  Beispiele: *Comment on this statement: "Teenagers should not have their own computers because it is too dangerous."*
  There is a lot of discussion in the media about genetic engineering. What do you think? Write a composition in about 150 words.
- Befassen Sie sich argumentativ mit dem vorgegebenen Thema/Problem, beleuchten Sie alle Seiten des Themas/Problems und fassen Sie die wichtigsten Aspekte zusammen. Gewichten Sie die Argumente, bevor Sie eine eigene begründete Meinung abgeben.
  Beispiel: *Discuss the sentence, "The world is getting smaller." Use information from the texts and your own ideas to write a comment in about 250 words."*

Vorbereitung der Stellungnahme

- Definieren Sie das Thema eindeutig unter Berücksichtigung der Aufgabenstellung.
- Schreiben Sie stichpunktartig alle Ideen auf, die Sie zu dem Thema haben.
- Sortieren Sie Ihre Ideen in einer Tabelle, einem Diagramm oder einem Word web.
  ► SF 21 Word webs
- Falls notwendig und möglich, sammeln Sie weitere Fakten, Argumente, Statistiken zu dem Thema, z. B. im Internet oder in der Bücherei.
- Formulieren Sie Ihre eigene Meinung zu dem Thema.

Verfassen der Einleitung

- Ihre Einleitung soll das Thema/Problem darstellen und das Interesse des Lesers wecken. Sie können z. B.
  - ein bedeutsames Zitat anführen,
  - eine provokative Aussage machen,
  - eine persönliche Erfahrung schildern,
  - die aktuelle öffentliche Meinung darstellen,
  - aktuelle Statistiken benennen.
- Zudem sollen Sie in Ihrer Einleitung:
  - den Inhalt Ihres Kommentars kurz vorstellen.
  - einen kurzen Überblick über das Thema/Problem zum gegenwärtigen Zeitpunkt und in der Vergangenheit geben.

Redewendungen

- Einleitungssätze:

According to the latest statistics …
It is a well-known fact that …
Today there is a lot of discussion about …
Today many people are worried about …

Verfassen des Hauptteils

- Ordnen Sie zunächst Ihre gesammelten Argumente. Eine Möglichkeit ist es, die Argumente vom schwächsten Argument zum stärksten Argument anzuordnen.
- Der Hauptteil muss übersichtlich gegliedert sein. Deshalb sollten Sie für jedes neue Argument mit einem neuen Absatz beginnen. Innerhalb eines Absatzes nennen Sie Ihr Argument und in den weiteren Sätzen erläutern Sie dieses anhand von Beispielen, Statistiken und/oder gesammelten Fakten.
- Setzen Sie Ihre Sätze in Bezug zueinander, indem Sie passende Bindewörter verwenden. ► SF 19 Connectives
- Verwenden Sie geeignete Adverbien, um Argumente hervorzuheben oder abzuschwächen.

Redewendungen

- Argumente strukturieren:

Firstly …, secondly …, finally …
Moreover …

In addition …
Next …
Then …

- Gegensätze ausdrücken:

On the one hand … on the other hand …
However …
In contrast …

- Begründungen angeben:

That's why …
It follows that …
Because (of)…
So …
Therefore …

- Adverbien:

absolutely – after all – almost – at least – completely – extremely – fortunately – hardly – in fact – mainly – of course – particularly – perhaps – really – sadly – very

Verfassen des Schlussteils

- Im letzten Teil Ihrer Stellungnahme, ziehen Sie Schlussfolgerungen aus den im Hauptteil aufgeführten Argumenten. Die Schlussfolgerungen sollen das Gesagte kurz zusammenfassen.
- Im Anschluss daran geben Sie Ihre eigene Meinung zu dem Thema. Nennen Sie keine neuen Argumente im Schlussteil.

Redewendungen

- Schlussfolgerungen:

In conclusion …
As a result …
All in all …
In short …
On the whole …
In my opinion …
In my view …
To my mind …

17 Writing a summary
Eine Inhaltsangabe schreiben

Eine Inhaltsangabe ist ein kurzer Text, in dem Sie die wichtigsten Aspekte eines vorliegenden Textes mit eigenen Worten wiedergeben. Wenn Sie die Inhaltsangabe zu einem Text schreiben, zeigen Sie, dass Sie das Wesentliche des Textes verstanden haben. Eine Inhaltsangabe ist immer eine objektive Darstellung/Version des Originaltextes.

Regeln zum Schreiben einer Inhaltsangabe

- Interpretieren oder kommentieren Sie den Text nicht, sondern schreiben Sie objektiv, worum es in dem Text geht.
- Berücksichtigen Sie wichtige Fakten, Aspekte, Ereignisse.
- Klammern Sie alle unwichtigen Details des Textes aus. Verwenden Sie keine Statistiken, Zahlen oder Zitate.
- Kürzen Sie lange Sätze und vereinfachen Sie den Wortschatz des Textes.
- Schreiben Sie Ihre Inhaltsangabe im Präsens (Gegenwart).
- Fassen Sie sich kurz! Ihre Inhaltsangabe sollte maximal ein Fünftel bis ein Drittel der Länge des Originaltextes haben.

Inhaltsangaben von nicht-fiktionalen Texten

Wenn Sie eine Inhaltsangabe von einem nicht-fiktionalen Text, z. B. Zeitungsartikel, Bericht, Sachtext usw. schreiben sollen, dann folgen Sie den folgenden Schritten:

- Lesen Sie den Originaltext sorgfältig, um das Hauptthema herauszufinden.
- Unterstreichen Sie den Satz, in dem das Hauptthema/die Hauptthese genannt wird.
- Formulieren Sie einen Einleitungssatz für Ihre Inhaltsangabe, der, wenn möglich, Textsorte, Titel des Textes, Autor, Erscheinungsort, Erscheinungsdatum und Hauptthema beinhalten sollte.
  Beispiel: *The newspaper article* "The answer is blowing in the wind" *written by Rick Martin and published in* The Daily USA *on November 12, 2010 is about the first big wind farm project in Nebraska.*
- Lesen Sie nun den Text ein zweites Mal und unterstreichen Sie alle wichtigen Fakten, Ideen, Argumente im Text, die das Hauptthema hervorheben. Hinweis: Keine vollständigen Sätze, sondern nur Stichpunkte.
- Fassen Sie nun die Hauptideen des Textes mit eigenen Worten zusammen. Sie können entweder eine Liste mit Stichpunkten erstellen oder einen Satz zu jedem Abschnitt des Originaltextes schreiben.
- Schreiben Sie einige oder alle Ihrer Sätze um, indem Sie die Intention des Autors hinzufügen. (Siehe Formulierungen zur Autorenintention.)
- Setzen Sie Ihre Sätze in Bezug zueinander, indem Sie passende Bindewörter verwenden.
  ► SF 19 Connectives

Redewendungen

- Formulierungen zur Autorenintention:

The author/writer opens with …
He/she points out that …
He/she suggests that …
He/she shows that …
He/she emphasizes …
He/she explains …
He/she concludes with …
He/she finishes with …

Inhaltsangaben von fiktionalen Texten

Wenn Sie eine Inhaltsangabe von einem fiktionalen Text, z. B. Kurzgeschichte, Romanauszug, Gedicht usw. schreiben sollen, dann folgen Sie den nachstehenden Schritten:

- Lesen Sie den Originaltext einmal sorgfältig, um herauszufinden, wer der Hauptcharakter ist und in welcher Situation sich dieser gerade befindet.
- Unterstreichen Sie den/die Hauptcharakter(e) und den Satz, der die Situation am besten beschreibt, in der der Hauptcharakter sich gerade befindet.
- Formulieren Sie einen Einleitungssatz für Ihre Inhaltsangabe, der folgende Punkte beinhalten sollte: Textsorte, Titel des Textes, Autor, Erscheinungsort, Erscheinungsdatum und Hauptcharakter/Situation.
  Beispiel: *The extract from the novel* "Cloning Miranda" *written by Carol Matas deals with Miranda, a teenage girl, who finds that she has a sister who has been cloned only to save Miranda's life.*
- Lesen Sie nun den Text ein zweites Mal und unterteilen Sie den Text – wenn möglich – in zwei Teile. Der zweite Teil beginnt, wenn sich in der Handlung/Situation etwas ändert oder ein neuer Aspekt hinzukommt. Unterstreichen Sie den Wendepunkt im Text.
- Fassen Sie nun die Handlung des Textes mit eigenen Worten zusammen. Beschreiben Sie hierzu, was passiert und wie die Ereignisse miteinander verbunden sind. Die untenstehenden Redewendungen können dabei hilfreich sein.
- Setzen Sie Ihre Sätze in Bezug zueinander, indem Sie passende Bindewörter verwenden.
  ► SF 19 Connectives

Redewendungen

The scene/story/extract/action takes place in …
It is set in …
It takes place in the present/past/future.

The main character is …
There are two/three/etc. main characters.
We get to know … by …
He/She is confronted with …

There is a conflict between …
The turning point …
At the beginning … / at the end …

18 Writing the minutes
Ein Protokoll schreiben

Ein Protokoll hält die Inhalte einer Konferenz, Besprechung, Diskussion, eines Referats oder einer Unterrichtsstunde fest. Dadurch ist es den Teilnehmern zu einem späteren Zeitpunkt möglich, die besprochenen Punkte nachzuvollziehen.

Formen des Protokolls

Es gibt verschiedene Formen des Protokollierens, die sich für verschiedene Anlässe eignen. Die beiden geläufigsten Formen – das Verlaufsprotokoll und das Ergebnisprotokoll – finden Sie im Folgenden erklärt:

	Verlaufsprotokoll	Ergebnisprotokoll
Kopfteil	Der Kopfteil sollte möglichst folgende Basisinformationen enthalten: Datum • Uhrzeit (Beginn und Ende) • Ort • Anwesende/Teilnehmer bzw. auch Abwesenheit eingeladener Personen • Leiter der Veranstaltung • Anlass/Thema der Veranstaltung • Tagesordnung	
Hauptteil	• Das Verlaufsprotokoll ist die ausführlichere Form des Protokolls. Es wird Wert gelegt auf den Prozess der Ergebnisfindung. • Geben Sie das Gehörte in zeitlicher Reihenfolge wieder. Dazu gehört auch der Inhalt von Vorschlägen, Diskussionen, Beschlüssen und Abstimmungsergebnissen.	• Das Ergebnisprotokoll ist die Kurzform des Protokolls. Es wird Wert gelegt auf das Festhalten der Ergebnisse der Veranstaltung. • Geben Sie nur die Ergebnisse des Gehörten wieder. Sie müssen deutlich formuliert sein und in der Reihenfolge der Tagesordnungspunkte dokumentiert werden.
Schlussteil	Der Schlussteil Ihres Protokolls sollte Ihre elektronische Signatur oder Kürzel sowie das Datum der Veranstaltung enthalten. Am Ende Ihres Protokolls weisen Sie auf mögliche Anlagen hin, z. B. Arbeitsblätter, die dem Protokoll angehängt werden.	

Protokolle schreiben

- Hören Sie erst genau zu, bevor Sie anfangen zu schreiben. Schreiben Sie erst dann, wenn ein Teilabschnitt beendet ist.
- Reduzieren Sie das Gehörte auf die Hauptaspekte und schreiben Sie diese stichpunktartig auf.
- Verwenden Sie Abkürzungen, die für Sie zu einem späteren Zeitpunkt aber auch noch verständlich sind. Schreiben Sie Namen und wichtige Begriffe möglichst vollständig auf.
- Schreiben Sie knapp und sachlich. Die eigene Meinung oder Wertungen gehören nicht in ein Protokoll.
- Verfassen Sie das Protokoll im Präsens (Gegenwart) in ganzen Sätzen.
- Gliedern Sie das Protokoll durch sinnvolle Absätze.

19 Connectives
Bindewörter (Konjunktionen)

Bindewörter sind Wörter oder Formulierungen, die Satzglieder, Sätze oder Textabschnitte miteinander verbinden. Diese Bindewörter geben Ihrem Text eine klare Struktur und sie erleichtern es dem Leser, Ihren Ausführungen zu folgen.

Die folgenden Bindewörter sind nur eine kleine Auswahl. Sie sollten eine persönliche Liste mit Bindewörtern führen, die Sie immer wieder erweitern können.

- Eine Reihenfolge anzeigen / Gliederung:

firstly …, secondly …, finally …
first of all
next
then
later
ultimately

Beispiel: Next the author describes the activities of the different organizations which help in Zimbabwe.

- Gedanken/Argumente hinzufügen:

another
also
as well
in addition / additionally
too
moreover
furthermore
last but not least

Beispiel: Another significant advantage of solar energy is that it doesn't pollute our air.

- Beispiele geben:

for example
for instance

Beispiel: The government of the USA is a good example of a presidential federal government.

- Die eigene Einstellung verdeutlichen:

obviously
undoubtedly/ doubtlessly
clearly
generally
luckily
fortunately
unfortunately
happily/sadly for …

Beispiel: Obviously it is wrong to say that tourism always damages our environment.

- Eine eigene Meinung abgeben:

in my opinion
in my view
to my mind
Without a doubt

Beispiel: To my mind this is not the solution to the economic problems of the people living in this area.

- Begründungen angeben:

consequently
therefore
as a result
this is why
because of
so

Beispiel: This is why more than thirty food companies in Britain have signed a promise to reduce their food transport miles.

- Vergleiche anstellen:

compared with
on the one hand … on the other hand …
in the same way
similarly

Beispiel: Compared with the situation five years ago children watch TV for longer periods of time.

- Gegensätze ausdrücken:

in contrast to
however
despite / in spite of

Beispiel: Despite all of the arguments mentioned in the text I do not agree with the author's position.

- Schluss:

in conclusion
as a result
all in all
in short
on the whole
finally
to sum up

Beispiel: To sum up, I am absolutely against the author's demand that pupils in German schools wear uniforms.

20 Collecting words
Vokabeln systematisch lernen

Wenn Sie eine Sprache lernen, ist es unerlässlich, dass Sie Vokabeln lernen. Je mehr Vokabeln Sie kennen, desto leichter wird es Ihnen fallen, Texte zu verfassen.

Tipps: Neue Vokabeln systematisch sammeln

Alphabetisch (A – Z): Diese Methode ist geeignet, wenn Sie Vokabeln schnell nachschlagen möchten. Allerdings müssen Sie das englische Wort bereits kennen. Wenn Sie einen Text verfassen möchten, ist dies meist nicht der Fall. Deshalb sollten Sie diese Methode mit einer der folgenden kombinieren.

Synonyme oder Antonyme: Sammeln Sie alle Synonyme, d. h. bedeutungsgleichen Wörter, und schreiben Sie diese zusammen auf.
Beispiel: *small, little, tiny*
Oder Sie schreiben Antonyme, d. h. Gegensätze, zusammen auf.
Beispiel: *small ≠ big.*

Wortfamilien: Wenn Sie sich ein Wort notieren, können Sie die anderen Formen (Wortarten) dieses Wortes hinzufügen, d. h. Nomen, Verb, Adjektiv, Adverb. Dadurch erweitern Sie Ihren Wortschatz besonders schnell.
Beispiel: *economy, to economize, economical, economically, economic.*

Wortfelder: Sammeln Sie Vokabeln anhand von thematischen Zusammenhängen.
Beispiel: das Wortfeld *globalisation: industry, travelling, culture, communication, brands, poverty, culture, technology, environment, multiculturalism* usw.

Word webs: Beginnen Sie mit dem Wortfeld, zu dem Sie Vokabeln sammeln möchten, z. B. *globalisation*, und schreiben Sie alles auf, was Ihnen zu diesem Wortfeld einfällt. Strukturieren Sie Ihre Einfälle in einem Word web. ► SF 21 Word webs

Kollokationen: Machen Sie sich eine Liste von Wörtern, die oft im Zusammenhang miteinander verwendet werden.
Beispiele: *to draw a conclusion, to make a promise* (Verb + Nomen), *extremely beautiful* (Adverb + Adjektiv), *a handsome man, a tall woman, a powerful computer* (Adjektiv + Nomen) usw.

21 Word webs
Wortnetze

Ein Wortnetz eignet sich überall dort, wo Gedanken zu einem bestimmten Thema gesammelt und dargestellt werden sollen, um sich das Thema sinnvoll zu erschließen oder um einen Überblick zu erhalten. Die Grundstruktur eines Wortnetzes ist immer gleich.

Wozu nutzt man Wortnetze?

Brainstorming: Um Ideen zu einem Thema zu sammeln und zusammenzutragen.
Erörterung von Themen: Um Argumente zu strukturieren. Beginnen Sie mit dem Thema der Diskussion und fügen Sie *arguments for* (Thesen) und *arguments against* (Antithesen) hinzu.
Vokabellernen: Um sich neue Wortfelder zu erschließen. Beginnen Sie mit einem Oberthema und fügen Sie alle Wörter hinzu, die sich auf diesen Begriff beziehen.

Erstellen eines Wortnetzes

Sie benötigen ausreichend Platz zum Erstellen des Wortnetzes, z. B. ein ausreichend großes Blatt Papier, Plakat, Tapete, Flipchart. Außerdem brauchen Sie Stifte in verschiedenen Farben.

1. Im Mittelpunkt steht das Hauptthema, zu dem Ideen gesammelt werden sollen, in einem aufgemalten Kreis. Das Thema kann als Stichpunkt formuliert werden, aber auch als Fragestellung.

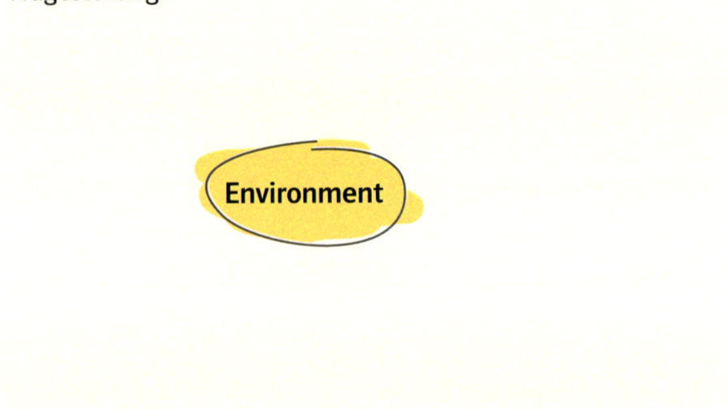

2. Sammeln Sie nun Ideen und fügen Sie diese in aufgemalten Kreisen mit einer Linie an das Hauptthema an. Wichtig ist, dass die Ideen bzw. Hauptpunkte noch relativ allgemein gehalten sind.

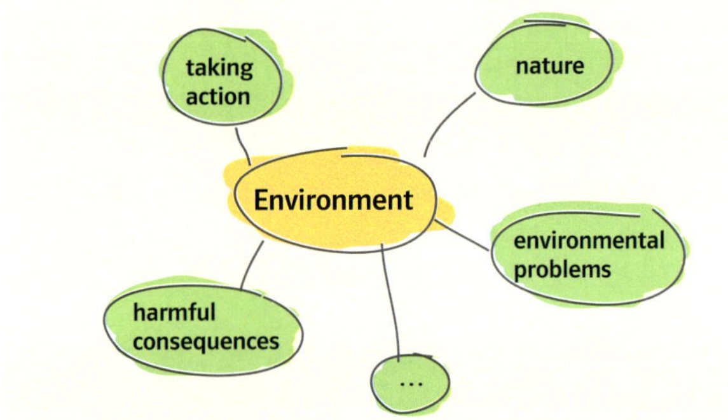

3. Wenn Sie genügend Hauptpunkte gefunden haben, dann hängen Sie daran Unterpunkte in aufgemalten Kreisen an, die sich thematisch auf die Hauptpunkte beziehen.

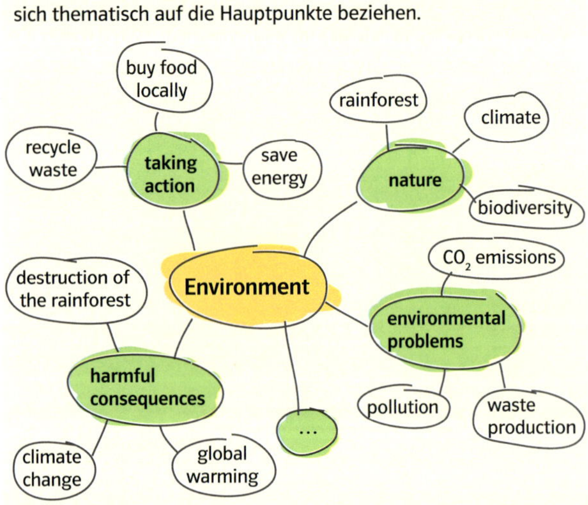

4. Anstelle von Kreisen können Sie auch Linien für die Haupt- und Unterpunkte verwenden.

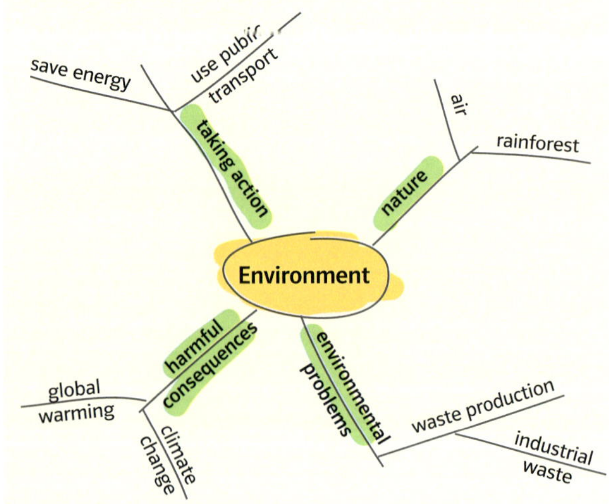

22 Mediation/translation
Mediation/Übersetzung

Mediation ist die sinngemäße Übertragung der wichtigsten Inhaltspunkte eines Textes in eine andere Sprache. Der Sinn einer Mediation besteht nicht darin, den Text wortwörtlich zu übersetzen (vgl. Übersetzung), sondern bei einer Mediation geht es darum, die wesentliche Botschaft eines Textes oder einer Äußerung in eine andere Sprache zu übertragen.

Bearbeitung einer Mediationsaufgabe

- Überfliegen Sie den Text, um sich einen allgemeinen Überblick über den Text zu verschaffen *(Skimming)*. ► SF 9 Anticipating, skimming, scanning
  Um welche Textsorte handelt es sich? Worum geht es in dem Text? (Hauptthema)
- Lesen Sie die Aufgabenstellung sorgfältig durch. Finden Sie heraus, welche Art von Text Sie verfassen und welches Sprachniveau Sie verwenden sollen.
  Beispiele für Textsorten sind informativer Text, Gedicht, Geschäftsbrief, Handzettel, Werbeanzeige, Schaubild usw. Wer ist der Adressat Ihrer Mediation? Z. B. Geschäftspartner, Freund, Chef usw.
- Lesen Sie nun den Text ein zweites Mal. Während Sie lesen, sollten Sie die wichtigsten Begriffe notieren, um die Aufgabe zu bearbeiten *(Scanning)*.
  ► SF 9 Anticipating, skimming, scanning
  Schreiben Sie sich nur Schlüsselbegriffe auf, keine ganzen Sätze. Achten Sie auf Bindewörter wie *but*/aber; *however*/jedoch; *in contrast* / im Gegensatz usw. Diese Bindewörter leiten oft neue Gesichtspunkte ein.
- Wählen Sie nur die für die Aufgabenstellung relevanten Punkte aus und fassen Sie diese mit Ihren eigenen Worten zusammen.
  Die Gliederung Ihres Textes muss nicht übereinstimmen mit der Gliederung des Originaltexts. Achten Sie darauf, dass Sie den Text nicht einfach übersetzen.
- Lesen Sie sich nun Ihren Text noch einmal durch und überprüfen Sie, ob Sie alle relevanten Punkte des Originaltexts in eigenen Worten verständlich wiedergegeben haben.
  Überprüfen Sie, ob Sie:
  - alle wichtigen Aspekte des Originaltexts genannt haben,
  - keine Beispiele, die im Originaltext genannt werden, einbezogen haben,
  - den Text adressatengerecht verfasst haben,
  - die Textsorte berücksichtigt haben,
  - den Text in der Zielsprache verständlich verfasst haben. (vgl. auch „Falsche Freunde" auf Seite 164),
  - den Text übersichtlich gestaltet haben.

Bearbeitung einer Übersetzungsaufgabe

Die **Übersetzung** eines Textes von einer Sprache in eine andere Sprache unterscheidet sich grundlegend von der Mediation. Wenn Sie einen Text übersetzen, dann müssen Sie diesen Wort für Wort in die andere Sprache übertragen. Der Sinn einer Übersetzung besteht darin, den Text so genau wie möglich in der Zielsprache wiederzugeben. Manchmal müssen Sie dazu die Satzstellung ändern oder idiomatische Ausdrücke sinnvoll anpassen.

- Überfliegen Sie den Text, um sich einen allgemeinen Überblick über den Text zu verschaffen *(Skimming)*.
- Schreiben Sie sich stichpunktartig auf, worum es in dem Text geht, bevor Sie mit der detaillierten Übersetzung beginnen. Verwenden Sie hierzu bereits die Zielsprache des zu verfassenden Texts.

Rohfassung

- In der Rohfassung Ihrer Übersetzung sollten Sie nicht wortwörtlich übersetzen. Versuchen Sie aber, sich so nah wie möglich an die Wortwahl des Originaltextes zu halten. Lassen Sie keine Lücken in Ihrer Übersetzung. Wenn Sie die genaue Übersetzung nicht kennen, dann schreiben Sie zunächst das Wort in der Sprache des Originaltexts auf.
- Für eine Übersetzungsaufgabe erhalten Sie in der Regel eine längere Bearbeitungszeit. Schreiben Sie deshalb Ihre erste Fassung mit einem Bleistift oder am PC, so dass Sie Wörter ändern und verbessern können.

Zweite Fassung

- Lesen Sie die erste Fassung sorgfältig durch und versuchen Sie die noch fehlenden Wörter oder Satzteile zu übersetzen.
- Versuchen Sie zunächst die Bedeutung der noch fehlenden Wörter aus dem Kontext zu erschließen. ► SF 10 Surviving without a dictionary
  Wenn es Ihnen nicht gelingt, die Wörter aus dem Kontext zu erschließen, dann schlagen Sie diese in einem Wörterbuch nach. ► SF 11 Using a dictionary
- Dann vergleichen Sie Ihre zweite Fassung Wort für Wort mit dem Originaltext. Stellen Sie sicher, dass Sie keine Satzteile ausgelassen haben.

Endfassung

- Lesen Sie Ihre Übersetzung noch einmal sorgfältig und überprüfen Sie, ob sie einwandfrei deutsch bzw. englisch klingt. Falls nicht, überarbeiten Sie diese Passagen noch einmal. Überlegen Sie hier genau, was Sie sagen möchten und wie Sie dies auf Deutsch bzw. Englisch normalerweise ausdrücken würden.
- Lesen Sie sich nun Ihren Text noch einmal durch und überprüfen Sie, ob Ihr Text dem Originaltext entspricht. Überprüfen Sie, ob Sie:
  - sinngemäß alles übersetzt haben. Nur wenn Sie ein Wort nicht übersetzen können und dieses nicht im Wörterbuch finden, dann paraphrasieren Sie, d. h. umschreiben Sie das Wort.
  - den Schreibstil des Originaltexts übernommen haben.
  - keine falschen Freunde in Ihren Zieltext eingebaut haben (vgl. auch „Falsche Freunde" unten).
  - Redewendungen richtig übersetzt haben.

Falsche Freunde

Falsche Freunde *(false friends)* sind Wörter, die in zwei verschiedenen Sprachen zwar ähnlich aussehen oder ähnlich klingen, aber dennoch unterschiedliche Bedeutungen haben.

Beispiele:

actual ≠ aktuell; = tatsächlich
become ≠ bekommen; = werden
brave ≠ brav; = mutig
gift ≠ Gift; = Geschenk

handy ≠ Handy; = geschickt, handlich
rent ≠ Rente; = Miete
sensible ≠ sensibel; = vernünftig
still ≠ still; = immer noch

23 Formal letters and e-mails
Formelle Briefe und E-Mails

Formelle Briefe

Wenn Sie einen Brief an einen Geschäftspartner verfassen möchten, müssen Sie sich an bestimmte formale Vorgaben halten. Diese Vorgaben sind nicht einheitlich geregelt, sondern unterscheiden sich in den verschiedenen Kulturkreisen – auch innerhalb des englischsprachigen Raums. Bei englischsprachigen Geschäftsbriefen sollten Sie sich an den britischen Vorgaben orientieren, es sei denn, Sie schreiben an ein Unternehmen in den USA.

Es gibt verschiedene Anlässe für formelle Briefe: Anfragen, Angebote, Beschwerden, Bestellungen, Bewerbungsschreiben, Mahnungen, Mitteilungen, Rechnungen und Reservierungen.

Your Books

342 Beaconsfield Road
Liverpool L256EE
England
Tel +44(0)151-1092687
Fax +44(0)151-1092688
www.yourbooks.co.uk
info@yourbooks.com

1 Your ref:
2 Our ref: Ab/Bc

3 15 March 20_

4 Confetti & Co
80 Tottenham Court Road
London WI6 8HR
England

5 Dear Sir or Madam

6 **Your advertisement for balloons on the Internet**

We refer to your advertisement for your balloons, which we found on the Internet last week.

We are a well established publishing company with subsidiaries all over the world. Our company is planning an introductory day for our new trainees. Therefore we would like to order your balloons for decoration.

Furthermore we saw your special March offer on the Internet and would be pleased if you could send us a confirmation of the validity of your stated prices. Moreover we would be grateful for information about terms of delivery and payment.

We look forward to receiving your answer soon.

7 Yours faithfully

8 Matt Smith

9 Matthew Smith
10 Training Manager

1 Im Amerikanischen stehen die Bezugszeichen ganz am Ende des Briefs unter den Anlagen.

2 Bezugszeichen des Absenders

3 Das Datum steht normalerweise unterhalb der Bezugszeichen. Es kann aber auch in der ersten Zeile oberhalb der Adressen oder in der ersten Zeile unterhalb der Adressen stehen.
Schreibweisen im Britischen Englisch: Tag, Monat, Jahr; im Amerikanischen Englisch: Monat, Tag, Jahr

4 Die Empfängeradresse steht unter dem Datum.

5 Anrede

6 Betreffzeile

7 Grußformel am Ende des Briefes

8 Unterschrift

9 Vollständiger Name

10 Position

Der folgende Beispielbrief zeigt Ihnen, wie ein Bewerbungsschreiben in Großbritannien in der Regel aufgebaut ist.

1 Lessingstr. 84
44147 Dortmund
Germany

Ms Angela Kelly
Maytree Nursery School
14 Moss Way
Leeds
LS2 9NQ
England

15 February 20_

Dear Ms Kelly

2 **Your advertisement in the Leeds Times of 6 February**

3 With reference to your advertisement in the Leeds Times of 6 February, I would like to apply for the position of a nursery school teacher.

4 After completing my education at Cologne College for Social Care I have been working with *Kindertagesstätte Regenbogenland* in Dortmund since August 20_. I now have great experience in developing the nursery learning environment and developing lesson plans. I feel well qualified for the position advertised.

5 I am particularly interested in this job as I would very much like to gain work experience abroad. As well as speaking fluent English and Spanish, I have working knowledge of French. My mother tongue is of course German.

I can supply references from former employers if you wish.

6 I enclose my curriculum vitae and certified translations of my certificates. Please do not hesitate to contact me if you should require further information.

7 I look forward to hearing from you.

Yours sincerely

Jasmin Kramer
Jasmin Kramer

8 Encs.

1 Ihre Adresse ohne Angabe des Namens gehört in die Ecke oben links.

2 Betreffzeile

3 Sagen Sie, worauf Sie sich beziehen (z. B. Anzeige, Telefonat), und nennen Sie den Anlass für den Brief.

4 Stellen Sie sich vor, indem Sie die wichtigsten Qualifikationen und Erfahrungen benennen.

5 Nennen Sie weitere Qualifikationen.

6 Erwähnen Sie die Anlagen Ihres Briefes und weisen Sie darauf hin, dass Sie weitere Zeugnisse usw. senden können.

7 Abschlussworte

8 Encs. = Enclosures (Anlagen)

Formelle E-Mails

Mittlerweile werden verstärkt keine formellen Briefe mehr geschrieben, sondern formelle E-Mails. Sie nehmen zum einen weniger Zeit in Anspruch und sie sind zum anderen schneller beim Empfänger.

Wenn Sie eine formelle E-Mail schreiben, dann müssen Sie den gleichen Kommunikationsregeln folgen wie beim formellen Brief.

Beim Aufbau Ihrer formellen E-Mail gibt es jedoch Unterschiede zum formellen Brief. Das Beispiel zeigt Ihnen, wie eine formelle E-Mail in Großbritannien in der Regel aufgebaut ist:

From: 1 matthew.smith@yourbooks.com
To: 2 info@confettiandco.com
CC: 3
Sent: 4 15 March 20_ 11:34
Subject: 5 Your advertisement for balloons on the Internet
Attachments: 6

7 Dear Sir or Madam

8 …

9 Kind regards

Matt Smith
Training Manager

– –
10 Your Books
342 Beaconsfield Road
Liverpool L256EE
England
Tel +44(0)151-1092687
Fax +44(0)151-1092688
www.yourbooks.co.uk
info@yourbooks.com

11 Your ref:
Our ref: Ab/Bc

1 Ihre E-Mail-Adresse

2 Die E-Mail-Adresse des Empfängers

3 Wenn Sie eine Kopie der E-Mail an eine weitere Person versenden möchten, dann geben Sie die E-Mail-Adresse unter cc (Carbon Copy = Kopie an …) ein.

4 Beim Versenden der E-Mail erscheinen das Datum sowie die Uhrzeit automatisch.

5 Betreffzeile

6 Die Anlagen bei E-Mails heißen nicht *enclosures*, sondern *attachments*.

7 Anrede

8 Text der E-Mail – wie bei Geschäftsbriefen achten Sie auch hier auf Höflichkeit.

9 Grußformel am Ende der E-Mail

10 Angaben zu Ihren Kontaktdetails

11 Die Bezugszeichen des Empfängers und des Absenders stehen am Ende der E-Mail.

→ **Redewendungen finden Sie auf der folgenden Seite.**

Redewendungen

- Anreden:

Dear Sir or Madam
Dear Sir
Dear Madam
Dear Mr Albee
Dear Ms Howard

- Schlussformeln:

Yours faithfully (Britisch)
Yours sincerely (Britisch; wenn Sie die Person namentlich kennen)
Best wishes / Best regards / Kind regards (Britisch und Amerikanisch)
Sincerely (Amerikanisch)

- Bezugnahme:

We refer to your advertisement …
Referring to your advertisement …
We refer to your offer of August 26, 2010.
Your firm has been recommended to us by …

- Briefanlass und Geschäftsvorstellung:

We wish to point out that …
We should appreciate it if you would …
We are a medium-sized company importing a wide range of …

- Informationen/Services erbitten:

Would you please send us …?
We would be grateful for details of …
We would like to ask for/to …
A visit by your representative would be appreciated.

- Nachrichten übermitteln:

We are pleased to inform you that …
You will be pleased to hear that …
We are really sorry to inform you that …

- Abschlussworte:

We hope to hear from you soon.
We look forward to hearing from you soon.
We look forward to an early reply.
We hope this information will help you.

- Struktur:

therefore / for this reason
if / provided that
however/but
besides / in addition
so far / up to now
still
as
so that

24 Letter to the editor
Der Leserbrief

Der Leserbrief gehört zu den formellen Briefen. In der Regel schreibt man einen Leserbrief an eine Zeitung oder Zeitschrift, wenn man einen Artikel über ein umstrittenes Thema gelesen hat und seine Sichtweise zu diesem Thema äußern möchte. ► SF 23 Formal letters

Tipps: Verfassen eines Leserbriefs

Lesen Sie den Zeitungsartikel sorgfältig durch und machen Sie sich Notizen zu Aspekten, auf die Sie in Ihrem Leserbrief eingehen möchten.

Sammeln Sie Ideen für Ihre Argumente und strukturieren Sie diese.

Fassen Sie sich kurz. Der Stil eines Leserbriefs ist knapp und klar. Wichtig ist, dass Sie sachlich bleiben.

Schreiben Sie den Leserbrief auf dem Computer und senden Sie ihn per E-Mail.

Bevor Sie Ihren Leserbrief absenden, lesen Sie ihn nochmals sorgfältig durch und korrigieren Sie alle gefundenen Fehler.

Aufbau des Leserbriefs und Redewendungen

- Anrede:

To the editor
Editor:
Dear editor
Dear Sir / Dear Madam / Dear Sir or Madam

- In der Einleitung sollten Sie zunächst den Bezug zu dem Zeitungsartikel herstellen. Nennen Sie neben dem Thema auch die Quelle des Artikels, auf den Sie sich beziehen.

I refer to your report/article on energy consumption in today's / last week's edition of *USA Worldwide*.
With reference to the article on energy consumption (*USA Worldwide*, 12 June 2010) I would like to point out that …
I am writing with reference to the article on energy consumption you published in yesterday's issue of *USA Worldwide*.

- Machen Sie Ihre eigene Position zu dem Thema deutlich.

I completely agree with your statements on …
I entirely disagree with …
I am completely opposed to …

- Im Hauptteil begründen Sie Ihre Position sachlich und zeigen Hintergrundwissen.

- Der Hauptteil besteht aus klar voneinander abgrenzbaren Argumenten, die Sie bestenfalls mit Beispielen veranschaulichen.

One should not forget that …
My first/second/final argument …
Another aspect is that …
To my mind …

- Im Schlussteil bekräftigen Sie noch einmal Ihre Position zu dem Thema, indem Sie Schlussfolgerungen ziehen und Forderungen aufstellen bzw. Lösungsvorschläge machen.

I am sure many readers will agree with me when I claim that …
In conclusion, I would say that …
All in all, …
Together, we can …

- Achtung: Wiederholen Sie Ihre Argumente nicht!

- Der Leserbrief endet ohne Grußformel nur mit Vornamen und Familiennamen.

► SF 16 Composition ► SF 19 Connectives

Beispiel:

From: michael.martin@webs.com
To: james.sullivan@press.com
Subject: Letter to the editor: "Food pantries falling short"

To the editor

I am writing about the article "Food pantries falling short" in the Aug. 10 *Press*. The Stanton family represents one in 10 of Michigan households that suffer from hunger. These households are a fraction of the 38 million who go hungry every day in the United States.

These are not statistics; they are humans in the image of God going hungry. The U.S. Conference of Mayors reported that requests for food assistance increased by an average of 12 percent in 24 cities surveyed. More than half of those in need had children, and while many were employed they were unable to put food on their table.

So what can we do? We cannot continue to read articles like this and remain idle. How we treat the hungry in our midst speaks volumes about our hearts, our character and our priorities. This is indeed a moral issue, an issue of justice and one that demands our immediate action.

In addition to donating food to local pantries, we can also call on our legislators to make a difference. A new piece of legislation called the Hunger-Free Communities Act would commit the federal government to cutting hunger in the U.S. in half by 2015, and eliminate it by 2020. This bill needs to be passed as soon as possible.

Together, we can end hunger. The question is only when we will choose to solve this problem.

Michael Martin

25 Personal letters and e-mails
Persönliche Briefe und E-Mails

Persönliche E-Mails

In den meisten Fällen werden keine persönlichen Briefe mehr geschrieben und mit der Post verschickt, sondern E-Mails. Sie können Ihre E-Mail zwanglos formulieren, so als würden Sie ein Gespräch mit der Person führen. Im Allgemeinen sollten Sie aber denselben Regeln folgen, die für das Schreiben eines Briefes gelten. Bedenken Sie, dass der ausländische Freund einen bestimmten Kommunikationsstil von Ihnen erwarten könnte.

Beispiel:

From: nicole.volk@webs.de
To: sandra_brown@fast.ca
Subject: Hey there! :-)

1 Hi Susan

2 Just a few lines to let you know I'm still alive!

3 How are things in Canada? You're on your snowboard every day, aren't you?
4 I really must say, I envy you having so much snow!!! We don't, so I haven't gone snowboarding this winter yet.

Suppose I won't go snowboarding this winter anyway, cause now I'm busy at college with exams. I've been working really hard at school. Hopefully I'll remember everything!

Last weekend I stayed at Sandra's place. :-) Do you remember that girl from volleyball classes? We studied together and went to a party that really rocked. I met this guy … :D We'll see how things work out …

Please drop me a line when you have a minute ASAP. We must keep in touch.

5 Love

Nicole

6 Königstr. 34
70173 Stuttgart
Germany

1 Beginnen Sie Ihre E-Mail mit einer Anrede: *Dear + name* (formell) *Hi + name* (informell).

2 Das erste Wort nach der Anrede wird immer groß geschrieben.

3 Gruppieren Sie Ihre Informationen in Sinnabschnitten.

4 Sie können Frageanhängsel verwenden, z. B. *aren't you?, don't you?*

5 Beenden Sie Ihre E-Mail mit einer entsprechenden Schlussfloskel, z. B. *All the best / Best wishes / Bye for now / Love / Lots of love and kisses …*

6 Sie schreiben Ihre Adresse nicht zu Beginn der E-Mail, sondern erst am Ende unterhalb Ihres Namens. Es ist auch üblich die Adresse wegzulassen.

Persönliche E-Mails verfassen

- Wenn Sie eine persönliche E-Mail schreiben, müssen Sie nicht in vollständigen Sätzen schreiben.
  Beispiel: Suppose I won't go snowboarding this winter anyway, cause I'm busy at college with exams.

Redemittel

- Freundliche Formulierungen:

Well, …	go back to a topic
Anyway …	summarize the topic
By the way …	change the topic
Of course …	say something is obvious
(Un)luckily …	show good or bad fortune
To be honest …	say what you really mean

- Abkürzungen und Emoticons:

Beispiele für Abkürzungen:	
LOL	laughing out loud
2BCTND	to be continued
AKA	also known as
ASAP	as soon as possible
CM	call me
F2F	face to face

Beispiele für Emoticons/ Smileys:	
:-)	smiling, happy
:D	large grin
:o	shocked, surprised
:O	shouting

Persönliche Briefe

Einen persönlichen Brief schreiben Sie an jemanden, den Sie gut kennen, z. B. an einen Freund oder einen Verwandten. Es gibt ebenfalls keine festen Regeln.

Es gibt verschiedene Kommunikationsanlässe: Freundschaftlicher Brief, Liebesbrief, Einladung, Entschuldigung, Glückwunsch/Kondolenz und Danksagung.

26 Describing illustrations and photographs
Bilder und Fotos beschreiben

Wenn Sie ein Bild analysieren möchten, dann beschreiben Sie das Bild sowohl optisch, d. h. das Aussehen des Bildes, als auch inhaltlich, d. h. den Informationsgehalt. Die Bildanalyse soll so genau sein, dass sich ein blinder Mensch theoretisch das Bild genau vorstellen kann.

Erster Eindruck

- Beschreiben Sie zunächst die Bildart, die Sie sehen, und welche Situation das Bild zeigt.
- Wenn angegeben, nennen Sie die Quellenangabe des Bildes, z. B.: Von wem stammt das Bild? Wer hat es erstellt? Wann ist das Bild entstanden? Welchen Titel trägt das Bild? Wo wurde es veröffentlicht?

Beschreibung des Bildes / des Fotos

- Beschreiben Sie nun detailliert, was Sie auf dem Bild sehen können. Gehen Sie hierbei so vor, dass Sie mit dem wichtigsten Aspekt des Bildes beginnen (im Vordergrund, im Fokus), und nennen Sie erst dann die Details, die im Hintergrund zu sehen sind.
- Achten Sie darauf, dass Sie nur beschreiben und noch nicht interpretieren!
- Was genau zeigt das Bild? Beantworten Sie möglichst die w-Fragen „wer?", „wo?", „was?".
- Beschreiben Sie zudem, wenn möglich, die Körpersprache der Menschen, d. h. Gestik und Mimik, die Beziehung der Menschen zueinander, die Verwendung von Farben, Licht und Symbolen.

Interpretation und Intention

- Versuchen Sie nun, das Bild zu interpretieren, d.h. ziehen Sie Schlussfolgerungen aus dem Beschriebenen hinsichtlich der Intention (Absicht) des Malers/Fotografen.
  - Welche Atmosphäre vermittelt das Bild? Warum wird diese Atmosphäre vermittelt?
  - Welche Botschaft möchte der Maler/Fotograf weitergeben? Und was möchte er/sie damit bewirken?
  - Welche Zielgruppe wird angesprochen?

Wirkung / persönliche Meinung

- Im letzten Teil Ihrer Bildanalyse formulieren Sie Ihren persönlichen Eindruck, den das Bild bei Ihnen hinterlassen hat. Versuchen Sie hierzu immer Beispiele dafür zu geben, welche Elemente des Bildes genau zu Ihrer persönlichen Meinung über das Bild geführt haben.
  - Wie wirkt das Bild auf Sie? Ablehnend oder anziehend?
  - Welche Gefühle weckt das Bild in Ihnen?
  - Bestätigt das Bild die Wirklichkeit oder zeigt es Widersprüche?

Tempus

- Wenn Sie beschreiben, welchen Gegenstand / welche Person Sie in einem Bild sehen, dann verwenden Sie die einfache Form des Präsens. ► GF16 Present simple
  Beispiele:
  There is a young person in the foreground.
  The photo shows …
- Wenn Sie jedoch beschreiben, was die Person in dem Bild gerade tut, dann müssen Sie die Verlaufsform des Präsens verwenden. ► GF17 Present continuous
  Beispiel: *The young person is holding a sign with one hand.*

Redemittel: Bilder und Fotos beschreiben

- Beschreibung der Bildart und der gezeigten Situation:

The picture is a/an illustration/painting/collage/still (from a film) / electronic image …
The (colour/black-and-white) photograph shows …
This is a (painting) showing a typical … scene/ situation …
This (collage) illustrates …
In this (still) you can see (that) …

- Beschreibung von Farben und Licht:

The colours are bright/dark.
The photograph is clear / in focus / blurred / not in focus / well-lit.
The day the photograph was taken on was sunny/ cloudy.

- Beschreiben, wo sich etwas im Bild befindet:

on the right-hand/left-hand side of the illustration
At the top/bottom of the photo you can find …
in the upper right-hand corner
in the lower left-hand corner
In the centre of the picture there is …
In the foreground/background you can see …

- Interpretation und Intention:

The person in the picture looks … (+ adjective)
The painting gives you the impression that …
The artist wants to express that …
Perhaps his/her intention is to show that …
The illustration is aimed at children …
Considering the … in the photo you could draw the conclusion that …

- Beschreibung der Atmosphäre:

This creates a/an … atmosphere.
The main factors that contribute to this atmosphere are …
The atmosphere is cosy, friendly, funny, happy, lively, peaceful, warm …
It is chilly, dark, depressing, desperate, sad, scary, serious, terrifying …
The atmosphere is boring, exotic, hectic, mysterious …
The … in the photo conveys an atmosphere of great sadness/happiness.

- Persönliche Meinung:

The impression I get from this illustration is that …
The illustration makes me feel …
The colours/light the artist has chosen make/makes me feel … (+ adjective)
In my opinion the painting is supposed to …
To my mind the photograph would be better if … (+ past simple)
My first thought when I saw the (photograph) was …
The (collage) is shocking/brilliant/breathtaking/terrifying/impressive/realistic …
The (painting) reminds me of …

27 Describing cartoons
Karikaturen beschreiben

Eine Karikatur ist eine satirische (spöttische) Darstellung von Menschen oder gesellschaftlichen Situationen. Charakteristisch für Karikaturen ist, dass sie die Realität übertrieben und verformt darstellen mit dem Ziel, einen gesellschaftlichen Zustand, eine Person oder eine Institution zu kritisieren. Meistens besteht eine Karikatur aus einem Bild und einem kurzen Text innerhalb des Bildes, z. B. als Sprechblase, oder unterhalb des Bildes als Bildunterschrift.

Eine Karikatur bedient sich in der Regel zahlreicher Stilmittel, um die Komik einer Situation oder die Eigenheiten einer Person überspitzt darzustellen.

Beispiele:

exaggeration	Übertreibung	Eigenschaften werden überdimensioniert und überzogen dargestellt.
irony	Ironie	Das Gegenteil des Gesagten ist gemeint.
pun	Wortspiel	Beruht auf der Mehrdeutigkeit und Verdrehung von Wörtern
simile	Vergleich	Veranschaulichung einer Aussage, indem sie durch *like* oder *as* mit einem anderen Bereich in Beziehung gesetzt wird
symbol	Symbol	Etwas Konkretes verweist auf etwas Abstraktes.

Wenn Sie eine Karikatur beschreiben und analysieren möchten, beachten Sie „Redemittel: Bilder und Fotos beschreiben" auf Seite 172.
► SF 26 Describing illustrations and photographs

→ **Redemittel finden Sie auf der folgenden Seite.**

Redemittel: Karikaturen beschreiben

- Die Karikatur beschreiben:

The cartoon consists of an illustration of …
The illustration shows …
There is a caption below the cartoon, which says "…".
In the (first) speech bubble it says "…"
The text in the speech bubble is spoken by …

- Die Botschaft der Karikatur:

The cartoonist's message might be that …
His point seems to be that …
Probably his intention is to show that …
The cartoonist is criticizing the behaviour of …
He is making fun of …
He is making a sarcastic comment on …

- Interpretation der Karikatur:

The figure is a caricature of …
The cartoonist exaggerates character traits.
The person's body language shows that …
From his/her facial expression you can conclude that …
… symbolizes / stands for / is a symbol of …

- Persönliche Meinung:

I think / I don't think the cartoon is (very) funny because …
I think / I don't think the cartoon is easy to understand because …
I agree / I don't agree with the point the cartoonist is making because …

28 Describing diagrams
Diagramme beschreiben

Diagramme sind graphische Darstellungen von numerischen Daten oder Informationen. Sie veranschaulichen Informationen und erleichtern es dem Leser, komplizierte Sachverhalte aufzunehmen.

Je nachdem, was ein Diagramm verdeutlichen soll, werden unterschiedliche Arten von Diagrammen eingesetzt. Im Folgenden finden Sie eine Auswahl der am häufigsten verwendeten Arten von Diagrammen.

Pie chart: Ein Tortendiagramm ist in mehrere Kreissektoren unterteilt, die Teile des Ganzen anzeigen. Es eignet sich besonders, um Anteile darzustellen.	**Bar chart:** Ein Säulendiagramm oder Balkendiagramm ist ein Diagramm, das die Häufigkeitsverteilung verschiedener Sektoren veranschaulicht. Es eignet sich besonders, um einige wenige Daten miteinander zu vergleichen.	**Line graph:** Ein Liniendiagramm stellt den funktionellen Zusammenhang von zwei Merkmalen graphisch dar. Es eignet sich besonders gut, um die Entwicklung von Werten graphisch darzustellen.

Diagramme beschreiben

- Nennen Sie zunächst die Art des Diagramms, den Titel, die Quelle, Erscheinungsort und -jahr sowie die Maßeinheiten und Parameter.
- Beschreiben Sie das Diagramm nun detailliert. Machen Sie sich zunächst Notizen. Je nach Art des Diagramms können Sie:
  - den Verlauf der Entwicklung differenziert beschreiben,
  - Einzelwerte vergleichen,
  - Gemeinsamkeiten und Unterschiede benennen,
  - den Kurvenverlauf, die Säulenverteilung, die Sektorverteilung beschreiben,
  - Maximal- und Minimalwerte angeben.
- Achten Sie darauf, dass Ihre Beschreibung nicht zu detailliert ausfällt. Konzentrieren Sie sich nur auf auffällige Entwicklungen oder Zahlen.
- Mit Hilfe Ihrer Notizen formulieren Sie vollständige Sätze, um das Diagramm zu beschreiben.
- Versuchen Sie nun, das Diagramm zu interpretieren, d.h. ziehen Sie Schlussfolgerungen aus dem Beschriebenen und überprüfen Sie gegebenenfalls die Zuverlässigkeit der Quelle.
- Fassen Sie die wichtigsten Ergebnisse des Diagramms in ein bis zwei Sätzen zusammen.

Redemittel: Diagramme beschreiben

- Bestandsaufnahme der Informationen:

The pie chart "US Exports" published in *The Daily USA* in New York in 20… shows in percentage terms what the USA exported in the year 20…

- Beschreibung:

The chart/graph/diagram shows …
It shows the development from … to …
The table shows the change of … from … to …
The chart gives an overview of …
The time scale runs vertically.
The weight scale runs horizontally.
On the y-axis/x-axis you can see …

- Einen Anstieg beschreiben:

There is a noticeable upward trend between … and …
By 2009 figures reached their highest level.
The number grew/increased.
The number of … rose slightly/sharply/slowly.

- Eine Abnahme beschreiben:

We notice a downward trend between … and …
By 20 … figures reached their lowest level.
The number declined/decreased.
The number fell slightly / slowly / sank sharply.
The number of … remained unchanged/steady.

- Unveränderte Werte:

Figures remained steady / Figures did not change.

- Zahlen und Daten:

the figures for the last year / the last month, etc.
the latest figures
the total number of …
a significant / an insignificant number of …
a high percentage of …
a majority/minority of …
percentage/amount

- Mengenbezeichnungen:

a total of	from over/under
over/under	one in five
nearly/almost/ approximately	half / a third / a quarter / two thirds
exactly	100 per cent
more/less than	twice/three times as many
the same number as	on average
the same amount of	

- Interpretation:

The biggest change can be seen in …
This leads to the assumption that …
This suggests a relation between … and …

- Schlussfolgerung:

The drastic change may be due to …
All in all you can say that …
To sum up … we can say that …

29 Analyzing films
Filmanalyse

Die Filmanalyse unterscheidet sich nicht wesentlich von der Analyse von geschriebenen Texten und auch Bildern. Bei der Textanalyse untersuchen Sie z. B. die Charaktere, den Handlungsverlauf und den Handlungsort; bei der Bildanalyse beschreiben und interpretieren Sie z. B. die Körpersprache von Menschen, die Verwendung von Farben und Licht und die Atmosphäre. ► SF 26 Describing illustrations and photographs

Diese Aspekte werden Sie auch bei der Filmanalyse näher betrachten.
In der Regel untersuchen Sie in der Schule keine ganzen Filme, sondern nur kurze Filmausschnitte, sogenannte Filmsequenzen.

Filmarten

Spielfilm *(feature film)* Ein Spielfilm ist ein Film mit einer fiktionalen Handlung, die manchmal auch der Wirklichkeit (z. B. realen Personen oder Ereignissen) nachempfunden sein kann.

Dokumentarfilm *(documentary)* Ein Dokumentarfilm befasst sich mit tatsächlichen Gegebenheiten und Ereignissen. Deshalb können Sie den Dokumentarfilm nicht genauso analysieren wie den Spielfilm: Es gibt in der Regel keinen Handlungsverlauf, weil keine Geschichte erzählt wird, sondern der Schwerpunkt liegt auf der Sachlichkeit des Films. Ein Dokumentarfilm soll Informationen zu einem bestimmten Thema bereitstellen.
Deshalb analysieren Sie bei einem Dokumentarfilm zunächst vor allem die Darstellung des Themas, die Vorgehensweise und Intention des Regisseurs und die Wirkung des Filmes auf den Zuschauer.
Zusätzlich müssen Sie die Gestaltungselemente des Dokumentarfilms analysieren, die denen des Spielfilms gleichen.

Werbefilm *(commercial)* Ein Werbefilm ist ein kurzer Film, in dem für ein Produkt oder eine Dienstleistung geworben wird. Charakteristisch für den Werbefilm ist, dass er Menschen beeinflussen soll, ein bestimmtes Produkt zu kaufen. (Siehe AIDA-Formel zur Analyse von Werbefilmen.) ► Unit 3, Seite 31

Quellenangabe

- Schreiben Sie eine Quellenangabe.
  Beispiel: The feature film "Twilight", directed by Catherine Hardwicke and produced in the USA in 2008, is about a teenage girl who falls in love with a vampire.

Gesamteindruck und Empfindungen

- Welchen Gesamteindruck haben Sie von der Filmsequenz? Welche Empfindungen ruft sie in Ihnen hervor?

My first thought when I saw the film sequence was …
The film sequence is shocking/brilliant/breathtaking/terrifying/impressive/realistic …

- Worum geht es in der Sequenz grob? Achten Sie auf Handlungsverlauf *(plot)*; Einsatz eines Erzählers *(narrator)*; Handlungsort und -zeit *(setting)*; Spannungsaufbau *(suspense)*; Atmosphäre *(atmosphere)*.

This sequence is about …
This sequence presents the different aspects of …
This sequence discusses the problem of … / the theme of …
The film makes use of a narrator.
The narrator wants to inform/influence/manipulate/convince the viewer.
The director makes use of voiceover with the aim of …
The story/extract is set in …
The scene/action takes place in the present/past/future …
Suspense is created by / arises from …
The main cause of suspense is …
The conflict between … and … creates suspense.
The atmosphere in this sequence is …
► SF 26 Describing illustrations and photographs

Die Charaktere bzw. Darsteller

- Beschreiben Sie die Charaktere (Spielfilm) bzw. die Darsteller (Dokumentarfilm) der Filmsequenz.

The main character is …
There are two/three/etc. main characters.
We get to know … by …
He/She is confronted with …

- Achten Sie auf das Aussehen *(appearance)*.

general: pretty, handsome, beautiful, ugly
body: fat, obese, slim, thin, tall, small
face: round/square/wrinkled face; pale/tanned skin; bright/dull eyes; long/pointed/flat nose; curly/straight/short/long hair
clothes: jacket, trousers, shirt, skirt, dress; fashionable, clean, dirty, tidy, neat, worn-out

- Achten Sie auf das Verhalten und die Beziehungen der Charaktere zueinander *(behaviour and relationships)*.

negative character traits: aggressive, anxious, bad-tempered, dishonest, narrow-minded, pessimistic, rude, shy, unfair
positive character traits: brave, friendly, honest, open-minded, optimistic, polite, reasonable, self-confident
This character represents …
The character is in a conflict (with) …
The character finds himself/herself in an inner conflict …
There is a relationship between … and …

- Achten Sie auf die Sprache *(language and how the characters communicate with one another)*.

The character has got a soft/loud/pleasant/coarse/funny voice.
The character speaks quietly/loudly.
There is little dialogue in this sequence.
There is a long dialogue between … and … in this sequence.
They are shouting at each other.
The character's monologue is focusing (mainly) on …
The scene begins/ends with a monologue.
This scene presents an important dialogue between … and …

Die Szene im Kontext des Films

- Setzen Sie die Filmszene in den Kontext des Gesamtfilms.

- Führt die Szene dazu, dass die Handlung voranschreitet? / …, dass Spannung aufgebaut wird? / … , dass neue Charaktere eingeführt werden? / … , dass ein Konflikt aufkommt? / …, dass ein Wendepunkt eingeleitet wird?

The course of the action is …
There is a conflict between …
The turning-point …
At the beginning … / at the end …
The film sequence introduces new characters.

Gestaltungselemente

- Wie wird die Filmszene gefilmt? Achten Sie auf:
  - Kameraabstände *(distance between the camera and the object)*
  - die Kameraperspektive *(camera position)*
  - Kamerabewegung *(camera movement)*

The director uses a long shot / static shot / over-the-shoulder shot in order to show …
The scene is shot from … point of view / high-angle / eye-level.
The medium shot / close-up / tracking shot is used to create a/an … effect.
The viewer sees this scene in a … shot.

- Wie wird das gefilmte Material am Ende nachbearbeitet?
  - Montage-Technik: Schnitt-Technik *(cut)*; Übergänge *(fade, wipe etc.)*
  - Special effects, z. B. Farben *(black-and-white, coloured)*; Zeitraffer, Zeitlupe *(fast motion, slow motion)*; Standbild *(freeze frame)*; Bildteilung *(split screen)*; Texteinblendungen *(text inserts)*

The intensity of the colour green/red/blue in this scene puts emphasis on …
The director's use of black-and-white stresses …
The use of slow motion emphasizes the moment / the character's situation.
The use of fast motion highlights the speed of the scene.
The text inserts add authenticity to the documentary.

- Wie werden die gefilmten Szenen vertont? Achten Sie auf:
  - Dialoge, Monologe, Erzählerkommentar
  - den Einsatz von Filmmusik
  - sonstige Geräusche, z. B. Straßenlärm, Anrufbeantworter
  - Lautstärken

The film music/sound builds suspense …
The film music/sound provides a shift from one scene to another.
There is light piano music in the background.
The music/sound makes the scene more cheerful/ sad/melancholic/aggressive/romantic/ authentic/dramatic, etc.
The background noises give the scene more authenticity.
The background noises / the sound effects stress the atmosphere.

- Wie werden Beleuchtungseffekte eingesetzt?

- Gibt es wiederkehrende Objekte als Symbole?

There is hardly any light in the scene.
The director makes use of back light / semi-darkness / darkness / artificial illumination …
The director makes use of symbols.
The … symbolizes / stands for / is a symbol of …

30 Group work and projects
Gruppenarbeit und Projekte

Gruppenarbeit

Die Arbeit in Gruppen bietet die Chance, sich mit einem Unterrichtsinhalt im Team auseinanderzusetzen. Viele Aufgaben lassen sich besser und schneller in einer Gruppe lösen. Gruppenarbeit dient dem Zweck, gemeinsam zu einer Lösung zu kommen, indem Sie miteinander kommunizieren und Ideen austauschen.

Gruppenzusammensetzung

- Die optimale Gruppengröße beträgt in der Regel 3–5 Personen.
- Gruppen können nach verschiedenen Prinzipien gebildet werden: nach Interesse, nach Sympathie, nach Zufall, nach Stärken und Schwächen. Dabei sollte darauf geachtet werden, dass die Gruppen ungefähr gleich stark gebildet werden und dass sie sich gegenseitig unterstützen.

Vorbereitung der Gruppenarbeit

- Richten Sie sich Ihren Arbeitsplatz so ein, dass Sie gut arbeiten, aber auch gut miteinander kommunizieren können.
- Erstellen Sie sich einen Arbeitsplan. Berücksichtigen Sie hierbei die Zeit, die Ihnen zur Bearbeitung der Aufgabe zur Verfügung steht.
- Verteilen Sie Aufgaben an die einzelnen Gruppenmitglieder. Beachten Sie, dass jeder ungefähr dieselbe Menge an Arbeit hat. Manchmal ist es sinnvoll, schriftlich festzuhalten, wer welche Aufgabe übernimmt.
- Für den Interaktionsprozess in der Gruppe kann es hilfreich sein, dass Sie den einzelnen Gruppenmitgliedern Funktionen zuordnen, z. B. Gruppenleiter, Zeitwächter, Schriftführer, Streitschlichter usw.
- Stellen Sie fest, welche Materialien Sie benötigen, und legen Sie fest, wer welche Materialien besorgt.
  Wenn die Gruppenarbeit über eine Unterrichtseinheit hinausgeht, sollten Sie sich überlegen, ob es eine Möglichkeit gibt, die Materialien aufzubewahren, so dass Sie immer Zugang dazu haben.
- Einigen Sie sich auf eine geeignete Form, um die Ergebnisse zu präsentieren, wenn sie nicht bereits vorgegeben wurde.

Durchführung der Gruppenarbeit

- Gehen Sie immer höflich und respektvoll miteinander um. Lassen Sie alle ausreden und fallen Sie niemandem ins Wort.
- Sie tragen alle die Verantwortung für die Qualität Ihrer Arbeitsergebnisse. Deshalb unterstützen Sie sich gegenseitig und helfen Sie einander bei Problemen.
- Wichtige Arbeitsergebnisse sollten von jedem Gruppenmitglied schriftlich festgehalten werden und nicht nur von einem Schriftführer. So kann es Ihnen nicht passieren, dass Ihnen bei der Präsentation der Arbeitsergebnisse Informationen fehlen.
- Bemühen Sie sich als Arbeitssprache Englisch einzusetzen.

Redemittel

- Die eigene Meinung ausdrücken:

In my opinion/view …
I think (that) …
I would like to …
We should …
It would be a good idea to …

- Jemanden unterbrechen:

Sorry, may I interrupt you for a second?
Wait a minute …
I'm sorry to interrupt but …

- Das Thema wechseln:

Before I forget …
There is something else I wanted to say …
By the way …

- Zum eigentlichen Thema zurückkehren:

Let's get back to …
To get back to what we were talking about …
As I was saying …

- Überraschung ausdrücken:

Really?
Are you serious?
I don't believe it!

- Zugeständnisse machen:

I (partly) agree with you, but …
Yes, that's true, but …

- Interesse zeigen:

Tell me about your idea.
Absolutely …
I'd love to …

- Rückmeldung geben:

That's very kind of you.
Are you sure?
I see.
I like your idea.

- Jemanden auffordern, etwas zu tun:

Could you possibly …?
Could I ask you to …?
Do you think you could … please?

- Vorschläge machen:

If I were you I would …
You could try …
How about …?

- Füllwörter:

Well, …
Anyway …
Actually …
I mean …
In fact …

- Höflichkeitsfloskeln:

Please.
You're welcome.
Thank you.
No worries.
Don't worry.

Projekte

Projekte zeichnen sich dadurch aus, dass Sie mit dem Lehrer gemeinsam ein Thema und die Arbeitsziele festlegen. Bei der Lösung der Aufgabe, der Beschaffung der Materialien/ Informationen und der Erstellung eines Produktes arbeiten Sie jedoch selbstständig in Gruppen.

Erfolgreiche Durchführung eines Projektes

- Lesen Sie die Aufgabenstellung sorgfältig und stellen Sie sicher, dass alle Gruppenmitglieder die Aufgabe verstanden haben. Oft ist es bei Projekten der Fall, dass zu Beginn nur das allgemeine Ziel bekannt ist und sich die detaillierten Ziele erst in der Gruppe ergeben, z. B. durch spezifische Betrachtungsweisen des Themas.
  Folgende Fragestellungen zum Verstehen des Arbeitsauftrags können hilfreich sein:
  - Was sollen Sie genau tun und mit welchem Ziel?
  - Gibt es eine zeitliche Begrenzung?
  - Welche Entscheidungen können Sie frei treffen?
  - Sind noch Fragen offen?
- Führen Sie in der Gruppe ein Brainstorming durch:
  - Was wissen Sie bereits über das Thema? Erstellen Sie ein Word web. ► SF 21 Word webs
  - Welche Aspekte des Themas möchten Sie bearbeiten?
  - Wo finden Sie die Informationen zu dem Thema?
- Planen Sie die Arbeit in Gruppen:
  - Erstellen Sie einen Plan, auf dem festgehalten wird, wer welche Aufgabe übernimmt.
  - Erstellen Sie einen Terminplan, auf dem Sie festhalten, wann bestimmte Aufgaben erledigt sein müssen.
  - Legen Sie fest, wie Sie Ihre Arbeit koordinieren. Wann treffen Sie sich, evtl. auch außerhalb des Unterrichts? Wie tauschen Sie Informationen aus?
- Entscheiden Sie gemeinsam in der Gruppe, wie Sie Ihre Arbeitsergebnisse präsentieren möchten, falls dies nicht in der Aufgabenstellung festgelegt ist.
  Ideen für Präsentationen: Handzettel, Broschüre, Poster, Plakat, Wandzeitung, Video, Hörspiel, Kurzvortrag, PowerPoint-Präsentation …
- Vergessen Sie nicht, alle Quellen zu notieren, die Sie verwendet haben. Sie müssen immer angeben können, wo Sie Informationen, Bilder usw. gefunden haben.

31 Internet research
Suche im Internet

Es gibt mittlerweile Millionen von Webseiten im Internet. Das Problem ist jedoch, unter der Vielzahl die gewünschten Informationen zu finden. Sie werden nur sofort fündig, wenn Sie die einschlägige Internet-Adresse bereits kennen oder Sie durch einen Link direkt weitergeleitet werden. Falls beides nicht der Fall ist, müssen Sie auf Suchmaschinen zurückgreifen. Suchmaschinen sind Spezialprogramme, mit deren Hilfe Sie sich Ihrem Ziel durch die Eingabe entsprechender Stichwörter nähern können.

Thema formulieren und eingrenzen

- Bevor Sie sich an den PC setzen, um im Internet nach Informationen zu suchen, sollten Sie sich genau überlegen, welche Informationen Sie benötigen, damit Sie nicht die Orientierung verlieren. Denn das Hauptproblem bei der Recherche im Internet liegt darin, dass man viel Zeit damit verbringt, eine Fülle an unwichtigen und überflüssigen Informationen zu sichten. Um dies zu vermeiden, können Sie z. B. …
  - das Thema präzisieren und evtl. eingrenzen,
  - sinnvolle Stichwörter zum Thema sammeln,
  - themenbezogene Wortfelder erstellen.

Suchanfragen richtig stellen

- Wenn Ihre Suchanfrage zu ungenau ist, werden Sie eine Vielzahl von Informationen erhalten, die zu allgemein sind. Wenn Sie z. B. Informationen zum Thema *TV viewing habits of children* suchen, reicht es nicht aus, das Stichwort *Media* einzugeben. Suchmaschinen bedienen sich teilweise leider unterschiedlicher Suchbegriffe.
  Folgende Eingabearten sind bei den meisten Suchmaschinen möglich:
  - Mehrere Wörter ohne Anführungszeichen
    Beispiel: *TV viewing habits*
    Ergebnis: Alle Texte, in denen entweder *TV* oder *viewing* oder *habits* vorkommen, werden angezeigt.
  - Mehrere Wörter mit Anführungszeichen
    Beispiel: *„TV viewing habits"*
    Ergebnis: Es werden nur Texte angezeigt, in denen die exakte Wortfolge vorkommt.
- Wenn Sie zu wenige Treffer erlangen, überprüfen Sie die Schreibweise, verwenden Sie weniger Begriffe oder versuchen Sie es mit einem anderen Stichwort.
- Wenn Sie zu viele Treffer erlangen, verwenden Sie spezifischere Begriffe oder fügen Sie Stichwörter hinzu.
- Spezielle Begriffe, die aber nicht zu ausgefallen sind, bringen meist gute und eingegrenzte Ergebnisse.

Informationen finden

- Um möglichst schnell und gezielt Informationen zu finden, können Sie Techniken wie Skimming und Scanning verwenden.
  ► **SF 9 Anticipating, skimming, scanning**
- Wenn Sie nach einzelnen Wörtern auf einer Seite suchen möchten, können Sie auch Strg+F drücken. Es erscheint dann ein Suchfeld, in das Sie das betreffende Wort eingeben können.

Informationen verarbeiten

- Denken Sie daran, dass jeder User beliebige Informationen im Internet veröffentlichen kann. Die von Ihnen gefundenen Informationen müssen also nicht immer korrekt sein. Um wertloses Material von wertvollem Material zu unterschieden, können folgende Fragen hilfreich sein:
  - Wer hat die Webseite veröffentlicht? (z. B. kommerziell vs. nicht kommerziell, Privatperson vs. öffentliche Institution, usw.)
  - Verfolgen die Autoren ein bestimmtes Interesse? (Soll z. B. etwas verkauft werden?)
  - Werden Fakten dargelegt oder Meinungen?
  - Sind die Informationen aktuell? (Wann z. B. wurde die Webseite zum letzten Mal aktualisiert? Von wann sind die Jahreszahlen/Statistiken?)

Favoriten

- Wenn Sie die gesuchten Informationen gefunden haben und später noch einmal auf die Seite zurückgreifen möchten, können Sie die Seite in die Liste der Favoriten aufnehmen. Ihr Browser speichert diese Liste, so dass Sie die Seite jederzeit anzeigen können, ohne erneut suchen zu müssen. Je nach Browser kann diese Liste auch Lesezeichen oder Bookmark heißen. Sie finden die Favoriten in der Menüleiste. Dort klicken Sie auf „Lesezeichen hinzufügen", während Sie die Seite, die Sie speichern möchten, geöffnet haben. Sie können die Seite auch direkt auf dem Desktop speichern, sodass Sie schnell auf diese Seite zugreifen können.

32 Giving a talk or presentation
Ein Referat halten, Arbeitsergebnisse präsentieren

Eine Präsentation oder ein Referat ist eine vorbereitete Vorstellung von Inhalten oder Ergebnissen zu einem bestimmten Thema. Ziel einer Präsentation ist es, die Zuhörer zu informieren.

In der Schule finden häufig Gruppenpräsentationen statt, so dass Sie sich untereinander absprechen sollten, wer welchen Teil übernimmt. ► SF 30 Projects and group work

Brainstorming

- Verschaffen Sie sich zunächst einen Überblick über das Thema, indem Sie ein Wortnetz zu dem Themenbereich erstellen. ► SF 21 Word webs
- Sie sollten sich auch Folgendes genau überlegen:
  - Welches Ziel verfolge ich mit der Präsentation?
  - An wen ist die Präsentation adressiert?
  - Welche Hilfsmittel und Medien kann ich verwenden, um erfolgreich zu präsentieren?

Materialsuche

- Sammeln Sie Informationen zu dem Thema. Sie können z. B. in Bibliotheken, Zeitungen, Schulbüchern, Lexika oder dem Internet recherchieren. Oder Sie befragen einen Experten zu dem Thema. ► SF 31 Internet research

Konzipierung und Aufbau der Präsentation

- Da Sie möglichst frei sprechen sollten und dies in der Fremdsprache noch etwas schwerer fällt, ist es sinnvoll, wenn Sie sich einen Ablaufplan Ihrer Präsentation erstellen. Sie können z.B. eine Tabelle erstellen, in der die Gliederung, der zeitliche Ablauf und der Einsatz von Medien ersichtlich werden. Den Ablaufplan können Sie sich auf Ihren Rednertisch legen, um während der Präsentation bei Bedarf einen Blick darauf werfen zu können.
- In der Regel können Sie Ihre Präsentation anhand der klassischen Dreiteilung aufbauen: Einstieg – Hauptteil – Schlussteil, wobei Sie den Einstieg und den Schlussteil kurz halten sollten, der Hauptteil kann ausführlicher sein.
- Einstieg: Anrede der Zuhörer und sich vorstellen – Thema vorstellen – Gliederung vorstellen. Dabei ist es sinnvoll, das Interesse der Zuhörer zu wecken. Beginnen Sie z.B. mit einem Zitat, einer Karikatur oder einer provokanten Frage, um die volle Aufmerksamkeit zu erhalten.
- Hauptteil: Gut strukturierte Ausführungen (z.B. chronologische Anordnung der Hauptaspekte) – Beispiele geben – visuelle Hilfsmittel hinzuziehen
- Schlussteil: Zusammenfassung der Hauptaspekte – Dank an die Zuhörer.

Stichwortkarten

- Reduzieren Sie Ihren Vortrag auf die wichtigsten Stichpunkte und schreiben Sie diese auf Karteikarten. Die Stichwortkarten sollten keinesfalls den ganzen Text Ihres Vortrags enthalten. Sie sollten es auch vermeiden, vollständige Sätze aufzuschreiben. Sie können sich auch Stichworte zu Beispielen oder Vokabeln auf den Stichwortkarten notieren.
- Sie sollten die Stichwortkarten so aufteilen, dass Sie während des Vortrags nicht durcheinander geraten. Es ist sinnvoll, für den Einstieg und den Schlussteil jeweils eine Stichwortkarte vorzubereiten. Für den Hauptteil sollten Sie je nach Länge Ihres Vortrags mehrere Karten vorbereiten, z.B. je Hauptaspekt eine Karte.

Visuelle Hilfsmittel

- Die meisten Menschen nehmen nur 30% über das Ohr auf, aber ca. 70% über das Auge. Überlegen Sie sich deshalb, welche visuellen Hilfsmittel Ihre Präsentation angemessen unterstützen können.
- Weniger ist mehr! Überfrachten Sie Tafelanschrieb, Plakate, Folien, Handzettel usw. möglichst nicht. Strukturieren Sie diese übersichtlich. ►SF 34 Creating a poster

Vortragsweise

- Wenn Sie nur ablesen, werden sich Ihre Zuhörer schnell langweilen. Sie sollten daher möglichst frei sprechen und nur hin und wieder auf Ihre Stichwortkarten zurückgreifen.
- Sprechen Sie nicht so, wie Sie schreiben, sondern versuchen Sie, natürlich zu sprechen, so dass Ihre Zuhörer Ihnen folgen können. Formulieren Sie möglichst kurze und unkomplizierte Sätze. Verzichten Sie, wenn möglich, auf Fachbegriffe, die Ihren Zuhörern unbekannt sind. Falls Sie doch auf Fachbegriffe zurückgreifen müssen, schreiben Sie diese an die Tafel.
- Nutzen Sie Wiederholungen, um Wichtiges zu betonen.

Stimme und Körpersprache

- Sprechen Sie langsam: So haben Sie länger Zeit, um Ihre Sätze im Englischen zu formulieren.
- Machen Sie Pausen: Die Zuhörer hören das Gesagte vielleicht zum ersten Mal.
- Halten Sie Blickkontakt mit den Zuhörern. Achten Sie auch auf die Reaktionen der Zuhörer.
- Versuchen Sie, Ihre Aussagen durch Gestik und Mimik zu unterstreichen.

Redemittel für die Präsentation

- Einstieg:

Good morning, my name is …
Good morning, let me introduce our group. …
Can everybody hear me alright?
Can everybody see the board/poster/screen?
Let me start by saying a few words about …
The topic of my presentation today is …

- Hauptteil:

Let me give you an example.
If you look at the screen, you'll see that …
As you can see on the board/poster/screen …
That proves my point.
I'd like to move on to …
Before we go any further, let's look at …

- Struktur und Zeitangaben:

My presentation will last fifteen minutes.
I will talk for fifteen minutes.
My presentation is split into four key areas.
Firstly, … Secondly, … Thirdly, … Finally, …
There will be time for questions at the end.
If you have any questions, feel free to interrupt me.

- Schlussteil:

Finally …
I'd like to finish/conclude by saying that …
To summarize … / To conclude …
Thank you very much for your attention.
Thank you very much for listening.
If you have any questions, please feel free to ask.

33 Taking notes
Die Mitschrift im Unterricht

Informationen, die im Unterricht mündlich präsentiert werden, sind in der Regel die zentralen Lerngegenstände und beinhalten einen großen Teil des prüfungsrelevanten Materials. Mitschriften entstehen im Unterricht durch das Aufschreiben der relevanten Informationen von verschiedenen Quellen, z. B. Unterrichtsgesprächen, Referaten, Hörverständnistexten, Interviews, Filmanalysen usw.

Unabhängig von der Quelle ist bei der Mitschrift besonders wichtig, dass Sie lernen, richtig zuzuhören. In der Regel kann der Mensch nämlich lediglich 30 % des Gehörten behalten. Da die englische Sprache nicht Ihre Muttersprache ist, wird es Ihnen noch schwerer fallen, das gesprochene Englisch zu verstehen und Informationen aufzunehmen. Die folgenden Tipps helfen Ihnen, Ihr Zuhörerverhalten zu verbessern.

Tipps zum richtigen Zuhören

Wenn Sie nichts oder nur schlecht hören können, verändern Sie Ihre Position. Setzen Sie sich dorthin, wo Sie den Sprecher sehen können und wo Sie nicht von Ablenkungen gestört werden.

Akzeptieren Sie die Tatsache, dass Sie nicht alles verstehen werden.

Achten Sie auf die Hauptaussagen des Gesprochenen. Versuchen Sie, Wichtiges von Unwichtigem zu unterscheiden. Konzentrieren Sie sich erst auf Details, wenn Sie die Hauptaussagen verstanden haben.

Auch wenn Sie für eine Zeit lang dem Gesprochenen nicht folgen können, lassen Sie sich nicht ablenken. Bleiben Sie konzentriert bei der Sache. Oft werden die wichtigen Informationen vom Sprecher im weiteren Verlauf wiederholt.

Machen Sie sich Notizen, während Sie zuhören. Scheuen Sie sich nicht nachzufragen, wenn Sie etwas nicht verstanden haben.

Übertragen Sie das Gehörte nicht in Ihre Muttersprache.

Vorbereitung

- Vor Unterrichtsbeginn sollten Sie kurz Ihre Notizen zur vorangegangen Unterrichtsstunde lesen. Dadurch werden Sie sich an den bereits besprochenen Lernstoff erinnern und es wird Ihnen helfen, dem neuen Lernstoff zu folgen.
- Sie sollten immer die Materialien für die Unterrichtsstunde vollständig mitbringen, d.h. Bücher, Hefte, verschiedenfarbige Stifte, Papier, usw.

Notizen erstellen

- Hören Sie erst genau zu, bevor Sie anfangen zu schreiben. Wenn Sie sofort drauflos schreiben, kann es passieren, dass Sie die wichtigste Information verpassen, weil Sie sich gerade auf die Mitschrift konzentrieren.
- Hören Sie auf „Signalsätze", die anzeigen, dass das Folgende besonders wichtig ist, z.B. *Remember that ..., The most important point ..., In conclusion ...*
- Schreiben Sie so schnell und effizient wie möglich, indem Sie nur das Wesentliche schreiben und Kurzsätze bzw. Stichworte aufschreiben. Verwenden Sie Abkürzungen, Symbole und Wortverkürzungen (siehe Tabelle).

Symbole		**Abkürzungen**		**Wortverkürzungen**	
&, +	and	p., l.	page, line	med	medicine
=	the same as	i.e.	that is	govt	government
≠	not the same as	e.g.	for example	impt	important
♀	female	cf	compare	yth	youth
♂	male	w/	with	tgt	target
%	percent	w/o	without	cert	certificate

- Informationen, die Sie beim Zuhören nicht verstanden haben, markieren Sie mit einem Fragezeichen (?), so dass Sie später nachfragen oder nachschlagen können.

Überarbeiten der Notizen

- Formulieren Sie Kurzsätze und Stichworte in längere Sätze um.
- Abkürzungen, Symbole und Wortverkürzungen sollten ausgeschrieben werden.
- Beantworten Sie Fragen zu Wörtern oder Informationen, die Sie nicht verstanden haben. Schlagen Sie nach oder fragen Sie Ihre Mitschüler oder Ihren Lehrer.
- Vergleichen Sie Ihre Mitschrift mit der Mitschrift Ihrer Mitschüler. So können Sie Ihre Mitschriften gegenseitig ergänzen.

34 Creating a poster
Ein Plakat erstellen

Ein Plakat ist eine informative, großformatige und übersichtlich gestaltete Form, Arbeitsergebnisse zu präsentieren. In der Regel stehen Plakate nicht für sich alleine, sondern sind als visuelle Unterstützung von Präsentationen gedacht.

Informationen beschaffen und verarbeiten

Bevor Sie mit der Gestaltung des Plakats beginnen, müssen Sie sich mit dem Inhalt beschäftigen. Sammeln Sie Informationen zu Ihrer Aufgabe, lesen Sie Texte, trennen Sie wichtige Informationen von Unwichtigem und fassen Sie schließlich die Inhalte zusammen.

Gliederung der Inhalte

- Auf einem Plakat sollten nie vollständige Sätze stehen, sondern Stichpunkte oder Halbsätze. Deshalb überarbeiten Sie Ihre Zusammenfassungen nun noch einmal, indem Sie Sätze umformulieren und kürzen oder durch Bilder und Symbole ersetzen. Fragen Sie sich an dieser Stelle immer: Welche Botschaft soll das Plakat vermitteln?
- Finden Sie eine passende Überschrift für das Plakat. Die Überschrift sollte nicht zu lang sein, aber für den Leser verständlich. Verwenden Sie also nur Abkürzungen in Überschriften, die allgemein bekannt sind.

Aufbau und Anordnung planen

- Überlegen Sie, ob die Inhalte Ihres Plakats besser im Hochformat oder im Querformat zur Geltung kommen und wie Sie die Überschriften, Textelemente und Bilder anordnen.
- Wenn Sie sich für eine klassische Anordnung der Inhalte entscheiden, dann halten Sie sich an den Aufbau, so wie er im nebenstehenden Schaubild dargestellt ist.
  - Überschrift: über den gesamten Kopf des Plakats,
  - Einleitung: oben links,
  - Schlussfolgerungen: unten links,
  - Sachinformationen und Ergebnisse: füllen den restlichen Platz.

Schrift und Farben

- Ihre Schrift sollte so groß sein, dass sie von allen Positionen des Raumes lesbar ist. Versuchen Sie, gerade zu schreiben. Verwenden Sie möglichst Druckbuchstaben und dicke Stifte.
- Heben Sie Wichtiges durch Farben, Unterstreichungen, Umrahmungen oder Schraffierungen hervor. Verwenden Sie jedoch maximal 3 Farben pro Plakat.

Grammar files

1 **Indefinite article**
Unbestimmter Artikel

2 **Definite article**
Bestimmter Artikel

3 **Plural**
Mehrzahl

4 **Some important prepositions**
Zeitliche und Räumliche Präpositionen, Präpositionen der Art und Weise

5 **Possessive case**
Genitiv

6 **Comparison of adjectives**
Steigerung der Adjektiven

7 **Adjective and adverb**
Adjektiv und Adverb

8 **Word order with adverbs and adverbials**
Wortstellung bei Adverbien und adverbialen Bestimmungen (a. B.)

9 **Some or any?**

10 **Some/any + -one/-body/-thing/-where**

11 **Much – many – a lot of**

12 **Little / a little – few / a few**

13 **Modal auxiliaries**
Modale Hilfsverben

14 **Defining relative clauses**
Notwendige Relativsätze

15 **Non-defining relative clauses**
Nicht notwendige Relativsätze

The tenses Die Zeiten

16 **Present simple**

17 **Present continuous**

18 **Past simple**

19 **Past continuous**

20 **Present perfect simple**

21 **Present perfect continuous**

22 **Past perfect simple**

23 **Future with 'going to'**

24 **Will-future**

25 **Question tags**
Frageanhängsel

26 **Reported speech**
Indirekte Rede

27 **Conditionals**
Bedingungssätze

28 **Passive voice**
Passiv

29 **Infinitive**
Infinitiv

30 **Gerund**
Gerundium

31 **Participle**
Partizip

1 Indefinite article
Unbestimmter Artikel

Form

a	college student university	vor **gesprochenen** Konsonanten
an	interview address hour	vor **gesprochenen** Vokalen

Verwendung

I have bought **a** book for you.	für zählbare Begriffe in der Einzahl
He is **a** teacher.	vor Berufsbezeichnungen

2 Definite article
Bestimmter Artikel

Form

the	course language European	vor **gesprochenen** Konsonanten Aussprache [ðə]
the	engineer office hour	vor **gesprochenen** Vokalen Aussprache [ði:]

Verwendung

the people of London **the** life of Lucy Jordan **the** University of Manchester	bei Substantiven (Personen, Dingen, Abstrakta), wenn sie näher bestimmt sind oder werden
the United States	für Ländernamen im Plural
the Thames, **the** North Sea	für Flüsse und Meere
the Browns	für Eigennamen im Plural
On their tour they visited **the** church.	für die konkrete Bedeutung als Gebäude

Verwendung von Substantiven ohne Artikel

Der Artikel wird abweichend vom Deutschen **nicht** verwendet:

nature, life, time, people	für abstrakte Begriffe und Sammelbezeichnungen, wenn sie nicht näher bestimmt sind oder werden
Trafalgar Square, Buckingham Palace	für Ortsbezeichnungen, bei Eigennamen
Switzerland, Normandy, Lake Windermere	für Länder, Berge und Seen im Singular
church, school, college When does church begin?	für Gebäudebezeichnungen, wenn die normale Nutzung gemeint ist

3 Plural
Mehrzahl

Form

student college	student**s** college**s**	Die meisten Nomen bilden den Plural durch Anhängen von -s.
universit**y** cit**y**	universit**ies** cit**ies**	Konsonant + y wird zu -ies.
addre**ss** mat**ch**	address**es** match**es**	Nach Zischlauten (z. B. s, ss, ch, sh) wird -es angehängt.
man woman child life	**men** **women** **children** **lives**	Einige Nomen haben unregelmäßige Pluralformen.

Verwendung

information, weather, nature, knowledge, work, furniture	Einige Nomen treten nur im Singular auf.
trousers, jeans, glasses, clothes, thanks, customs, savings	Einige Nomen treten nur im Plural auf.
news, the United States, the United Nations, economics, mathematics, electronics **Example:** No news **is** good news.	Einige Nomen treten nur in der Pluralform auf, das Verb steht jedoch im Singular.
family, government, staff, team, band	Sammelnamen – Plural, wenn eher auf die einzelnen Mitglieder hingewiesen wird – Singular, wenn die Gruppe eher in ihrer Gesamtheit gemeint ist

4 Some important prepositions
Zeitliche und Räumliche Präpositionen, Präpositionen der Art und Weise

Zeitliche Präpositionen

on 20th September **on** Saturday **on** weekdays	**at** six o'clock **at** the age of 16 **at** night **at** noon **at** midnight **at** the weekend	**by** day, **by** Wednesday
in 1992 **in** the morning **in** the evening		twelve minutes **to** five
		(a) quarter **past** six, half **past** nine

Räumliche Präpositionen

go **to** the cinema go **to** college I've been **to** Scotland
at home **at** school **at** the supermarket

Präpositionen der Art und Weise

go **by** bus, car, bike
go **on** foot

5 Possessive case
Genitiv

's-Genitiv

Verwendung bei Personen, Tieren, Zeiten, Personenkollektiven

Henry**'s** exam the baker**'s** (shop)	Nomen im Singular + **'s**
his parents' computer shop the Greens' house	Nomen im Plural + '
people**'s** faces children**'s** books	bei Nomen im Plural **ohne** s Anhängung von **'s**
today**'s** newspaper two weeks' pay	Bei Zeiten gelten die gleichen Regeln.
Britain's social problems the party's policy	häufig auch bei Staaten, Städten und Institutionen

of-Genitiv

Verwendung bei Sachen

the title **of** the book the price **of** the computers	Der *of*-Genitiv wird im Singular und im Plural verwendet.

6 Comparison of adjectives
Steigerung von Adjektiven

Form

cheap small	cheap**er** small**er**	cheap**est** small**est**	Steigerung der kurzen Adjektive mit -er und -est
nice	nic**er**	nic**est**	stummes -e entfällt
heavy	heav**ier**	heav**iest**	-y wird zu -ier und -iest
big	bigg**er**	bigg**est**	Nach kurzen Vokalen wird der Endkonsonant verdoppelt.
good bad little	**better** **worse** **less**	**best** **worst** **least**	Einige Adjektive haben unregelmäßige Steigerungsformen.
careful difficult	**more** careful **more** difficult	**most** careful **most** difficult	Alle dreisilbigen und mehrsilbigen Adjektive und alle zweisilbigen Adjektive, die nicht auf -er, -le, -y, -ow enden, werden mit *more* und *most* gesteigert.
careful difficult	**less** careful **less** difficult	**least** careful **least** difficult	Eine Verminderung der Adjektive ist mit *less* und *least* möglich.

Verwendung

In town centres walking is often **as fast as** going by car.	Gleichheit wird mit *as … as* ausgedrückt.
Travelling by plane is **faster than** travelling by train. Travelling by car is **more expensive than** walking.	Ungleichheit kann mit Hilfe des Komparativs und *than* ausgedrückt werden.
A bicycle is **not so expensive as** (isn't **as expensive as**) a car. A bicycle is **less expensive than** a car.	Eine andere Form Ungleichheit auszudrücken, ist *not so … as* oder umgangssprachlich *not as … as*. Wie im Deutschen kann man auch „weniger als" verwenden.
The Concorde was **the fastest** airliner from Paris to New York.	Der Superlativ wird nur benutzt, wenn mehr als zwei Dinge miteinander verglichen werden.

7 Adjective and adverb
Adjektiv und Adverb

Form

Adjective	Adverb	
cheap	cheap**ly**	Das Adverb wird gebildet aus Adjektiv + *-ly*.
lazy	laz**ily**	*-y* wird zu *-ily*
horrible	horrib**ly**	*-le* wird zu *-ly*
economic	econom**ically**	*-ic* wird zu *-ically*
fast good	**fast** **well**	Einige Adverbien bilden unregelmäßige Formen.

Adjective	Adverb	Adverb	
late	**late** (spät)	**lately** (in letzter Zeit)	Einige Adverbien bilden mehrere Formen.
hard	**hard** (hart)	**hardly** (kaum)	
near	**near** (nah)	**nearly** (beinahe)	

Steigerung von Adverbien

quickly carefully	more quickly more carefully	most quickly most carefully	Alle abgeleiteten Adverbien auf -ly werden mit *more* und *most* gesteigert.
well badly fast	better worse faster	best worst fastest	Unregelmäßige Adverbien haben eigene Steigerungsformen.

Verwendung

There are many **new computers** on the market. **They** are still **expensive**.	Adjektive beziehen sich auf Nomen oder Pronomen.
We can't **control** the technology **exactly**. Comics are **really popular** with children. Modern computers work **extremely quickly**. **Fortunately, she e-mailed the information to me in time.**	Adverbien beziehen sich auf Verben, … Adjektive, … Adverbien, … und ganze Sätze.
He **felt nervous** about his new job.	Nach Verben, die einen Zustand beschreiben (z. B. *feel, look* (= aussehen), *smell, taste, sound, be, become, get, seem, appear, keep*) folgt ein Adjektiv.

8 Word order with adverbs and adverbials
Wortstellung bei Adverbien und adverbialen Bestimmungen (a. B.)

Die folgenden Satzstellungen sind üblich.

At nine o'clock he caught the bus **to work.**	Adverbien / a. B. der Zeit stehen am Anfang oder Ende des Satzes. Adverbien / a. B. des Ortes stehen in der Regel am Ende des Satzes.
Mr Woods **always** travels to work by train. He has **never** missed a train in his life. The train arrives **punctually**.	Adverbien / a. B. der Häufigkeit (z. B. *never*, *sometimes*, *often*, *usually*, *always*) stehen vor dem Vollverb. Adverbien / a. B. der Art und Weise stehen in der Regel nach dem Verb (den Verben).
The bus drove **slowly** through **London during the rush hour**.	Treten mehrere Adverbien / a. B. zur gleichen Zeit auf, gilt die Regel: Art und Weise vor Ort und Zeit.

9 Some or any?

Verwendung

I need **some** help with this program. **Some** newspapers in Britain only appear on Sundays.	in Aussagesätzen vor unbestimmten Mengen (etwas) oder Anzahlen (einige)
They didn't make **any** money with the new campaign. Some TV stations do not show **any** adverts.	in verneinten Sätzen vor unbestimmten Mengen oder Anzahlen (kein oder keine)
Have they done **any** research on the new product? Have you got **any** ideas for a new logo?	in Fragesätzen vor unbestimmten Mengen (etwas) oder Anzahlen (welche?)
Would you like me to show you **some** examples?	in Fragesätzen, wenn sie eine Aufforderung, Bitte oder ein Angebot enthalten und wenn die Antwort „ja" erwartet wird.
We never needed **any** electronic devices in the past.	nach Wörtern mit negativer Bedeutung

10 Some/any + -one/-body/-thing/-where

Somebody wants to see you. We haven't been **anywhere** this weekend. Have you got **anything** to say?	Die Regeln zum Gebrauch von *some* und *any* gelten auch für diese Formen.

11 Much – many – a lot of

Form

much **a lot of**	viel	nicht zählbar
many **a lot of**	viele	zählbar

Verwendung

He spends **a lot of** time practising his communication skills. **A lot of** (many) people have computers in their homes.	In Aussagesätzen wird in der Regel *a lot of* bevorzugt.
I don't have **a lot of/much** money to spend on computers. There aren't **a lot of/many** experts on the staff.	In verneinten Sätzen kann man beide Formen gebrauchen.
How **much** money do you earn? How **many** adverts did they show? They spend too **much** time in front of the screen.	Nach *how* und *too* muss *much* oder *many* stehen.

12 Little/a little – few/a few

Form

We had **little** help during our training. John had only **a little** time to explain. Last week I spent **less** money than the week before. His latest film made the **least** money.	wenig ein bisschen weniger am wenigsten	unzählbar
Few computers never break down. There are **a few** good adverts on TV. There are **fewer** cars on the roads on Sundays. **The fewest** immigrants are from Norway.	wenige ein paar weniger die wenigsten	zählbar

13 Modal auxiliaries
Modale Hilfsverben

Form

Modale Form	Ersatzform	Bedeutung
must	**have to**	müssen
can	**be able to**	können
can	**be allowed to**	dürfen
mustn't **can't**	**not be allowed to**	nicht dürfen
can't	**not be able to**	nicht können
needn't	**not have to**	nicht brauchen/nicht müssen

Verwendung

Cars **must/have to** stop when the lights are red. You **needn't/don't have to** pay in that car park. John **can't/isn't able to** find a parking space.	In der Gegenwart kann entweder die modale Form oder die Ersatzform benutzt werden.
We **had to** turn right at the traffic lights. He **didn't have to** wait as the lights were green. Jane **couldn't/wasn't allowed to** leave her car outside the house, as there was a "No Parking" sign.	Mit Ausnahme von *could* oder *couldn't* können die modalen Hilfsverben keine anderen Zeiten bilden. Für die anderen Zeiten werden die Ersatzformen verwendet.
You **should** go home now. There **may** be some rain today. You **might** even lose your job.	Für einige modale Hilfsverben gibt es keine genau passenden Ersatzformen.

14 Defining relative clauses
Notwendige Relativsätze

Verwendung

Ein Relativsatz ist notwendig, wenn die darin enthaltene Information nötig ist, um zu erkennen, welche Person oder Sache gemeint ist.

The man **who/that** is getting on the bus is on his way to the office. The boy **who/that** was on the platform was waiting for a friend.	Bei Personen werden die Relativpronomen *who* oder *that* verwendet.
The bus **which/that** is at the lights is going to London. The train **which/that** is leaving right now is heading for Bristol.	Bei Sachen wird *which* oder *that* verwendet.
He greeted the man **(who)** he saw on the platform. He read the paper **(which)** he had bought that morning.	Wenn das Relativpronomen Objekt des Relativsatzes ist, kann es weggelassen werden.
The woman **whose** name I always forget is coming to see us.	*Whose* (dessen/deren) wird als possessives Relativpronomen gebraucht.

15 Non-defining relative clauses
Nicht notwendige Relativsätze

Verwendung

Ein Relativsatz ist nicht notwendig, wenn die darin enthaltene Information nicht nötig ist, um zu erkennen, welche Person oder Sache gemeint ist.

Henry's wife, **who is 58**, was waiting for him at the station.	Ein Relativsatz wird durch Kommas vom Hauptsatz getrennt.
The train, **which was an Intercity**, left punctually.	*that* darf hier nicht verwendet werden.
Henry, **who I met at the station**, is retiring next week.	In nicht-notwendigen Relativsätzen darf das Relativpronomen nicht entfallen.

The Tenses
Die Zeiten

16 Present simple

Form

I/you/we/they he/she/it	**live** **lives**	in Leeds.	Aussage
I/you/we/they he/she/it	**do not (don't) live** **does not (doesn't) live**	in Birmingham.	Verneinung

Do **Does**	I/you/we/they he/she/it	**(not)**	**live**	in Liverpool?	(verneinte) Frage
Why Why	**do** you **does** she	**(not)** **(not)**	**work** **like**	on Saturdays? baseball?	

Besonderheiten

Who **How many students**	**likes** **live**	basketball? at home?	Ist das Fragewort Subjekt oder Teil des Subjekts, wird *do/does* nicht verwendet.

Besonderheiten bei der Schreibung der s-Endung

watch, kiss	watch**es**, kiss**es**	*-es* nach Zischlauten
carry, try	carr**ies**, tr**ies**	*-ies*, wenn die Endung *-y* in der Grundform hinter einem Konsonanten steht
go, do	go**es**, do**es**	Ausnahmen beachten!

Verwendung

She **has** a brother.	bei einem Dauerzustand
She **(usually) goes** to college by bus. He **(often) helps** at home.	bei regelmäßigen oder wiederholten Handlungen (oft mit Häufigkeitsadverbien wie *usually, normally, often, sometimes, never, always* – sogenannte *tense markers*)
She **doesn't smoke**.	bei Gewohnheiten
He **has** a flat in Mayfield. I **think** that this **is** a good idea.	bei bestimmten Verben, wenn sie einen Zustand beschreiben, z. B. *be, have, look, think, see, know, like, want*
The train **arrives** at 8 o'clock tomorrow morning.	bei Fahrplänen und Veranstaltungsprogrammen (mit Zukunftsbezug)

17 Present continuous

Form

I you/we/they he/she/it	**am** **are** **is**	**(not)**	**reading** a book.	Aussage und Verneinung
Am **Are** **Is**	I you/we/they he/she/it	**(not)**	**reading** a magazine?	Frage und verneinte Frage Die Kurzform der Verneinung wird mit *aren't* und *isn't* gebildet.

Besonderheiten bei der Schreibung

come, take	com**ing**, tak**ing**	*-e* entfällt
sit, run	sit**t**ing, run**n**ing	Verdoppelung der Konsonanten am Wortende nach kurzen Vokalen

Verwendung

They **are talking** about their courses.	bei Handlungen, die im Moment des Sprechens stattfinden
She **is studying** for her exam this year. She **is working** at home today.	bei Handlungen, die vorübergehend stattfinden, nicht aber unbedingt im Augenblick
She **is having** a good time. A lot of people **are thinking** about their future.	bei bestimmten Verben (siehe *present simple*), wenn sie eine vorübergehende Handlung und keinen Zustand beschreiben
I **am meeting** him tomorrow.	bei zukünftigen Handlungen (mit Zeitbestimmung)
Some students **are always complaining**.	zur gefühlsbetonten Darstellung von Handlungen in Verbindung mit *always*

18 Past simple

Form

She You	work**ed** need**ed**	in Glasgow a new car.	last year.	Aussagen Grundform + -ed (Infinitiv)

Besonderheiten

mov**e**	mov**ed**	stummes -e entfällt
tr**y**	tr**ied**	Konsonant + y wird zu ie
sto**p**	sto**pped**	Lautverdopplung
go meet	**went** **met**	unregelmäßige Verben haben besondere Formen für das *simple past* dabei wird die 2. Form verwendet

He We	**did not** **(didn't)**	**need** **lose**	special software. the money.	Verneinung

Did	you they it	**(not)**	**move** **live** **take**	to Glasgow? in Birmingham? more than six months?	(verneinte) Frage
Why did	he	**(not)**	**stop**	in Liverpool?	

Verwendung

Jane **moved** to Glasgow seven years ago. First she **worked** for a computer company.	bei Handlungen zu einem bestimmten Zeitpunkt oder in einem abgeschlossenen Zeitraum in der Vergangenheit (oft mit einer Zeitbestimmung wie z. B. *yesterday, last year, in 1988, … ago, from … until – tense markers*)

19 Past continuous

Form

I/He/She/It	**was**	**(not)** **(wasn't)**	**standing**	on the platform.	(verneinte) Aussage
We/You/They	**were**	**(not)** **(weren't)**			

Verwendung

As/while he **was driving** to the airport, it started to rain. A lot of passengers **were waiting** at the counter when Jason went into the bank.	Für eine Handlung, die schon im Gange war, als eine neue Handlung eintrat, wird die Verlaufsform verwendet.
While **I was reading** a book, my friend **was writing** a letter.	Bei gleichzeitigem Verlauf zweier Handlungen steht die Verlaufsform in beiden Fällen.
What **did** you **do** when Susan **came** in? When she **came** in **I put down** my newspaper and talked to her.	Für Handlungen, die nacheinander stattfanden, wird in beiden Fällen *past simple* benutzt.

20 Present perfect simple

Form

I/You/We/They	**have**	**(not)** **(haven't)**	**had** a car for three years.	(verneinte) Aussage *have/has* + 3. Form
He/She/It	**has**	**(not)** **(hasn't)**	**sold** 20 million CDs. **been** to Scotland.	
Have	I/you/we/they	**(not)**	**made** a loss? **taken** a photo? **been** here?	(verneinte) Frage
Has	he/she/it			

Verwendung

I **have repaired** the car.	bei Handlungen in der Vergangenheit ohne Zeitangabe – das Ergebnis ist oft wichtiger als die Zeitangabe
They **have sold** 50,000 cars **up till now**.	mit Zeitbestimmungen, die einen Zeitraum beschreiben, der noch andauert, z. B. *today, this week, so far, in the last ten years – tense markers*
He has **already paid** the bill.	mit bestimmten Adverbien wie z. B. *ever, never, always, yet, just, already – tense markers*
How long have you **known** about this particular book? The Browns **have lived** there **for** over three years. We **have lived** here **since** 2006.	bei nicht abgeschlossenen Zuständen mit *how long, since* und *for* – *since* bezieht sich dabei auf einen Zeitpunkt, *for* auf einen Zeitraum Im Deutschen wird hier das Präsens verwendet, z. B. Wir leben hier seit 2006.

21 Present perfect continuous

Form

I/you/we/they	**have**	**been standing.**	*Present simple* von *have* + *been* + *-ing*-Form

Verwendung

How long have you been waiting? I've been waiting … – for half an hour. – since ten o'clock.	bei Handlungen, die in der Vergangenheit begonnen haben und noch andauern – meist in Verbindung mit *how long, since, for* Im Deutschen wird hier das Präsens verwendet – z. B. Ich warte schon seit 10 Uhr.

22 Past perfect simple

Form

I/You/He/She/ It/We/They	**had**	**(not)** **(-n't)**	**travelled** to Paris.	(verneinte) Aussage

Verwendung

After he **had arrived** at the hotel, he went to his room. When **I** arrived at the station, the ticket office **had** already **closed**.	für Handlungen oder Zustände, die vor einem Zeitpunkt in der Vergangenheit abgeschlossen waren

23 Future with 'going to'

Form

I He/She/It We/You/They	**am ('m)** **is ('s)** **are ('re)**	**(not)**	**going to** watch TV.	(verneinte) Aussage
Am **Is** **Are**	I he/she/it we/you/they	**going to have**	a cup of coffee?	Frage

Verwendung

She **is going to answer** the phone.	bei Absichten und Vorhaben
That fax machine **is going to break** down.	bei Vorhersagen, die aufgrund bereits bekannter Fakten oder bisheriger Erfahrungen sicher oder logischerweise in Erfüllung gehen müssen

24 Will-future

Form

I/You/He/She/It We/They	**will** **will not (won't)**	**use** alternative energy. **waste** water.	Aussage Verneinung
Will	I/you/he/she/it we/they	**use** talking computers?	Frage

Verwendung

Computers **will probably do** most of the work.	bei Vorhersagen mit *hope/suppose/expect* und *probably*
Just a minute, **I'll help** you with your shopping.	bei Entscheidungen, die im Moment des Sprechens getroffen werden
I'll phone you tomorrow, I promise.	bei Versprechen
Will you **make** some coffee, please?	um eine Bitte auszudrücken

25 Question tags
Frageanhängsel

Form

Aussagesatz	Frageanhängsel	
You can drive, Pollution is increasing, Trams will improve our public transport service,	**can't you?** **isn't it?** **won't they?**	Das Hilfsverb wird in dem Frageanhängsel wiederholt. Ist der Aussagesatz positiv, so wird das Frageanhängsel verneint.
Statistics aren't always correct,	**are they?**	Ist der Aussagesatz verneint, so wird das Frageanhängsel bejaht.
We enjoyed the journey, She usually goes to Britain,	**didn't we?** **doesn't she?**	Wenn der Aussagesatz kein Hilfsverb enthält, wird das Frageanhängsel mit *to do* in der Zeit des Aussagesatzes gebildet.

Verwendung

Frageanhängsel werden verwendet:

Air travel is really comfortable, **isn't it?**	beim Wunsch nach Bestätigung
You didn't walk here, **did you?**	bei Überraschung
Oh, it's not another traffic jam, **is it?**	bei Verärgerung
Well, that's a really new idea, **isn't it?**	bei ironischen Aussagen

26 Reported speech
Indirekte Rede

Form

Bei Aussagen ändern sich die Zeitformen, wenn das einleitende Verb in der Vergangenheit steht.

"We are protesting about pollution." → Harry said they **were protesting** about pollution. "He doesn't buy cans." → June told me he **didn't buy** cans.	*Present tenses* werden zu *past tenses*.
"Watson's opened four supermarkets in 2008." → Fred pointed out that Watson's **had opened** four supermarkets in 2008. "They have started a bus service." → He added that they **had started** a bus service.	*Simple past* und *present perfect* werden zu *past perfect*.
"There will be more 'green' products." → Sue went on to say that there **would be** more 'green' products.	*will* wird zu *would*.

Weitere Änderungen bei Aussagen

"I can save more energy." → Harry told me that **he** could save more energy.	Die Pronomen werden angepasst.
"We are meeting the town planner tomorrow." → Sue added that they were meeting the town planner **the next day**. "I bought the car three days ago." → He said that he had bought the car **three days before**.	Orts- (z. B. *here* wird zu *there*) und Zeitbestimmungen werden angepasst.

Fragen

"What are you doing about waste?" → **They asked what we were doing** about waste. "When did you introduce bicycle routes?" → **We wanted to know when they had introduced** bicycle routes.	Bei Fragen wird die Wortstellung geändert.

Verwendung

Indirekte Rede wird benutzt, wenn berichtet werden soll, was jemand gesagt oder gefragt hat.

27 Conditionals
Bedingungssätze

Form

Typ 1

If-Satz	Hauptsatz	
If **we fit** a shower, If **you go** to Paris,	**we will** save water. **you can** see the Eiffel Tower.	*Present simple* wird für das Verb im If-Satz, Futur mit *will* für das Verb im Hauptsatz verwendet.
If **you want** to stay alive,	don't drink and drive!	Im Hauptsatz kann in manchen Fällen ein modales Hilfsverb mit Verb oder ein Imperativ stehen.

Typ 2

If-Satz	Hauptsatz	
If the government **developed** solar energy,	there **would be** less pollution.	*Past simple* wird für das Verb im If-Satz, *Conditional I (would)* für das Verb im Hauptsatz verwendet.
If I **were** Environment Minister,	I **could** put my ideas about energy into practice.	*could* oder *might* sind Alternativen zu *would* im Hauptsatz.

Typ 3

If-Satz	Hauptsatz	
If Tom and Kate **had insulated** their roof years ago,	they **would have saved** a lot of money.	*Past perfect* wird für das Verb im If-Satz, *Conditional II (would have)* für das Verb im Hauptsatz verwendet.

Verwendung

Typ 1 wird verwendet, wenn es sich um eine erfüllbare Bedingung in der Gegenwart oder Zukunft handelt: "Was passiert / wird passieren, wenn …?"

Typ 2 wird verwendet, wenn es sich um eine unerfüllbare Bedingung in der Gegenwart handelt: "Was würde passieren, wenn …?"

Typ 3 wird verwendet, wenn über eine nicht mehr erfüllbare Bedingung in der Vergangenheit gesprochen wird: "Was wäre passiert, wenn …?"

28 Passive voice
Passiv

Form

The robots **are equipped** with sensors. This motor **was not made** in Great Britain. **Will** the new car **be sold** in Japan?	Form von *be* in der jeweiligen Zeit + Partizip Perfekt (3. Form) des Verbs
Now the wheels **can be fitted**. The car **must be tested** first.	Bei der Benutzung von Hilfsverben wird das Hilfsverb + *be* + Partizip Perfekt (3. Form) des Verbs verwendet.

Verwendung

These cars **were made** in Germany. The handbook **is written** in English.	hauptsächlich in der Schriftsprache, wenn der Ausführende unbekannt, unwichtig oder selbstverständlich ist
This information **is checked by** the central computer.	Wenn der Ausführende allerdings genannt werden soll, dann benutzt man die Präposition *by (by-agent)*.
It is said **It is reported** **It is believed** **It is supposed** that computers will become even more important in the future. **He is said** to be rich.	bei Verben des Meinens und Berichtens
English **is spoken** here. = Man spricht Englisch. We **will be told** the result later. = Man wird uns später das Ergebnis sagen.	Im Deutschen wird ein Aktivsatz mit ‚man' bevorzugt.

29 Infinitive
Infinitiv

Verwendung

ohne *to*

We **must write** a report about our trip to England.	nach den meisten Hilfsverben
Our new teachers **make us work** very hard, but on Friday they **let us go** home early.	nach *make* und *let* + direktem Objekt

mit *to*

The teacher **asked me to show** my photos of Newcastle. She **told them to wait** outside for a moment.	nach bestimmten Verben (*ask/tell/advise/expect* etc.)
This is not **easy to understand**. I am **surprised to hear** that.	nach Adjektiven
I do not know **what to do**.	nach Fragewörtern

30 Gerund
Gerundium

Verwendung

Drinking and **driving** is dangerous.	als Subjekt
I **enjoy swimming.**	als Objekt nach Verben ohne Präpositionen, wenn eine allgemeingültige Situation beschrieben wird: z. B. *enjoy/like/dislike/hate/stop/start/avoid/suggest/mind/love/recommend/prefer*
I **look forward to seeing** you again. He is **tired of waiting** here. They saw the **danger of destroying** the environment.	nach Verben/Adjektiven/Substantiven mit Präpositionen
He has helped me a lot **by giving** me that map of Newcastle. The child crossed the road **without looking**.	nach Präpositionen mit adverbialer Bedeutung, z. B. *by/without/instead of*
Normally I enjoy swimming but today I **would prefer to play** tennis. I **remember learning** those rules. = *Ich erinnere mich daran, dass ich die Regeln gelernt habe.* I **must remember to learn** these rules. = *Ich muss daran denken, diese Regeln zu lernen.*	Statt des Gerundiums wird der Infinitiv verwendet, wenn es sich um eine Ausnahmesituation handelt (oft mit *would*) oder wenn die Bedeutung des Satzes die Verwendung des Gerundiums nicht zulässt, z. B. bei *stop/start/remember*.
After talking to the press they started their demonstration.	als Verkürzung von Adverbialsätzen *(after/before)*

31 Participle
Partizip

Form

Es gibt zwei Formen des Partizips.

waiting/going/watching	Partizip Präsens
waited/gone/watched	Partizip Perfekt

Verwendung

The weather forecast for the **coming** week … The weather in New York last week was rather **mixed**.	als Adjektiv
You can find several families **living** in one flat. There are a lot of restaurants there especially **built** for the tourists.	anstelle von Relativsätzen
While talking to his children the minister wrote a note to his secretary. **Feeling tired** the President lay down for a rest.	als Verkürzung von Adverbialsätzen *(while/when/because/as)*

Online-Link
808201-1000

Unit vocabulary

Videotraining: Englische Aussprache

Perfekte englische Aussprache leicht gemacht: Mit dem Lernprogramm zur englischen Lautschrift können Sie alle Laute einüben. Wählen Sie einfach in der Navigation rechts den entsprechenden Reiter (*Vowels* oder *Consonants*) aus und dann klicken Sie auf das gewünschte phonetische Symbol. Sprechen Sie die Wörter laut nach.
Unter www.klett.de geben Sie einfach den Online-Link 808201-1000 ein. Von dort aus können Sie die Webanwendung online starten.

Abkürzungen und Zeichen

etw.	=	etwas	
pl	=	Plural	
s.o.	=	someone	
s.th.	=	something	
BE	=	britisches Englisch	
AE	=	amerikanisches Englisch	

=	entspricht
↔	ist das Gegenteil von
→	verwandt mit
blue	Vokabel aus Hörtext

Vor den Vokabeln finden Sie immer die jeweiligen Übungsnummer.

1 Young people in Europe

A	**above** [ə'bʌv]	oben, über	above = over. There's a nice picture above the table in Becky's room.
	impression [ɪm'preʃn]	Eindruck	She has made a good impression.
	blog [blɒg]	Internet-Tagebuch	a diary on the Internet
	statement ['steɪtmənt]	Aussage	to make a statement = to say something
	current ['kʌrənt]	aktuell	The current situation is difficult.
	part-time job [ˌpɑːt‿taɪm 'dʒɒb]	Teilzeitjob	part-time job ↔ full-time job
	below [bɪ'ləʊ]	unten, unter(halb)	below = under. The TV magazine is on the shelf below the TV. Look, down there!
	mum [mʌm]	Mutter, Mama	mum *(BE)* → mom *(AE)*
	National Diploma [ˌnæʃənl dɪ'pləʊmə]	2-jährige Schulzeit am College	National Diploma of sport
	to finance ['faɪnæns]	finanzieren	My dad paid for our trip to Hawaii, so he financed it.
	technician [tek'nɪʃn]	Techniker(in)	technician → technical → technology
	to attend [ə'tend]	teilnehmen	to take part
	IT [ˌaɪ'tiː]	Informationstechnik	information technology
	full-time [ˌfʊl'taɪm]	Vollzeit	full-time ↔ part-time
	to achieve [ə'tʃiːv]	erreichen	If you work hard and are ambitious, you can achieve a lot.
	musician [mjuː'zɪʃn]	Musiker(in)	musician → music → musical
	guy [gaɪ]	Typ	Our new classmate is a really cool guy.
	general ['dʒenrəl]	allgemein	Do you want details or just general information?
	to chill out [tʃɪl‿'aʊt]	sich entspannen	to relax

	style [staɪl]	Stil	Do you like this style? It's very cool this year.
	social care [ˌsəʊʃl 'keə]	Sozialwissenschaft, Sozialwesen	People who really care about people often study social care.
	campaigning [kæm'peɪnɪŋ]	Aktionen; Wahlkampf führen	campaigning → campaign
	primary school ['praɪmərɪ ˌsku:l]	Grundschule	the first school you go to
	environmental [ɪnˌvaɪərən'mentl]	Umwelt-	environment → environmental
	pet [pet]	Haustier	A typical pet is a dog or a cat.
	chicken ['tʃɪkɪn]	Huhn	a farm bird
	concerning [kən'sɜ:nɪŋ]	betreffend, bezüglich	regarding
	aim [eɪm]	Ziel	My aim is to get really good at basketball.
	dislike ['dɪslaɪk]	Abneigung	What are your likes and dislikes? = What do you like and what don't you like?
	personality [ˌpɜ:sn'ælətɪ]	Persönlichkeit	personality → person
	social networking website [ˌsəʊʃl 'netwɜ:kɪŋ ˌwebsaɪt]	Internetseite für ein soziales Netzwerk	Examples are: MySpace, StudiVZ, Twitter
B 1	**leaver** ['li:və]	Schulabgänger(in)	The student left school. He is a school leaver.
	adult ['ædʌlt]	Erwachsene(r)	Tickets cost $3 for children (under 18) and $5 for adults.
	science [saɪəns]	Wissenschaft, Naturwissenschaft	*Achtung Aussprache: Das erste ‚c' wird nicht gesprochen.*
	Biology [baɪ'ɒlədʒɪ]	Biologie	You learn about animals and trees in Biology lessons.
	Physics ['fɪzɪks]	Physik	Science = Biology, Chemistry, Physics
	Geography [dʒɪ'ɒgrəfɪ]	Geographie	In Geography lessons we learn about different countries.
	project ['prɒdʒekt]	Projekt, Vorhaben	I'm busy with the school project.
	presentation [prezn'teɪʃn]	Präsentation	We've got lots of information for our presentation to the class.
	essay ['eseɪ]	Aufsatz	In school I had to write an essay about why children are not allowed to smoke.
	term [tɜ:m]	Trimester, Begriff, Bedingung	In Britain, one of the three periods of time between the school holidays: the autumn term, the spring term and the summer term.
	placement ['pleɪsmənt]	Praktikum, Platzierung, Vertriebspolitik	During a work placement you can see if you like the job.
	prompt [prɒmpt]	Stichwort	keyword
	website ['websaɪt]	Website, Internetseite	You can find lots of information about London on the website.
B 3	**lunchtime** ['lʌntʃtaɪm]	Mittagszeit	lunchtime → lunch
	normally ['nɔ:məlɪ]	normalerweise	usually, regularly
C	**nationality** [ˌnæʃn'ælətɪ]	Nationalität	nationality → national
	cosmopolitan atmosphere [kɒsməˌpɒlɪtn 'ætməsfɪə]	weltoffene Atmosphäre	New York City has a cosmopolitan atmosphere because of the different cultures living there.
	multicultural [ˌmʌltɪ'kʌltʃərəl]	multikulturell	London and New York are multicultural cities.
	cleaner ['kli:nə]	Raumpfleger(in)	a cleaner → to clean
	chef [ʃef]	Koch, Köchin	A false friend: *der Chef* = the boss; *der Koch* = the chef
	to socialize ['səʊʃəlaɪz]	ausgehen	If you socialize, you go out with or meet your friends.
	to settle ['setl]	einleben	I have just moved here. I still have not settled in.
	suitable ['su:təbl]	geeignet	Warm jackets and thick shoes are suitable for cold weather.
	fashion designer ['fæʃn dɪˌzaɪnə]	Modeschöpfer(in)	Paris and New York are the best places for fashion designers to study.
	salesperson ['seɪlzˌpɜ:sn]	Verkäufer(in)	A salesperson can be a salesman or saleswoman.
	architect ['ɑ:kɪtekt]	Architekt(in)	An architect plans and designs buildings.
	to install [ɪn'stɔ:l]	installieren	to put a new thing in its place
	journalist ['dʒɜ:nəlɪst]	Journalist(in)	A journalist writes for a newspaper.
	to interview ['ɪntəvju:]	befragen	The journalist interviewed Brad Pitt about his latest movie.
	role [rəʊl]	Rolle	Brad Pitt plays a role in the new film.
	country of origin [ˌkʌntrɪ‿əv 'ɒrɪdʒɪn]	Herkunftsland	Your country of origin is the country you were born in.
	workplace ['wɜ:kpleɪs]	Arbeitsplatz	workplace → work → worker → to work

D 1	**sales talk** ['seɪlz ˌtɔ:k]	Verkaufsgespräch	The salesman is very good at sales talk: he sells a lot of products.
	top [tɒp]	Top, Oberteil	Hannah wore her new top last night.
	salad ['sæləd]	Salat	Would you like vegetables or a green salad?
	right-hand ['raɪthænd]	rechtsseitig, rechts stehend	In Germany the cars drive on the right-hand side of the road.
	the background [ðə 'bækgraʊnd]	der Hintergrund	You can see mountains in the background of the picture.
	left-hand ['lefthænd]	linksseitig, links stehend	In England the cars drive on the left-hand side of the road.
	foreground ['fɔ:graʊnd]	Vordergrund	foreground ↔ background
	to scream [skri:m]	schreien	Don't scream at me!
	to consist of [kən'sɪst ɒv]	bestehen aus	to be made up of
	to get changed [get‿'tʃeɪndʒd]	sich umziehen	It is getting warmer. I think I will get changed and put a T-shirt on.
	to take orders [teɪk 'ɔ:dəz]	Bestellungen entgegennehmen	The waiter took our orders. We wanted some cake and tea.
	tip [tɪp]	Tipp, Hinweis, Spitze, Trinkgeld	Before you leave a café or restaurant, you normally leave a tip.
D 2	**corresponding** [ˌkɒrɪ'spɒndɪŋ]	entsprechend, zugehörig	similar, comparable, like
	lifestyle ['laɪfstaɪl]	Lebensstil	the way you live your life
	subculture ['sʌbˌkʌltʃə]	Subkultur	A subculture is a culture within a culture.
	behaviour [bɪ'heɪvjə]	Verhalten	behaviour → to behave
	attitude ['ætɪtju:d]	Haltung	Your attitude to/towards life is the way you feel about it.
	scene [si:n]	Szene, Kulisse	This is a very quiet scene in the play, nothing much is happening.
	identity [aɪ'dentətɪ]	Identität	Your true identity is who you really are.

2 Getting a job

A 1	**personnel** [ˌpɜ:sən'el]	Personal	The personnel manager looks for the right person for the right job.
	manufacturing [ˌmænjə'fæktʃərɪŋ]	Herstellung	manufacturing → to manufacture
	research [rɪ'sɜ:tʃ]	Forschung	research → to research
	to operate ['ɒpəreɪt]	bedienen	If you operate a machine, you make it do its work.
	raw material [ˌrɔ: mə'tɪərɪəl]	Rohstoff	Germany must import a lot of its raw materials.
	recipe ['resɪpɪ]	Rezept	I have a good recipe for chocolate cookies.
	sweet [swi:t]	Süßigkeit	The children eat too many sweets.
	phrase [freɪz]	Ausdruck	'Good' is a word, 'be good at' is a phrase.
	brand [brænd]	Marke	The Levis brand is known all over the world.
	headquarters [ˌhed'kwɔ:təz]	Zentrale, Stammsitz	Many international companies have their headquarters in the USA.
	home-made [ˌhəʊm'meɪd]	hausgemacht	Did you buy that cake? – No, it's home-made.
	huge [hju:dʒ]	riesig	very big
	confectionery [kən'fekʃənrɪ]	Süßwaren	sweets and chocolates
	ever since [ˌevə 'sɪns]	seitdem	I've been a fan of Tokio Hotel ever since I heard their first song.
	frozen ['frəʊzn]	gefroren	The lake was frozen in the cold weather.
	business field ['bɪznɪs ˌfi:ld]	Geschäftsbereich	Big companies often operate in different business fields (production, banking, insurance).
	convenience food [kən'vi:nɪəns ˌfu:d]	Fertiggericht	food which is frozen or dried so that it can be cooked easily
A 2	**sharp** [ʃɑ:p]	steil, stark, scharf	sharp → sharply
	steady ['stedɪ]	stetig	steady → steadily
B 1	**to expand** [ɪk'spænd]	(sich) ausdehnen, expandieren	to expand → expansion
	superstore ['su:pəstɔ:]	großer Supermarkt	In a superstore you can buy nearly everything.
	independent [ˌɪndɪ'pendənt]	unabhängig	independent → to depend → independence
	dealer ['di:lə]	Händler(in)	A dealer buys and sells things.
	retailer ['rɪ:teɪlə]	Einzelhändler(in)	A retailer is a person who sells goods to consumers.
	letter ['letə]	Buchstabe	There are four letters in the word 'joke'.

B 3	**yourself** [jɔ:'self]	selbst	You shouldn't talk about yourself all the time.
	fluency ['flu:ənsɪ]	Sprachebeherrschung, Sprachgewandtheit	fluency → fluent
B 4	**bracket** ['brækɪt]	Klammer	These are brackets: ( ).
	chain [tʃeɪn]	Kette	A supermarket chain is a large number of shops that belong to the same person.
	to type [taɪp]	tippen	It's easier to read a text that has been typed than one that has been written by hand.
	loaf of bread [ˌləʊf‿əv 'bred]	Brotlaib	I went to the bakery and bought a loaf of bread.
C	**application** [ˌæplɪ'keɪʃn]	Bewerbung	application → to apply → applicant
	curriculum vitae [kəˌrɪkjələm 'vi:taɪ]	Lebenslauf	curriculum vitae (CV) = résumé
	permanent ['pɜ:mənənt]	dauerhaft	for a longer time
	fluent [flu:ənt]	flüssig	If you are fluent in English, you can speak it easily and well.
	ignorant ['ɪgnərənt]	ignorant	ignorance → to ignore → ignorant
	qualification [ˌkwɒlɪfɪ'keɪʃn]	Qualifikation	If you have a driving licence you have the qualification to be a driver.
	housekeeping ['haʊsˌki:pɪŋ]	Haushaltsführung, Raumpflege	housekeeping → housekeeper
	essential [ɪ'sentʃl]	wichtig	very important
	requirement [rɪ'kwaɪəmənt]	Anforderung	requirement → to require
	with reference to [wɪð 'refrəns tu:]	betreffend, bezüglich	reference → to refer
	advert ['ædvɜ:t]	Anzeige	advert → advertisement
	open-minded [ˌəʊpn'maɪndɪd]	aufgeschlossen, unvoreingenommen	tolerant
	long-term [ˌlɒŋ'tɜ:m]	langfristig	Tomorrow I will do an English test, but in the long term I hope that I will get my GCSEs.
	high-class [ˌhaɪ'klɑ:s]	erstklassig	It is a high-class hotel. You must pay a lot of money to stay there.
	facility [fə'sɪlətɪ]	Einrichtung	All the hotels have great facilities.
	rewarding [rɪ'wɔ:dɪŋ]	lohnend	rewarding → reward
	to enclose [ɪn'kləʊz]	beifügen	When you enclose something, you put it in with the letter you want to send.
	challenge ['tʃælɪndʒ]	Herausforderung	His new job was a real challenge.
	active ['æktɪv]	aktiv	active → action → to act out
	driving licence ['draɪvɪŋ ˌlaɪsəns]	Führerschein	When you have passed your driving test, you are given a driving licence.
D 1	**candidate** ['kændɪdət]	Bewerber(in)	someone who is trying to get a job
	motor mechanic ['məʊtə mɪˌkænɪk]	Kfz-Mechaniker(in)	someone who repairs cars
	nursery school ['nɜ:sərɪ ˌsku:l]	Vorschule	a school for young children between three and five years of age
	bank clerk ['bæŋk‿klɑ:k]	Bankkaufmann/-frau	person who works in a bank
	electrician [ˌelɪk'trɪʃn]	Elektriker(in)	someone who repairs electric equipment
	on offer [ɒn 'ɒfə]	im Angebot	There is 50% off the shoes. They are on offer.
	applicant ['æplɪkənt]	Bewerber(in)	applicant → to apply → application
	catering firm ['keɪtərɪŋ ˌfɜ:m]	Catering-Firma	A catering firm delivers food and drink for a large number of people at a party.
	feature ['fi:tʃə]	Einrichtung, Eigenschaft, Merkmal, Kennzeichen	character, characteristic
	convinced [kən'vɪnst]	überzeugt	sure something is true
	to support [sə'pɔ:t]	unterstützen	If you support people, you agree with them and help them.
D 2	**word web** ['wɜ:d ˌweb]	Wortnetz	a diagram you can make to collect ideas about a topic
	reliable [rɪ'laɪəbl]	zuverlässig	someone you can depend on is reliable
D 3	**plant** [plɑ:nt]	Fabrikanlage	factory

3 The youth market

A 1	**target** ['tɑ:gɪt]	Ziel	aim, goal
A 2	**heading** ['hedɪŋ]	Überschrift	Each part of the article has got a different heading.
	ending ['endɪŋ]	Ende	ending → to end
	lonely ['ləʊnlɪ]	einsam	I'm often alone, but I don't feel lonely.
	cafeteria [kæfə'tɪərɪə]	Kantine, Cafeteria	cafeteria → café
	truthful ['tru:θfəl]	ehrlich	honest
	trainer ['treɪnə]	Turnschuh	running shoe
	similar ['sɪmɪlə]	ähnlich	similar ↔ different; similar → similarly
	logo ['ləʊgəʊ]	Firmenemblem	a design or symbol that a company uses to advertise its products
	tick [tɪk]	Häkchen	Put a tick next to the correct answer.
	stripe [straɪp]	Streifen	The US flag is called 'the stars and stripes'.
	silver ['sɪlvə]	Silber	Rings are made of gold or silver.
	confused [kən'fju:zd]	verwirrt	If you are confused, you do not understand what is happening.
A 3	**no-name product** [ˌnəʊneɪm 'prɒdʌkt]	Billigprodukt, Produkt ohne Markenname	no-name product ↔ branded product
	packaging ['pækɪdʒɪŋ]	Verpackungsmaterial	packaging → to pack
A 4	**consumer** [kən'sju:mə]	Konsument(in), Verbraucher(in)	someone who buys or uses goods or services
	item ['aɪtəm]	Punkt, Gegenstand	thing
	mobile phone [ˌməʊbaɪl 'fəʊn]	Mobiltelefon, Handy	mobile phone *(BE)* = mobile, cellphone *(AE)*. False friend: handy *(English)* = *praktisch (German)*
	cosmetics [kɒz'metɪks]	Kosmetik	make-up
	common ['kɒmən]	gemeinsam, gebräuchlich	What do these boys have in common? – They both play football; common → commonly
B 1	**portrait** ['pɔ:trət]	Portrait, Konterfei	painting or photograph of a person
	art [ɑ:t]	Kunst	Becky likes art at school because she's good at drawing.
	unlimited [ʌn'lɪmɪtɪd]	grenzenlos, unbegrenzt	His knowledge seemed unlimited.
	to try on [traɪ‿'ɒn]	anprobieren	That's a nice T-shirt, Lisa. Why don't you try it on?
	to exchange [ɪks'tʃeɪndʒ]	umtauschen, austauschen	This CD doesn't work. I would like to exchange it.
B 2	**dialogue** ['daɪəlɒg]	Dialog, Gespräch	dialogue *(BE)* = dialog *(AE)*
	underlined [ˌʌndə'laɪnd]	unterstrichen	underlined → to underline
	to act out [ækt 'aʊt]	aufführen	The actor acted out his role perfectly.
B 3	**to drop** [drɒp]	(herunter-)fallen, fallen lassen	to drop → drop (of water)
B 4	**to unpack** [ʌn'pæk]	auspacken	unpack ↔ pack
	commercial [kə'mɜ:ʃl]	Werbespot	During TV shows there are commercials for cars, coffee, mobiles …
C 1	**advertiser** ['ædvətaɪzə]	Inserent(in), Werbefachmann/-frau	advertiser → to advertise → advertisment
	to behave [bɪ'heɪv]	sich benehmen	You're silly! You behave like a little child.
	in particular [ɪn pə'tɪkjʊlə]	im Besonderen	in particular = especially
	at risk [ət 'rɪsk]	gefährdet	at risk → to risk → risk (of death)
	County Council [ˌkaʊntɪ 'kaʊnsəl]	etwa Kreisverwaltung	local government of a county in Britain
	tip [tɪp]	Tipp, Hinweis, Spitze, Trinkgeld	I can give you tips for your trip to England.
	extract ['ekstrækt]	Auszug	An extract from a book is just a small part of the story.
	right [raɪt]	Recht	Children don't have the right to drive cars. It's illegal.
	trader ['treɪdə]	Händler(in)	trader → to trade → trade
	additional [ə'dɪʃənl]	zusätzlich	additional → to add → additionally
	confirmation [ˌkɒnfə'meɪʃn]	Bestätigung	The confirmation comes as an e-mail.
	to cancel ['kænsəl]	absagen	One of the singers was ill, so the concert was cancelled.
	regulation [ˌregjʊ'leɪʃn]	Regelung, Vorschrift	Don't risk accidents, watch the traffic regulations!
	cooling-off period [ˌku:lɪŋ'ɒf ˌpɪərɪəd]	Widerspruchsfrist	Within the cooling-off period the buyer can get his money back.
	auction ['ɔ:kʃn]	Versteigerung	You can buy things cheaply in an auction.

	platform ['plætfɔ:m]	Plattform	The train leaves from platform 3.
	to trust [trʌst]	vertrauen	to trust someone = to believe that someone is honest
	feedback ['fi:dbæk]	Rückmeldung, Feedback	You get feedback when the other person says something about what you said or did.
	to be based [bɪ 'beɪst]	Geschäftssitz haben	Your company is based in London.
	bid [bɪd]	Gebot	an offer to pay a particular sum of money in an auction; bid → to bid
	postage ['pəʊstɪdʒ]	Porto, Postgebühr	If you don't want your letter to come back, put enough postage on it.
	payment ['peɪmənt]	Bezahlung	payment → to pay
	scam [skæm]	Betrug	a banking scam
	text message ['tekst ˌmesɪdʒ]	Textmitteilung, SMS	SMS = short message service
	premium rate number [ˌpri:mɪəmˌreɪt 'nʌmbə]	Sonderrufnummer	At a premium rate of £2.50 you can buy a game for your mobile phone.
	to delete [dɪ'li:t]	löschen	When you type a wrong letter on your PC, you can delete it again.
	ringtone ['rɪŋtəʊn]	Klingelton	My best friend has his favourite song as a ringtone on his mobile phone.
	wallpaper ['wɔ:lˌpeɪpə]	Hintergrundbild, Tapete	My boyfriend has my picture as a wallpaper on his computer screen.
	alert [ə'lɜ:t]	Alarm	a signal that warns of a danger
	short code ['ʃɔ:t ˌkəʊd]	Kurzwahlnummer	To get the latest football news send an SMS with 'football' to the short code 72404.
	to change one's mind [ˌtʃeɪndʒ wʌnz‿'maɪnd]	seine Meinung ändern	I've changed my mind. I don't want to go out with you anymore.
	summary ['sʌmərɪ]	Zusammenfassung	a very short version of a text which gives only the most important points
	certain ['sɜ:tn]	bestimmt, gewiss	If you say you have certain things to do, you mean definite things, but you don't say what they are.
	relevant ['reləvənt]	relevant, bedeutend	relevant ↔ irrelevant
	to purchase ['pɜ:tʃəs]	kaufen	to purchase → a purchase
	local council [ˌləʊkl 'kaʊnsəl]	etwa Gemeinderat	government of a town in Britain
C 2	**contract** ['kɒntrækt]	Vertrag	to agree in a contract *(= einen Vertrag abschließen)*
	to persuade [pə'sweɪd]	überreden	If you want to persuade someone to do something, it's important to find good arguments.
D 1	**slogan** ['sləʊgən]	Slogan, Werbespruch	a short phrase that a company uses to advertise its products
	gender ['dʒendə]	Geschlecht	The gender of a girl is female.
	to create [krɪ'eɪt]	schaffen	to create → creative → creativity
	flyer ['flaɪə]	Flugblatt	flyer → to fly
	expert ['ekspɜ:t]	Experte/Expertin	a person who knows a lot about a subject
	quiet [kwaɪət]	Ruhe	quiet ↔ noise
	cooking ['kʊkɪŋ]	Kochen	cooking → to cook → the cook
	missing ['mɪsɪŋ]	fehlend, vermisst	Not all the letters have arrived. Two are missing.
	crime [kraɪm]	Verbrechen, Kriminalität	Stealing money is a crime.
	to be on [bɪ‿'ɒn]	zu sehen sein (Sendung)	to be shown
	fascinated ['fæsɪneɪtɪd]	fasziniert	fascinated → fascinating → fascination
	climate ['klaɪmət]	Klima	The kind of weather that is typical of a country or an area.
	extreme [ɪk'stri:m]	extrem	Extreme weather means that it is very cold, very hot and/or very windy in an area.
	catastrophic [ˌkætə'strɒfɪk]	katastrophal	catastrophic → catastrophe
	hurricane ['hʌrɪkən]	Wirbelsturm, Hurrikan	Tornados and hurricanes are very bad storms.
	level ['levl]	Niveau, Pegelstand	He plays football at a very high level.
	lifetime ['laɪftaɪm]	Lebensdauer, Lebenszeit, Lebzeiten	as long as a person lives
	planet ['plænɪt]	Planet	The Earth is a planet.

D 2	**agency** ['eɪdʒənsɪ]	Agentur	NASA is the US space agency.
	jingle ['dʒɪŋgl]	Jingle, kurze Tonfolge in der Werbung	a short melody which is easy to remember
	storyline ['stɔ:rɪlaɪn]	Handlung	The movie has a boring storyline.
	script [skrɪpt]	Drehbuch	The actor didn't want to act in the film because he didn't like the script.
	to market ['mɑ:kɪt]	vermarkten, verkaufen	to sell
	promotion [prə'məʊʃn]	Werbung, Promotion	promotion → to promote
	uniqueness [jʊ'ni:knəs]	Einzigartigkeit	uniqueness → unique
	discount ['dɪskaʊnt]	Rabatt, Nachlass	Let's buy this MP3 player, it's really cheap. There's a 50% discount on it!
	billboard ['bɪlbɔ:d]	Plakatwand, Werbetafel	board on which posters and adverts are displayed outdoors
	merchandising ['mɜ:tʃəndaɪzɪŋ]	Verkaufsförderung, Merchandising, Vermarktung	In a merchandising campaign a football club sells products with the club's logo.
	sponsoring ['spɒnsərɪŋ]	Sponsoring, Förderung, finanzielle Unterstützung	A famous beer brand is the sponsor of the tennis championship.
	distribution [ˌdɪstrɪ'bju:ʃn]	Vertrieb, Verteilung	distribution → to distribute
	retailing ['ri:teɪlɪŋ]	Einzelhandel	retailing → to retail → retailer
D 3	**formula** ['fɔ:mjələ]	Formel	You need formulas in mathematics.
	theory ['θɪərɪ]	Theorie	theory ↔ practice
	marketing ['mɑ:kɪtɪŋ]	Marketing	using advertisements etc. in order to sell products
	to attract [ə'trækt]	anziehen	to attract → attraction → attractive
	to analyze ['ænəlaɪz]	analysieren	to examine the details of something carefully, in order to understand or explain it
D 4	**to ban** [bæn]	verbieten	In Germany they have banned smoking in schools.
	representative [ˌreprɪ'zentətɪv]	Vertreter(in)	representative → to represent
	ban [bæn]	Verbot	a ban → to ban

4 Media in our lives

A 1	**bar chart** ['bɑ: ˌtʃɑ:t]	Säulendiagramm, Balkendiagramm	bar graph
A 2	**to tend (to)** [tend]	zu etwas neigen	to tend → tendency
	screen [skri:n]	Bildschirm	TVs and computers have screens.
	monitor ['mɒnɪtə]	Monitor, Bildschirm	You can see pictures or texts on the monitor of a PC.
	electronic [ˌelek'trɒnɪk]	elektronisch	Electronic equipment includes things like televisions, computers etc.
	surprising [sə'praɪzɪŋ]	überraschend	surprising → surprise → to surprise
	educational [ˌedʒʊ'keɪʃnl]	lehrreich, bildend	There's a lot of rubbish on TV, but there are also some educational programmes.
	constant ['kɒnstənt]	beständig, andauernd, konstant	constant → constantly
	average ['ævərɪdʒ]	Durchschnitt	a typical amount
	scientist ['saɪəntɪst]	Wissenschaftler(in)	scientist → science → scientific
	brain [breɪn]	Gehirn	Your brain controls your feelings, and how you think and move.
	to confuse [kən'fju:z]	verwirren	to confuse → confused
	aged [eɪdʒd]	im Alter von	aged → age
	overweight [ˌəʊvə'weɪt]	übergewichtig	overweight → weight → to weigh
	dramatic [drə'mætɪk]	dramatisch	dramatic → drama
	conclusion [kən'klu:ʒn]	Schlussfolgerung	conclusion → to conclude
	to summarize ['sʌməraɪz]	zusammenfassen	to summarize → summary
	consequence ['kɒnsɪkwəns]	Konsequenz, Folge	the result of something
	to affect [ə'fekt]	auswirken, beeinflussen	to influence
B 1	**to influence** ['ɪnflʊəns]	beeinflussen	to influence → the influence
B 2	**messaging service** ['mesɪdʒɪŋ ˌsɜ:vɪs]	Dienst zur Versendung von (Sofort-)Nachrichten	ICQ and Skype are instant messaging services.
	browser ['braʊzə]	Browser	a computer program that helps to find and read documents on the Internet

	icon ['aɪkɒn]	Icon, Symbol, Bildschirmsymbol	You find icons for the computer programs on the desktop.
	to click [klɪk]	klicken	to press for a short time
	desktop ['desktɒp]	Desktop, Benutzeroberfläche	the background image on your computer screen
B 3	**managing director** [ˌmænɪdʒɪŋ dɪ'rektə]	Geschäftsführer(in), Mitglied der Geschäftsführung	managing director → to manage → management
	telecommunications [ˌtelɪkəˌmju:nɪ'keɪʃnz]	Telekommunikation	communications → to communicate
	to go ahead [ˌgəʊ‿ə'hed]	fortfahren	to continue
	to secure [sɪ'kjʊə, sɪ'kjɔ:]	absichern, bewirken, schützen	to secure → security
	mobile ['məʊbaɪl]	mobil, beweglich	mobile → mobile phone
	web [web]	Netz	*(short form of)* World Wide Web
	server ['sɜ:və]	Server, zentrale Einheit im Netzwerk	server → to serve → service
	to update [ʌp'deɪt]	aktualisieren	The server needed to have the latest software so I updated it.
	innovation [ˌɪnəʊ'veɪʃn]	Neuerung	innovation → to innovate
B 4	**button** ['bʌtn]	Knopf, Taste	It's easy to take a picture – just press the button.
	to download ['daʊnləʊd]	herunterladen	You can download interesting information from the Internet.
	file [faɪl]	Datei, Hefter, Akte	Don't forget to save the file!
	wireless ['waɪələs]	drahtlos	WLAN = wireless local area network
	to steal [sti:l]	stehlen	Robin Hood stole money from rich people and gave it to poor families.
	recyclable [ˌri:'saɪkləbl]	wiederverwertbar, wiederverwendbar	recyclable → to recycle → recycling
	harmful ['hɑ:mfəl]	schädlich, nachteilig	damaging, bad
	toxic ['tɒksɪk]	giftig	poisonous
	to print [prɪnt]	drucken	to print → printer
	complicated ['kɒmplɪkeɪtɪd]	kompliziert	not easy, difficult
	whereas [weə'ræz]	während	People can think for themselves, whereas a computer cannot.
	publishing date ['pʌblɪʃɪŋ ˌdeɪt]	Veröffentlichungsdatum	publishing date → to publish → publication
C	**according to** [ə'kɔ:dɪŋ tə]	laut, entsprechend	According to the weather forecast, it will be warm and sunny tomorrow.
	comment ['kɒment]	Kommentar, Stellungnahme	a statement of your opinion
	to comment ['kɒment]	kommentieren, Stellung nehmen	to give one's opinion on something
	World Wide Web [ˌwɜ:ld waɪd 'web]	weltweites Netz innerhalb des Internets	WWW
	network ['netwɜ:k]	Netz, Netzwerk	Which network does your mobile phone use?
	programming language ['prəʊgræmɪŋ ˌlæŋgwɪdʒ]	Programmiersprache	programming language → program → programmer
	HTML [ˌeɪtʃti:em'el]	eine Programmiersprache für das World Wide Web	Hypertext Markup Language
	software ['sɒftweə]	Software (Computerprogramme)	software ↔ hardware
	worldwide [ˌwɜ:ld'waɪd]	weltweit	worldwide → world
	games console ['geɪmz ˌkɒnsəʊl]	Spielekonsole, Bedienungsgerät für Computerspiele	an electronic device used to play video games
	to propose [prə'pəʊz]	vorschlagen	to propose → proposal
	classification system [ˌklæsɪfɪ'keɪʃn ˌsɪstəm]	Klassifizierungssystem, Ordnungssystem	classification → class → to classify
	illegal [ɪ'li:gl]	illegal, gesetzeswidrig	illegal ↔ legal
	to recommend [ˌrekə'mend]	empfehlen	We recommend that young children do not play this game.
	to act [ækt]	handeln, sich verhalten	to act → active → activity
	teenage ['ti:neɪdʒ]	im Alter von 13 bis 19	Your teenage years are the time from the age of 13 to the age of 19.

	instant messaging [ˌɪnstənt 'mesɪdʒɪŋ]	sofortige Nachrichtenübermittlung, Chatten	communication in real time, live chat
	to chat [tʃæt]	chatten, sich online unterhalten	to chat → a chat
	to turn up [tɜ:n‿'ʌp]	auftauchen, erscheinen	to appear, to arrive
	frightened ['fraɪtənd]	verängstigt, erschrocken	to be frightened = to be afraid
	video clip ['vɪdiəʊ ˌklɪp]	Videoclip, kurze Videoaufnahme	Short music videos are also called video clips.
	sleepless ['sli:pləs]	schlaflos	sleepless → to sleep → sleep → sleepy
	provider [prə'vaɪdə]	Anbieter(in)	provider → to provide → provision
	measure ['meʒə]	Maßnahme	measure → to measure
	piracy ['paɪrəsɪ]	Piraterie, Raubkopieren	piracy → pirate
	to keep an eye on [ˌki:p‿ən 'aɪ‿ɒn]	im Auge behalten	Please keep an eye on the children while I am doing the shopping.
	court [kɔ:t]	Gericht, Hof, Spielfeld	Before people can be sent to prison, they have to appear in court.
	prison ['prɪzn]	Gefängnis	Many criminals have to go to prison.
	responsible (for) [rɪ'spɒnsəbl]	verantwortlich (für), haftbar	responsible → responsibility
D 1	**report** [rɪ'pɔ:t]	Bericht	report → reporter → to report
	to crash [kræʃ]	abstürzen	The plane crashed in the Rocky Mountains.
	flame [fleɪm]	Flamme	When you make a fire, the flames go up and turn into smoke.
	crash [kræʃ]	Absturz, Unfall	crash → to crash
	killing ['kɪlɪŋ]	Tötung	killing → to kill → killer
	murder ['mɜ:də]	Mord	murder → to murder → murderer
	shower ['ʃaʊə]	Schauer, Dusche	The rain soon stopped – it was only a shower.
	thunderstorm ['θʌndəstɔ:m]	Gewitter	What was the weather like? – Not so good. There were some very bad thunderstorms.
	temperature ['temprətʃə]	Temperatur	the amount of heat in a place
	degree [dɪ'gri:]	Grad	On a hot summer's day the temperature can rise to 30 degrees.
	Celsius ['selsɪəs]	Celsius	centigrade = C
	bright [braɪt]	hell	In the summer the sun is very bright.
	sunny ['sʌnɪ]	sonnig	sunny → sun
	motorway ['məʊtəweɪ]	Autobahn	a wide road where you can drive faster than on other roads
	lane [leɪn]	Fahrspur	The road around the city has four lanes.
	closed [kləʊzd]	gesperrt, geschlossen	closed ↔ open
	radio station ['reɪdɪəʊ ˌsteɪʃn]	Radiosender	The DJ works for a radio station.
	to come on air [ˌkʌm ɒn 'eə]	auf Sendung sein	to broadcast
	aircraft ['eəkrɑ:ft]	Flugzeug	plane
	youngster ['jʌŋkstə]	Jugendliche(r)	young person
	skiing ['ski:ɪŋ]	Skifahren	You can go skiing in Scotland in the winter.
	witness ['wɪtnəs]	Zeugin, Zeuge	witness → to witness
	truck [trʌk]	Lastwagen	truck *(AE)* = lorry *(BE)*
	to do poorly [du: 'pɔ:lɪ]	schlecht abschneiden	If you do not work hard at school, you will do poorly.
	to pay attention [ˌpeɪ‿ə'tenʃn]	Aufmerksamkeit schenken	to pay attention at school to what the teacher says
	westerly ['westəlɪ]	aus westlicher Richtung	coming from the west
	southbound ['saʊθbaʊnd]	in Richtung Süden	southbound ↔ northbound
	junction ['dʒʌŋkʃn]	Kreuzung	a place where roads meet
	keypad ['ki:pæd]	Tastatur	keyboard
D 2	**analysis** [ə'næləsɪs]	Analyse	analysis → to analyze
	cartoonist [kɑ:'tu:nɪst]	Karikaturist(in)	cartoonist → cartoon
	to point out [pɔɪnt‿'aʊt]	hinweisen auf	If you point out a fact, you tell someone about it.
	to observe [əb'zɜ:v]	beobachten	to watch carefully
D 3	**yard** [jɑ:d]	Hof	Between lessons students often meet in the schoolyard.
	corridor ['kɒrɪdɔ:]	Gang, Flur, Korridor	The students walked down the corridor to their classroom.

CCTV (closed circuit television) [ˌsi:si:ti:ˈvi:]	Videoüberwachungsanlage	In dangerous areas of the town the police has installed CCTV cameras.
head teacher [ˌhed‿ˈti:tʃə]	Schulleiter(in)	If pupils behave badly, the teacher can send them to the head teacher.
officer [ˈɒfɪsə]	Beamter, Beamtin	A police officer is a man or woman in the police.
pros and cons [ˌprəʊz‿ən ˈkɒnz]	Argumente für und gegen etwas	advantages and disadvantages
to suggest [səˈdʒest]	vorschlagen	to suggest → suggestion
in favour of [ɪn ˈfeɪvər‿əv]	für, zugunsten	to support
to reduce [rɪˈdju:s]	reduzieren, vermindern	to increase ↔ to reduce

5 Social change

A **society** [səˈsaɪətɪ]	Gesellschaft	society → social
western [ˈwestən]	westlich	western → west
past [pɑ:st]	letzte(r, s), vergangen	past 100 years ↔ next 100 years
to refer (to) [rɪˈfɜ:]	sich beziehen auf	refer → reference
section [ˈsekʃn]	Abschnitt, Abteilung	department
bookshop [ˈbʊkʃɒp]	Buchhandlung	The bookshop has got books and CDs, but they haven't got magazines.
Indian [ˈɪndɪən]	indisch	Mrs Brooks comes from India, so she cooks Indian food.
origin [ˈɒrɪdʒɪn]	Herkunft, Ursprung	An immigrant who comes from India is of Indian origin.
conventional [kənˈvenʃənl]	konventionell, normal	normal, typical
idyll [ˈɪdəl]	Idylle	a romantic scene
countryside [ˈkʌntrɪsaɪd]	Landschaft, Land	Some people like living in the city, others prefer the countryside.
strawberry [ˈstrɔ:brɪ]	Erdbeere	sweet, red fruit
wage [weɪdʒ]	Lohn	money that is paid for work
proper [ˈprɒpə]	angemessen, passend, richtig	An Englishman's idea of a proper breakfast is eggs with bacon, tomatoes and sausages, and tea to drink.
salary [ˈsælərɪ]	Gehalt	money that is paid every month for work
deduction [dɪˈdʌkʃn]	Abzug, Nachlass	We can offer you a price deduction of 20%.
accommodation [əˌkɒməˈdeɪʃn]	Unterbringung	a place where you can stay, e.g. for a holiday
fee [fi:]	Gebühr	payment for services
left [left]	übrig	If you spend all your money, nothing will be left.
picker [ˈpɪkə]	Pflücker(in)	picker → to pick
meanness [ˈmi:nnəs]	Gemeinheit, Knauserigkeit	meanness → mean
chemist's [ˈkemɪsts]	Apotheke, Drogerie	chemist's *(BE)* = drugstore *(AE)*
condom [ˈkɒndɒm]	Kondom	You can have safer sex, if you use a condom.
way beyond [ˌweɪ bɪˈjɒnd]	weit entfernt, weit darüber hinaus	farther than
missus [ˈmɪsɪz]	umgangssprachliche Anrede für eine Frau	missus → Mrs
anyway [ˈenɪweɪ]	jedenfalls, trotzdem	The weather was bad but we went to the football match anyway.
to realize [ˈrɪəlaɪz]	erkennen, bemerken	On the way to the airport I suddenly realized I'd forgotten my passport.
to spot [spɒt]	entdecken	to notice
neither [ˈnaɪðə, ˈni:ðə]	keine(-r/-s) (von beiden)	Both my parents have bicycles, but neither of them cycles to work.
pregnancy [ˈpregnənsɪ]	Schwangerschaft	period when a woman expects her baby
embarrassment [ɪmˈbærəsmənt]	Peinlichkeit, Verlegenheit	embarrassment → to embarrass → embarrassed
kit [kɪt]	Ausrüstung	special clothes or equipment
engaged [ɪnˈgeɪdʒd]	verlobt	They are engaged and are going to get married next month.
right now [ˌraɪt ˈnaʊ]	in diesem Augenblick	What is he doing right now?
could do with [ˌkʊd‿ˈdu: wɪð]	gebrauchen können, vertragen können (Getränk)	need
resentful [rɪˈzentfəl]	aufgebracht, grollend	angry

	to snap [snæp]	blaffen	to speak in a sharp, unfriendly way
	to shut s.o. up [ˌʃʌt ˌsʌmwʌn 'ʌp]	jemanden dazu bringen, den Mund zu halten	to stop s.o. talking
	to head off [hed 'ɒf]	sich aufmachen	The family headed off early on their holidays.
	colloquial [kə'ləʊkwɪəl]	umgangssprachlich	informal, everyday language
	superdrug ['su:pədrʌg]	Name einer britischen Drogeriekette	You can buy cosmetics at Superdrug.
	drugstore ['drʌgstɔ:]	Apotheke, Drogerie	drugstore *(AE)* = chemist *(BE)*
	satisfied ['sætɪsfaɪd]	zufrieden	You are satisfied because you have received what you wanted.
	treatment ['tri:tmənt]	Behandlung	treatment → to treat
	definition [ˌdefɪ'nɪʃn]	Definition, Erklärung	'A subject which teaches you about the past' is a definition of the word 'history'.
	medicine ['medsɪn]	Medizin	what your doctor may give you when you're ill
B 1	**feminist** ['femɪnɪst]	Feministin, Frauenrechtlerin	Feminists fight for women's rights.
	drill [drɪl]	Bohrer	You need a drill to make holes in the wall.
	documentary [ˌdɒkjʊ'mentərɪ]	Dokumentarfilm	documentary → document
	to accommodate [ə'kɒmədeɪt]	Unterkunft bieten, versorgen	accommodate → accommodation
	to hand out [hænd 'aʊt]	aushändigen, verteilen	Please, hand out the papers to the other students.
	credit card ['kredɪt ˌkɑ:d]	Kreditkarte	plastic card with which you can pay
	beauty ['bju:tɪ]	Schönheit	beauty → beautiful
	topic ['tɒpɪk]	Thema	subject
B 2	**non-defining relative clause** [ˌnɒndɪfaɪnɪŋ 'relətɪv ˌklɔ:z]	nicht notwendiger Relativsatz	non-defining ↔ defining
	Europe ['jʊərəp]	Europa	Britain is in Europe.
	various ['veərɪəs]	verschieden	different
	affair [ə'feə]	Affäre	She had an affair with a married man.
	social ['səʊʃl]	sozial, gesellschaftlich	Rich people and poor people often come from different social backgrounds.
	norm [nɔ:m]	Norm, Regel	a way of behaving that people expect from you
	to force [fɔ:s]	zwingen	If you force someone to do something, you make them do it.
	poverty ['pɒvətɪ]	Armut	poverty → poor
	comedian [kə'mi:dɪən]	Komiker(in)	a person whose job is to make people laugh
	to leave out [li:v‿'aʊt]	auslassen	leave out ↔ fill in
	Muslim ['mʊzlɪm]	Moslem(in)	a person who believes in Islam (also Moslem)
	profession [prə'feʃn]	Beruf	the profession of teaching
	comprehensive school [ˌkɒmprɪ'hensɪv ˌsku:l]	Gesamtschule	Comprehensive schools are for people from 11 to 16 or 18 years old.
	tradition [trə'dɪʃn]	Tradition	tradition → traditional
	columnist ['kɒləmnɪst]	Schreiber(in), Kolumnist(in)	a journalist who writes regular articles in a newspaper or magazine
	award [ə'wɔ:d]	Preis, Auszeichnung	an important prize
	religious [rɪ'lɪdʒəs]	religiös	Our neighbours go to church very often. They are religious people.
B 3	**to take on** [teɪk‿'ɒn]	aufgreifen, übernehmen	to pick, to accept
B 4	**modal auxiliary** [ˌməʊdl‿ɔ:g'zɪljərɪ]	Hilfsverb	Must, need and can are modal auxiliaries.
	substitute ['sʌbstɪtju:t]	Ersatz	Can you play tennis for Becky on Saturday? She needs a substitute.
C	**to anticipate** [æn'tɪsɪpeɪt]	vorhersehen, erwarten	to expect something before it happens
	to skim [skɪm]	überfliegen	to read very quickly
	to scan [skæn]	scannen, durchsuchen	to look at something (a text etc.) carefully because you are looking for special details
	subheading ['sʌbˌhedɪŋ]	Zwischenüberschrift	Subheadings divide a text into shorter parts.
	interaction [ˌɪntə'rækʃn]	Interaktion	communicating and working together
	campus ['kæmpəs]	Campus, (Hoch-)Schulgelände	area of land with the buildings of a university or school

	What is he like? [ˌwɒt ɪz hiː 'laɪk]	Wie ist er?	What's your little sister like? – She's very sweet.
	scarf [skɑːf]	Schal, Halstuch, Kopftuch	a piece of cloth that you wear round your neck or head
	to guide [gaɪd]	führen, leiten	guide → guidebook
	formal ['fɔːml]	formell, formal	Spoken English is less formal than written English.
	blind [blaɪnd]	blind	not able to see
	to found [faʊnd]	gründen	to establish, to set up
	European [jʊərə'piːən]	europäisch	Germany and Britain are European countries.
	commission [kə'mɪʃn]	Kommission, Provision	The European Commission has one member from each state of the European Union.
	European [jʊərə'piːən]	Europäer(in)	European → Europe
	commitment [kə'mɪtmənt]	Engagement, Verpflichtung, Bekenntnis	When you work towards something you show your commitment to it.
	unpaid [ʌn'peɪd]	unbezahlt	You don't get any money for unpaid work.
	voluntary ['vɒləntrɪ]	freiwillig	When you do voluntary work, you aren't paid for what you do.
	volunteer [ˌvɒlən'tɪə]	Freiwillige(r)	Volunteers are not paid for their work.
	board [bɔːd]	Verpflegung	You have to pay 100 dollars for room and board in that hotel.
	involved (in) [ɪn'vɒlvd]	beteiligt	to take part in
	Scottish ['skɒtɪʃ]	schottisch	Glasgow is a big Scottish city.
	visual ['vɪʒʊəl]	bildlich, visuell, das Sehen betreffend	If you are visually handicapped, you cannot see well.
	handicapped ['hændɪkæpt]	behindert, benachteiligt	handicapped → handicap
	outdoor [ˌaʊt'dɔː]	im Freien, draußen	Skateboarding and camping are outdoor activities.
	sense [sens]	Sinn, Sinnesempfindung, Bedeutung	You use your senses to hear, see and taste things.
	community [kə'mjuːnətɪ]	Gemeinde, Gemeinschaft	We don't live in a big city: our village is just a small community.
	opportunity [ˌɒpə'tjuːnətɪ]	Gelegenheit	chance
	organizational [ˌɔːgənaɪ'zeɪʃənl]	organisatorisch	organizational → organization → to organize
	structure ['strʌktʃə]	Struktur, Aufbau	the way something is arranged
	disabled [dɪ'seɪbld]	behindert	handicapped
	to enable [ɪ'neɪbl]	ermöglichen, in die Lage versetzen	to make something possible
	communicative [kə'mjuːnɪkətɪv]	kommunikativ, gesprächig	communicative → communication
	situation [ˌsɪtjʊ'eɪʃn]	Situation	what is happening at the moment
	focus ['fəʊkəs]	Blickpunkt, Mittelpunkt, Fokus	a central point of attention
	care [keə]	Pflege, Sorge	Nurses and doctors work in healthcare.
	mechanical [mə'kænɪkl]	mechanisch, technisch	mechanical → mechanic
	musical ['mjuːzɪkl]	musikalisch	Sue is very musical. She plays three different musical instruments.
	talent ['tælənt]	Talent	If you have a talent, you are – or can become – very good at something.
	creative [krɪ'eɪtɪv]	kreativ, schöpferisch	You can use your own ideas in creative writing exercises.
	to get along with [ˌget ə'lɒŋ wɪð]	auskommen mit, sich verstehen mit	to be friendly and work well with someone
	detailed ['diːteɪld]	detailliert, ausführlich	detailed → detail
	motivation [ˌməʊtɪ'veɪʃn]	Motivation, Leistungsbereitschaft	motivation → to motivate
	routine [ruː'tiːn]	Routine, Tagesablauf	regular tasks in a fixed order
	task [tɑːsk]	Aufgabe	a piece of work that is difficult or that you don't enjoy doing
	to get dressed [get‿'drest]	sich anziehen	to put clothes on
	to clean up [kliːn 'ʌp]	aufräumen	to make something tidy
D 1	**female** ['fiːmeɪl]	weiblich	a female singer = a singer who is a woman
	special needs [ˌspeʃl 'niːdz]	Sonderschul-	When someone has learning difficulties a special needs teacher can help them.

	on one's own [ˌɒn wʌnz‿ˈəʊn]	(ganz) allein(e)	Her friends didn't want to go to the cinema, so she went on her own.
	shift [ʃɪft]	(Arbeits-)Schicht	a period of work, e.g. in a factory or hospital
	single parent [ˌsɪŋgl ˈpeərənt]	Alleinerziehende(r)	a parent who cares for a child or children without another parent in the home
	to combine [kəmˈbaɪn]	kombinieren	combine → combination
	unit [ˈjuːnɪt]	Abteilung, Station, Kapitel	department at a hospital
	private [ˈpraɪvɪt]	privat	private ↔ public
	to treat [triːt]	behandeln	treat → treatment
	patient [ˈpeɪʃnt]	Patient(in)	There are a lot of patients in this hospital.
	single mum [ˌsɪŋgl ˈmʌm]	alleinerziehende Mutter	woman who is a single parent
	demanding [dɪˈmɑːndɪŋ]	anspruchsvoll	demanding → to demand → the demand
	perspective [pəˈspektɪv]	Blickwinkel, Perspektive	way of thinking of or seeing something
D 2	**concept** [ˈkɒnsept]	Entwurf, Konzept	plan, idea
	secondary school [ˈsekəndrɪ ˌskuːl]	weiterführende Schule	high school
	to be located [bɪ ləʊˈkeɪtɪd]	gelegen sein, sich befinden	to be situated
	courtyard [ˈkɔːtjɑːd]	(Innen-)Hof	a flat, open area with buildings around it
	canteen [kænˈtiːn]	Kantine, Mensa	a place in a school or factory where people can eat and drink
	storey [ˈstɔːrɪ]	Stock(werk)	The house has got three storeys.
	library [ˈlaɪbrərɪ]	Bibliothek, Bücherei	There are lots and lots of books in a library.
	conference [ˈkɒnfrəns]	Konferenz	a meeting to discuss something
	gym [dʒɪm]	Sporthalle	sports hall
	wheelchair [ˈwiːltʃeə]	Rollstuhl	wheelchair → chair and wheels
	access [ˈækses]	Zugang	If you have access to something, it is possible for you to use it.
	environment [ɪnˈvaɪərənmənt]	Umgebung, Umfeld	the people and things around you
	range [reɪndʒ]	Angebot, Produktpalette, Reichweite	The supermarket offers a wide range of sweets.
	clinic [ˈklɪnɪk]	Klinik	hospital
	contraception [ˌkɒntrəˈsepʃn]	Schwangerschaftsverhütung	Safe methods of contraception help women not to have babies.
	relating to [rɪˈleɪtɪŋ tuː]	in Bezug auf	in relation to, concerning
	in addition [ɪn əˈdɪʃn]	zusätzlich, außerdem	When Sarah fell, she broke her arm and, in addition, she broke her glasses.
	social worker [ˈsəʊʃl ˌwɜːkə]	Sozialarbeiter(in)	A social worker helps people in need.
	twin town [ˌtwɪnˈtaʊn]	Partnerstadt	London and Berlin are twin towns.
	imagination [ɪˌmædʒɪˈneɪʃn]	Vorstellungskraft, Phantasie	the ability to form pictures and ideas in your mind
	function [ˈfʌŋkʃn]	Funktion, Aufgabe(nbereich)	role, purpose, task
	to interact [ˌɪntəˈrækt]	interagieren, zusammenwirken, einander beeinflussen	to interact → interaction
	medical [ˈmedɪkl]	medizinisch	When you see a doctor, you get medical treatment.

6 Ecology

A 1	**to flash** [flæʃ]	blinken, blitzen	to create a sudden light
	to breathe [briːð]	atmen	to take air into the lungs
	ecology [ɪˈkɒlədʒɪ]	Ökologie	the relation between plants, animals, people and their environment
	to recycle [ˌriːˈsaɪkl]	recyceln, wiederverwerten	If you recycle used products, you can save raw materials.
	vandalism [ˈvændəlɪzm]	Vandalismus, mutwillige Beschädigung	destruction of useful or beautiful things for fun
	global [ˈgləʊbl]	global	A global problem is one that the whole world shares.
	warming [ˈwɔːmɪŋ]	Erwärmung	warming → warm
	worry [ˈwʌrɪ]	Sorge, Ärger	the worry → to worry
	rainfall [ˈreɪnfɔːl]	Niederschlag, Regen	rain + fall = rainfall

	use [ju:s]	Verwendung, Verwendungsmöglichkeit	the use → to use
	concern [kən'sɜ:n]	Bedenken, Sorge, Anliegen	concern → concerning
	day by day [ˌdeɪbaɪ'deɪ]	jeden Tag, täglich	every day
	increasing [ɪn'kri:sɪŋ]	zunehmend, steigend, wachsend	increasing → to increase
	worried ['wʌrɪd]	beunruhigt	"Are you happy?" – "No, I'm worried."
	issue ['ɪʃu:]	Angelegenheit, Problem, Ausgabe (einer Zeitung)	topic
	aspect ['æspekt]	Aspekt, Gesichtspunkt	This aspect of the problem is most important.
	fossil fuel [ˌfɒsl 'fjʊəl]	fossiler Brennstoff	Coal and oil are fossil fuels.
	to emit [ɪ'mɪt]	emittieren, ausstoßen	to give out or send out
	gas [gæs]	Gas, Benzin	Most people in Europe use gas or electricity for cooking.
	carbon dioxide [ˌkɑ:bndaɪ'ɒksaɪd]	Kohlendioxyd, CO_2	You get CO_2 gases when you burn coal or wood.
	to contribute [kən'trɪbju:t]	beitragen	to contribute → contribution
	complex ['kɒmpleks]	komplex, vielfältig, kompliziert	consisting of many parts
	likely ['laɪklɪ]	wahrscheinlich, voraussichtlich	Are you sure you want to spend your holidays in Majorca in August? It's likely to be very crowded.
	resource [rɪ'zɔ:s]	Ressource, Bodenschatz, Rohstoff	It is important not to waste the world's natural resources.
	improvement [ɪm'pru:vmənt]	Verbesserung	to improve → improvement
	responsibility [rɪˌspɒnsə'bɪlətɪ]	Verantwortung	responsibility → responsible
	to encourage [ɪn'kʌrɪdʒ]	unterstützen, fördern, ermutigen	to support
	conservation [ˌkɒnsə'veɪʃn]	Erhaltung, Schutz	conservation → to conserve
	natural ['nætʃərl]	natürlich	natural → nature
	to identify (with) [aɪ'dentɪfaɪ wɪð]	herausfinden, (sich) identifizieren (mit)	to identify → identification
	to range [reɪndʒ]	sich bewegen, reichen	to range → the range
	control [kən'trəʊl]	Kontrolle	the control → to control
	to aim [eɪm]	anstreben, zielen	to aim → the aim
	to provide s.o. with [prəʊ'vaɪd ˌsʌmwʌn wɪð]	jmdn. versorgen mit	We'll provide you with money.
	to save [seɪv]	sparen	We can save money by walking instead of driving.
A 2	**to punish** ['pʌnɪʃ]	bestrafen	Is it right to punish a child who has done something wrong?
	organic [ɔ:'gænɪk]	biologisch angebaut, organisch	natural
	to survive [sə'vaɪv]	überleben	He survived for days at sea in a small boat.
	concerned [kən'sɜ:nd]	betroffen	concerned → concerning → the concern
B 1	**developing world** [dɪˌveləpɪŋ 'wɜ:ld]	Entwicklungsländer	Most people in the developing world are poor.
	water-related disease [ˌwɔ:tərɪˌleɪtɪd‿dɪ'zi:z]	Krankheit, die durch (unsauberes) Wasser verursacht wird	In Africa you find many water-related diseases.
	thirst [θɜ:st]	Durst	thirst → thirsty, hunger → hungry
	gamble ['gæmbl]	Risiko	risk
	heartbreaking ['hɑ:tˌbreɪkɪŋ]	herzzerreißend	It breaks your heart to see young children dying, it is heartbreaking.
	to benefit (from) ['benəfɪt frɒm]	Nutzen ziehen (aus), profitieren (von)	Oil-producing countries benefit from the high price of oil.
	to conclude [kən'klu:d]	schließen, folgern	to say the last thing that you are going to say
B 2	**donation** [dəʊ'neɪʃn]	Spende	money that you give to an organization such as the Red Cross
	to donate [dəʊ'neɪt]	spenden	to donate → donation
	surname ['sɜ:neɪm]	Nachname	last name
	postcode ['pəʊstkəʊd]	Postleitzahl	postcode *(BE)* = zip code *(AE)*

B 3	**tuna,** pl. **tuna** ['tju:nə]	Thunfisch	large fish that lives in warm seas and is caught for food
	salmon, pl. **salmon** ['sæmən]	Lachs	a tasty kind of fish which looks pink when you cut it open
	menu ['menju:]	Speisekarte	Waiter, what's on the menu today?
	seafood ['si:fu:d]	Fisch und Meeresfrüchte	Seafood is healthy.
	protein ['prəʊti:n]	Protein, Eiweiß	Protein can be found in meat, eggs and milk.
	apart from [ə'pɑ:t frəm]	abgesehen von, außer	I'm going to the supermarket later. What else do we need apart from bread, milk and sugar?
	algae pl. ['ælgi:]	Algen, Tang	plants that live in the water
	to avoid [ə'vɔɪd]	(ver)meiden	to keep away (from)
	disaster [dɪ'zɑ:stə]	Katastrophe, Desaster	A disaster is a very bad accident.
	catastrophe [kə'tæstrəfɪ]	Katastrophe	an extremely bad thing that happens to you
B 4	**World Nature Fund** [ˌwɜ:ld 'neɪtʃə ˌfʌnd]	Fonds zum Schutz der Natur	an organization that helps to protect nature
	branch [brɑ:ntʃ]	Zweigstelle, Zweig, Abzweigung, Sektor	part of something
	major ['meɪdʒə]	bedeutend, groß, Haupt-	major → majority
	membership ['membəʃɪp]	Mitgliedschaft	membership → member
B 5	**drop** [drɒp]	Tropfen; Abnahme, Verringerung	Oh, I think that was a drop of rain. Let's go before it really starts.
	meaningful ['mi:nɪŋfəl]	sinnvoll, aussagekräftig	meaningful → meaning → to mean
	to run out [rʌn 'aʊt]	ablaufen, auslaufen, zu Ende gehen	Time or money can run out so that there is no more left.
	overfishing [ˌəʊvə'fɪʃɪŋ]	Überfischung	overfishing → fishing → fish
	exotic [ɪg'zɒtɪk]	exotisch	I love exotic dishes, but I don't always want to know exactly what I'm eating.
	economic [ˌi:kə'nɒmɪk]	ökonomisch, wirtschaftlich	economic → economy
	fisherman, pl. **fishermen** ['fɪʃəmən]	Fischer	fisherman → fishing → fish
C	**pie chart** ['paɪ ˌtʃɑ:t]	Kreisdiagramm	pie chart → bar chart
	non-food [ˌnɒn'fu:d]	Nichtlebensmittel, Güter, die nicht zum Verzehr gedacht sind	non-food ↔ food
	retail ['ri:teɪl]	Einzelhandel	selling goods to the public in small quantities
	home food related [ˌhəʊmˌfu:drɪ'leɪtɪd]	im Zusammenhang mit der häuslichen Nahrungszubereitung	connected with food preparation at home
	fertiliser ['fɜ:tɪlaɪzə]	Dünger	It makes plants grow more successfully.
	agriculture ['ægrɪkʌltʃə]	Landwirtschaft	farming
	air mile ['eə ˌmaɪl]	Flugmeile	air + mile = air mile
	South African [ˌsaʊθ'æfrɪkən]	südafrikanisch	African → Africa
	Argentinian [ˌɑ:dʒən'tɪnɪən]	argentinisch	Argentinian → Argentina
	beef [bi:f]	Rindfleisch	meat that comes from cows
	Spanish ['spænɪʃ]	spanisch	Spanish → Spain
	Brazilian [brə'zɪlɪən]	brasilianisch	Brazilian → Brazil
	pineapple ['paɪnæpl]	Ananas	A pineapple is a fruit.
	Indonesian [ˌɪndə'ni:ʒn]	indonesisch	Indonesian → Indonesia
	king prawn [ˌkɪŋ 'prɔ:n]	Königskrabbe	seafood, similar to a shrimp but bigger
	banana [bə'nɑ:nə]	Banane	Apples, oranges, strawberries and bananas are all fruit.
	transportation [ˌtrænspɔ:'teɪʃn]	Transport, Beförderung	transportation → transport
	enormous [ɪ'nɔ:məs]	riesig, enorm	very large
	to harm [hɑ:m]	schaden, verletzen	to damage
	rail [reɪl]	Bahn, Eisenbahn, Schiene	rail → railway
	shipping ['ʃɪpɪŋ]	Schifffahrt, Versand	shipping → the ship → to ship
	to label ['leɪbl]	beschriften	to put a piece of paper on a bottle, box etc. that tells you what it is and what's in it
	label ['leɪbl]	Etikett	the label → to label
	researcher [rɪ'sɜ:tʃə]	Forscher(in)	researcher → the research → to research

process ['prəʊsəs]	Prozess	methods of producing goods in factories
negative ['negətɪv]	negativ	bad, harmful
so-called [ˌsəʊ'kɔ:ld]	so genannte	so-called → to call
citizen ['sɪtɪzn]	Bürger(in), Staatsangehörige(r)	London has about 7.2 million citizens.
eco- ['i:kəʊ]	Öko-	Our car is eco-friendly.
to cut [kʌt]	senken, verringern, kürzen	to reduce
consumption [kən'sʌmpʃn]	Verbrauch	consumption → consumer → to consume
as well as [əz 'wel‿əz]	sowohl … als auch	We've got two cats as well as a dog.
rather than ['rɑ:ðə ðən]	eher … als, besser … als	Rather than sitting on the couch all day they should do some sport.
calorie ['kæləri]	Kalorie	If you work hard, you use up more calories.
impact ['ɪmpækt]	Wirkung, Aufprall	effect
vegetable ['vedʒtəbl]	Gemüse	The Burtons eat lots of vegetables from their garden.
season ['si:zn]	Saison, Jahreszeit	Summer is the warmest season.
advisor [əd'vaɪzə]	Berater(in), Ratgeber(in)	advisor → advice
solar ['səʊlə]	Sonnen-, Solar-	solar → sun
to divide [dɪ'vaɪd]	teilen	to divide → division
effort ['efət]	Mühe, Leistung, Versuch	It will take a lot of effort to win the match.
to compete [kəm'pi:t]	konkurrieren, mithalten, teilnehmen	to compete → competition
to argue ['ɑ:gju:]	diskutieren, streiten, argumentieren	Young people sometimes argue with their parents.
assistance [ə'sɪstəns]	Hilfe	assistance → to assist → assistant
physical ['fɪzɪkl]	körperlich, physisch	connected with a person's body
pain [peɪn]	Schmerz	the feeling you have when something hurts a lot
object ['ɒbdʒekt]	Gegenstand, Objekt	you can see and touch it
to mark [mɑ:k]	markieren, kennzeichnen, korrigieren	to label
declaration [ˌdeklə'reɪʃn]	Erklärung	the American Declaration of Independence
definite ['defɪnɪt]	bestimmt, klar, definitiv	definite ↔ indefinite
context ['kɒntekst]	Kontext, Zusammenhang	The words and sentences before and after a word; it helps you to show the meaning of the word.
strict [strɪkt]	streng	"Have a biscuit." – "No, thanks, I'm on a strict diet."
the elderly [ðɪ‿'eldəlɪ]	ältere Menschen	elderly → old
to challenge ['tʃælɪndʒ]	herausfordern	to invite s.o. to compete in a fight or game
to beat, beat, beaten [bi:t, bi:t, bi:tn]	besiegen, schlagen	We're winning, come on, we can beat the other team!
D 1 **to go clubbing** [gəʊ 'klʌbɪŋ]	Nachtclubs besuchen	to go to clubs or discos
to generate ['dʒenəreɪt]	erzeugen, entwickeln, schaffen	to generate → generator
conscience ['kɒnʃəns]	Gewissen, Bewusstsein	sense of what is right and wrong
nuclear ['nju:klɪə]	nuklear, Atom-	atomic
low-flush toilet [ˌləʊflʌʃ 'tɔɪlɪt]	Toilette mit geringem Wasserverbrauch	You can save water by using low-flush toilets.
waterless ['wɔ:tələs]	ohne Wasser, trocken	without water
urinal [jʊ'raɪnl]	Pissoir, Urinal	part of men's toilets
automatic [ˌɔ:tə'mætɪk]	automatisch	Automatic cars are easy to drive.
tap [tæp]	Wasserhahn	Turn off the tap. The water is still running.
lighter ['laɪtə]	Feuerzeug, Anzünder	lighter → the light → to light
dancer ['dɑ:nsə]	Tänzer(in)	dancer → to dance → the dance
electricity [ˌelɪk'trɪsətɪ]	Elektrizität	electricity → electric → electrician
battery ['bætərɪ]	Batterie	My alarm clock did not ring. The battery must be dead.
to power [paʊə]	mit Strom versorgen, antreiben	to power → the power → powerful
neighbourhood ['neɪbəhʊd]	Nachbarschaft	neighbourhood → neighbour
shiny ['ʃaɪnɪ]	glänzend	shiny → to shine
to entertain [ˌentə'teɪn]	unterhalten	to entertain → entertainment
clubber ['klʌbə]	Clubbesucher(in)	clubber → club

	entry ['entrɪ]	Eintritt, Eingang, Eintrag	No entry!
	ecological [ˌi:kə'lɒdʒɪkl]	ökologisch	ecological → ecology
	material [mə'tɪərɪəl]	Material	things which help you to make or write something
	poly-carbon [ˌpɒlɪ'kɑbn]	aus Polycarbonat	A poly-carbon cup can be recycled.
	futuristic [ˌfju:tʃə'rɪstɪk]	futuristisch	futuristic → future
	crazy ['kreɪzɪ]	verrückt	strange, foolish
	piezoelectric [ˌpi:zəʊɪ'lektrɪk]	piezoelektrisch	piezoelectric → electric → electricity
	piezoelectricity [ˌpi:zəʊɪˌlek'trɪsətɪ]	Piezoelektrizität	You produce electricity by pressing a crystal.
	crystal ['krɪstl]	Kristall	a mineral (e.g. diamond) that has a regular shape
	pressure ['preʃə]	Druck	pressure → to press
	motion ['məʊʃn]	Bewegung	motion → to move
	turbine ['tɜ:baɪn]	Turbine	You can use a turbine to produce electricity.
	location [ləʊ'keɪʃn]	Einrichtung, Standort, Lage	location → to be located
	wave [weɪv]	Welle	When there is a storm at sea there are big waves.
	unforgettable [ˌʌnfə'getəbl]	unvergesslich	unforgettable → to forget
	sort [sɔ:t]	Sorte, Art	a sort of = a kind of
	armchair ['ɑ:mtʃeə]	Sessel	a comfortable chair which supports your arms on each side
	lounge [laʊndʒ]	Salon, Gesellschaftszimmer	a room with comfortable furniture in a house or hotel where you can sit and relax
	folks [fəʊks]	Leute (Anrede)	On the radio: “That's all for tonight, folks.“
	to prove [pru:v]	beweisen	to show that something is true
D 2	**sustainable** [sə'steɪnəbl]	nachhaltig, kontinuierlich	Only sustainable development can save the environment for our children.
	flag [flæg]	Fahne, Flagge	The colours of the American flag are red, white and blue.
	non-profit [ˌnɒn'prɒfɪt]	gemeinnützig, keinen Gewinn anstrebend	making no profit
	foundation [faʊn'deɪʃn]	Stiftung, Gründung, Fundament	foundation → to found
	to concentrate ['kɒnsəntreɪt]	konzentrieren	If you don't concentrate on the traffic while you're driving, you might have an accident.
	workshop ['wɜ:kʃɒp]	Werkstatt	workshop → work → to work
	it's your turn [ɪts ˌjɔ: 'tɜ:n]	du bist an der Reihe	It's your turn now to buy a round of drinks for everyone.
	phase [feɪz]	Phase, (Zeit-)Abschnitt	Parents and their teenage children often go through a difficult phase of life.
	critique [krɪ'ti:k]	Kritik	examination of a situation or idea
	positive ['pɒzətɪv]	positiv	positive ↔ negative
	fantasy ['fæntəsɪ]	Fantasie	Harry Potter lives in a fantasy world.
	vision ['vɪʒn]	Vorstellung, (Zukunfts-)Vision	A good politician must have visions of the future.
	realisation [ˌrɪəlaɪ'zeɪʃn]	Verwirklichung, Realisierung, Erkenntnis	realisation → real → to realise
	regarding [rɪ'gɑ:dɪŋ]	in Bezug auf	with regard to
	practicability [ˌpræktɪkə'bɪlətɪ]	Durchführbarkeit, Praktikabilität	practicability → practical → practice
	suggestion [sə'dʒestʃn]	Vorschlag	suggestion → to suggest
	collage [kɒ'lɑ:ʒ]	Collage	Let's put lots of different pictures together and make a collage.
	stall [stɔ:l]	Stand, Box, Parkett	On market day, people sell different things at different stalls.

7 Man and technology

A	**installation** [ˌɪnstə'leɪʃn]	Installation, Anlage, Einrichtung	installation → to install
	favourable ['feɪvrəbl]	günstig, vorteilhaft	favourable → favour
	to blow, blew, blown [bləʊ, blu:, bləʊn]	wehen, blasen	The wind is blowing.
	annual ['ænjʊəl]	jährlich	every year
	official [ə'fɪʃl]	Beamter, Beamtin	a person in an official position

	Nebraska Public Power District [nɪˌbræskə ˌpʌblɪk ˈpaʊə ˌdɪstrɪkt]	verantwortliche Stelle für die Stromversorgung in Nebraska	Nebraska Public Power District is responsible for wind farms and power stations.
	to flow [fləʊ]	fließen, strömen	The Rhine flows into the North Sea.
	right [raɪt]	richtig	right ↔ wrong
	thief, pl. **thieves** [θiːf, θiːvz]	Dieb(in)	a person who has stolen s.th.
	power [paʊə]	Energie, Strom	Electricity is a form of power.
	dozen [ˈdʌzn]	Dutzend	twelve
	beside [bɪˈsaɪd]	neben	next to
	to graze [greɪz]	grasen	to eat grass
	cattle (pl. only) [ˈkætl]	Vieh	The cattle (cows and bulls) are in the field.
	beneath [bɪˈniːθ]	unterhalb, unter	under, below
	ton [tʌn]	Tonne (Gewicht)	A metric ton is 1,000 kg, but an American ton only weighs 907 kg.
	blade [bleɪd]	Flügel, Klinge, Blatt	A modern wind turbine usually has two or three blades.
	wind farm [ˈwɪnd ˌfɑːm]	Windpark	You can find many wind farms near the coast.
	mayor [meə]	Bürgermeister(in)	the head of a town or city
	to view [vjuː]	besichtigen, betrachten, sehen	to look at s.th. with great interest
	impressive [ɪmˈpresɪv]	beeindruckend	impressive → impression
	view [vjuː]	Aussicht, Sicht	You get a nice view of the city from the top of the church.
	steel [stiːl]	Stahl	Steel is used to make things like bridges, cars, knives and forks.
	to complain [kəmˈpleɪn]	sich beschweren, klagen	My coffee was cold, so I complained to the waiter.
	trend [trend]	Trend, Mode, Richtung, Tendenz	If you follow the newest trends, you are trendy.
	demand [dɪˈmɑːnd]	Bedarf, Nachfrage, Forderung	the demand → to demand
	wonder [ˈwʌndə]	Wunder	You say, “No wonder!” when you are not surprised by s.th.
	biofuel [ˈbaɪəʊˌfjʊəl]	Biotreibstoff	bio(logical) + fuel = biofuel
	hydro power [ˈhaɪdrəʊ ˌpaʊə]	Wasserkraft	Hydro power is used to make electricity in a power station.
	renewable [rɪˈnjuːəbl]	erneuerbar	renewable → new
	exhaustible [ɪgˈzɔːstəbl]	begrenzt, sich erschöpfend	limited
	dependent (on) [dɪˈpendənt ɒn]	abhängig	dependent → independent
B 1	**passive voice** [ˌpæsɪv ˈvɔɪs]	Passiv (Grammatik)	passive voice ↔ active voice
	to promote [prəˈməʊt]	(be)fördern, veranstalten, werben für	to support
	efficient [ɪˈfɪʃnt]	leistungsfähig, wirksam, effizient	An efficient person or machine works quickly and well.
	deposit [dɪˈpɒzɪt]	Lagerstätte, Guthaben, Anzahlung	You can find deposits of coal or oil in the ground.
B 2	**coal-fired** [ˌkəʊlˈfaɪəd]	mit Kohle betrieben, Kohle-	A coal-fired power station uses coal to produce electricity.
	power plant [ˈpaʊə ˌplɑːnt]	Kraftwerk	power station
	steam [stiːm]	Dampf	When water boils, you get steam.
	magnet [ˈmægnət]	Magnet	a piece of iron which attracts iron
	power line [ˈpaʊə ˌlaɪn]	Starkstromleitung, Überlandleitung	Power lines provide big cities with electricity.
	to cool (down) [kuːl ˈdaʊn]	(ab)kühlen	to cool down ↔ to heat up
B 3	**sweater** [ˈswetə]	Pullover	The boy was wearing blue jeans and a sweater.
	cap [kæp]	Kappe, Mütze	Boys often wear baseball caps.
	earring [ˈɪərɪŋ]	Ohrring	The girl was wearing big earrings at the party.
B 5	**steam engine** [ˈstiːm ˌendʒɪn]	Dampfmaschine, Dampflokomotive	The modern steam engine was designed by James Watt.
	hybrid [ˈhaɪbrɪd]	Hybrid-	A hybrid car usually has a petrol engine and an electric motor.
	hydrogen [ˈhaɪdrədʒən]	Wasserstoff	We can produce hydrogen from water.
C 1	**to clone** [kləʊn]	klonen	to make a copy of a person or animal
	novel [ˈnɒvl]	Roman	There are seven ‘Harry Potter’ novels.
	in a rush [ˌɪn ə ˈrʌʃ]	in Eile	Hi, Bob! Can you help me? – Sorry, I’m in a rush!

	to be bound to (happen) [bɪ ˌbaʊnd‿tə 'hæpn]	etwas wird bestimmt (passieren)	it is certain to happen
	to upset, upset, upset [ʌp'set, ʌp'set, ʌp'set]	aus der Fassung bringen, bestürzen, aufregen	to make somebody worried or unhappy
	breath [breθ]	Atemzug, Atem	He took a deep breath and then started running.
	duplicate ['dju:plɪkət]	Duplikat, Kopie	copy
	DNA [ˌdi:en'eɪ]	DNS, DNA (Träger der Erbinformationen)	*(short form of)* deoxyribonucleic acid
	policy ['pɒlɪsɪ]	(Versicherungs-)Police, Versicherungsschein, Politik	the document you get from an insurance company
	horrible ['hɒrəbl]	schrecklich	terrible
	replacement [rɪ'pleɪsmənt]	Ersatz, Vertretung	a person or thing that takes the place of another
	organ ['ɔ:gən]	Organ	part of your body e.g. your heart
	bone marrow ['bəʊnˌmærəʊ]	Knochenmark	the inside part of a bone
	determined [dɪ'tɜ:mɪnd]	entschlossen	when you have made a decision to do s.th. and nothing will stop you
	to suffer ['sʌfə]	leiden, erleiden	to experience pain
	fate [feɪt]	Schicksal	your fate is what happens to you
	sole [səʊl]	einzig, ausschließlich	single, exclusive
	wobbly ['wɒblɪ]	wackelig, zittrig	She felt wobbly so she had to sit down.
	shaky ['ʃeɪkɪ]	wackelig, unsicher	shaky → to shake
	to topple ['tɒpl]	wackeln, stürzen, umwerfen	to shake and fall
	liver ['lɪvə]	Leber	The liver is an organ.
	barely ['beəlɪ]	kaum	He was so drunk that he could barely stand.
	whisper ['wɪspə]	Wispern, Flüstern	a very quiet voice
	defiant [dɪ'faɪənt]	trotzig, herausfordernd	showing aggression or independence
	to sacrifice ['sækrɪfaɪs]	opfern	to give up s.th. for s.o. else
	to raise [reɪz]	großziehen	Parents raise their children until they are grown up.
	lab [læb]	Labor(atorium)	*(short form of)* laboratory
	nonsense ['nɒnsəns]	Unsinn	If s.o. says s.th. stupid, you might say: "Nonsense!"
	shocked [ʃɒkt]	bestürzt, geschockt	shocked → to shock → the shock
	joke [dʒəʊk]	Witz	If you're good at telling jokes, you can make people laugh.
	silence ['saɪləns]	Schweigen, Stille	silence → silent
	to demand [dɪ'mɑ:nd]	verlangen, fordern	to demand → the demand
	awake [ə'weɪk]	wach	Someone who is awake is not sleeping.
	to be about to [ˌbɪ‿ə'baʊt‿tə]	im Begriff sein zu	to be going to do s.th. very soon
	blackness ['blæknəs]	Schwärze	blackness → black
	reaction [rɪ'ækʃn]	Reaktion	reaction → to react
	motive ['məʊtɪv]	Beweggrund, Absicht, Motiv	reason for doing s.th.
	character ['kærəktə]	(Roman-)Figur, Charakter	A character is a person in a book or story.
	emotion [ɪ'məʊʃn]	Gefühl, Emotion	Some people like to show their emotions, some don't.
	adjective ['ædʒɪktɪv]	Adjektiv	The word 'happy' is an adjective.
	to react [rɪ'ækt]	reagieren	to react → reaction
	transplant ['trænsplɑ:nt]	Transplantation, Übertragung	Mr Lee went to hospital for a heart transplant last week.
C 2	**genetic** [dʒə'netɪk]	genetisch, Gen-	Many people are afraid of what genetic engineering can do.
	composition [ˌkɒmpə'zɪʃn]	Aufsatz, Komposition	a piece of written work especially one that you do at school
	childless ['tʃaɪldləs]	kinderlos	not having any children of one's own
	to control [kən'trəʊl]	kontrollieren	to control → the control → controlled
	human ['hju:mən]	menschlich	It's only human to make mistakes, we all do.
	being ['bi:ɪŋ]	(Lebe-)Wesen, Geschöpf	being → to be
	deadly ['dedlɪ]	tödlich	deadly → dead → death → to die
	disease [dɪ'zi:z]	Krankheit	AIDS is a terrible disease which kills millions of people each year.
	God [gɒd]	Gott	You hear about God at church.
	freedom (no pl.) ['fri:dəm]	Freiheit	freedom → free

	scientific [ˌsaɪən'tɪfɪk]	wissenschaftlich	scientific → science → scientist
	embryo ['embrɪəʊ]	Embryo	an unborn human being in the first three months
	laboratory [lə'bɒrətrɪ]	Labor	a building or room with scientific equipment
	connective [kə'nektɪv]	Bindewort	word or words that connect clauses e.g. and, or, but
	contrast ['kɒntrɑ:st]	Gegensatz, Kontrast	There is a sharp contrast between life in the country and in a big city.
	point of view [ˌpɔɪnt‿əv‿'vju:]	Standpunkt, Ansicht	Your point of view is your way of seeing things.
	in short [ɪn 'ʃɔ:t]	kurz gesagt, kurzum	in a few words
	on the whole [ˌɒn ðə 'həʊl]	im Großen und Ganzen, alles in allem	all in all
D 1	**to give birth to** [ˌgɪv 'bɜ:θ tu:]	zur Welt bringen, gebären	She gave birth to a sweet, little girl.
	marriage ['mærɪdʒ]	Heirat, Hochzeit	marriage → to marry
	pregnant ['pregnənt]	schwanger	when a woman carries a baby in her body
	gradual ['grædʒʊəl]	schrittweise, allmählich, graduell	gradual ↔ sudden
	twin [twɪn]	Zwilling	She's got twins, a boy and a girl.
	in-vitro fertilisation [ɪnˌvi:trəʊ ˌfɜ:tɪlaɪ'zeɪʃn]	In-vitro-Befruchtung (im Reagenzglas)	In-vitro fertilisation (IVF) takes place in a laboratory.
	buffalo ['bʌfələʊ]	Büffel	A bison is a buffalo.
	despite [dɪ'spaɪt]	trotz	She likes working in a restaurant, despite the low wages.
D 2	**gene** [dʒi:n]	Gen, Erbfaktor	A gene test can be used to find a child's father.
	biotechnology [ˌbaɪəʊtek'nɒlədʒɪ]	Biotechnologie	the use of living organisms e.g. in the production of medicine
	fertility [fə'tɪlɪtɪ]	Fruchtbarkeit	the ability to have children
	puppy ['pʌpɪ]	junger Hund, Welpe	young dog
D 3	**FDA** [ˌefdi:'eɪ]	Behörde für Lebens- und Arzneimittelsicherheit	Food and Drug Administration (responsible for public health in the USA)
D 4	**to modify** ['mɒdɪfaɪ]	verändern, modifizieren	to change
	dairy ['deərɪ]	Molkerei	Milk and butter are dairy products.
	to spray [spreɪ]	sprühen	We sprayed the car blue.
	pesticide ['pestɪsaɪd]	Schädlingsbekämpfungsmittel, Pflanzenschutzmittel	chemical especially used to kill harmful insects
	rainforest ['reɪnfɒrɪst]	Regenwald	The world's rainforests are important for our climate.

8 The tourist industry

A	**tourism** ['tʊərɪzm]	Tourismus	tourism → tourist
	series, pl. **series** ['sɪəri:z]	Serie	A TV series is a number of programs with the same title.
	sporting ['spɔ:tɪŋ]	sportlich, Sport-	sporting → sport
	day off [deɪ‿'ɒf]	arbeitsfreier Tag	day without work
	inexpensive [ˌɪnɪk'spensɪv]	preiswert, billig	cheap
	catalogue ['kætəlɒg]	Katalog	In a catalogue you find illustrations, descriptions of products and their prices.
	travel ['trævl]	das Reisen	travel → to travel
	attractive [ə'træktɪv]	attraktiv	attractive → to attract → attraction
	infrastructure ['ɪnfrəˌstrʌktʃə]	Infrastruktur	the system of a country with regard to transport, communication, education, energy supply etc.
	consequent ['kɒnsɪkwənt]	folgend, folgerichtig	consequent → consequence
	destination [ˌdestɪ'neɪʃn]	Ziel, Reiseziel	What's your destination?
	accessible [ək'sesəbl]	zugänglich, befahrbar	accessible → access
	faraway [ˌfɑ:rə'weɪ]	fern, weit entfernt	When you are in Germany Australia is a faraway continent.
	booking ['bʊkɪŋ]	Buchung, Reservierung	booking → to book
	Spain [speɪn]	Spanien	the country between Portugal and France
	Far East [ˌfɑ:r‿'i:st]	Ferner Osten	China and Japan belong to the Far East (East Asia).
	adventure [əd'ventʃə]	Abenteuer	I like reading stories about adventures in foreign countries.

	cultural ['kʌltʃərl]	kulturell	There are cultural differences between people who come from different countries.
	airline ['eəlaɪn]	Fluggesellschaft	a company that owns planes and organises air travel
	sector ['sektə]	Sektor	part
	primary ['praɪmərɪ]	primär, hauptsächlich, Erst-	first
	extraction [ɪk'strækʃn]	Gewinnung, Förderung, Entnahme	taking raw materials out of the ground
	mining ['maɪnɪŋ]	Bergbau	mining → (coal) mine → miner
	secondary ['sekəndrɪ]	sekundär, Zweit-	secondary → second
	tertiary ['tɜ:ʃərɪ]	tertiär	third
B 1	**sightseeing** ['saɪtˌsi:ɪŋ]	Besichtigungstour	looking at tourist attractions
	square [skweə]	Platz, Quadrat	Trafalgar Square is in the centre of London.
	opera ['ɒprə]	Oper	All of the parts in an opera are sung.
	Statue of Liberty [ˌstætʃu:‿əv 'lɪbətɪ]	Freiheitsstatue	You can see the Statue of Liberty in New York.
	Moscow ['mɒskəʊ]	Moskau	the capital of Russia
	France [frɑ:ns]	Frankreich	France → French
	Russia ['rʌʃə]	Russland	Russia is in the east of Europe.
	conditional [kən'dɪʃənl]	Konditional	conditional → condition
B 2	**Australian** [ɒsˌtreɪlɪən]	Australier(in)	Australian → Australia
	to depart [dɪ'pɑ:t]	abfliegen, abfahren	to leave
	departure [dɪ'pɑ:tʃə]	Abflug, Abfahrt	the time when a flight or train leaves
B 3	**fuel** [fjʊəl]	Brennstoff, Treibstoff, Benzin	The cost of fuel is high.
	to hire [haɪə]	mieten	You can hire a car at the airport.
	bin [bɪn]	Mülleimer, Mülltonne	Put your rubbish in the bin, please.
	litter ['lɪtə]	Abfall	rubbish
B 4	**lottery** ['lɒtərɪ]	Lotterie	If you buy a lottery ticket and the numbers you have chosen come up, you may win a lot of money.
B 5	**honeymoon** ['hʌnɪmu:n]	Hochzeitsreise	journey after one's wedding
	Ireland ['aɪələnd]	Irland	Dublin is the capital of Ireland.
	argument ['ɑ:gjəmənt]	Streit, Argument	Tom had an argument with his girlfriend.
	otherwise ['ʌðəwaɪz]	sonst	Let's buy that music magazine. Otherwise we can't get the special CD.
	trendy ['trendɪ]	modisch, trendig	trendy → trend
	jealous (of) ['dʒeləs]	eifersüchtig	If you are jealous of s.o., you feel angry with them because they have s.th. you would like to have.
	perfect ['pɜ:fekt]	vollkommen, perfekt	ideal
	to go wrong [gəʊ 'rɒŋ]	schiefgehen	to turn out badly
	Majorca [mə'jɔ:kə]	Mallorca	island that belongs to Spain
	never mind! [ˌnevə 'maɪnd]	macht nichts! schon gut! bitte!	= Forget it! It doesn't matter.
C	**initiative** [ɪ'nɪʃətɪv]	Initiative, Entschlusskraft	action you take to solve a problem
	support [sə'pɔ:t]	Unterstützung	support → to support
	nature ['neɪtʃə]	Natur	all of the animals and plants in the world
	to preserve [prɪ'zɜ:v]	bewahren, erhalten, schonen	to keep in the original state
	priority [praɪ'ɒrətɪ]	Vorrang, Dringlichkeit, Priorität	Something that is a priority must be done as soon as possible.
	to establish [ɪ'stæblɪʃ]	aufbauen, (be)gründen	to establish → establishment
	backup ['bækʌp]	Unterstützung, Sicherung	support
	central ['sentrl]	zentral	central → centre
	barrier reef [ˌbærɪə 'ri:f]	der Küste vorgelagertes Riff	The Great Barrier Reef is near the coast of Australia.
	southern ['sʌðən]	südlich	southern → south
	native ['neɪtɪv]	eingeboren, einheimisch	People who were born in a country are its native people.
	guide [gaɪd]	Führer(in)	a person or a book that gives you information (for example about a city or a museum)
	fascinating ['fæsɪneɪtɪŋ]	faszinierend	very, very interesting
	legend ['ledʒənd]	Legende	an old story which may be true in parts

	Caribbean [ˌkærɪ'bi:ən, kə'rɪbɪən]	Karibik, karibisch	The Caribbean islands are between North and South America.
	condor ['kɒndɔ:]	Kondor	a big bird
	bioreserve ['baɪəʊrɪˌzɜ:v]	(Bio-)Reservat	an area where nature is protected
	variety [və'raɪətɪ]	Vielfalt, Auswahl	a number of different types
	attraction [ə'trækʃn]	Attraktion, Anziehungspunkt, Anziehungskraft	attraction → to attract → attractive
	thermal ['θɜ:ml]	Thermal-, Wärme-	producing heat or caused by heat
	spring [sprɪŋ]	Quelle, Brunnen	water coming from the earth
	forest ['fɒrɪst]	Wald	an area covered with trees
	carving ['kɑ:vɪŋ]	Schnitzarbeit	cutting wood in order to form s.th.
	alive [ə'laɪv]	lebendig	alive → to live → life
	to exploit [ɪk'splɔɪt]	ausbeuten	to take unfair advantage of s.o., e.g. by not paying them enough
	surroundings [sə'raʊndɪŋz]	Umgebung	the world around us
	sensitive ['sensətɪv]	einfühlsam, sensibel	sensitive → sense
	untouched [ʌn'tʌtʃt]	unberührt, unversehrt	untouched → touch
	unknown [ʌn'nəʊn]	unbekannt	unknown → to know
	race [reɪs]	Rasse	group of people who have the same history, language, nationality etc.
	to rephrase [ˌri:'freɪz]	umformulieren	to say in different words
D 1	**to associate** [ə'səʊʃɪeɪt]	verbinden, assoziieren	to connect with s.th. else
	jet-skiing ['dʒetˌski:ɪŋ]	Wassermotorrad fahren	going by jet-ski
	paragliding ['pærəˌglaɪdɪŋ]	Gleitschirm fliegen	a special way of flying
	to hike [haɪk]	wandern	to go for a long walk in the country
	volcano, pl. **volcanoes** [vɒl'keɪnəʊ]	Vulkan	a mountain out of which material sometimes comes from inside the earth
	once in a while [ˌwʌns ɪn‿ə 'waɪl]	ab und zu, gelegentlich	from time to time
	to cool off [ku:l 'ɒf]	(sich) abkühlen	to become cooler
	motorboat ['məʊtəbəʊt]	Motorboot	a boat with an engine or a motor
	alright [ɔ:l'raɪt]	in Ordnung	OK, fine
	resort [rɪ'zɔ:t]	Ferienort, Badeort	We're going to a beautiful resort in the Rocky Mountains for our holidays.
	peaceful ['pi:sfəl]	friedlich	peaceful → peace
	wild [waɪld]	wild	These ponies don't live on a farm. They're wild.
	monkey ['mʌŋkɪ]	Affe	Monkeys are always children's favourite animals at the zoo.
	to float [fləʊt]	treiben, gleiten, mit dem Floß fahren	to move on a river
	overnight [ˌəʊvə'naɪt]	über Nacht	during the night
D 4	**investor** [ɪn'vestə]	Kapitalanleger, Investor	investor → to invest → investment
	to mine [maɪn]	abbauen, fördern	You can mine coal or gold.

9 Globalisation and multiculturalism

A	**globalisation** [ˌgləʊblaɪ'zeɪʃn]	Globalisierung	Companies, labour, products, transport become more and more international.
	chance [tʃɑ:ns]	Chance	She lost the race because the others were too fast. She did not have a chance.
	risk [rɪsk]	Risiko	I used the traffic lights because there was a risk of being hit by a car if I didn't.
	labour ['leɪbə]	Arbeits-	work
	Austrian ['ɒstrɪən]	österreichisch	The Austrian mountains are a great place to go skiing.
	unfashionable [ʌn'fæʃnəbl]	unmodisch, unmodern	The clothes from last year are already unfashionable this year.
	sneaker ['sni:kə]	Turnschuh	I always wear sneakers when I have to walk a lot.
	MP3 player [ˌempi:'θri: ˌpleɪə]	MP3 Spieler	MP3 is the abbreviation for Moving Picture Experts Group (MPEG) Audio Layer 3.
	India ['ɪndɪə]	Indien	India is a country in the east.

	textile ['tekstaɪl]	textil	A textile factory is a place where cloth is manufactured.
	to dye [daɪ]	färben	I would like to have blue hair. I think I will dye it.
	dyer [daɪə]	Färber(in)	A dyer is someone whose job is to change the colour of things.
	chemical ['kemɪkl]	Chemikalie	A chemical is material which is used in industry to change the appearance of a product.
	to risk [rɪsk]	riskieren	I do my job as well as I can because I don't want to risk losing it.
	to make money [meɪk 'mʌnɪ]	Geld verdienen	The top football players make a lot of money.
	whatever [wɒt'evə]	was auch immer	Take whatever you want out of the fridge if you are hungry!
	accessory [ək'sesərɪ]	Zubehör, Accessoire	A handbag or a scarf are nice accessories for women.
	stuff [stʌf]	Zeug	things; We've had that old stuff in the garage for years!
	standard ['stændəd]	Standard, Norm, Maßstab	You can't judge an amateur's work by professional standards.
	apprenticeship [ə'prentɪʃɪp]	Ausbildung	If you want to do a job like working in a bank, you can do an apprenticeship. In Germany this takes between 2 and 3 ½ years.
	manufacturer [ˌmænjə'fæktʃərə]	Hersteller	manufacturer → manufacturing → to manufacture
	Czech Republic [ˌtʃek rɪ'pʌblɪk]	Tschechische Republik	The Czech Republic is to the east of Germany.
	either way [ˌaɪðə'weɪ, ˌiːðə'weɪ]	so oder so	It does not matter what you do, either way you end up the loser.
B	**New Zealand** [ˌnjuː 'ziːlənd]	Neuseeland	New Zealand is a country that is close to Australia.
	tutor ['tjuːtə]	Klassenlehrer(in), Betreuer(in)	My tutor says where I need to go to get my papers done.
	host [həʊst]	Gastgeber(in)	The host at a party is the person who has invited the people.
	ice hockey ['aɪs ˌhɒkɪ]	Eishockey	Ice hockey is a popular sport in Canada.
	preposition [ˌprepə'zɪʃn]	Präposition	Examples: of, in, at, on, beneath, under, above
	to apologize [ə'pɒlədʒaɪz]	sich entschuldigen	to say "I'm sorry!"
	logistics [lə'dʒɪstɪks]	Logistik, Versorgung	Logistics deals with the transportation of goods.
	guideline ['gaɪdlaɪn]	Richtlinie	If you follow the guidelines you will not have any problems.
	polite [pə'laɪt]	höflich	It is polite to say 'thank you' when you are given a present.
	busy ['bɪzɪ]	besetzt, belegt	Please call another time, the line is busy right now.
	caller ['kɔːlə]	Anrufer(in)	caller → to call
C	**habit** ['hæbɪt]	Gewohnheit, Angewohnheit	Tracy always uses her mobile in restaurants. That's an annoying habit.
	authentic [ɔː'θentɪk]	authentisch	real
	takeaway ['teɪkəweɪ]	Restaurant, das Speisen zum Mitnehmen verkauft	a place where you can buy dishes and take them home to eat
	industrialized [ɪn'dʌstrɪəlaɪzd]	industrialisiert	industrialized countries ↔ developing countries
	radical ['rædɪkl]	radikal, drastisch, durchgreifend	Radical changes are needed to solve the problem of pollution.
	textiles ['tekstaɪlz]	Textilien	cloth
	merchant ['mɜːtʃənt]	Händler, Kaufmann, Handelsmann	salesperson
	original [ə'rɪdʒənl]	original, ursprünglich, unbearbeitet	original → origin
	generation [ˌdʒenə'reɪʃn]	Generation	You think of your parents as the older generation.
	ironical [aɪ'rɒnɪkl]	ironisch	I didn't really mean what I said. It was meant ironically.
	nevertheless [ˌnevəðə'les]	dennoch, trotzdem, nichtsdestotrotz	There is no solution. Nevertheless we still hope that things will get better.
	to carry on [ˌkærɪ‿'ɒn]	weiterführen	I want to carry on playing the guitar.
	racial ['reɪʃl]	Rassen-	racial → race
	diverse [daɪ'vɜːs]	unterschiedlich, vielfältig, verschieden	different
	to escape (from) [ɪ'skeɪp]	flüchten (vor)	The sheriff didn't catch Robin Hood because he escaped at the last minute.

	Latvian ['lætvɪən]	lettisch	People from Latvia are called Latvians.
	Russian ['rʌʃn]	russisch	Russian → Russia
	Asian ['eɪʒən]	asiatisch	Chinese people and people from India are Asians.
	option ['ɒpʃn]	Alternative, Möglichkeit	possibility
	ethnic ['eθnɪk]	ethnisch	An ethnic group shares the same culture, religion, language etc.
	to eliminate [ɪ'lɪmɪneɪt]	beseitigen, entfernen, eliminieren	to cancel
	credit ['kredɪt]	Guthaben, Punkte, Vertrauen, Anerkennung	I can't phone Emily because I've got no credit on my mobile.
	mixture ['mɪkstʃə]	Mischung, Vermischung, Gemenge	A fruit salad is a mixture of different fruits.
D 2	**podcast** ['pɒdkɑ:st]	Podcast, aus dem Internet herunterladbare Film- bzw. Hörsequenz	You can download the latest news podcasts from the Internet.
	aid [eɪd]	Hilfe	help
	to sum up [sʌm 'ʌp]	zusammenfassen	If you sum up what happens in a story, you explain it in a few sentences.
	cocoa ['kəʊkəʊ]	Kakao	Chocolate is made from cocoa.
	hut [hʌt]	Hütte	a little house made out of wood and/or metal
	listener ['lɪsnə]	Zuhörer(in)	listener → to listen
	insight ['ɪnsaɪt]	Einblick	insight → sight → to see

10 International politics

A	**united** [jʊ'naɪtɪd]	vereint	United Nations (= *Vereinte Nationen)*
	humanitarian [hju:ˌmænɪ'teərɪən]	humanitär, menschenfreundlich	humanitarian → humanity → human
	peacekeeping ['pi:sˌki:pɪŋ]	Friedenserhaltung, Friedensbewahrung	making sure that a war does not break out
	operation [ˌɒpər'eɪʃn]	Operation, Handlung, Verfahren, Arbeitsgang	act, action, activity
	budget ['bʌdʒɪt]	Haushalt, Etat	for example, the amount of money a company has to spend on its advertising
	Zimbabwe [zɪm'bɑ:bweɪ]	Simbabwe	Zimbabwe is a country in southeast Africa.
	maize [meɪz]	Mais	a tall plant that produces sweetcorn
	pill [pɪl]	Pille, Tablette	one form of medicine
	to prevent s.th. from happening/s.o. from doing s.th. [prɪ'vent]	verhindern	The rain prevented us from finishing the match.
	stomach ['stʌmək]	Magen	You shouldn't go swimming on a full stomach.
	non-governmental [ˌnɒngʌvən'mentl]	nichtregierungs-, nichtstaatlich	non-governmental organization = NGO
	two-thirds [ˌtu:'θɜ:dz]	zwei Drittel	Two-thirds plus one-third equals one.
	ration ['ræʃn]	Zuteilung, Ration	The man has to survive on a ration of a piece of bread and a cup of water a day.
	Zimbabwean [zɪm'bɑ:bwɪən]	simbabwisch, Simbabwer	People living in Zimbabwe are called Zimbabweans.
	to flee, fled, fled [fli:, fled, fled]	fliehen	The animals fled from the fire.
	inflation [ɪn'fleɪʃn]	Inflation, Geldentwertung	If a country introduces too much money, inflation may rise.
	harvest ['hɑ:vɪst]	Ernte	In the autumn the farmers usually bring in the harvest.
	seed [si:d]	Saat, Samen	A lot of plants can be grown from seed.
	cholera ['kɒlərə]	Cholera	Cholera is a disease which can result from drinking unclean water.
	infection [ɪn'fekʃn]	Infektion, Ansteckung	infection → to infect → infectious
	to infect [ɪn'fekt]	infizieren, anstecken	to infect → infection
	grandchild ['grændtʃaɪld]	Enkelkind, Enkel(in)	grandchild → grandson → granddaughter
	furthermore [ˌfɜ:ðə'mɔ:]	überdies; außerdem	moreover, additionally

	TLD (top-level domain) [ˌtiːelˈdiː, ˌtɒplevl dəˈmeɪn]	Bereich oberster Ebene	The last letters of an internet address show its top-level domain. The TLD for Germany is 'de'.
	condition [kənˈdɪʃn]	Kondition, Zustand, Situation, Bedingung	on one condition *(= unter einer Bedingung)*
	illiterate [ɪˈlɪtərət]	nicht lesen oder schreiben können	John never went to school. He is illiterate.
	desperate [ˈdespərət]	verzweifelt, aussichtslos	If you are desperate, you don't know what to do and you need help.
	barefoot [ˈbeəfʊt]	barfuß	not wearing shoes or socks
	to persecute [ˈpɜːsɪkjuːt]	verfolgen	to persecute → persecution → persecutor
	refuge [ˈrefjuːdʒ]	Asyl, Zufluchtsstätte	a place you can go to if you are in danger
	abbreviation [əˌbriːviˈeɪʃn]	Abkürzung	the short form of a term or of a name, for example USA
	cross [krɒs]	Kreuz	cross → to cross → crossing
B 1	**eastern** [ˈiːstən]	östlich, ost-	The sun rises in the eastern part of the world.
	to fail [feɪl]	versagen	to fail → failure
	rice [raɪs]	Reis	Risotto is made with rice.
	slave [sleɪv]	Sklave/Sklavin	Slaves are not paid for their work and they must do what their owners tell them.
	Senegalese [ˌsenɪgəˈliːz]	senegalesisch, Senegalese/-in	A person from Senegal is a Senegalese.
	industrial [ɪnˈdʌstriəl]	industriell	industrial → industry
B 2	**to rewrite** [ˌriːˈraɪt]	umschreiben	to rewrite → to write
	to carry out [ˌkæri‿ˈaʊt]	ausführen	If you carry s.th. out, you do or complete it.
	short-term [ˌʃɔːtˈtɜːm]	kurzfristig, befristet, kurzzeitig	short-term ↔ long-term
	committee [kəˈmɪtiː]	Komitee, Ausschuss, Gremium	The committee decided to help poor children in Africa.
	zone [zəʊn]	Zone, Gebiet, Bereich	area
B 3	**presenter** [prɪˈzentə]	Präsentator(in), Moderator(in)	presenter → to present → presentation
	thanks [θæŋks]	danke	'Thanks' is short for 'thank you'.
	to arrange [əˈreɪndʒ]	organisieren, ausmachen	I've arranged to meet Rob at seven o'clock.
C	**presidential** [ˌprezɪˈdenʃl]	Präsidentschafts-, präsidial	presidential → president
	federal [ˈfedərəl]	Bundes-	belonging to the central government of a country and not just to a region or state
	parliament [ˈpɑːləmənt]	Parlament	The people vote for the members of parliament.
	president [ˈprezɪdənt]	Präsident(in)	the person who has the highest political position in a country
	parliamentary [ˌpɑːləˈmentəri]	parlamentarisch	parliamentary → parliament
	majority [məˈdʒɒrəti]	Mehrheit	the majority of us = most of us
	to make up (s.th.) [meɪk ˈʌp]	etwas bilden, zusammenstellen, erfinden	The party makes up over fifty percent of the parliament.
	separation of powers [sepəˌreɪʃn‿əv ˈpaʊəz]	Gewaltenteilung	The separation of powers is one of the main principles of German politics.
	legislative [ˈledʒɪslətɪv]	legislativ, gesetzgebend	Parliament belongs to the legislative branch.
	executive [ɪgˈzekjətɪv]	exekutiv, ausführend, leitend	When we talk about the executive branch in politics we usually mean the government.
	judicial [dʒuːˈdɪʃl]	gerichtlich, rechtsprechend	Judges belong to the judicial branch.
	checks and balances [ˌtʃeks‿ən ˈbælənsɪz]	gegenseitige Kontrolle, Gewaltenteilung	Checks and balances is an important part of the American system of government.
	concentration [ˌkɒnsənˈtreɪʃn]	Ansammlung, Verdichtung, Konzentration	concentration → to concentrate
	to represent [ˌreprɪˈzent]	repräsentieren, vertreten	to stand for, to act in the place of
	Congress [ˈkɒŋgres]	Congress (Parlament in den USA)	Congress makes the laws in the United States.
	to pass [pɑːs]	(ein Gesetz) verabschieden, bestehen, weitergeben	to agree on a law
	bill [bɪl]	Gesetzesvorlage, Banknote, Entwurf, Rechnung	We would like to pay. Can you bring us the bill, please?
	congressional [kənˈgreʃənl]	Kongress-, den Kongress betreffend	congressional → Congress

	judiciary [dʒuː'dɪʃərɪ]	Judikative, Justizgewalt, Gerichtswesen	judiciary → judicial
	to impeach [ɪm'piːtʃ]	anklagen	to impeach the president = to say that the president has done something illegal
	to reverse [rɪ'vɜːs]	umkehren	to change back
	veto ['viːtəʊ]	Veto, Einspruchsrecht, Einspruch	veto ↔ approval
	to approve [ə'pruːv]	anerkennen, bestätigen, zustimmen, akzeptieren	to approve → approval
	appointment [ə'pɔɪntmənt]	Berufung, Termin	I have an appointment at the bank at 9 am tomorrow morning.
	judge [dʒʌdʒ]	Richter(in), Wettkampfrichter(in)	The judge decides in court and competitions.
	Commander-in-Chief [kəˌmɑːndər‿ɪn 'tʃiːf]	Oberbefehlshaber	The Commander-in-Chief is the top leader of the military.
	armed forces [ˌɑːmd 'fɔːsɪz]	Militär, Streitkräfte	The airforce, the army and the navy are all part of a country's armed forces.
	leader ['liːdə]	Führer(in)	The group has to follow the leader.
	treaty ['triːtɪ]	Vertrag	When two countries or nations agree on s.th., there is an official treaty between them.
	to permit [pə'mɪt]	erlauben, zulassen, genehmigen	to permit → permission
	to declare [dɪ'kleə]	erklären	declaration → to declare
	permission [pə'mɪʃn]	Erlaubnis	My mom gave me permission to stay overnight.
	to limit ['lɪmɪt]	begrenzen	to limit → limit
	to nominate ['nɒmɪneɪt]	ernennen, nominieren, aufstellen	Bruce Willis was nominated for an Oscar.
	Supreme Court [suːˌpriːm 'kɔːt]	Oberstes Bundesgericht	The Supreme Court is the highest court in the United States of America.
	constitution [ˌkɒnstɪ'tjuːʃn]	Verfassung	The constitution is a set of rules for the government.
	unconstitutional [ʌnˌkɒnstɪ'tjuːʃənl]	verfassungswidrig	It is unconstitutional to treat men and women differently.
	indirect [ˌɪndaɪ'rekt]	indirekt, mittelbar	indirect ↔ direct
	delegate ['delɪgət]	Delegierte(r), Abgeordnete(r), Bevollmächtigte(r)	People vote for the delegates who then represent the people's interests.
	voter ['vəʊtə]	Wähler(in)	The voters elect the people who form the parliament.
	citizenship ['sɪtɪzənʃɪp]	Staatsangehörigkeit, Nationalität, Bürgerrecht	Most of the people living in Germany have German citizenship.
	to register ['redʒɪstə]	registrieren, einschreiben, anmelden	Students who want to study at the university need to register for their courses first.
	residence ['rezɪdns]	Wohnsitz, Wohnhaus	His main residence is in Switzerland.
	mediation [ˌmiːdɪ'eɪʃn]	Sprachmittlung, Vermittlung, Schlichtungswesen	repeating the main ideas of a text in another language
	to paraphrase ['pærəfreɪz]	paraphrasieren, mit anderen Worten ausdrücken, umschreiben	to express in a different way but the meaning stays the same
D 1	**Italy** ['ɪtəlɪ]	Italien	Italian → Italy
	Slovenia [slə'viːnɪə]	Slowenien	Slovenia → Slovenian
	Norway ['nɔːweɪ]	Norwegen	Norway → Norwegian
	Latvia ['lætvɪə]	Lettland	Latvia is located in the north-east of Europe.
	Netherlands ['neðələndz]	Niederlande	The Netherlands is on the western border of Germany.
	Bulgaria [bʌl'geərɪə]	Bulgarien	Bulgaria is the third-largest country in south-east Europe.
	Turkey ['tɜːkɪ]	Türkei; Truthahn	Turkey → Turkish
	Greece [grɪːs]	Griechenland	Greece → Greek
	Switzerland ['swɪtsələnd]	Schweiz	the country between France, Germany and Italy
	international [ˌɪntə'næʃənl]	international	interaction between two or more countries
	Irish ['aɪrɪʃ]	irisch	of Ireland; There are lots of nice Irish songs.
	enlargement [ɪn'lɑːdʒmənt]	Vergrößerung, Erweiterung, Erhöhung	enlargement → to enlarge

continent ['kɒntɪnənt]	Kontinent, Erdteil	Europe is a continent.
stable ['steɪbl]	stabil	stable ↔ unstable
countryman ['kʌntrɪmən]	Landsmann	someone who comes from your country
corruption [kə'rʌpʃn]	Korruption, Bestechlichkeit	People use their power to make themselves rich.
bankrupt ['bæŋkrʌpt]	bankrott, insolvent	When a company can no longer pay its production costs or its workers it is bankrupt.
potential [pə'tentʃl]	potenziell, eventuell	possible
accession [æk'seʃn]	Beitritt, Einwilligung, Zuwachs	the point at which a country becomes a member of an organization
criterion, criteria [kraɪ'tɪərɪən, kraɪ'tɪərɪə]	Kriterium, Kriterien	standard
Italian [ɪ'tælɪən]	italienisch	In Italy people speak Italian.
Rome [rəʊm]	Rom	Rome is the capital of Italy.
hometown ['həʊmtaʊn]	Heimatstadt	the town that you come from
decisive [dɪ'saɪsɪv]	entscheidend, bestimmend, entscheidungsfreudig	decisive → decision → to decide
to respect [rɪ'spekt]	respektieren	If you respect s.o.'s rights, you accept them.
democracy [dɪ'mɒkrəsɪ]	Demokratie	One major feature of a democracy is its free elections.
to function ['fʌŋkʃn]	funktionieren	to work
to define [dɪ'faɪn]	definieren	When you define something, you explain what it is.
ally ['ælaɪ]	Alliierte(r), Verbündete(r)	partner, friend
thankful ['θæŋkfəl]	dankbar	thankful → to thank → thanks
to foresee [fə'siː]	vorhersehen, absehen	to expect something to happen and then it does
to by-pass ['baɪpɑːs]	überbrücken, umgehen	You by-pass a law when you break it.
to disappear [ˌdɪsə'pɪə]	verschwinden	I can't find my MP3 player. It has disappeared.
to afford [ə'fɔːd]	sich leisten	That's too expensive. I can't afford to buy it.
bureaucracy [bjʊə'rɒkrəsɪ]	Bürokratie	Bureaucracy usually means a lot of rules and paperwork.
to orientate ['ɔːrɪənteɪt]	orientieren, ausrichten	to orientate → orientation
2 **hostile** ['hɒstaɪl]	feindlich	People who are hostile like to fight.
European Monetary Union [ˌjʊərə'piːən ˌmʌnətrɪ‿'juːnɪən]	Europäische Wirtschafts- und Währungsunion	*(short form)* = EMU
referendum [ˌrefə'rendəm]	Referendum, Abstimmung, Volksbefragung	a direct vote in which citizens can say "yes" or "no" to a special issue
opponent [ə'pəʊnənt]	Gegner(in)	opponent ↔ supporter
supporter [sə'pɔːtə]	Anhänger(in), Befürworter(in)	A supporter agrees with you and helps you.
institution [ˌɪnstɪ'tjuːʃn]	Institution, Einrichtung, Anstalt	Hospitals and schools are examples of institutions.
commissioner [kə'mɪʃənə]	Beauftragte(r), Bevollmächtigte(r), Auftraggeber(in)	a person who acts officially for his/her government
to implement ['ɪmplɪment]	ausführen, verwirklichen, realisieren	to carry out, to fulfil
council ['kaʊnsl]	Gremium, Rat	committee
intergovernmental [ˌɪntəˌɡʌvən'mentl]	zwischenstaatlich, international	international
official [ə'fɪʃl]	offiziell	Where can I get information about McFly? – Try their official website.
to vary ['veərɪ]	variieren	If your feelings vary a lot, they change a lot.
European Court of Justice [ˌjʊərəpiːən ˌkɔːt‿əv 'dʒʌstɪs]	Europäischer Gerichtshof	The European Court of Justice is the highest court in the European Union.
stability [stə'bɪlətɪ]	Stabilität, Beständigkeit	stability → stable

11 Living and working in Britain

1	**German** ['dʒɜ:mən]	Deutsch	I can speak German. I can say: *Guten Tag!*
	partnership ['pɑ:tnəʃɪp]	Partnerschaft	Dortmund has a partnership with the city of Leeds.
	to be delighted [bɪ dɪ'laɪtɪd]	glücklich sein, sehr zufrieden sein	to be delighted = to be very happy
	Scotland ['skɒtlənd]	Schottland	Scotland is to the north of England.
	ourselves [ˌaʊə'selvz]	uns, selbst	We made all the food for the party ourselves.
	exclusive [ɪks'klu:sɪv]	exklusiv	When a hotel is exclusive, it is usually expensive.
	custom ['kʌstəm]	Gewohnheit, Sitte, Brauch	It is a custom in Scotland that men wear a special kind of skirt.
	restaurant ['restərɒnt]	Restaurant, Gaststätte	If you want to go out for a meal, you can go to a restaurant.
	attachment [ə'tætʃmənt]	Anhang, Anbringung	If you want to send a file with an e-mail, you send it as an attachment.
	draft [drɑ:ft]	Entwurf, Skizze	draft → to draft → draftsman
	to appreciate [ə'pri:ʃɪeɪt]	schätzen	If you appreciate s.th., you notice its positive characteristics.
	sincerely [sɪn'sɪəlɪ]	Mit freundlichen Grüßen	Yours sincerely = Yours faithfully
	salutation [ˌsæljə'teɪʃn]	Begrüßung, Anrede	You always start a letter with a salutation.
	scheme [ski:m]	Programm	scheme = programme = schedule
	request [rɪ'kwest]	Nachfrage, Anfrage	a request is when you ask someone to do s.th.
	apology [ə'pɒlədʒɪ]	Entschuldigung	to apologize → apology
	reference ['refrəns]	Referenz, Bezug	1. a letter that is written by s.o. who knows you to say you are suitable for a job; 2. s.th. you refer to for information
	complimentary close [ˌkɒmplɪmentərɪ 'kləʊz]	Grußformel	Yours ...; Yours sincerely ...; Sincerely ...; Kind regards ... are examples of complimentary closes.
2	**to come over** [kʌm 'əʊvə]	herüberkommen	Can you come over this afternoon?
	vacancy ['veɪkənsɪ]	Stellenangebot, Leere, Lücke	The hotel does not have any vacancies, it's full up.
	bed and breakfast [ˌbed‿n 'brekfəst]	Pension	A bed and breakfast is cheaper than a hotel.
	to charge [tʃɑ:dʒ]	in Rechnung stellen, berechnen	Although they charged us a large sum of money for the tickets, the show was very poor.
	reduction [rɪ'dʌkʃn]	Reduzierung	to reduce → reduction
	dot [dɒt]	Punkt	A sentence ends with a dot.
	availability [əˌveɪlə'bɪlətɪ]	Verfügbarkeit, Verwendbarkeit	availability → available → to avail
	rate [reɪt]	Rate, Preis	the level of s.th., e.g. of unemployment in a certain area
	reservation [ˌrezə'veɪʃn]	Reservierung	I have got a reservation for a seat in the train.
	to catch s.th. [kætʃ]	etwas akustisch verstehen	to hear and understand something
	to be in touch [bɪ‿ɪn 'tʌtʃ]	mit jemandem in Verbindung stehen, mit jemandem in Kontakt bleiben	I'd like to meet you again. Let's keep in touch.
3	**to cut a long story short** [tə kʌt ə ˌlɒŋ ˌstɔ:rɪ 'ʃɔ:t]	langer Rede kurzer Sinn	
	to give s.o. a buzz [bʌz]	jemanden anrufen	colloquial way of saying 'to call s.o.'
	New Year's Eve [ˌnju:ˌjɪəz'i:v]	Silvesterabend	the night before the first of January
	informal [ɪn'fɔ:ml]	informell	formal ↔ informal

12 Meeting people

1	**colleague** ['kɒli:g]	Kollege/Kollegin	a person who works with you in a company
	to shake [ʃeɪk]	schütteln, zittern	1. shake + object *(= schütteln)*; 2. shake (without object) *(= zittern)*
	pleased [pli:zd]	erfreut	happy = glad = pleased
	to cover for s.o. ['kʌvə]	jemanden vertreten	There is no one to cover for me, everyone is sick.
	response [rɪ'spɒns]	Reaktion, Antwort	He's still waiting for your response.
2	**conversation** [ˌkɒnvə'seɪʃn]	Gespräch, Unterhaltung, Konversation	When people talk to each other, they have a conversation.

executive suite [ɪɡˌzekjətɪv ˈswiːt]	Führungsloge, Vorstandsetage	The executive suite is usually on the top floor of the building.
on duty [ɒn ˈdjuːtɪ]	im Dienst	The policeman on duty gave me a ticket.
ought to [ɔːt]	sollte, müsste	ought to = must, should
foyer [ˈfɔɪeɪ]	Vorhalle, Foyer	foyer = entrance
general office [ˌdʒenrəl ˈɒfɪs]	Zentrale, Allgemeine Verwaltung	All of the information relating to this project must go to the general office.
paperwork [ˈpeɪpəwɜːk]	Schreibarbeit, Büroarbeit	She likes working in an office. She is good at paperwork.
general manager [ˌdʒenrəl ˈmænɪdʒə]	Generaldirektor(in), Geschäftsführer(in)	The general manager is the head of a company.
onto [ˈɒntə]	auf … hinauf	on + to = onto
3 **straight** [streɪt]	gerade, direkt	We're late. Let's go straight to our class.
4 **rainbow** [ˈreɪnbəʊ]	Regenbogen	rain → rainbow
trout, pl. **trout** [traʊt]	Forelle	one trout – lots of trout
haggis [ˈhæɡɪs]	Haggis (traditionelles schottisches Gericht)	
prawn [prɔːn]	Garnele	Prawns are a very delicious seafood.
lager (beer) [ˈlɑːɡə ˌbɪə]	helles Bier, Lagerbier	lager beer ↔ dark beer
shrimp [ʃrɪmp]	Krabbe, Schrimp	A shrimp is a smaller form of a prawn.
beer [bɪə]	Bier	
dish [dɪʃ]	Gericht	There are many vegetarian dishes on the menu in this café.
spicy [ˈspaɪsɪ]	würzig, pikant, scharf	spicy = hot
starter [ˈstɑːtə]	Vorspeise	to start → starter
soup [suːp]	Suppe	A bowl of hot soup on a cold day does you good.
cocktail [ˈkɒkteɪl]	Cocktail	A lot of young people like beer and cocktails.
main course [ˌmeɪn ˈkɔːs]	Hauptgericht	I'd like lamb curry for my main course, please.
pea [piː]	Erbse	Peas and carrots are two very common vegetables.
fried [fraɪd]	in der Pfanne gebraten	Fried food is delicious but you mustn't eat too much of it.
dessert [dɪˈzɜːt]	Dessert, Nachtisch	Children often like the dessert more than the main course.
pie [paɪ]	gedeckter Obstkuchen	In England you often get apple pie with ice-cream for dessert.
custard [ˈkʌstəd]	Vanillesoße	Custard is a sweet sauce which is yellow in colour.
cream [kriːm]	Sahne, Creme	You can buy cream at the supermarket.
spirit [ˈspɪrɪt]	Spirituose	a drink with a lot of alcohol in it
soft drink [ˌsɒft ˈdrɪŋk]	alkoholfreies Getränk	Children are not allow to drink alcohol in restaurants therefore they have to order soft drinks instead.
to fancy [ˈfænsɪ]	angetan sein von	She fancies him. = She likes him and would like him to be her boyfriend.
to impress [ɪmˈpres]	beeindrucken	I hoped to impress my new boss by working really hard.
Roman [ˈrəʊmən]	Römer(in)	The Romans were really good soldiers.
sparkling water [ˌspɑːklɪŋ ˈwɔːtə]	Mineralwasser mit Kohlensäure	Many people prefer drinking sparkling water to plain water.
order [ˈɔːdə]	Bestellung, Befehl, Reihenfolge	They waited an hour for their order to come.
5 **orange** [ˈɒrɪndʒ]	Orange	Oranges are usually orange in colour.
pint [paɪnt]	Pinte (englisches Hohlmaß: 0,57 l)	In England you drink beer in pints instead of litres.
emotional [ɪˈməʊʃnl]	emotional, gefühlvoll, gerührt	He gets emotional when he hears sad songs on the radio.
intense [ɪnˈtens]	angestrengt, intensiv	His reaction was very intense. It really hurt him.
trainee [ˌtreɪˈniː]	Praktikant(in), Auszubildende(r)	trainee → to train → training
to circulate [ˈsɜːkjəleɪt]	zirkulieren, herumgehen	to circulate → circle → circulation
stopover [ˈstɒpˌəʊvə]	Zwischenlandung	to stop → stopover
marital status [ˌmærɪtl ˈsteɪtəs]	Ehestand, Familienstand	He has just got married so his marital status has changed.

13 Working in a hotel

1	**single** ['sɪŋgl]	einzeln, einfach	1. not a single person (= *kein einziger Mensch*); 2. a single room (= *ein Einzelzimmer*); 3. I'm single. (= *Ich bin alleinstehend.*)
	double ['dʌbl]	Doppel-, Doppelgänger	He looks like me. He's my double.
	time-consuming ['taɪmkən,sju:mɪŋ]	zeitraubend	It's so time-consuming when I must do things that I'm not interested in.
	security [sɪ'kjʊərətɪ]	Sicherheit	security → to secure
	expiry [ɪk'spaɪrɪ]	Fälligwerden, Ablauf, Verfall	expiry → to expire
	stay [steɪ]	Aufenthalt	stay → to stay
	to require [rɪ'kwaɪə]	benötigen	If you require s.th., it means that you need to have it.
2	**diary** ['daɪərɪ]	Tagebuch, Terminkalender	Some people write what they have done during the day in a diary. A small diary is just for things you plan to do.
	businessman ['bɪznɪsmən]	Geschäftsmann	I could have got more money when I sold my car, but I'm not a very good businessman.
	fairly ['feəlɪ]	relativ	The test was fairly difficult but I think that I passed.
	flexible ['fleksɪbl]	flexibel, biegsam, anpassungsfähig	I can cope with very different people. I'm really flexible.
	what a pity [,wɒt ə 'pɪtɪ]	wie schade!	He didn't get the job. What a pity!
	available [ə'veɪləbl]	frei, erhältlich	If s.th. is available, you can get it or buy it.
	midday [,mɪd'deɪ]	Mittag	We normally eat lunch around midday.
	to be on business [bɪ‿ɒn 'bɪznɪs]	auf Geschäftsreise sein	I'm sorry the manager can't speak to you. He is away on business.
	to confirm [kən'fɜ:m]	bestätigen, bestärken, konfirmieren	Would you please confirm our meeting on Monday?
3	**utensil** [ju:'tensl]	Gerät, Geschirr, Gefäß	A utensil is something you use daily.
	ladle ['leɪdl]	Kelle, Schöpflöffel	The cook served the soup with a ladle.
	saucepan ['sɔ:spən]	Kochtopf	The potatoes were boiled in a saucepan.
	to fry [fraɪ]	braten	You fry an egg, you bake a cake and you boil potatoes.
	pan [pæn]	Pfanne	The meat was fried in a pan.
	lamb [læm]	Lamm	
	to stew [stju:]	dämpfen, schmoren, sich aufregen	Stewed vegetables are very healthy.
	ingredient [ɪn'gri:dɪənt]	Zutat	Something is missing in this cake. What ingredient have I forgotten?
	cubed [kju:bd]	in Würfeln geschnitten, zur dritten Potenz erhoben	to cube → cube → cubic
	onion ['ʌnjən]	Zwiebel	When I cut onions, I always have to cry.
	finely ['faɪnlɪ]	dünn	If you cut the vegetables finely, they would cook more quickly.
	to chop [tʃɒp]	zerhacken, hauen, spalten	The cook uses chopped tomatoes in the tomato soup.
	leek [li:k]	Lauch	vegetable that is related to the onion
	carrot ['kærət]	Karotte	a long, orange vegetable
	stock [stɒk]	Brühe	It is easy to make your own stock with a few vegetables.
	thyme [taɪm]	Thymian	Thyme leaves are used in cooking.
	to melt [melt]	schmelzen	Butter melts if you leave it out for a little while.
	to stir [stɜ:]	(um)rühren, sich regen	The chef is stirring the soup in the pot.
	pepper ['pepə]	Pfeffer	Salt and pepper are part of every good meal.
	crusty ['krʌstɪ]	knusprig	Bread that has just been baked is crusty on top.
4	**to check in** [tʃek‿'ɪn]	einchecken, anmelden	The guest is checking in to the hotel.
6	**to inquire** [ɪn'kwaɪə]	sich erkundigen, fragen	to inquire → inquiry
	rental ['rentl]	Miet-, Verleih	rental → to rent → rent
	saloon [sə'lu:n]	Limousine, Salon, Saal	It is more expensive to rent a saloon car than a Mini.
	shoulder bag ['ʃəʊldə ,bæg]	Umhängetasche	
	toll [təʊl]	Maut	If you want to drive through the tunnel, you must pay a toll.
	tube [tju:b]	U-Bahn, Röhre	Another name for the London Underground is the Tube.

7 **to give s.o.'s regards to s.o.** [gɪv ˌsʌmwʌnz rɪ'gɑ:dz tʊ ˌsʌmwʌn]	herzliche Grüße an jemanden ausrichten	Please give Daniel my best regards.
take care [teɪk 'keə]	Pass auf dich auf.	Friends often say this when they say goodbye to one another.

14 Different countries, different cultures

1 **culture** ['kʌltʃə]	Kultur	culture → cultural
look [lʊk]	Blick, Aussehen	look → to look
monster ['mɒnstə]	Monster, Ungetüm	What colour is the monster? – It's blue.
distillery [dɪ'stɪlərɪ]	Brennerei	Spirits are produced in a distillery.
North Sea [ˌnɔ:θ 'si:]	Nordsee	The North Sea is off the north coast of Germany.
scenery ['si:nərɪ]	Landschaft	The scenery in Canada is great. There are mountains, lakes, trees …
its [ɪts]	sein(e), ihr(e)	I like its colours.
tartan ['tɑ:tən]	Schottenkaro (bestimmtes Muster eines Clans)	The kilts of different families are in tartans of different colours.
instant ['ɪnstənt]	sofort	An instant message is something you get right away.
unique [ju:'ni:k]	einzig, einzigartig	s.th. unique is the only one of its kind
pattern ['pætən]	Muster	1. the way in which s.th. is done or repeated; 2. a design of lines, colours, shapes, etc.
fashionable ['fæʃənəbl]	modisch	fashion → fashionable
alongside [əˌlɒŋ'saɪd]	nebenher, entlang, an der Seite, nebenstehend	alongside = next to
thistle ['θɪsl]	Distel	a wild plant with thorns; It hurts if you touch it.
identifiable [aɪ'dentɪfaɪəbl]	identifizierbar, erkennbar, feststellbar, belegbar	identifiable → to identify → identification
warrior ['wɒrɪə]	Krieger(in)	war → warrior
to attack [ə'tæk]	angreifen	Let's play "Robin Hood". We can attack Nottingham Castle.
Viking ['vaɪkɪŋ]	Wikinger	people who used to live in the North of Europe and were really good naval warriors
to defend oneself [dɪ'fend wʌnˌself]	sich verteidigen	
to defeat [dɪ'fi:t]	besiegen	to defeat = to beat
lung [lʌŋ]	Lunge	You take a breath of air into your lungs.
sheep, pl. **sheep** [ʃi:p]	Schaf	one sheep – a lot of sheep
oatmeal ['əʊtmi:l]	Haferflocken, Hafermehl	Some people like to eat oatmeal with milk for breakfast.
spice [spaɪs]	Gewürz, Beigeschmack	Spices are used to make food taste more interesting.
to stuff (into) [stʌf‿'ɪntə]	stopfen (in)	Peter was in a hurry. He stuffed his school things into his bag and left.
to celebrate ['seləbreɪt]	feiern	"How do you celebrate your birthday?" – "I usually have a party."
national ['næʃənl]	national	of a country
poet ['pəʊɪt]	Dichter(in), Poet(in)	poet → poetry → poem
to accompany [ə'kʌmpənɪ]	begleiten	If you accompany a person, you go somewhere with them.
bagpiper ['bægˌpaɪpə]	Dudelsackspieler(in)	a person who plays a traditional Scottish instrument
prayer [preə]	Gebet	People in church usually sing and say prayers.
fan [fæn]	Fan, Anhänger(in)	He's a big football fan.
talk [tɔ:k]	Vortrag, Gespräch, Unterhaltung	to talk → a talk
2 **handout** ['hændaʊt]	Informationsblatt, Handout	hand → handout; a piece of paper that gives important information (e. g. from a talk)
impolite [ˌɪmpə'laɪt]	unhöflich	impolite ↔ polite
to swear, swore, sworn [sweə, swɔ:, swɔ:n]	fluchen; schwören	It's not very polite to swear at people.
unnatural [ʌn'nætʃərəl]	unnatürlich	unnatural ↔ natural
foreigner ['fɒrənə]	Ausländer(in)	foreign → foreigner
in general [ɪn 'dʒenrəl]	im Allgemeinen, generell	In general I am interested in all sports.

stranger ['streɪndʒə]	Fremde(r)	I don't know that man – he's a stranger.
rank [ræŋk]	Rang, Stellung, Rangordnung	A general is the highest rank in the military.
standing ['stændɪŋ]	Ansehen, Stellung	Paul is the best student in his class. He has a very good standing with the other students.
queue [kju:]	Warteschlange	a line of people who are waiting, e.g. in a shop or at a bus stop
Brit [brɪt]	umgangssprachlicher Ausdruck für einen Engländer	a person who comes from Britain
dress code ['dres ˌkəʊd]	Kleiderordnung	The dress code tells you what you have to wear.
tie [taɪ]	Krawatte; (Spiel) unentschieden enden	The game ended in a tie: 58-58.
showy ['ʃəʊɪ]	auffallend, prächtig, protzig	Everybody looked at her because she was wearing a very showy skirt.
pedestrian [pə'destrɪən]	Fußgänger(in)	When you walk down the street, you are a pedestrian.
disciplined ['dɪsɪplɪnd]	diszipliniert	If you do what you should do all of the time, then you are very disciplined.
tactic ['tæktɪk]	Taktik	a plan how to do s.th.
3 **quiz** [kwɪz]	Quiz, Ratespiel	quiz = a game to see what you know
incoming ['ɪnˌkʌmɪŋ]	eingehend, ankommend	We couldn't receive any incoming calls because the phone lines were down.
4 **overseas** [ˌəʊvə'si:z]	Übersee-, in Übersee	If you go to the USA, you travel overseas.
floor [flɔ:]	Stock, Etage	This building has lots of floors.
cell phone ['sel ˌfəʊn]	Handy, Mobiltelefon	cell phone *(AE)* = mobile phone *(BE)*
check [tʃek]	Rechnung (im Restaurant) *(AE)*, Scheck *(AE)*, Prüfung	check → to check
bill [bɪl]	Rechnung, Banknote, Schnabel	a piece of paper that shows how much you must pay for s.th.
out of order [ˌaʊt‿əv 'ɔ:də]	außer Betrieb, gestört	The lift doesn't work anymore. It is out of order.
closet ['klɒzɪt]	Wandschrank, Kammer	I put all of my clothes into the bedroom closet.
elevator ['eləveɪtə]	Aufzug	elevator *(AE)* = lift *(BE)*
wedding ['wedɪŋ]	Hochzeit	Paul and Jane really love each other. Their wedding is on Friday.
anniversary [ˌænɪ'vɜ:sərɪ]	Jubiläum, Hochzeitstag	a day when you remember s.th. that happened on the same date one or more years ago
restroom ['restrʊm]	Toilette	restroom *(AE)* = toilet(s) *(BE)*
gas [gæs]	Benzin	gas *(AE)* = petrol *(BE)*
Mountie ['maʊntɪ]	berittene kanadische Polizei	a Canadian policeman on horseback
Gaelic football [ˌgeɪlɪk 'fʊtbɔ:l]	eine Sportart, die vorwiegend in Irland gespielt wird	a type of football played in Ireland
leprechaun ['leprəkɔ:n]	ein kleiner Kobold aus der irischen Mythologie	a type of fairy said to be found in Ireland
billboard ['bɪlbɔ:d]	Plakatwand	outdoor board on which posters and adverts are displayed
dingo ['dɪŋgəʊ]	Dingo (australischer Wildhund)	Dingoes look like pet dogs, but they are wild animals which kill other animals for food.
kiwi ['ki:wi:]	ein flugunfähiger Vogel, eine Fruchtsorte, eine Eigenbezeichnung der Bewohner Neuseelands	A kiwi can be a bird, a type of fruit or an informal name for a person from New Zealand.
Aussie *(informal)* ['ɒzɪ]	Australier(in)	Aussie = Australian
All Blacks [ˌɔ:l 'blæks]	die neuseeländische Rugby-Union-Nationalmannschaft	the New Zealand national rugby union team
to settle up [ˌsetl 'ʌp]	bezahlen, Rechnung begleichen	to settle up = to pay
account [ə'kaʊnt]	Konto, Abrechnung, Berechnung, Wert	Where do you have your bank account?
wanna (= *informal form of* **want to**) ['wɒnə]	will/wollen	I really wanna go to that party tomorrow.
pretty ['prɪtɪ]	ziemlich	s.th. that is 'pretty good' is 'quite good'

maintenance ['meɪntənəns]	Wartung, Pflege, Instandhaltung, Unterhalt, Verwaltung	maintenance → to maintain
inconvenience [ˌɪnkən'vi:nɪəns]	Unannehmlichkeit, Belästigung, Unbequemlichkeit	inconvenience → inconvenient
pleasant ['pleznt]	angenehm	I like having him around. He is a very pleasant person.
French fry ['frentʃ ˌfraɪ]	Pommes frites	French fries *(AE)* = chips *(BE)*
to accommodate [ə'kɒmədeɪt]	unterbringen, anpassen, aushelfen	to accommodate → accommodation

15 Youth unemployment

1 **figure** ['fɪgə]	Zahl, Ziffer	figure = number
rejection [rɪ'dʒekʃn]	Ablehnung, Absage	I wasn't qualified for the job so I got a rejection in the post.
expert ['ekspɜ:t]	Experte/Expertin	James really knows everything about that subject. He is an expert on it.
to get used to (+gerund) [get‿'ju:zd tə]	sich gewöhnen (an)	It takes time to get used to living in a new place.
to gain [geɪn]	gewinnen	to get s.th. positive or an advantage from doing s.th.
failure ['feɪljə]	Versagen	failure → to fail
homelessness ['həʊmləsnəs]	Obdachlosigkeit	not having a home
factor ['fæktə]	Faktor, Einfluss	Those factors influenced my decision.
unhelpful [ʌn'helpfəl]	nutzlos, nicht hilfreich	unhelpful ↔ helpful
lack of ['læk‿əv]	Mangel an, mangelnd, fehlend	His lack of experience was the reason why he was fired.
qualified ['kwɒlɪfaɪd]	qualifiziert	A qualified teacher has learnt how to teach in a college.
coaching ['kəʊtʃɪŋ]	Nachhilfeunterricht, Coaching	He isn't good at football so I am giving him some coaching.
sufficient [sə'fɪʃənt]	ausreichend, genügend	sufficient = enough
eager ['i:gə]	eifrig	She's always so eager to be the best at everything she does; it really drives me crazy sometimes.
downhill [ˌdaʊn'hɪl]	abwärts, bergab	He climbed the mountain and then went downhill on his bike.
teaching assistant ['ti:tʃɪŋ əˌsɪstənt]	Lehrkraft, die einen Lehrer im Unterricht unterstützt, kleinen Schülergruppen Nachhilfe gibt bzw. Kinder mit Behinderungen betreut	assistant → to assist
childcare ['tʃaɪldkeə]	Kinderbetreuung	She really likes children so she wants to go into childcare.
appealing [ə'pi:lɪŋ]	ansprechend, reizvoll	The girl is very good-looking. She is very appealing to the boys.
critic ['krɪtɪk]	Kritiker(in)	critic → to criticise → criticism → critical
to hang around [ˌhæŋ‿ə'raʊnd]	herumhängen	If you hang around, you stay in one place and don't really do anything.
lifelong ['laɪflɒŋ]	lebenslang, lebenslänglich	People have to learn all of the time. Learning is a lifelong task.
2 **based on** ['beɪst ɒn]	basierend auf	This adventure story is based on the life of a real person.

16 New jobs

rundown [ˌrʌn'daʊn]	abgewirtschaftet, verwahrlost	The building was empty and completely rundown.
1 **district** ['dɪstrɪkt]	Distrikt, Bezirk, Stadtteil	Harlem is a district in New York City.
regeneration [rɪˌdʒenə'reɪʃn]	Erneuerung, Wiederherstellung, Regeneration	If you bring new life to s.th. it is called 'regeneration'.
deprived [dɪ'praɪvd]	sozial benachteiligt	= disadvantaged in some way
investment [ɪn'vestmənt]	Investition, Geldanlage	I have too much money in my account. I need a good form of investment so that I can make money.
benefit ['benɪfɪt]	Nutzen, Gewinn, Sozialhilfe, Rente	His parents don't have jobs. They get benefits from the state.
model ['mɒdl]	Model, Vorbild, Modell	A lot of young girls dream of becoming models.

activist ['æktɪvɪst]	Aktivist(in), jemand, der sich für etwas engagiert	active → activity → activist
to transform [træns'fɔ:m]	verwandeln	to transform → transformation → transformer
forum ['fɔ:rəm]	Forum, öffentliche Diskussion	I'm sorry, but this is the wrong forum for that kind of discussion. Can we talk about it another time?
convenience store [kən'vi:nɪəns‿stɔ:]	kleiner Lebensmittelladen	convenience → convenient
to dismiss [dɪ'smɪs]	entlassen, freistellen, ablehnen	to dismiss = to fire
retail ['ri:teɪl]	Einzelhandel(s-)	retail → to retail
fear [fɪə]	Angst	the feeling you have when you are scared
turnover ['tɜ:nˌəʊvə]	Absatz, Umsatz	Just because the company has a big turnover it doesn't mean that you earn a lot.
2 **basic** ['beɪsɪk]	grundlegend	In the first two years of English you learn a lot of basic words and phrases.

17 Modern technology

modern ['mɒdən]	modern	a new school = a modern school
1 **fairy tale** ['feərɪ ˌteɪl]	Märchen	In fairy tales the youngest of the three sons is often the hero.
powerful ['paʊəfəl]	stark	powerful → power
search engine ['sɜ:tʃ ˌendʒɪn]	Suchmaschine	A search engine helps you to find information on the Internet.
domain [dəʊ'meɪn]	Domain	part of a website address
misspelling [mɪs'spelɪŋ]	falsche Schreibweise, Rechtschreibfehler	misspelling → to spell
googol ['gu:gɒl, 'gu:gəl]	Googol	1×10^{100}
zero ['zɪərəʊ]	Null	the figure '0'
to google ['gu:gəl]	googeln	to search for information on the Internet using the Google search engine
to obtain [əb'teɪn]	erlangen	to get
pop-up advertising [ˌpɒpʌp 'ædvətaɪzɪŋ]	Werbung in einem Pop-up-Fenster (auf einem Monitor)	an online advertisement that is shown in a new window
user ['ju:zə]	Benutzer(in)	user → to use
design [dɪ'zaɪn]	Design, Entwurf, Gestaltung	to design → designer → design
to be related to [bɪ rɪ'leɪtɪd‿tu:]	sich beziehen auf, betreffen	related → relation → to relate
to enter ['entə]	eingeben	enter → entrance → entry
to be targeted [bɪ 'tɑ:gɪtɪd]	gezielt sein	to target → the target
click [klɪk]	Klicken	when you press a key or mouse button quickly
link [lɪŋk]	Verbindung, Link	connection
ingenious [ɪn'dʒi:nɪəs]	genial, raffiniert	very clever
earnings ['ɜ:nɪŋz]	Einnahmen, Erträge	earnings → to earn
criticism ['krɪtɪsɪzm]	Kritik	criticism → to criticize
with regard to [wɪð rɪ'gɑ:d‿tə]	in Bezug auf	referring to
privacy ['prɪvəsɪ; 'praɪvəsɪ]	Privatsphäre	privacy → private
image ['ɪmɪdʒ]	Bild, Image	picture
doubt [daʊt]	Zweifel	without doubt = certainly
search [sɜ:tʃ]	Suche	the search → to search
theoretical [θɪə'retɪkl]	theoretisch	theoretical ↔ practical
to assign [ə'saɪn]	zuordnen	to relate
data ['deɪtə]	Daten	facts, items of information
individual [ˌɪndɪ'vɪdʒʊəl]	Einzelperson	Each individual is a unique person.
third party [ˌθɜ:d 'pɑ:tɪ]	Dritte	other people
in the long run [ɪn ðə 'lɒŋ ˌrʌn]	auf lange Sicht	in the end

18 Plastic money for young people

	plastic ['plæstɪk]	Plastik	material that is light and doesn't break easily
1	**cool** [ku:l]	cool, kühl	School is cool!
	pre-paid [ˌpri:'peɪd]	vorausbezahlt	You must pay for it before you can use it.
	must-have ['mʌsthæv]	etwas Unentbehrliches	something that people think is very important and fashionable
	massive ['mæsɪv]	massiv, umfangreich	very large
	campaign [kæm'peɪn]	Kampagne	planned activity carried out over a period of time
	logical ['lɒdʒɪkl]	logisch	Mathematics is a logical science.
	step [step]	Schritt, Stufe	It's only a few more steps to their house.
	to withdraw (withdrew, withdrawn) [wɪð'drɔ:, wɪð'dru:, wɪð'drɔ:n]	abheben, (sich) entfernen	If you need cash, you can withdraw money from your bank account.
	cash machine ['kæʃ məˌʃi:n]	Bankautomat	an appliance that lets you get money from your account
	to top up [tɒp 'ʌp]	füllen, aufladen	to make something full again
	personal identification number [ˌpɜ:sənl aɪˌdentɪfɪ'keɪʃn‿ˌnʌmbə]	persönliche Identifikationsnummer	secret number that you use with a bank card, for example
	transaction [træn'zækʃn]	Übertragung, Transaktion, Geschäft	a piece of business
	debt [det]	Schulden	a sum of money that you owe somebody
	to consider [kən'sɪdə]	nachdenken über, überlegen, betrachten	to think about
	to issue ['ɪʃu:]	herausgeben	to give out
	monthly ['mʌnθlɪ]	monatlich	every month
	to reload [ˌri:'ləʊd]	wieder aufladen	to load again, to top up
	to discover [dɪ'skʌvə]	entdecken	to find s.th. for the first time; to find s.th. out
	notification [ˌnəʊtɪfɪ'keɪʃn]	Benachrichtigung, Meldung	information
	database ['deɪtəbeɪs]	Datenbank	collection of data stored in a computer
	sensible ['sensɪbl]	vernünftig	based on reason and not on feelings
	to handle ['hændl]	umgehen mit, handhaben	to deal with
	virtual ['vɜ:tʃʊəl]	virtuell	In a computer game, everything you do is virtual, it's not real.
3	**clothing** ['kləʊðɪŋ]	Kleidung	clothing = clothes
	movie ['mu:vɪ]	Film	A movie is a film.
	jewelry *(AE)*, **jewellery** *(BE)* ['dʒu:əlrɪ]	Schmuck	rings or earrings made of gold or silver
	comic ['kɒmɪk]	Comic(heft)	*Spiderman* and *Superman* are comics.

19 Young people and society

1	**normal** ['nɔ:ml]	normal	It's normal to feel tired after a long day.
	well-dressed [ˌwel'drest]	gut angezogen	wearing nice clothes
	past [pɑ:st]	vorbei	I didn't go into the café. I just walked past it.
	row [rəʊ]	Reihe	We have tickets for the cinema. We are going to sit in row 9.
	shocking ['ʃɒkɪŋ]	schockierend	shocking → a shock
	to terrorize ['terəraɪz]	terrorisieren	to terrorize → terror → terrorist
	gang [gæŋ]	Bande, Gang	a gang of thieves
	mental ['mentl]	geistig, mental	related to the mind, for example, a mental illness
	rabbit ['ræbɪt]	Kaninchen	Roger Rabbit plays a role in a film of the same name.
	fire fighter ['faɪəˌfaɪtə]	Feuerwehrmann, Feuerwehrfrau	The fire fighter tried to get the children out of the burning house.
	Halloween [ˌhæləʊ'i:n]	Halloween, Tag vor Allerheiligen	Halloween is celebrated on October 31.
	hell [hel]	Hölle	Some people believe that if you live an evil life, you'll go to hell.

climax ['klaɪmæks]	Höhepunkt	The climax is the most exciting point in a story, the highlight of a story.
trick or treat [ˌtrɪkɔ:'tri:t]	Streich oder Leckereien, Süßes oder Saures	On Halloween children go to neighbours and use this phrase.
firework ['faɪəwɜ:k]	Feuerwerk, Feuerwerkskörper	People often have fireworks on December 31.
letter box ['letəbɒks]	Briefkasten	a box for the delivery of post to a house
to urinate ['jʊərɪneɪt]	urinieren	urinate → urine
to abuse [ə'bju:z]	beschimpfen, misshandeln, missbrauchen	to use wrongly
dirt [dɜ:t]	Schmutz	dirt → dirty
depressed [dɪ'prest]	niedergeschlagen, deprimiert	depressed → depression
to take action [teɪk 'ækʃn]	handeln, eingreifen	If you don't reply, we will have to take action.
to wander ['wɒndə]	umherstreifen, wandern	to walk around
to bring up [brɪŋ 'ʌp]	großziehen, aufbringen	to care for children
moreover [mɔ:r'əʊvə]	überdies; außerdem	in addition
to maintain [meɪn'teɪn]	behaupten, erhalten, pflegen	to declare to be true
minority [maɪ'nɒrətɪ]	Minderheit	minority ↔ majority
tolerance ['tɒlərəns]	Toleranz	tolerance → to tolerate
jungle ['dʒʌŋgl]	Dschungel	a wild area of land, for example, the rain forest
scenario [sɪ'nɑ:rɪəʊ]	Szenario, Drehbuch	situation
tragic ['trædʒɪk]	tragisch	tragic → tragedy
to wonder ['wʌndə]	sich fragen, sich Gedanken machen, sich wundern	I wonder what it was like to live in the 16th century.
to commit [kə'mɪt]	begehen (Verbrechen, Mord)	to commit a crime
suicide ['su:ɪsaɪd]	Selbstmord	killing oneself
bullying ['bʊlɪɪŋ]	Mobbing, Schikanieren	being aggressive towards s.o. weaker
to cope (with) [kəʊp]	zurechtkommen (mit)	to manage
to claim [kleɪm]	behaupten, beanspruchen	to say that s.th. is true although it has not been proved
ghost [gəʊst]	Geist	Some people believe that there are ghosts in old houses and castles.
nasty ['nɑ:stɪ]	schlimm, böse	nasty ↔ nice
unsure [ʌn'ʃɔ:]	unsicher	unsure ↔ sure
contented [kən'tentɪd]	zufrieden	pleased, happy, satisfied
3 **anti-social** [ˌæntɪ'səʊʃl]	asozial	which hurts other people

20 Young people and alcohol

alcohol ['ælkəhɒl]	Alkohol	Whisky, gin or vodka contain alcohol.
1 **excessive** [ek'sesɪv]	maßlos, exzessiv, zu viel	going over a reasonable limit
binge drinking ['bɪndʒ ˌdrɪnkɪŋ]	Besäufnis, Komasaufen	the consumption of large quantities of alcohol within a few hours
evidence ['evɪdəns]	Beweis, Beweismaterial	something that makes something clear or that proves something
irresponsible [ˌɪrɪ'spɒnsəbl]	unverantwortlich	irresponsible ↔ responsible
double ['dʌbl]	doppelt	twice as much, twice as large
injury ['ɪndʒərɪ]	Verletzung	to injure → injury
drunken ['drʌŋkən]	betrunken	having had too much alcohol
violence ['vaɪələns]	Gewalt	Violence is when people try to hurt or even kill others.
by [baɪ]	um	The world population has grown by about 12 per cent over the last ten years.
to alarm [ə'lɑ:m]	beängstigen, beunruhigen, alarmieren	to warn of danger
increase ['ɪnkri:s]	Zunahme	the increase → to increase
attempt [ə'tempt]	Versuch	an effort
to halt [hɒlt]	halten, anhalten, unterbrechen	to stop
awareness [ə'weənəs]	Bewusstsein, Bewusstheit	awareness → to be aware
certificate [sə'tɪfɪkət]	Zertifikat, Bescheinigung, Zeugnis, Urkunde	When you pass the exam, you will get a certificate.

	on the one hand [ˌɒn ðə ˈwʌn ˌhænd]	einerseits, auf der einen Seite	on the one hand ↔ on the other hand
	excess [ekˈses, ˈekses]	Übermaß, Maßlosigkeit	excess → excessive
	impotence [ˈɪmpətəns]	Impotenz, Unvermögen, Zeugungsunfähigkeit	impotence → impotent
	inability [ˌɪnəˈbɪləti]	Unfähigkeit, Unvermögen	inability → ability → able
	on the other hand [ɒn ðɪ‿ˈʌðə ˌhænd]	andererseits, auf der anderen Seite	When you say 'on the other hand', you mention another aspect of a situation.
	legal [ˈliːgl]	rechtlich, gesetzlich, legal	legal ↔ illegal
	to focus (on) [ˈfəʊkəs]	sich konzentrieren (auf)	to concentrate on
	penalty [ˈpenəltɪ]	Strafe, Elfmeter (Fußball)	The penalty for his crime was to do community work at the weekends.
	under-age [ˌʌndərˈeɪdʒ]	minderjährig, unmündig	not being old enough to vote, to buy alcohol, to drive, etc.
	to resist [rɪˈzɪst]	widerstehen	to fight back or to refuse to accept s.th. and try to prevent it from happening
	dehydrated [ˌdiːhaɪˈdreɪtɪd]	entwässert, dehydriert	to lose water from the body
	to poison [ˈpɔɪzn]	vergiften	to poison → the poison → poisonous
	to choke [tʃəʊk]	ersticken, drosseln	When you can't get any air, you choke.
	vomit [ˈvɒmɪt]	Erbrochenes	food which comes up again through the mouth
	fatal [ˈfeɪtl]	tödlich	causing death, deadly
	GCSE [ˌdʒiːsiːesˈiː]	Prüfung zum Abschluss der Sekundarstufe	General Certificate of Secondary Education
	valuable [ˈvæljʊbl]	wertvoll	Picasso's pictures are very valuable.
	myth [mɪθ]	Mythos, Märchen, Gerücht	a story or version of the truth that is often still believed, even though it is not founded on fact
	conscious [ˈkɒnʃəs]	bewusst, bei Bewusstsein	aware, awake
	blind drunk [ˌblaɪnd‿ˈdrʌŋk]	stark betrunken, sternhagelvoll	very drunk
3	**episodic** [ˌepɪˈsɒdɪk]	gelegentlich	which happens now and again

21 Biotechnology

	cloning [ˈkləʊnɪŋ]	Klonen	process of producing an identical copy from a parent
	dimension [daɪˈmenʃn]	Größenordnung, Dimension, Ausmaß	= size
1	**cell** [sel]	Zelle	very small structure in the body
	capable (of) [ˈkeɪpəbl]	fähig	= able (to)
	adulthood [ˈædʌlthʊd]	Erwachsensein, Erwachsenenalter	the state or time of being an adult
	Chinese [tʃaɪˈniːz]	chinesisch; Chinese, Chinesin	from China
	specific [spəˈsɪfɪk]	spezifisch, bestimmt, speziell	special
	tissue [ˈtɪʃuː]	Gewebe, Papiertaschentuch	a large number of cells which have the same function and can be used in medicine
	cancer [ˈkænsə]	Krebs	often deadly illness
	copycat [ˈkɒpɪkæt]	Nachahmer(in)	a person that copies another person
	offspring [ˈɒfsprɪŋ]	Nachwuchs, Nachkommen	child, children
	clone [kləʊn]	Klon, Nachbau	an identical copy of a person, animal or cell
	era [ˈɪərə]	Ära, Zeitalter	period of time
	mouse, pl. **mice** [maʊs, maɪs]	Maus	a little animal with a long tail
	previous [ˈpriːvɪəs]	vorherig, früher, vorausgegangen	previous ↔ later
	extent [ɪkˈstent]	Ausmaß, Größe, Umfang	size
	breakthrough [ˈbreɪkθruː]	Durchbruch	My English was bad. The breakthrough was a trip to the USA. Now I can speak well.
	stem cell [ˈstem ˌsel]	Stammzelle	an unspecialized cell that can develop into different cells
	skin [skɪn]	Haut	Too much sun is bad for your skin.
	to convert (into) [kənˈvɜːt]	umwandeln, konvertieren	to change into, to turn into
	embryonic-like [embrɪˌɒnɪkˈlaɪk]	wie von einem Embryo	embryonic → embryo
	adult [ˈædʌlt]	erwachsen	adult → an adult

	to reprogram [ˌri:'prəʊgræm]	umprogrammieren, neu programmieren	reprogram → program
	applicable [ə'plɪkəbl]	anwendbar, geeignet	applicable → to apply → application
	technique [tek'ni:k]	Methode, Technik	method, skill
	to transfer [træns'fɜ:]	übertragen, transferieren	to move s.o. or s.th. from one place to another
	ethics ['eθɪks]	Moral, ethische Grundsätze	moral principles
	human ['hju:mən]	Mensch	human ↔ alien
	designer [dɪ'zaɪnə]	Designer(in), Gestalter(in)	A designer baby is created according to its parents' wishes.
	application [ˌæplɪ'keɪʃn]	Anwendung, Einsatz, Bewerbung	application → to apply
	ethical ['eθɪkl]	ethisch, moralisch	ethical → ethics
2	**to illustrate** ['ɪləstreɪt]	illustrieren, darstellen	The photos illustrate the company's history.
	to justify ['dʒʌstɪfaɪ]	rechtfertigen	to give good reasons for s.th.
	prohibition [ˌprəʊhɪ'bɪʃn]	Verbot	a law that makes s.th. illegal
3	**blessing** ['blesɪŋ]	Segen	benefit, advantage
	curse [kɜ:s]	Fluch	evil, disadvantage

22 Modern transport

1	**carbon** ['kɑ:bən]	Kohlenstoff	element in coal or petroleum
	claim [kleɪm]	Anspruch, Behauptung	claim → to claim
	traveller ['trævələ]	Reisende(r)	traveller → to travel
	footprint ['fʊtprɪnt]	Fußabdruck	a mark that is left in earth or sand by a foot
	i.e. [ˌaɪ'i:]	das heißt	*(short form of)* id est (that is)
	remarkable [rɪ'mɑ:kəbl]	beachtlich, bemerkenswert, auffallend	extraordinary
	strike [straɪk]	Treffer, Schlag	attack, hit
	lead [li:d]	Führung	the lead → to lead
	to commission [kə'mɪʃn]	in Dienst stellen, bestellen, bevollmächtigen	to put into service
	wing [wɪŋ]	Flügel	Birds and planes have wings.
	span [spæn]	Spannweite, Spanne	It refers to how wide the wings of a plane are.
	extraordinary [ɪk'strɔ:dɪnrɪ]	außergewöhnlich	much better or worse than is usual
	construction [kən'strʌkʃn]	Bau, Konstruktion	Skyscrapers and huge bridges must be dream projects for people who are interested in construction.
	maximum ['mæksɪməm]	maximal, größte(r, s)	the greatest quantity
	partly ['pɑ:tlɪ]	teilweise	partly → part
	to construct [kən'strʌkt]	bauen, konstruieren	to construct → construction
	deck [dek]	Deck	level on a ship, bus or plane; upper deck ↔ lower deck
	body ['bɒdɪ]	Rumpf, Karosserie	main outer part of a plane or car
	elliptical [ɪ'lɪptɪkl]	elliptisch	An egg has an elliptical shape.
	uplift ['ʌplɪft]	Auftrieb	act of raising a plane up into the air
	shape [ʃeɪp]	Form	form
	angle ['æŋgl]	Winkel	direction from which s.th. comes
	current ['kʌrənt]	Strömung, Strom	Be careful, the current here is very strong.
	given the fact [ˌgɪvn ðə 'fækt]	angesichts der Tatsache	considering the fact
	exhaust [ɪg'zɔ:st]	Abgas, Auspuff	emissions from a car or plane
	amazing [ə'meɪzɪŋ]	unglaublich, erstaunlich	That's amazing! I've never seen anything like it.
	capacity [kə'pæsɪtɪ]	Kapazität	The fuel tank of the car has a capacity of 60 litres.
	technological [ˌteknə'lɒdʒɪkl]	technisch, technologisch	technology → technological
	to look like ['lʊk laɪk]	aussehen wie	The London Eye looks like a big spinning wheel.
	inventiveness [ɪn'ventɪvnəs]	Einfallsreichtum, Ideenreichtum	inventiveness → to invent → invention
	to hold true [həʊld‿'tru:]	gelten	to be true
3	**delayed** [dɪ'leɪd]	verspätet, aufgeschoben	later than expected
	fine print [ˌfaɪn 'prɪnt]	das Kleingedruckte	terms in a document which are printed in small letters

23 Sport for health

1 **to draw up** ['drɔː ʌp]	entwerfen, aufstellen	to prepare and write something
obesity [əʊ'biːsətɪ]	Fettleibigkeit	the condition of being very overweight
related [rɪ'leɪtɪd]	in Beziehung stehend, verwandt, ähnlich	connected
study ['stʌdɪ]	Studie	research, examination
addicted to [ə'dɪktɪd‿tʊ]	süchtig nach	If you watch TV all the time you must be addicted to it.
to tackle ['tækl]	angreifen	to tackle → a tackle (in football, rugby)
parkour [pɑː'kɔː]	Parkour, schnelle Fortbewegung ohne Hilfsmittel	a sport in which you try to move as quickly as possible by running, jumping and climbing
pilot programme ['paɪlət ˌprəʊgræm]	Modellprojekt	test period
the Midlands [ðə 'mɪdləndz]	Midlands (zentrale Region Englands um Birmingham)	area in central England around Birmingham
to balance ['bæləns]	balancieren	to keep your body in a certain position without falling over
to swing [swɪŋ]	schwingen	to swing → the swing
rooftop ['ruːftɒp]	(Haus-)Dach	the outside of a roof of a building
stairs [steəz]	Treppe	a series of steps from one floor to another in a building
to search (for) ['sɜːtʃ fə]	suchen (nach)	When you search for s.th. you look for s.th. that is difficult to find.
obstacle ['ɒbstəkl]	Hindernis	s.th. that is in the way
gymnastics [dʒɪm'næstɪks]	Gymnastik, Turnen	exercises done in a sports hall or gym
freestyle ['friːstaɪl]	Freistil, Kür	All kinds of movements are allowed in freestyle.
thoughtless ['θɔːtləs]	gedankenlos, unbedacht	Sorry! What I said was thoughtless.
to land [lænd]	landen	to bring a plane or helicopter down to earth again
precise [prɪ'saɪs]	präzise, genau	exact, perfect
to supervise ['suːpəvaɪz]	beaufsichtigen	to watch s.o. to make sure they do everything correctly
supervision [ˌsuːpə'vɪʒn]	Aufsicht	supervision → supervise → supervisor
to perform [pə'fɔːm]	aufführen	If you perform, you act in front of people who come specially to watch.
to show off [ʃəʊ‿'ɒf]	angeben, sich aufspielen	to behave in a way that attracts people's attention
aware (of) [ə'weə]	bewusst	Are you aware of the problem?
to exclude [ɪks'kluːd]	ausschließen	to include ↔ to exclude
curriculum [kə'rɪkjələm]	Lehrplan	subjects one studies at college
severe [sɪ'vɪə]	ernst	serious
bone [bəʊn]	Knochen	There are 206 bones in the body.

24 Social lives and computers

1 **gaming** ['geɪmɪŋ]	Spielen	playing a video game
to fear [fɪə]	fürchten	to fear → fear
multiplayer [ˌmʌltɪ'pleɪə]	für viele Mitspieler	A multiplayer game can be played online by many people at the same time.
social network [ˌsəʊʃl 'netwɜːk]	soziales Netzwerk	Many young people meet online in a social network such as Facebook.
enemy ['enəmɪ]	Feind(in)	enemy ↔ friend
warfare ['wɔːfeə]	Krieg, Kriegführung	act of fighting a war
pastime ['pɑːstaɪm]	Zeitvertreib, Beschäftigung	s.th. that you do for fun in your free time
whenever [wen'evə]	wann immer, jedes Mal, wenn	every time s.th. happens
relationship [rɪ'leɪʃnʃɪp]	Beziehung	She has a good relationship with her sister. They are very close.
to quit, quit, quit [kwɪt, kwɪt, kwɪt]	aufgeben, mit etwas aufhören, kündigen	to leave, to stop
touch [tʌtʃ]	Kontakt, Verbindung, Berührung	contact
unreal [ʌn'rɪəl]	irreal, unwirklich	unreal ↔ real
untouchable [ʌn'tʌtʃəbl]	unantastbar, unberührbar, unerreichbar	unable to communicate properly with others

	barrier ['bærɪə]	Barriere	a wall or fence which protects s.o. or s.th.
	loneliness ['ləʊnlɪnəs]	Einsamkeit	If you have no friends and no one to talk to, you can suffer from loneliness.
	isolation [ˌaɪsə'leɪʃn]	Isolation	a situation in which you are separated from other people
	to end up [end 'ʌp]	enden	I don't want to end up doing a job I don't enjoy.
	to reinforce [ˌriːɪn'fɔːs]	verstärken	to make stronger
	similarity [ˌsɪmɪ'lærətɪ]	Ähnlichkeit, Gemeinsamkeit	similarity → similar
	face-to-face [ˌfeɪstə'feɪs]	von Angesicht zu Angesicht, persönlich	A face-to-face group is a group of people who are together in the same place.
	value ['væljuː]	Wert	a principle by which you live
	goal [gəʊl]	Ziel, Tor	target
	basis, pl. **bases** ['beɪsɪs; 'beɪsiːz]	Basis	This agreement is the basis of our future cooperation.
	disagreement [ˌdɪsə'griːmənt]	Meinungsverschiedenheit, Streitigkeit	disagreement ↔ agreement
	acceptance [ək'septəns]	Akzeptanz, Annahme	acceptance → to accept
	conflict ['kɒnflɪkt]	Konflikt	disagreement, argument, fighting
	to strengthen ['streŋkθn]	stärken, kräftigen	to make stronger
	to involve [ɪn'vɒlv]	beinhalten, zur Folge haben, verbunden sein mit	to include
	digital ['dɪdʒɪtl]	digital	storing information as numbers or electronic signals
	operator ['ɒpəreɪtə]	Betreiber(in)	operator → to operate
	transparent [træn'spærənt]	transparent, durchsichtig	when your data are not a secret
3	**percentage** [pə'sentɪdʒ]	Prozentsatz	percentage → per cent
	nationwide [ˌneɪʃn'waɪd]	landesweit	in all parts of the country
	console ['kɒnsəʊl]	Konsole, Bediengerät	a piece of electronic equipment for playing video games
	portal ['pɔːtl]	Portal	website on the Internet

25 Living in a multicultural society

1	**racism** ['reɪsɪzm]	Rassismus	racism → racist → racial
	racist ['reɪsɪst]	rassistisch	when s.o. thinks that their race is better than all others
	incident ['ɪnsɪdənt]	Vorfall	an event which can be dangerous or criminal
	child carer ['tʃaɪld ˌkeərə]	Erzieher(in), Kinderbetreuer(in)	a person who looks after other people's children
	to investigate [ɪn'vestɪgeɪt]	ermitteln	When the police investigate a crime, they often make inquiries.
	quarrel ['kwɒrəl]	Streit, Auseinandersetzung	an argument, often about s.th. unimportant
	to settle ['setl]	beilegen, ansiedeln, begleichen	to put an end to a fight
	confrontation [ˌkɒnfrən'teɪʃn]	Konfrontation, Auseinandersetzung	confrontation → to confront
	authority [ɔː'θɒrətɪ]	Behörde, Autorität	an organisation or public service that looks after a certain area
	offender [ə'fendə]	Angreifer(in), Täter(in)	s.o. who has done s.th. wrong
	to criticize ['krɪtɪsaɪz]	kritisieren	to point out what is negative or bad about s.th. or s.o.
	bar [bɑː]	Riegel, Schranke	a block (of chocolate)
	Paki ['pækɪ]	Abkürzung von ‚Pakistani', Schimpfwort für Menschen aus Asien	an offensive word for an Asian person
	trash [træʃ]	Abfall	rubbish
	appearance [ə'pɪərəns]	Aussehen, Erscheinung	appearance → to appear
	accent ['æksnt]	Akzent	It is difficult to understand s.o. who speaks with a strong accent.
	conforming (to) [kən'fɔːmɪŋ tuː]	übereinstimmend (mit), konform (mit)	in agreement with
	fortunately ['fɔːtʃnətlɪ]	zum Glück, glücklicherweise	luckily
	deliberately [dɪ'lɪbrətlɪ]	bewusst	He didn't do it deliberately. It was an accident.
	exaggerated [ɪg'zædʒəreɪtɪd]	übertrieben	describing s.th. in a way that makes it seem better or worse than it really is
	absurd [əb'sɜːd]	absurd, abwegig, lächerlich	unbelievably silly
	acceptable [ək'septəbl]	akzeptabel, zulässig	allowed, reasonable

division [dɪ'vɪʒn]	Aufspaltung, Teilung, Geschäftsbereich	the process of separating people into different groups
actual ['æktʃʊəl]	tatsächlich, wirklich	real, true
category ['kætəgrɪ]	Kategorie, Klasse, Bereich	a group of people and things that have similar qualities
Bollywood aerobics [ˌbɒlɪwʊd eə'rəʊbɪks]	Aerobic wie in indischen (Musik-)Filmen	special exercises to Indian music that help you get fit
multi-ethnic [ˌmʌltɪ'eθnɪk]	multiethnisch	with people from different ethnic groups
league [li:g]	Liga	Chelsea are at the top of the league.
inter-racial [ˌɪntə'reɪʃl]	zwischen Rassen, verschiedenen Rassen gemeinsam	consisting of people who belong to different races
relations [rɪ'ləɪʃnz]	Verhältnis, Beziehung	If you have good relations with your neighbours, it means you get on well with them.
discrimination [dɪˌskrɪmɪ'neɪʃn]	Diskriminierung, Benachteiligung	unfair treatment of a person because of their religion, race etc.
to examine [ɪg'zæmɪn]	untersuchen	to look at carefully
cruel ['kru:əl]	grausam	You mustn't hurt people or animals. It's not fair and it's cruel.
to tease [ti:z]	necken	If you tease a person, you try to make them feel embarrassed or annoyed just for fun.
to tell s.o. off [tel ˌsʌmwʌn 'ɒf]	tadeln, ausschimpfen	to criticize s.o. for doing s.th. wrong
to suspend [sə'spend]	suspendieren, ausschließen	to stop s.o. from doing their job or going to school for a limited time

26 Poverty and the welfare state

1 **one-bedroomed** [ˌwʌn'bedru:md]	mit einem Schlafzimmer	bedroomed → bedroom
stressful ['stresfəl]	anstrengend, stressig	My new job is very stressful.
oven ['ʌvn]	Backofen	large piece of equipment in the kitchen used to cook food, it often has a grill
belongings [bɪ'lɒŋɪŋz]	Habseligkeiten, Eigentum	belongings → to belong
cardboard ['kɑ:dbɔ:d]	Pappe	thick paper, especially used in boxes
to be carpeted [bɪ 'kɑ:pɪtɪd]	mit einem Teppichboden ausgestattet sein	having a carpet on the floor
rarely ['reəlɪ]	selten	not very often
tinned [tɪnd]	in Dosen, konserviert	I prefer fresh fruit to tinned.
slum [slʌm]	Slum, Elendsviertel	poor area of a town where the houses are in very bad condition
Ethiopia [ˌi:θɪ'əʊpɪə]	Äthiopien	a country in Africa
tragedy ['trædʒədɪ]	Tragödie	s.th. terrible or very sad that happens to a person
Africa ['æfrɪkə]	Afrika	the continent south of Europe
to ignore [ɪg'nɔ:]	ignorieren	If you don't look at s.th. and don't listen to it, even if you know it's there, you ignore it.
healthcare ['helθkeə]	Gesundheitsversorgung	health + care
unhealthy [ʌn'helθɪ]	ungesund	unhealthy ↔ healthy
limited ['lɪmɪtɪd]	begrenzt, beschränkt	limited → limit
poorly ['pɔ:lɪ]	schlecht	badly
standard ['stændəd]	Standard	level of s.th.
minimum ['mɪnɪməm]	Minimum, Mindest-	minimum ↔ maximum
to pay off [peɪ 'ɒf]	sich auszahlen	to have a benefit for s.o.
welfare ['welfeə]	Sozialhilfe, Wohl(ergehen)	money provided by the state to people who have no job
to halve [hɑ:v]	halbieren	to reduce s.th. to half its size or number
3 **non-working** [ˌnɒn'wɜ:kɪŋ]	nicht erwerbstätig	not having a job
lone parent [ˌləʊn 'peərənt]	Alleinerziehende(r)	single parent
fries [fraɪz]	Pommes frites	*(short form of)* French fries, chips
utility [ju:'tɪlətɪ]	Versorgung mit Wasser, Strom usw.	public service such as gas, water or electricity
paycheck *(AE)* ['peɪtʃek]	Gehaltsscheck, Lohnscheck	the money you get for the work you do
groceries ['grəʊsərɪz]	Lebensmittel	groceries → grocer

Video lounge

Video lounge 1

Applying for a job placement

to take a seat [ˌteɪk‿ə 'si:t]	Platz nehmen, sich hinsetzen	You don't need to stand. You can take a seat.
self-confidence [ˌself'kɒnfɪdəns]	Selbstbewusstsein	Debbie has got a lot of self-confidence. She believes that she can do anything.
exhausting [ɪg'zɔ:stɪŋ]	anstrengend, erschöpfend	The meeting lasted for four hours. It was exhausting for everyone.
coordination [kəʊˌɔ:dɪ'neɪʃn]	Koordination, Abstimmung	To be good at sport your hand-eye coordination must be good.
faux pas [ˌfəʊ'pɑ:]	Fehlgriff, Fehltritt, Entgleisung, Fauxpas	doing s.th. that is impolite
to embarrass [ɪm'bærəs]	verlegen machen, verwirren, blamieren	While I was kissing my boyfriend my mum came in. That was really embarrassing.
uncomfortable [ʌn'kʌmftəbl]	unbequem	uncomfortable ↔ comfortable
Japanese [ˌdʒæpə'ni:z]	japanisch	Japanese → Japan
to bow [baʊ]	sich verbeugen	When s.o. bows they show respect.
no matter [ˌnəʊ 'mætə]	egal	I will stay with you no matter what happens.
calm [kɑ:m]	ruhig	calm ↔ nervous
providing [prə'vaɪdɪŋ]	vorausgesetzt	providing → to provide

Video lounge 2

Environmental protection

river catchment ['rɪvə ˌkætʃmənt]	Flusseinzugsgebiet	area between the mountain and the sea through which a river flows
site [saɪt]	Ort	place, location
sewage ['su:ɪdʒ]	Abwasser	dirty waste water
licensed ['laɪsənst]	zugelassen, lizensiert	licensed → to license → licence *(BE)*, license *(AE)*
management ['mænɪdʒmənt]	Management, Geschäftsführung	to manage → manager → management
to discharge [dɪs'tʃɑ:dʒ]	entlassen, abladen, freisprechen	The members of the jury were discharged. They were allowed to leave.
consent [kən'sent]	Zustimmung	agreement
prone [prəʊn]	anfällig, geneigt	She is prone to colds because she never wears enough clothes.
bathing ['beɪðɪŋ]	Bade-	bathing → to bathe → bath
to monitor ['mɒnɪtə]	überwachen	to watch carefully
A level ['eɪˌlevl]	entspricht in etwa dem Abitur	Lisa is taking her A levels and then she wants to go to university.
Chemistry ['kemɪstrɪ]	Chemie	one of the science subjects
post-graduate [ˌpəʊst'grædʒʊət]	Nachdiplom-	If you continue studying after your graduation, you are a post-graduate student.
to get stuck [get 'stʌk]	hängen bleiben, stecken bleiben	Sorry I'm late! I got stuck in a meeting.
traffic jam ['træfɪk ˌdʒæm]	Stau	At eight o'clock in the morning there are usually traffic jams on the roads into big cities.
quarter to ['kwɔ:tə tə]	Viertel vor	7.45 = quarter to eight
to work to a nine-to-five clock [ˌwɜ:k tʊ‿ə ˌnaɪntʊfaɪv 'klɒk]	normale Geschäftszeiten einhalten	to keep to normal working hours
to alter ['ɒltə]	ändern	to change, to vary
isolated ['aɪsəleɪtɪd]	isoliert	Prisoners can feel isolated from the world outside.
plenty ['plentɪ]	eine Menge	plenty of food = a lot of things to eat
discipline ['dɪsɪplɪn]	Disziplin, Studienfach	discipline → to discipline → disciplined
problem solver ['prɒbləm ˌsɒlvə]	Problemlöser	solver → to solve → solution
resilient [rɪ'zɪlɪənt]	belastbar, stabil, robust	able to manage a problem situation
communicator [kə'mju:nɪkeɪtə]	Sprecher(in), Mitteilende(r)	communicator → to communicate → communication
operative ['ɒpərətɪv]	angelernte Arbeiterin, angelernter Arbeiter	a skilled worker

Video lounge 3

Ecology and/or economy?

to drill [drɪl]	bohren	to make a hole
unspoiled [ʌn'spɔɪlt]	unberührt, unbeschädigt	undamaged, intact
wilderness ['wɪldənəs]	Wildnis	wilderness → wild → wildlife
fragile ['frædʒaɪl]	zerbrechlich	Glass is very fragile. You need to take care.
undeveloped [ˌʌndɪ'veləpt]	nicht entwickelt	undeveloped ↔ developed
wildlife ['waɪldlaɪf]	Tierwelt (in freier Wildbahn)	all animals that don't live in zoos, people's homes or on farms
circle ['sɜ:kl]	Kreis	Please put the chairs into a circle.
coastal ['kəʊstl]	Küsten-	coastal → coast
plain [pleɪn]	Ebene, Fläche	a wide, open space
corporation [ˌkɔ:pə'reɪʃn]	Aktiengesellschaft	The corporation employs some 60,000 people worldwide.
to lobby for s.th. ['lɒbɪ]	sich für etwas einsetzen	to lobby → lobbyist
to exploit [ɪk'splɔɪt]	verwerten, ausbeuten	to use s.th. in order to make money
pristine ['prɪsti:n]	makellos	completely clean
haven ['heɪvən]	Zufluchtsort, Hafen	a place that is safe
musk ox ['mʌsk ˌɒks]	Moschusochse	a mammal that lives in the Arctic
wolf, pl. **wolves** [wʊlf; wʊlvz]	Wolf	Wolves belong to the dog family.
caribou ['kærɪbu:]	Rentier, Karibu	A caribou is a North American reindeer.
to keep out [ki:p 'aʊt]	abhalten, fernhalten	Keep out of my room! I want to be alone!
calving ground ['kɑ:vɪŋˌgraʊnd]	Gebiet, in dem Säugetiere ihre Jungen bekommen (gebären)	a place where wild animals give birth
hunt [hʌnt]	Jagd	hunt → to hunt → hunter
underway [ˌʌndə'weɪ]	unterwegs, im Gange	on the move
herd [hɜ:d]	Herde	many animals of one kind living together
to suspect [sə'spekt]	vermuten, misstrauen	to believe, to mistrust
migration [maɪ'greɪʃn]	Migration, Abwanderung, Umzug	migration ↔ immigration
sprawl [sprɔ:l]	Ausbreitung	expansion, spread
to stretch [stretʃ]	dehnen, strecken	Before you do any sport you should do some stretching exercises.
to extract [ɪk'strækt]	gewinnen, herausziehen, entnehmen	to take s.th. out (of the ground)
survival [sə'vaɪvl]	Überleben	to survive → survival → survivor

Video lounge 4

Brick Lane – past and present

blend [blend]	Mischung, Vermischung	mixture, cross
Jewish ['dʒu:ɪʃ]	jüdisch	Jewish → Jew
East End [ˌi:st'end]	Bezeichnung für die Bezirke in London, die sich östlich des mittelalterlichen Stadtkerns und nördlich der Themse befinden	traditionally the poorer part of London
jellied eel [ˌdʒelɪd 'i:l]	Aal in Aspik	a traditional dish in London's East End, eaten by poor people
side by side [ˌsaɪdbaɪ'saɪd]	Seite an Seite	We stood side by side and that way nothing could happen to us.
transformation [ˌtrænsfə'meɪʃn]	Umwandlung, Umgestaltung, Wandlung	transformation → to transform → transformer
newcomer ['nju:ˌkʌmə]	Neuling	s.o. who has just come to live in a place
upside down [ˌʌpsaɪd 'daʊn]	umgedreht	You cannot read the book upside down. You need to turn it around.
stunning ['stʌnɪŋ]	umwerfend	The film star looked absolutely stunning in real life.
gorgeous ['gɔ:dʒəs]	hinreißend	The man is really gorgeous. I would like to go out with him.
handsome ['hænsəm]	attraktiv	a handsome man = a good-looking man

lovely ['lʌvlɪ]	nett, hübsch, schön	Is your new neighbour nice? – Oh yes, she's lovely.
to take to s.o. ['teɪk tə ˌsʌmwʌn]	an jemandem Gefallen finden	to really like s.o.
hopeful ['həʊpfəl]	Hoffnungsträger	a hopeful → to be hopeful → to hope
encounter [ɪn'kaʊntə]	Begegnung, Treffen	meeting, reunion
disappointed [ˌdɪsə'pɔɪntɪd]	enttäuscht	I was very disappointed when my girlfriend didn't want to go out with me anymore.
religion [rɪ'lɪdʒn]	Religion, Glaube	religion → religious
to step [step]	treten	to step
opposition [ˌɒpə'zɪʃn]	Widerstand, Gegensatz, Widerspruch	opposition → opposite → to oppose
divide [dɪ'vaɪd]	Kluft, Trennlinie, Grenze	divide → to divide → division

Video lounge 5

American immigration

Mexican ['meksɪkn]	mexikanisch	a Mexican town = a town in Mexico
to thrive [θraɪv]	Erfolg haben, gedeihen, blühen	A thriving business can bring a lot of money into a town.
dusty ['dʌstɪ]	staubig	If you don't clean your room, everything starts to get dusty.
anticipation [ænˌtɪsɪ'peɪʃn]	Vorahnung, Erwartung	speculation, expectation
shadow ['ʃædəʊ]	Schatten	Shadows are longer in the evening than in the middle of the day.
to gather ['gæðə]	(sich) sammeln	to collect, to get together, to understand
brick [brɪk]	Ziegelstein	Nearly all of the houses in Germany are made of brick.
equipped [ɪ'kwɪpt]	ausgestattet, ausgerüstet	equipped → to equip → equipment
desert ['dezət]	Wüste	It doesn't rain very often in the desert.
exhaustion [ɪg'zɔ:stʃn]	Erschöpfung, Überanstrengung	I couldn't run anymore. I was crying from exhaustion.
urban ['ɜ:bn]	städtisch	Towns and cities are urban areas.
undergrowth ['ʌndəgrəʊθ]	Gestrüpp, Unterholz	We were not able to go through the undergrowth because it was too thick.
trick [trɪk]	Trick	an illusion is a kind of trick played on s.o.
to dig, dug, dug [dɪg, dʌg, dʌg]	graben	They dug a big hole in our garden for the new swimming pool.
border patrol ['bɔ:də pəˌtrəʊl]	Grenzschutz	The border patrol checks the borders day and night.
giant ['dʒaɪənt]	riesig	huge, big
fan [fæn]	Ventilator	It is very hot in this room. Could you please turn on the fan?
to give chase to s.o. [gɪv 'tʃeɪs]	jemanden verfolgen	to run after s.o. in order to catch them
tally ['tælɪ]	Summe, Anzahl	a number of things
on the lookout [ɒn ðə 'lʊkaʊt]	Ausschau haltend	watching for s.th.
terrorist ['terərɪst]	Terrorist(in)	terrorist → terror
to be deported [bɪ ˌdɪ'pɔ:tɪd]	abgeschoben werden	to make an immigrant leave a country he or she has entered illegally
to light up [laɪt 'ʌp]	beleuchten	to light up → light
flashlight ['flæʃlaɪt]	Taschenlampe	an electric light that you can hold in your hand
deer, pl. **deer** [dɪə]	Hirsch	If you are lucky, you may see a deer in the woods.
Minuteman, pl. **Minutemen** ['mɪnɪtmæn]	Freiwilliger, der auf Abruf bereit steht	We need the Minutemen to stop people crossing the border illegally.
determination [dɪˌtɜ:mɪ'neɪʃn]	Entschlossenheit	determination → to determine
night vision goggles [ˌnaɪtvɪʒn 'gɒglz]	Nachtsichtgerät	I need my night vision goggles to see in the dark.
migrant ['maɪgrənt]	Migrant(in), Übersiedler(in)	migrant → to migrate → migration
gun [gʌn]	Schusswaffe	A man with a gun went into a shop and said, "Give me the money!"
Dad's Army [ˌdædz'ɑ:mɪ]	englische Fernsehkomödie	
self-defence [ˌselfdɪ'fens]	Selbstverteidigung, Notwehr	The man attacked me so I hit him in self-defence.
to commit [kə'mɪt]	begehen, verüben	He committed suicide.
bitter ['bɪtə]	bitter, verärgert	When my friend lied to me I was very bitter.
battle ['bætl]	Schlacht	Armies fight in battles.

	migration [maɪˈgreɪʃn]	Migration, Wanderung, Umzug	migration → to migrate → migrant
	flimsy [ˈflɪmzɪ]	schwach, dünn, fadenscheinig	The walls are very flimsy. The next strong wind will blow them away.
	fence [fens]	Zaun	With a fence around the field, the cattle can't get out.
	economics [ˌi:kəˈnɒmɪks]	Volkswirtschaftslehre, Wirtschaftswissenschaften	economics → economy → economist
	leaf, pl. **leaves** [li:f; li:vz]	Blatt	leaf → to leaf (e.g. through a book)

Video lounge 6

A job placement at reception

	absolutely [ˌæbsəˈlu:tlɪ]	absolut	completely
	valid [ˈvælɪd]	gültig	The credit card isn't valid anymore, it expired last month.

Role cards

Unit 6

B5	**overfishing** [ˌəʊvəˈfɪʃɪŋ]	Überfischung	overfishing → fishing → fish
	exotic [ɪgˈzɒtɪk]	exotisch	I love exotic dishes, but I don't always want to know exactly what I'm eating.
	economic [ˌi:kəˈnɒmɪk]	ökonomisch, wirtschaftlich	economic → economy
	fisherman, pl. **fishermen** [ˈfɪʃəmən]	Fischer	fisherman → fishing → fish

Unit 8

D4	**economical** [ˌi:kəˈnɒmɪkl]	wirtschaftlich, sparsam	economically → economic → economical → economy

Unit 11

2	**full board** [ˌfʊlˈbɔ:d]	Vollpension, Vollverpflegung	full board ↔ half board
	half board [ˌhɑ:fˈbɔ:d]	Halbpension	half board ↔ full board

Unit 12

5	**ferry** [ˈferɪ]	Fähre	a boat that takes passengers and cars across a river or a narrow bit of sea
	ballroom dancing [ˌbɔ:lrʊm ˈdɑ:nsɪŋ]	Gesellschaftstanz	a formal kind of dancing

Alphabetical vocabulary

A

abbreviation Abkürzung 81
above oben, über 8
absolutely absolut 131
absurd absurd, abwegig, lächerlich 124
to abuse beschimpfen, misshandeln, missbrauchen 112
accent Akzent 124
acceptable akzeptabel, zulässig 124
acceptance Akzeptanz, Annahme 122
access Zugang 47
accessible zugänglich, befahrbar 65
accession Beitritt, Einwilligung, Zuwachs 86
accessory Zubehör, Accessoire 73
to accommodate unterbringen, anpassen, aushelfen 103
accommodation Unterbringung 41
to accompany begleiten 101
according to laut, entsprechend 36
account Konto, Abrechnung, Berechnung, Wert 103
to achieve erreichen 9
to act handeln, sich verhalten 37
active aktiv 21
activist Aktivist(in), jemand, der sich für etwas engagiert 106
to act out aufführen 27
actual tatsächlich, wirklich 124
addicted to süchtig nach 120
additional zusätzlich 28
adjective Adjektiv 61
adult Erwachsene(r) 10
adult erwachsen 116
adulthood Erwachsensein, Erwachsenenalter 116
adventure Abenteuer 65
advert Anzeige 21
advertiser Inserent(in), Werbefachmann/-frau 28
advisor Berater(in), Ratgeber(in) 52
aeroplane Flugzeug 52
affair Affäre 42
to affect auswirken, beeinflussen 33
to afford sich leisten 86
aged im Alter von 33
agency Agentur 30
agriculture Landwirtschaft 52
aid Hilfe 79
aim Ziel 9
to aim anstreben, zielen 49
aircraft Flugzeug 38
airline Fluggesellschaft 65
air mile Flugmeile 52
to alarm beängstigen, beunruhigen, alarmieren 114
alcohol Alkohol 114
alert Alarm 28
A level entspricht in etwa dem Abitur 128
algae pl. Algen, Tang 51
alive lebendig 68
ally Alliierte(r), Verbündete(r) 86
alongside nebenher, entlang, an der Seite, nebenstehend 101
alright in Ordnung 70
to alter ändern 128
amazing unglaublich, erstaunlich 118
to analyse analysieren 31
analysis Analyse 39
angle Winkel 118
anniversary Jubiläum, Hochzeitstag 103
annual jährlich 57
to anticipate vorhersehen, erwarten 44
anticipation Vorahnung, Erwartung 131
anti-social asozial 113
anyway jedenfalls, trotzdem 41
apart from abgesehen von, außer 51
to apologize sich entschuldigen 75
apology Entschuldigung 89
appealing ansprechend, reizvoll 104
appearance Aussehen, Erscheinung 124
applicable anwendbar, geeignet 116
applicant Bewerber(in) 22
application Anwendung, Einsatz, Bewerbung 117
appointment Berufung, Termin 84
to appreciate schätzen 89
apprenticeship Ausbildung 73
to approve anerkennen, bestätigen, zustimmen, akzeptieren 84
architect Architekt(in) 13
Argentinian argentinisch 52
to argue diskutieren, streiten, argumentieren 53
argument Streit, Argument 67
armchair Sessel 54
armed forces Militär, Streitkräfte 84
to arrange organisieren, ausmachen 83
art Kunst 26
Asian asiatisch 76
aspect Aspekt, Gesichtspunkt 49
to assign zuordnen 108
assistance Hilfe 53
to associate verbinden, assoziieren 70
as well as sowohl … als auch 52
at risk gefährdet 28
attachment Anhang, Anbringung 88
to attack angreifen 101
attempt Versuch 114
to attend teilnehmen 9
attitude Haltung 15
to attract anziehen 31
attraction Attraktion, Anziehungspunkt, Anziehungskraft 68
attractive attraktiv 65
auction Versteigerung 28
Aussie *(informal)* Australier(in) 103
Australian Australier(in) 66
Austrian österreichisch 72
authentic authentisch 76
authority Behörde, Autorität 124
automatic automatisch 54
availability Verfügbarkeit, Verwendbarkeit 90
available frei, erhältlich 97
average Durchschnitt 33
to avoid (ver)meiden 51
awake wach 60
award Preis, Auszeichnung 43
aware (of) bewusst 120
awareness Bewusstsein, Bewusstheit 114

B

backup Unterstützung, Sicherung 68
bagpiper Dudelsackspieler(in) 101
to balance balancieren 120
ballroom dancing Gesellschaftstanz 134
ban Verbot 31
to ban verbieten 31
banana Banane 52
bank clerk Bankkaufmann/-frau 22
bankrupt bankrott, insolvent 86
bar Riegel, Schranke 124
bar chart Säulendiagramm, Balkendiagramm 32
barefoot barfuß 81
barely kaum 60
barrier Barriere 122
based on basierend auf 105
basic grundlegend 107
basis, pl. **bases** Basis 122
bathing Bade- 128
battery Batterie 54
battle Schlacht 131
to be about to im Begriff sein zu 60
to beat, beat, beaten besiegen, schlagen 53
beauty Schönheit 42
to be based Geschäftssitz haben 28
to be bound to (happen) etwas wird bestimmt (passieren) 60
to be carpeted mit einem Teppichboden ausgestattet sein 126
bed and breakfast Pension 90
to be delighted glücklich sein, sehr zufrieden sein 89
to be deported abgeschoben werden 131
beef Rindfleisch 52
beer Bier 94
to behave sich benehmen 28
behaviour Verhalten 15
being (Lebe-)Wesen, Geschöpf 61

to be in touch mit jemandem in Verbindung stehen, mit jemandem in Kontakt bleiben 90
to be located gelegen sein, sich befinden 47
belongings Habseligkeiten, Eigentum 126
below unten, unter(halb) 8
beneath unterhalb, unter 57
benefit Nutzen, Gewinn, Sozialhilfe, Rente 106
to benefit (from) Nutzen ziehen (aus), profitieren (von) 50
to be on zu sehen sein (Sendung) 30
to be on business auf Geschäftsreise sein 97
to be related to sich beziehen auf, betreffen 108
beside neben 57
to be targeted gezielt sein 108
bid Gebot 28
bill Rechnung, Banknote, Schnabel 103
billboard Plakatwand 103
bin Mülleimer, Mülltonne 67
binge drinking Besäufnis, Komasaufen 114
biofuel Biotreibstoff 66
Biology Biologie 10
bioreserve (Bio-)Reservat 68
biotechnology Biotechnologie 62
bitter bitter, verärgert 131
blackness Schwärze 60
blade Flügel, Klinge, Blatt 57
blend Mischung, Vermischung 130
blessing Segen 117
blind blind 45
blind drunk stark betrunken, sternhagelvoll 114
blog Internet-Tagebuch 8
to blow, blew, blown wehen, blasen 57
board Verpflegung 45
body Rumpf, Karosserie 118
Bollywood aerobics Aerobic wie in indischen (Musik-)Filmen 124
bone Knochen 120
bone marrow Knochenmark 60
booking Buchung, Reservierung 65
bookshop Buchhandlung 40
border patrol Grenzschutz 131
to bow sich verbeugen 128
bracket Klammer 19
brain Gehirn 33
branch Zweigstelle, Zweig, Abzweigung, Sektor 51
brand Marke 17
Brazilian brasilianisch 52
breakthrough Durchbruch 116
breath Atemzug, Atem 60
to breathe atmen 48
brick Ziegelstein 131
bright hell 38
to bring up großziehen, aufbringen 112
Brit umgangssprachlicher Ausdruck für einen Engländer 102
browser Browser 34
budget Haushalt, Etat 80
buffalo Büffel 62
bullying Mobbing, Schikanieren 113
bureaucracy Bürokratie 86
business field Geschäftsbereich 17
businessman Geschäftsmann 97
busy besetzt, belegt 75
button Knopf, Taste 35
by um 114
to by-pass überbrücken, umgehen 86

C

cafeteria Kantine, Cafeteria 25
caller Anrufer(in) 75
calm ruhig 128
calorie Kalorie 52
calving ground Gebiet, in dem Säugetiere ihre Jungen bekommen (gebären) 129
campaign Kampagne 110
campaigning Aktionen; Wahlkampf führen 9
campus Campus, (Hoch-)Schulgelände 44
to cancel absagen 28
cancer Krebs 116
candidate Bewerber(in) 22
canteen Kantine, Mensa 47
cap Kappe, Mütze 59
capable (of) fähig 116
capacity Kapazität 118
carbon Kohlenstoff 118
carbon dioxide Kohlendioxyd, CO_2 49
cardboard Pappe 126
care Pflege, Sorge 45
Caribbean Karibik, karibisch 68
caribou Rentier, Karibu 129
carrot Karotte 97
to carry on weiterführen 76
to carry out ausführen 82
cartoonist Karikaturist(in) 39
carving Schnitzarbeit 68
cash machine Bankautomat 110
catalogue Katalog 64
catastrophe Katastrophe 51
catastrophic katastrophal 30
to catch s.th. etwas akustisch verstehen 90
category Kategorie, Klasse, Bereich 124
catering firm Catering-Firma 22
cattle (pl. only) Vieh 57
CCTV (closed circuit television) Videoüberwachungsanlage 39
to celebrate feiern 101
cell Zelle 116
cell phone Handy, Mobiltelefon 103
central zentral 68
certain bestimmt, gewiss 29
certificate Zertifikat, Bescheinigung, Zeugnis, Urkunde 114
chain Kette 19
challenge Herausforderung 21
to challenge herausfordern 53
chance Chance 72
to change one's mind seine Meinung ändern 29
character (Roman-)Figur, Charakter 61
to charge in Rechnung stellen, berechnen 90
to chat chatten, sich online unterhalten 37
check Rechnung (im Restaurant) (AE), Scheck (AE), Prüfung 103
to check in einchecken, anmelden 98
checks and balances gegenseitige Kontrolle, Gewaltenteilung 84
chef Koch, Köchin 12
chemical Chemikalie 73
Chemistry Chemie 128
chemist's Apotheke, Drogerie 41
chicken Huhn 9
childcare Kinderbetreuung 104
child carer Erzieher(in), Kinderbetreuer(in) 124
childless kinderlos 61
to chill out sich entspannen 9
Chinese chinesisch; Chinese, Chinesin 116
to choke ersticken, drosseln 114
cholera Cholera 81
to chop zerhacken, hauen, spalten 97
circle Kreis 129
to circulate zirkulieren, herumgehen 95
citizen Bürger(in), Staatsangehörige(r) 52
citizenship Staatsangehörigkeit, Nationalität, Bürgerrecht 84
claim Anspruch, Behauptung 118
to claim behaupten, beanspruchen 113
classification system Klassifizierungssystem, Ordnungssystem 37
cleaner Raumpfleger(in) 12
to clean up aufräumen 45
click Klicken 108
to click klicken 34
climate Klima 30
climax Höhepunkt 112
clinic Klinik 47
clone Klon, Nachbau 116
to clone klonen 60
cloning Klonen 116
closed gesperrt, geschlossen 38
closet Wandschrank, Kammer 103
clothing Kleidung 111
clubber Clubbesucher(in) 54
coach Reisebus 14
coaching Nachhilfeunterricht, Coaching 104
coal-fired mit Kohle betrieben, Kohle- 58
coastal Küsten- 129
cocktail Cocktail 94
cocoa Kakao 79
collage Collage 55
colleague Kollege/Kollegin 92
colloquial umgangssprachlich 41
columnist Schreiber(in), Kolumnist(in) 43
to combine kombinieren 46
comedian Komiker(in) 43

delegate Delegierte(r), Abgeordnete(r), Bevollmächtigte(r) 84
to delete löschen 28
deliberately bewusst 124
demand Bedarf, Nachfrage, Forderung 57
to demand verlangen, fordern 60
demanding anspruchsvoll 46
democracy Demokratie 86
to depart abfliegen, abfahren 66
departure Abflug, Abfahrt 66
dependent (on) abhängig 57
deposit Lagerstätte, Guthaben, Anzahlung 58
depressed niedergeschlagen, deprimiert 112
deprived sozial benachteiligt 106
desert Wüste 131
design Design, Entwurf, Gestaltung 108
designer Designer(in), Gestalter(in) 116
desktop Desktop, Benutzeroberfläche 34
desperate verzweifelt, aussichtslos 81
despite trotz 62
dessert Dessert, Nachtisch 94
destination Ziel, Reiseziel 65
detailed detailliert, ausführlich 45
determination Entschlossenheit 131
determined entschlossen 60
dialogue Dialog, Gespräch 27
diary Tagebuch, Terminkalender 97
to dig, dug, dug graben 131
digital digital 122
dimension Größenordnung, Dimension, Ausmaß 116
dingo Dingo (australischer Wildhund) 103
dirt Schmutz 112
disabled behindert 45
disagreement Meinungsverschiedenheit, Streitigkeit 122
to disappear verschwinden 86
disappointed enttäuscht 130
disaster Katastrophe, Desaster 51
to discharge entlassen, abladen, freisprechen 128
discipline Disziplin, Studienfach 128
disciplined diszipliniert 102
discount Rabatt, Nachlass 30
to discover entdecken 110
discrimination Diskriminierung, Benachteiligung 125
disease Krankheit 61
dish Gericht 94
dislike Abneigung 9
to dismiss entlassen, freistellen, ablehnen 106
distillery Brennerei 100
distribution Vertrieb, Verteilung 30
district Distrikt, Bezirk, Stadtteil 106
diverse unterschiedlich, vielfältig, verschieden 76
divide Kluft, Trennlinie, Grenze 130
to divide teilen 53
division Aufspaltung, Teilung, Geschäftsbereich 124
DNA DNS, DNA (Träger der Erbinformationen) 60
documentary Dokumentarfilm 42
domain Domain 108
to donate spenden 50
donation Spende 50
to do poorly schlecht abschneiden 38
dot Punkt 90
double doppelt 114
doubt Zweifel 108
downhill abwärts, bergab 104
to download herunterladen 35
dozen Dutzend 57
draft Entwurf, Skizze 89
dramatic dramatisch 33
to draw up entwerfen, aufstellen 120
dress code Kleiderordnung 102
drill Bohrer 42
to drill bohren 129
driving licence Führerschein 21
drop Tropfen; Abnahme, Verringerung 51
to drop (herunter-)fallen, fallen lassen 27
drugstore Apotheke, Drogerie 41
drunken betrunken 114
duplicate Duplikat, Kopie 60
dusty staubig 131
to dye färben 73
dyer Färber(in) 73

E

eager eifrig 104
earnings Einnahmen, Erträge 108
earring Ohrring 59
eastern östlich, ost- 82
eco- Öko- 52
ecological ökologisch 54
ecology Ökologie 48
economic ökonomisch, wirtschaftlich 133
economical wirtschaftlich, sparsam 134
economics Volkswirtschaftslehre, Wirtschaftswissenschaften 131
educational lehrreich, bildend 33
efficient leistungsfähig, wirksam, effizient 58
effort Mühe, Leistung, Versuch 53
either way so oder so 73
electrician Elektriker(in) 22
electricity Elektrizität 54
electronic elektronisch 33
elevator Aufzug 103
to eliminate beseitigen, entfernen, eliminieren 77
elliptical elliptisch 118
to embarrass verlegen machen, verwirren, blamieren 128
embarrassment Peinlichkeit, Verlegenheit 41
embryo Embryo 61
embryonic-like wie von einem Embryo 116
to emit emittieren, ausstoßen 49
emotion Gefühl, Emotion 61
emotional emotional, gefühlvoll, gerührt 95
to enable ermöglichen, in die Lage versetzen 45
to enclose beifügen 21
encounter Begegnung, Treffen 130
to encourage unterstützen, fördern, ermutigen 49
ending Ende 24
to end up enden 122
enemy Feind(in) 122
engaged verlobt 41
enlargement Vergrößerung, Erweiterung, Erhöhung 86
enormous riesig, enorm 52
to enter eingeben 108
to entertain unterhalten 54
entry Eintritt, Eingang, Eintrag 54
environment Umgebung, Umfeld 47
environmental Umwelt- 9
episodic gelegentlich 115
equipped ausgestattet, ausgerüstet 131
era Ära, Zeitalter 116
to escape (from) flüchten (vor) 76
essay Aufsatz 10
essential wichtig 20
to establish aufbauen, (be)gründen 68
ethical ethisch, moralisch 117
ethics Moral, ethische Grundsätze 116
ethnic ethnisch 77
European Europäer(in) 45
European europäisch 45
European Court of Justice Europäischer Gerichtshof 87
European Monetary Union Europäische Wirtschafts- und Währungsunion 87
ever since seitdem 17
evidence Beweis, Beweismaterial 114
exaggerated übertrieben 124
to examine untersuchen 125
excess Übermaß, Maßlosigkeit 114
excessive maßlos, exzessiv, zu viel 114
to exchange umtauschen, austauschen 26
to exclude ausschließen 120
exclusive exklusiv 89
executive exekutiv, ausführend, leitend 84
executive suite Führungsloge, Vorstandsetage 93
exhaust Abgas, Auspuff 118
exhaustible begrenzt, sich erschöpfend 57
exhausting anstrengend, erschöpfend 128
exhaustion Erschöpfung, Überanstrengung 131
exotic exotisch 133
to expand (sich) ausdehnen, expandieren 18
expert Experte/Expertin 104
expiry Fälligwerden, Ablauf, Verfall 96

to exploit verwerten, ausbeuten 129
extent Ausmaß, Größe, Umfang 116
extract Auszug 28
to extract gewinnen, herausziehen, entnehmen 129
extraction Gewinnung, Förderung, Entnahme 65
extraordinary außergewöhnlich 118
extreme extrem 30

F

face-to-face von Angesicht zu Angesicht, persönlich 122
facility Einrichtung 21
factor Faktor, Einfluss 104
to fail versagen 82
failure Versagen 104
fairly relativ 97
fairy tale Märchen 108
fan Ventilator 131
to fancy angetan sein von 95
fantasy Fantasie 55
faraway fern, weit entfernt 65
fascinated fasziniert 30
fascinating faszinierend 68
fashionable modisch 101
fashion design Modedesign 13
fatal tödlich 114
fate Schicksal 60
faux pas Fehlgriff, Fehltritt, Entgleisung, Fauxpas 128
favourable günstig, vorteilhaft 56
FDA Behörde für Lebens- und Arzneimittelsicherheit 63
fear Angst 106
to fear fürchten 122
feature Einrichtung, Eigenschaft, Merkmal, Kennzeichen 22
federal Bundes- 84
fee Gebühr 41
feedback Rückmeldung, Feedback 28
female weiblich 46
feminist Feministin, Frauenrechtlerin 42
fence Zaun 131
ferry Fähre 134
fertiliser Dünger, Düngemittel 52
fertility Fruchtbarkeit 62
figure Zahl, Ziffer 104
file Datei, Hefter, Akte 35
to finance finanzieren 9
finely dünn 97
fine print das Kleingedruckte 119
fire fighter Feuerwehrmann, Feuerwehrfrau 112
firework Feuerwerk, Feuerwerkskörper 112
fisherman, pl. **fishermen** Fischer 133
flag Fahne, Flagge 55
flame Flamme 38
to flash blinken, blitzen 48
flashlight Taschenlampe 131
flatmate Mitbewohner(in) 14
to flee, fled, fled fliehen 81
flexible flexibel, biegsam, anpassungsfähig 97
flimsy schwach, dünn, fadenscheinig 131
to float treiben, gleiten, mit dem Floß fahren 70
floor Stock, Etage 103
to flow fließen, strömen 57
fluency Sprachebeherrschung, Sprachgewandtheit 19
fluent flüssig 20
flyer Flugblatt 30
focus Blickpunkt, Mittelpunkt, Fokus 45
to focus (on) sich konzentrieren (auf) 114
folks Leute (Anrede) 54
footprint Fußabdruck 118
to force zwingen 42
foreground Vordergrund 14
foreigner Ausländer(in) 102
to foresee vorhersehen, absehen 86
forest Wald 68
formal formell, formal 44
formula Formel 31
fortunately zum Glück, glücklicherweise 124
forum Forum, öffentliche Diskussion 106
fossil fuel fossiler Brennstoff 49
to found gründen 45
foundation Stiftung, Gründung, Fundament 55
foyer Vorhalle, Foyer 93
fragile zerbrechlich 129
freedom (no pl.) Freiheit 61
freestyle Freistil, Kür 120
French fry Pommes frites 103
fried in der Pfanne gebraten 94
fries pl. Pommes frites 127
frightened verängstigt, erschrocken 37
frozen gefroren 17
to fry braten 97
fuel Brennstoff, Treibstoff, Benzin 67
full board Vollpension, Vollverpflegung 134
full-time Vollzeit 9
function Funktion, Aufgabe(nbereich) 47
to function funktionieren 86
furthermore überdies; außerdem 81
futuristic futuristisch 54

G

to gain gewinnen 104
gamble Risiko 50
games console Spielekonsole, Bedienungsgerät für Computerspiele 37
gaming Spielen 122
gang Bande, Gang 112
gas Gas, Benzin 49
to gather (sich) sammeln 131
GCSE Prüfung zum Abschluss der Sekundarstufe 114
gender Geschlecht 30
gene Gen, Erbfaktor 62
general allgemein 9
general manager Generaldirektor(in), Geschäftsführer(in) 93
general office Zentrale, Allgemeine Verwaltung 93
to generate erzeugen, entwickeln, schaffen 54
generation Generation 76
genetic genetisch 63
Geography Geographie 10
German Deutsch 88
to get along with auskommen mit, sich verstehen mit 45
to get changed sich umziehen 14
to get dressed sich anziehen 45
to get stuck hängen bleiben, stecken bleiben 128
to get used to (+gerund) sich gewöhnen (an) 104
ghost Geist 113
giant riesig 131
to give birth to zur Welt bringen, gebären 62
to give chase to s.o. jemanden verfolgen 131
given the fact angesichts der Tatsache 118
to give s.o. a buzz jemanden anrufen 91
to give s.o.'s regards to s.o. herzliche Grüße an jemanden ausrichten 99
global global 48
globalisation Globalisierung 72
to go ahead fortfahren 35
goal Ziel, Tor 122
to go clubbing Nachtclubs besuchen 54
God Gott 61
to google googeln 108
googol Googol 108
gorgeous hinreißend 130
to go wrong schiefgehen 67
gradual schrittweise, allmählich, graduell 62
grandchild Enkelkind, Enkel(in) 81
to graze grasen 57
groceries Lebensmittel 127
guide Führer(in) 68
to guide führen, leiten 44
guideline Richtlinie 75
gun Schusswaffe 131
guy Typ 9
gym Sporthalle 47
gymnastics Gymnastik, Turnen 120

H

habit Gewohnheit, Angewohnheit 76
haggis Haggis (traditionelles schottisches Gericht) 94
half board Halbpension 134
to halt halten, anhalten, unterbrechen 114
to halve halbieren 126
handicapped behindert, benachteiligt 45
to handle umgehen mit, handhaben 110
handout Informationsblatt, Handout 102
Halloween Halloween (Tag vor Allerheiligen) 112
to hand out aushändigen, verteilen 42

handsome attraktiv 130
to hang around herumhängen 104
to harm schaden, verletzen 52
harmful schädlich, nachteilig 35
harvest Ernte 81
haven Zufluchtsort, Hafen 129
heading Überschrift 24
to head off sich aufmachen 41
headquarters Zentrale, Stammsitz 17
head teacher Schulleiter(in) 39
healthcare Gesundheitsversorgung 126
heartbreaking herzzerreißend 50
hell Hölle 112
herd Herde 129
high-class erstklassig 21
to hike wandern 70
to hire mieten 67
to hold true gelten 118
home food related im Zusammenhang mit der häuslichen Nahrungszubereitung 52
homelessness Obdachlosigkeit 104
home-made hausgemacht 17
hometown Heimatstadt 86
honeymoon Hochzeitsreise 67
hopeful Hoffnungsträger 130
horrible schrecklich 60
host Gastgeber(in) 74
hostile feindlich 87
housekeeping Haushaltsführung, Raumpflege 20
HTML eine Programmiersprache für das World Wide Web 37
huge riesig 17
human Mensch 116
human menschlich 61
humanitarian humanitär, menschenfreundlich 80
hunt Jagd 129
hurricane Wirbelsturm, Hurrikan 30
hut Hütte 79
hybrid Hybrid- 59
hydrogen Wasserstoff 59
hydro power Wasserkraft 57

I

ice hockey Eishockey 75
icon Icon, Symbol, Bildschirmsymbol 34
identifiable identifizierbar, erkennbar, feststellbar, belegbar 101
to identify (with) herausfinden, (sich) identifizieren (mit) 49
identity Identität 15
idyll Idylle 40
i.e. das heißt 118
ignorant ignorant 20
to ignore ignorieren 126
illegal illegal, gesetzeswidrig 37
illiterate nicht lesen oder schreiben können 81
to illustrate illustrieren, darstellen 117
image Bild, Image 108
imagination Vorstellungskraft, Phantasie 47
impact Wirkung, Aufprall 52
to impeach anklagen 84
to implement ausführen, verwirklichen, realisieren 87
impolite unhöflich 102
impotence Impotenz, Unvermögen, Zeugungsunfähigkeit 114
to impress beeindrucken 95
impression Eindruck 8
impressive beeindruckend 57
improvement Verbesserung 49
inability Unfähigkeit, Unvermögen 114
in addition zusätzlich, außerdem 47
in a rush in Eile 60
incident Vorfall 124
incoming eingehend, ankommend 102
inconvenience Unannehmlichkeit, Belästigung, Unbequemlichkeit 103
increase Zunahme 114
increasing zunehmend, steigend, wachsend 49
independent unabhängig 18
Indian indisch 40
indirect indirekt, mittelbar 84
individual Einzelperson 108
Indonesian indonesisch 52
industrial industriell 82
industrialized industrialisiert 76
inexpensive preiswert, billig 64
in favour of für, zugunsten 39
to infect infizieren, anstecken 81
infection Infektion, Ansteckung 81
inflation Inflation, Geldentwertung 81
to influence beeinflussen 34
informal informell 91
infrastructure Infrastruktur 65
in general im Allgemeinen, generell 102
ingenious genial, raffiniert 108
ingredient Zutat 97
initiative Initiative, Entschlusskraft 68
injury Verletzung 114
innovation Neuerung 35
in particular im Besonderen 28
to inquire sich erkundigen, fragen 98
in short kurz gesagt, kurzum 61
insight Einblick 22
to install installieren 13
installation Installation, Anlage, Einrichtung 56
instant sofort 101
instant messaging sofortige Nachrichtenübermittlung, Chatten 37
institution Institution, Einrichtung, Anstalt 87
intense angestrengt, intensiv 95
to interact interagieren, zusammenwirken, einander beeinflussen 47
interaction Interaktion 44
intergovernmental zwischenstaatlich, international 87
international international 86
inter-racial zwischen Rassen, verschiedenen Rassen gemeinsam 124
to interview befragen 13
in the long run auf lange Sicht 109
inventiveness Einfallsreichtum, Ideenreichtum 118
to investigate ermitteln 124
investment Investition, Geldanlage 106
investor Kapitalanleger, Investor 71
in-vitro fertilisation In-vitro-Befruchtung (im Reagenzglas) 62
to involve beinhalten, zur Folge haben, verbunden sein mit 122
involved (in) beteiligt 45
Irish irisch 86
ironical ironisch 76
irresponsible unverantwortlich 114
isolated isoliert 128
isolation Isolation 122
issue Angelegenheit, Problem, Ausgabe (einer Zeitung) 49
to issue herausgeben 110
IT Informationstechnik 9
Italian italienisch 86
item Punkt, Gegenstand 25
its sein(e), ihr(e) 101
it's your turn du bist an der Reihe 55

J

Japanese japanisch 128
jealous (of) eifersüchtig 67
jellied eel Aal in Aspik 130
jet-skiing Wassermotorrad fahren 70
jewelry *(AE)*, **jewellery** *(BE)* Schmuck 111
Jewish jüdisch 130
jingle Jingle, kurze Tonfolge in der Werbung 30
joke Witz 60
journalist Journalist(in) 13
judge Richter(in), Wettkampfrichter(in) 84
judicial gerichtlich, rechtsprechend 84
judiciary Judikative, Justizgewalt, Gerichtswesen 84
junction Kreuzung 38
jungle Dschungel 112
to justify rechtfertigen 117

K

to keep an eye on im Auge behalten 37
to keep out abhalten, fernhalten 129
keypad Tastatur 38
killing Tötung 38
king prawn Königskrabbe 52
kit Ausrüstung 41
kiwi ein flugunfähiger Vogel, eine Fruchtsorte, eine Eigenbezeichnung der Bewohner Neuseelands 103

L

lab Labor(atorium) 60
laboratory Labor 61
label Etikett 52
to label beschriften 52
labour Arbeits- 72
lack of Mangel an, mangelnd, fehlend 104
ladle Kelle, Schöpflöffel 97
lager beer helles Bier, Lagerbier 94

lamb Lamm 97
to land landen 120
lane Fahrspur 38
Latvian lettisch 76
lead Führung 118
leader Führer(in) 84
leaf, pl. **leaves** Blatt 131
league Liga 124
to leave out auslassen 43
leaver Schulabgänger(in) 10
leek Lauch 97
left übrig 41
left-hand linksseitig, links stehend 14
legal rechtlich, gesetzlich, legal 114
legend Legende 68
legislative legislativ, gesetzgebend 84
leprechaun ein kleiner Kobold aus der irischen Mythologie 103
letter Buchstabe 18
letter box Briefkasten 112
level Niveau, Pegelstand 30
library Bibliothek, Bücherei 47
licensed zugelassen, lizensiert 128
lifelong lebenslang, lebenslänglich 105
lifestyle Lebensstil 15
lifetime Lebensdauer, Lebenszeit, Lebzeiten 30
lighter Feuerzeug, Anzünder 54
to light up beleuchten 131
likely wahrscheinlich, voraussichtlich 49
to limit begrenzen 84
limited begrenzt, beschränkt 126
link Verbindung, Link 108
listener Zuhörer(in) 79
litter Abfall 67
liver Leber 60
loaf of bread Brotleib 19
to lobby for s.th. sich für etwas einsetzen 129
local council etwa Gemeinderat 29
location Einrichtung, Standort, Lage 54
logical logisch 110
logistics Logistik, Versorgung 75
logo Firmenemblem 25
loneliness Einsamkeit 122
lonely einsam 25
lone parent Alleinerziehende(-r) 127
long-term langfristig 21
look Blick, Aussehen 100
to look like aussehen wie 118
lottery Lotterie 67
lounge Salon, Gesellschaftszimmer 54
lovely nett, hübsch, schön 130
low-flush toilet Toilette mit geringem Wasserverbrauch 54
low season Nebensaison 90
lunchtime Mittagszeit 11
lung Lunge 101

M

magnet Magnet 58
main course Hauptgericht 94
to maintain behaupten, erhalten, pflegen 112
maintenance Wartung, Pflege, Instandhaltung, Unterhalt, Verwaltung 103
maize Mais 81
major bedeutend, groß, Haupt- 51
majority Mehrheit 84
to make money Geld verdienen 73
to make up (s.th.) etwas bilden, zusammenstellen, erfinden 84
management Management, Geschäftsführung 128
managing director Geschäftsführer(in), Mitglied der Geschäftsführung 35
manufacturer Hersteller 73
manufacturing Herstellung 16
marital status Ehestand, Familienstand 95
to mark markieren, kennzeichnen, korrigieren 53
to market vermarkten, verkaufen 30
marketing Marketing 31
marriage Heirat, Hochzeit 62
massive massiv, umfangreich 110
material Material 54
maximum maximal, größte(r, s) 118
mayor Bürgermeister(in) 57
meaningful sinnvoll, aussagekräftig 51
meanness Gemeinheit, Knauserigkeit 41
measure Maßnahme 37
mechanical mechanisch, technisch 45
mediation Sprachmittlung, Vermittlung, Schlichtungswesen 85
medical medizinisch 47
medicine Medizin 41
to melt schmelzen 97
membership Mitgliedschaft 51
mental geistig, mental 112
menu Speisekarte 51
merchandising Verkaufsförderung, Merchandising, Vermarktung 30
merchant Händler, Kaufmann, Handelsmann 76
messaging service Dienst zur Versendung von (Sofort-)Nachrichten 34
Mexican mexikanisch 131
midday Mittag 97
migrant Migrant(in), Übersiedler(in) 131
migration Migration, Abwanderung, Umzug 129
to mine abbauen, fördern 71
minimum Minimum, Mindest- 126
mining Bergbau 65
minority Minderheit 112
missing fehlend, vermisst 30
misspelling falsche Schreibweise, Rechtschreibfehler 108
missus umgangssprachliche Anrede für eine Frau 41
mixture Mischung, Vermischung, Gemenge 77
mobile mobil, beweglich 35
mobile phone Mobiltelefon, Handy 25
modal auxiliary Hilfsverb 43
model Model, Vorbild, Modell 106
modern modern 108
to modify verändern, modifizieren 63
monitor Monitor, Bildschirm 33
to monitor überwachen 128
monkey Affe 70
monster Monster, Ungetüm 100
monthly monatlich 110
moreover überdies; außerdem 112
motion Bewegung 54
motivation Motivation, Leistungsbereitschaft 45
motive Beweggrund, Absicht, Motiv 61
motorboat Motorboot 70
motor mechanic Kfz-Mechaniker(in) 22
motorway Autobahn 38
Mountie berittene kanadische Polizei 103
mouse, pl. **mice** Maus 116
movie Film 111
MP3 player MP3 Spieler 72
multicultural multikulturell 12
multi-ethnic multiethnisch 124
multiplayer für viele Mitspieler 122
mum Mutter, Mama 9
murder Mord 38
musical musikalisch 45
musician Musiker(in) 9
musk ox Moschusochse 129
Muslim Moslem(in) 43
must-have etwas Unentbehrliches 110
myth Mythos, Märchen, Gerücht 114

N

nasty schlimm, böse 113
national national 101
National Diploma 2-jährige Schulzeit 9
nationality Nationalität 12
nationwide landesweit 123
native eingeboren, einheimisch 68
natural natürlich 49
nature Natur 68
negative negativ 52
neighbourhood Nachbarschaft 54
neither keine(-r/-s) (von beiden) 41
network Netz, Netzwerk 37
never mind! macht nichts! schon gut! bitte! 67
nevertheless dennoch, trotzdem, nichtsdestotrotz 76
newcomer Neuling 130
night vision goggles Nachtsichtgerät 131
no matter egal 128
to nominate ernennen, nominieren, aufstellen 84
no-name product Billigprodukt, Produkt ohne Markenname 25
non-defining relative clause nicht notwendiger Relativsatz 42
non-food Nichtlebensmittel, Güter, die nicht zum Verzehr gedacht sind 52
non-governmental nichtregierungs-, nichtstaatlich 81
non-profit gemeinnützig, keinen Gewinn anstrebend 55
nonsense Unsinn 60

non-working nicht erwerbstätig 127
norm Norm, Regel 42
normal normal 112
normally normalerweise 11
notification Benachrichtigung, Meldung 110
novel Roman 60
nuclear nuklear, Atom- 54
nursery school Vorschule 22

O

oatmeal Haferflocken, Hafermehl 101
obesity Fettleibigkeit 120
object Gegenstand, Objekt 53
to observe beobachten 39
obstacle Hindernis 120
to obtain erlangen 108
offender Angreifer(in), Täter(in) 124
officer Beamter, Beamtin 39
official Beamter, Beamtin 57
official offiziell 87
offspring Nachwuchs, Nachkommen 116
once in a while ab und zu, gelegentlich 70
on duty im Dienst 93
one-bedroomed mit einem Schlafzimmer 126
onion Zwiebel 97
on offer im Angebot 22
on one's own (ganz) allein(e) 46
on the lookout Ausschau haltend 131
on the one hand einerseits, auf der einen Seite 114
on the other hand andererseits, auf der anderen Seite 114
on the whole im Großen und Ganzen, alles in allem 61
onto auf … hinauf 93
open-minded aufgeschlossen, unvoreingenommen 21
opera Oper 66
to operate bedienen 16
operation Operation, Handlung, Verfahren, Arbeitsgang 80
operative angelernte Arbeiterin, angelernter Arbeiter 128
operator Betreiber(in) 122
opponent Gegner(in) 87
opportunity Gelegenheit 45
opposition Widerstand, Gegensatz, Widerspruch 130
option Alternative, Möglichkeit 77
orange Orange 95
order Bestellung, Befehl, Reihenfolge 95
organ Organ 60
organic biologisch angebaut, organisch 49
organizational organisatorisch 45
to orientate orientieren, ausrichten 86
origin Herkunft, Ursprung 40
original original, ursprünglich, unbearbeitet 76
otherwise sonst 67
ought to sollte, müsste 93
ourselves uns, selbst 89
outdoor im Freien, draußen 45
out of order außer Betrieb, gestört 103
oven Backofen 126
overfishing Überfischung 133
overnight über Nacht 70
overseas Übersee-, in Übersee 103
overweight übergewichtig 33

P

packaging Verpackungsmaterial 25
pain Schmerz 53
Paki Abkürzung von ‚Pakistani', Schimpfwort für Menschen aus Asien 124
pan Pfanne 97
paperwork Schreibarbeit, Büroarbeit 93
paragliding Gleitschirm fliegen 70
to paraphrase paraphrasieren, mit anderen Worten ausdrücken, umschreiben 85
parkour Parkour, schnelle Fortbewegung ohne Hilfsmittel 120
parliament Parlament 84
parliamentary parlamentarisch 84
partly teilweise 118
partnership Partnerschaft 89
part-time job Teilzeitjob 8
to pass (ein Gesetz) verabschieden, bestehen, weitergeben 84
passive voice Passiv (Grammatik) 58
past letzte(r, s), vergangen; vorbei 40; 112
pastime Zeitvertreib, Beschäftigung 122
patient Patient(in) 46
pattern Muster 101
to pay attention Aufmerksamkeit schenken 38
paycheck *(AE)* Gehaltsscheck, Lohnscheck 127
payment Bezahlung 28
to pay off sich auszahlen 126
pea Erbse 94
peaceful friedlich 70
peacekeeping Friedenserhaltung, Friedensbewahrung 80
pedestrian Fußgänger(in) 102
penalty Strafe, Elfmeter (Fußball) 114
pepper Pfeffer 97
percentage Prozentsatz 123
perfect vollkommen, perfekt 67
to perform aufführen 120
permanent dauerhaft 20
permission Erlaubnis 84
to permit erlauben, zulassen, genehmigen 84
to persecute verfolgen 81
personal identification number persönliche Identifikationsnummer 110
personality Persönlichkeit 9
personnel Personal 16
perspective Blickwinkel, Perspektive 46
to persuade überreden 29
pesticide Schädlingsbekämpfungsmittel, Pflanzenschutzmittel 63
pet Haustier 9
phase Phase, (Zeit-)Abschnitt 55
phrase Ausdruck 16
physical körperlich, physisch 53
Physics Physik 10
picker Pflücker(in) 41
pie gedeckter Obstkuchen 94
pie chart Kreisdiagramm 52
piezoelectric piezoelektrisch 54
piezoelectricity Piezoelektrizität 54
pill Pille, Tablette 81
pilot programme Modellprojekt 120
pineapple Ananas 52
pint Pinte (englisches Hohlmaß: 0,57 l) 95
piracy Piraterie, Raubkopieren 37
placement Praktikum, Platzierung, Vertriebspolitik 10
plain Ebene, Fläche 129
planet Planet 30
plant Fabrikanlage 23
plastic Plastik 110
platform Plattform 28
pleasant angenehm 103
pleased erfreut 92
plenty eine Menge 128
podcast Podcast, aus dem Internet herunterladbare Film- bzw. Hörsequenz 79
poet Dichter(in), Poet(in) 101
point of view Standpunkt, Ansicht 61
to point out hinweisen auf 39
to poison vergiften 114
policy (Versicherungs-)Police, Versicherungsschein, Politik 60
polite höflich 14
poly-carbon aus Polycarbonat 54
poorly schlecht 126
pop-up advertising Werbung in einem Pop-up-Fenster (auf einem Monitor) 108
portal Portal 123
portrait Portrait, Konterfei 26
positive positiv 55
postage Porto, Postgebühr 28
postcode Postleitzahl 50
post-graduate Nachdiplom- 128
potential potenziell, eventuell 86
poverty Armut 42
power Energie, Strom 57
to power mit Strom versorgen, antreiben 54
powerful stark 108
power line Starkstromleitung, Überlandleitung 58
power plant Kraftwerk 58
practicability Durchführbarkeit, Praktikabilität 55
prawn Garnele 94
prayer Gebet 101
precise präzise, genau 120
pregnancy Schwangerschaft 41
pregnant schwanger 62
premium rate number Sonderrufnummer 28

scam Betrug 28
to scan scannen, durchsuchen 44
scarf Schal, Halstuch, Kopftuch 44
scenario Szenario, Drehbuch 112
scene Szene, Kulisse 15
scenery Landschaft 101
scheme Programm 89
science Wissenschaft, Naturwissenschaft 10
scientific wissenschaftlich 61
scientist Wissenschaftler(in) 33
Scotland Schottland 89
Scottish schottisch 45
to scream schreien 14
screen Bildschirm 33
script Drehbuch 30
seafood Fisch und Meeresfrüchte 51
search Suche 108
search engine Suchmaschine 108
to search (for) suchen (nach) 120
season Saison, Jahreszeit 52
secondary sekundär, Zweit- 65
secondary school weiterführende Schule 47
section Abschnitt, Abteilung 40
sector Sektor 65
to secure absichern, bewirken, schützen 35
security Sicherheit 96
seed Saat, Samen 81
self-confidence Selbstbewusstsein 128
self-defence Selbstverteidigung, Notwehr 131
sense Sinn, Sinnesempfindung, Bedeutung 45
sensible vernünftig 110
sensitive einfühlsam, sensibel 68
separation of powers Gewaltenteilung 84
series, pl. **series** Serie 64
server Server, zentrale Einheit im Netzwerk 35
to settle beilegen, ansiedeln, begleichen 124
to settle up bezahlen, Rechnung begleichen 103
severe ernst 120
sewage Abwasser 128
shadow Schatten 131
to shake schütteln, zittern 92
shaky wackelig, unsicher 60
shape Form 118
sharp steil, stark, scharf 17
sheep, pl. **sheep** Schaf 101
shift (Arbeits-)Schicht 46
shiny glänzend 54
shipping Schifffahrt, Versand 52
shocked bestürzt, geschockt 60
shocking schockierend 112
short code Kurzwahlnummer 28
short-term kurzfristig, befristet, kurzzeitig 82
shoulder bag Umhängetasche 98
shower Schauer, Dusche 38
to show off angeben, sich aufspielen 120
showy auffallend, prächtig, protzig 102
shrimp Krabbe, Schrimp 94
to shut someone up jemanden dazu bringen, den Mund zu halten 41
side by side Seite an Seite 130
sightseeing Besichtigungstour 66
silence Schweigen, Stille 60
silver Silber 25
similar ähnlich 25
similarity Ähnlichkeit, Gemeinsamkeit 122
sincerely Mit freundlichen Grüßen 89
single einzeln, einfach 96
single mum alleinerziehende Mutter 46
single parent Alleinerziehende(r) 46
site Ort 128
situation Situation 45
skiing Skifahren 38
to skim überfliegen 44
skin Haut 116
slave Sklave/Sklavin 82
sleepless schlaflos 37
slogan Slogan, Werbespruch 30
slum Slum, Elendsviertel 126
to snap blaffen 41
sneaker Turnschuh 72
so-called so genannte 52
social sozial, gesellschaftlich 42
social care Sozialwissenschaft, Sozialwesen 9
to socialize ausgehen 12
social network soziales Netzwerk 122
social networking website Internetseite für ein soziales Netzwerk 9
social worker Sozialarbeiter(in) 47
society Gesellschaft 40
soft drink alkoholfreies Getränk 94
software Software (Computerprogramme) 37
solar Sonnen-, Solar- 52
sole einzig, ausschließlich 60
sort Sorte, Art 54
soup Suppe 94
South African südafrikanisch 52
southbound in Richtung Süden 38
southern südlich 68
span Spannweite, Spanne 118
Spanish spanisch 52
sparkling water Mineralwasser mit Kohlensäure 95
special needs Sonderschul- 46
specific spezifisch, bestimmt, speziell 116
spice Gewürz, Beigeschmack 101
spicy würzig, pikant, scharf 94
spirit Spirituose 94
sponsoring Sponsoring, Förderung, finanzielle Unterstützung 30
sporting sportlich, Sport- 64
to spot entdecken 41
sprawl Ausbreitung 129
to spray sprühen 63
spring Quelle, Brunnen 68
square Platz, Quadrat 66
stability Stabilität, Beständigkeit 87
stable stabil 86
stairs Treppe 120
stall Stand, Box, Parkett 55
standard Standard 126
standing Ansehen, Stellung 102
starter Vorspeise 94
statement Aussage 8
Statue of Liberty Freiheitsstatue 66
stay Aufenthalt 96
steady stetig 17
to steal stehlen 35
steam Dampf 58
steam engine Dampfmaschine, Dampflokomotive 59
steel Stahl 57
stem cell Stammzelle 116
step Schritt, Stufe 110
to step treten 130
to stew dämpfen, schmoren, sich aufregen 97
to stir (um)rühren, sich regen 97
stock Brühe 97
stomach Magen 81
stopover Zwischenlandung 95
storey Stock(werk) 47
storyline Handlung 30
straight gerade, direkt 94
stranger Fremde(r) 102
strawberry Erdbeere 40
to strengthen stärken, kräftigen 122
stressful anstrengend, stressig 126
to stretch dehnen, strecken 129
strict streng 53
strike Treffer, Schlag 118
stripe Streifen 25
structure Struktur, Aufbau 45
study Studie 120
stuff Zeug 73
to stuff (into) stopfen (in) 101
stunning umwerfend 130
style Stil 9
subculture Subkultur 15
subheading Zwischenüberschrift 44
substitute Ersatz 43
to suffer leiden, erleiden 60
sufficient ausreichend, genügend 104
to suggest vorschlagen 39
suggestion Vorschlag 55
suicide Selbstmord 113
suitable geeignet 13
Supreme Court Oberstes Bundesgericht 84
to summarize zusammenfassen 33
summary Zusammenfassung 29
to sum up zusammenfassen 79
sunny sonnig 38
superstore großer Supermarkt 18
to supervise beaufsichtigen 120
supervision Aufsicht 120
support Unterstützung 68
to support unterstützen 22
supporter Anhänger(in), Befürworter(in) 87

surname Nachname 50
surprising überraschend 33
surroundings Umgebung 68
survival Überleben 129
to survive überleben 49
to suspect vermuten, misstrauen 129
to suspend suspendieren, ausschließen 125
sustainable nachhaltig, kontinuierlich 55
to swear, swore, sworn fluchen; schwören 102
sweater Pullover 59
sweet Süßigkeit 16
to swing schwingen 120

T

to tackle angreifen 120
tactic Taktik 102
to take action handeln, eingreifen 112
to take a seat Platz nehmen, sich hinsetzen 128
takeaway Restaurant, das Speisen zum Mitnehmen verkauft 76
take care Pass auf dich auf. 99
to take on aufgreifen, übernehmen 43
to take orders Bestellungen entgegennehmen 14
to take to s.o. an jemandem Gefallen finden 130
talent Talent 45
talk Vortrag, Gespräch, Unterhaltung 101
tally Summe, Anzahl 131
tap Wasserhahn 54
target Ziel 24
tartan Schottenkaro (bestimmtes Muster eines Clans) 101
task Aufgabe 45
teaching assistant Lehrkraft, die einen Lehrer im Unterricht unterstützt, kleinen Schülergruppen Nachhilfe gibt bzw. Kinder mit Behinderungen betreut 104
to tease necken 125
technician Techniker(in) 9
technique Methode, Technik 116
technological technisch, technologisch 118
teenage im Alter von 13 bis 19 37
telecommunications Telekommunikation 35
to tell s.o. off tadeln, ausschimpfen 125
temperature Temperatur 38
to tend (to) zu etwas neigen 33
term Trimester, Begriff, Bedingung 10
terrorist Terrorist(in) 131
to terrorize terrorisieren 112
tertiary tertiär 65
textile textil 73
textiles Textilien 76
text message Textmitteilung, SMS 28
thankful dankbar 86
thanks danke 83
the background der Hintergrund 14
the elderly ältere Menschen 53
theoretical theoretisch 108
theory Theorie 31
thermal Thermal-, Wärme- 68
thief, pl. **thieves** Dieb(in) 57
third party Dritte 108
thirst Durst 50
thistle Distel 101
thoughtless gedankenlos, unbedacht 120
to thrive Erfolg haben, gedeihen, blühen 131
thunderstorm Gewitter 38
thyme Thymian 97
tick Häkchen 25
tie Krawatte, (Spiel) unentschieden enden 102
time-consuming zeitraubend 96
tinned in Dosen, konserviert 126
tip Tipp, Hinweis, Trinkgeld 28
tissue Gewebe, Papiertaschentuch 116
TLD (top-level domain) Bereich oberster Ebene 81
tolerance Toleranz 112
toll Maut 98
ton Tonne (Gewicht) 57
top Top, Oberteil 14
topic Thema 42
to top up füllen, aufladen 110
to topple wackeln, stürzen, umwerfen 60
touch Kontakt, Verbindung, Berührung 122
tourism Tourismus 64
toxic giftig 35
trader Händler(in) 28
tradition Tradition 43
traffic jam Stau 128
tragedy Tragödie 126
tragic tragisch 112
trainee Praktikant(in), Auszubildende(r) 95
trainer Turnschuh 25
transaction Übertragung, Transaktion, Geschäft 110
to transfer übertragen, transferieren 116
to transform verwandeln 106
transformation Umwandlung, Umgestaltung, Wandlung 130
transparent transparent, durchsichtig 122
transplant Transplantation, Übertragung 61
transportation Transport, Beförderung 52
trash Abfall 124
travel das Reisen 64
traveller Reisende(r) 118
to treat behandeln 46
treatment Behandlung 41
treaty Vertrag 84
trend Trend, Mode, Richtung, Tendenz 57
trendy modisch, trendig 67
trick Trick 131
trick or treat Streich oder Leckereien, Süßes oder Saures 112
trout, pl. **trout** Forelle 94
truck Lastwagen 38
to trust vertrauen 28
truthful ehrlich 25
to try on anprobieren 26
tube U-Bahn, Röhre 98
tuna, pl. **tuna** Thunfisch 51
turbine Turbine 54
turnover Absatz, Umsatz 106
to turn up auftauchen, erscheinen 37
tutor Klassenlehrer(in), Betreuer(in) 74
twin Zwilling 62
twin town Partnerstadt 47
two-thirds zwei Drittel 81
to type tippen 19

U

unconstitutional verfassungswidrig 84
under-age minderjährig, unmündig 114
undergrowth Gestrüpp, Unterholz 131
underlined unterstrichen 27
underway unterwegs, im Gange 129
undeveloped nicht entwickelt 129
unfashionable unmodisch, unmodern 72
unforgettable unvergesslich 54
unhealthy ungesund 126
unhelpful nutzlos, nicht hilfreich 104
unique einzig, einzigartig 101
uniqueness Einzigartigkeit 30
unit Abteilung, Station, Kapitel 46
united vereint 80
unknown unbekannt 69
unlimited grenzenlos, unbegrenzt 26
unnatural unnatürlich 102
to unpack auspacken 27
unpaid unbezahlt 45
unreal irreal, unwirklich 122
unspoiled unberührt, unbeschädigt 129
unsure unsicher 113
untouchable unantastbar, unberührbar, unerreichbar 122
untouched unberührt, unversehrt 68
to update aktualisieren 35
uplift Auftrieb 118
to upset, upset, upset aus der Fassung bringen, bestürzen, aufregen 60
upside down umgedreht 130
urban städtisch 131
urinal Pissoir, Urinal 54
to urinate urinieren 112
use Verwendung, Verwendungsmöglichkeit 48
user Benutzer(in) 108
utensil Gerät, Geschirr, Gefäß 97
utility Versorgung mit Wasser, Strom usw. 127

V

vacancy Stellenangebot, Leere, Lücke 90
valid gültig 131
valuable wertvoll 114
value Wert 122

vandalism Vandalismus, mutwillige Beschädigung 48
variety Vielfalt, Auswahl 68
various verschieden 42
to vary variieren 87
vegetable Gemüse 52
veto Veto, Einspruchsrecht, Einspruch 84
video clip Videoclip, kurze Videoaufnahme 37
view Aussicht, Sicht 57
to view besichtigen, betrachten, sehen 57
Viking Wikinger 101
vinegar Essig 14
violence Gewalt 114
virtual virtuell 110
vision Vorstellung, (Zukunfts-)Vision 55
visual bildlich, visuell, das Sehen betreffend 45
volcano, pl. **volcanoes** Vulkan 70
voluntary freiwillig 45
volunteer Freiwillige(r) 45
vomit Erbrochenes 114
voter Wähler(in) 84

W

wage Lohn 41
wallpaper Hintergrundbild, Tapete 28
to wander umherstreifen, wandern 112
wanna (= informal form of **want to**) will/ wollen 103
warfare Krieg, Kriegführung 122
warming Erwärmung 48
warrior Krieger(in) 101
waterless ohne Wasser, trocken 54
water-related disease Krankheit, die durch (unsauberes) Wasser verursacht wird 50
wave Welle 54
way beyond weit entfernt, weit darüber hinaus 41
web Netz 35
website Website, Internetseite 10
wedding Hochzeit 103
welfare Sozialhilfe, Wohl(ergehen) 126
well-dressed gut angezogen 112
westerly aus westlicher Richtung 38
western westlich 40
what a pity wie schade! 97
whatever was auch immer 73
What is he like? Wie ist er? 44
wheelchair Rollstuhl 47
whenever wann immer, jedes Mal, wenn 122
whereas während 35
whisper Wispern, Flüstern 60
wild wild 70
wilderness Wildnis 129
wildlife Tierwelt (in freier Wildbahn) 129
wind farm Windpark 57
wing Flügel 118
wireless drahtlos 35
to withdraw (withdrew, withdrawn) abheben, (sich) entfernen 110
with reference to betreffend, bezüglich 21
with regard to in Bezug auf 108
witness Zeugin, Zeuge 38
wobbly wackelig, zittrig 60
wolf, pl. **wolves** Wolf 129
wonder Wunder 57
to wonder sich fragen, sich Gedanken machen, sich wundern 112
word web Wortnetz 22
workplace Arbeitsplatz 13
workshop Werkstatt 55
to work to a nine-to-five clock normale Geschäftszeiten einhalten 128
worldwide weltweit 37
worried beunruhigt 49
worry Sorge, Ärger 48

Y

yard Hof 39
youngster Jugendliche(r) 38
yourself selbst 19

Z

zero Null 108
zone Zone, Gebiet, Bereich 82

Basic vocabulary

Abkürzung
AE = Gebrauch im amerikanischen Englisch

A

a couple of ein paar
a little etwas, ein bisschen
a lot of viel(e)
a number of einige
ability Fähigkeit
abroad im/ins Ausland
to accept annehmen, akzeptieren
accident Unfall
accurate genau
to achieve erreichen
active aktiv
activity Aktivität
to add hinzufügen, addieren
additional zusätzlich
address Adresse
advantage Vorteil
advert(isement) Werbeanzeige, Anzeige
to advertise werben, inserieren
advertiser Inserent, Werbefachmann
advertising Werbung
advice Rat, Ratschlag
to advise (be)raten
afternoon Nachmittag
afterwards danach
again wieder
against gegen
age Alter, Zeitalter
ago vor
to agree einverstanden sein, zustimmen
agreement Übereinstimmung, Übereinkunft
aim Ziel
air Luft
airport Flughafen
alert Alarm
all alle(s), ganz
to allow erlauben
almost fast, beinahe
alone allein
along entlang
already schon, bereits
also auch
alternative Alternative, Wahl; alternativ
although obwohl
always immer
among zwischen, unter
amount Betrag, Summe
to analyze analysieren
angry wütend
animal Tier
to announce bekannt geben, ansagen
announcement Bekanntgabe, Durchsage
another noch eine(r, s), ein(e) andere(r, s)
to answer; answer (be)antworten; Antwort
any irgendeine(r, s)
any time jederzeit
anybody irgendjemand
anyone irgendjemand
anything irgendetwas
to appear (er)scheinen
apple Apfel
applicant Bewerber(in)
application Bewerbung
to apply (for) sich bewerben (um)
area Gebiet
around um (herum), ungefähr
arrival Ankunft
to arrive ankommen
article Artikel
as wie, da, als
as well auch, ebenso gut
to ask (for) fragen, bitten (um)
at first anfangs
at home zu Hause
at last schließlich, endlich
at least wenigstens
at once sofort
at present im Augenblick, jetzt
at risk gefährdet
at the moment im Moment, jetzt
at work bei der Arbeit
atmosphere Atmosphäre
to attend (school) (Schule) besuchen
attention Aufmerksamkeit
attitude Haltung, Einstellung
to attract anziehen
aunt Tante
autumn Herbst
away weg
awful furchtbar, schrecklich

B

back Rücken; zurück
background Hintergrund
bad schlecht, schlimm, böse
bag Tasche, Tüte
baggage Gepäck
to bake backen
baker Bäcker(in)
balcony Balkon
to ban; ban verbieten, Verbot
bank Bank (Geldinstitut)
basket Korb
bathroom Badezimmer
to be able können
to be afraid (of) Angst haben (vor)
beach Strand
beard Bart
beautiful schön
because weil
because of wegen
to become, (became, become) werden
bed Bett
bedroom Schlafzimmer
before vor, bevor
to begin, (began, begun) anfangen, beginnen
beginning Anfang, Beginn
to behave sich benehmen, sich verhalten
behaviour Verhalten, Benehmen
behind hinter
to believe glauben
to belong to gehören zu
best beste(r, s), am besten
best wishes alles Gute
better besser
between zwischen
bicycle Fahrrad
big groß
bike Fahrrad (Kurzform)
bill Rechnung, Gesetzesvorlage, Banknote, Entwurf, Schnabel
bird Vogel
birth Geburt
birthday Geburtstag
bit Stückchen
to bite, (bit, bitten) beißen
black schwarz
blackboard (Wand-)Tafel
to blame (for) verantwortlich machen (für)
block of flats Wohnblock
blog Internet-Tagebuch
blood Blut
blue blau
board Brett, Verpflegung
boat Boot
body Körper
to boil kochen
to book; book buchen; Buch
boot Stiefel
border Grenze
bored gelangweilt
boring langweilig
to borrow sich ausleihen
both beide
bottle Flasche
bottom Boden
box Schachtel, Kiste, Karton
boy Junge
boyfriend Freund
bread Brot
break Pause
to break, (broke, broken); break (zer)brechen, kaputt machen; Pause
to break down zusammenbrechen
breakfast Frühstück
bridge Brücke
to bring, (brought, brought) bringen

to broadcast, (broadcast, broadcast) übertragen, senden
brochure Broschüre, Prospekt
brother Bruder
brown braun
to brush; brush bürsten; Bürste
to build, (built, built) bauen
building Gebäude
to burn, (burnt, burnt) brennen
business Geschäft
busy beschäftigt, besetzt, belegt
but aber
butcher Metzger(in)
to buy, (bought, bought) kaufen
buyer Käufer(in)
by durch, mit, bei, neben, bis, um
by the way übrigens

C

cake Kuchen
to calculate (be)rechnen
to call; call (an)rufen, nennen, heißen; Anruf
camera Kamera, Fotoapparat
to camp; camp zelten, lagern; Lager
to campaign; campaign Wahlkampf führen; Kampagne, Wahlkampf
can können; Büchse, Dose
capital Großbuchstabe, Hauptstadt
car Auto
card Karte
to care; care sorgen; Sorge
career Beruf, Laufbahn, Karriere
careful vorsichtig, sorgfältig
careless sorglos
cargo Fracht, Ladung
to carry tragen
case Fall, Koffer, Kiste
cash Bargeld
cat Katze
to catch, (caught, caught) fangen
to cause; cause verursachen; Ursache
ceiling Zimmerdecke
centre Zentrum, Mittelpunkt
century Jahrhundert
certain sicher, bestimmt, gewiss
chair Stuhl
chalk Kreide
to change; change wechseln, (sich) (ver)ändern; Änderung, Wechsel(geld)
channel Kanal
chart Schaubild, Tabelle, Karte
cheap billig
to check; check (über)prüfen, kontrollieren; Kontrolle, Rechnung (im Restaurant), *(AE)* Scheck, Prüfung
cheers Tschüs, zum Wohl
cheese Käse
child(ren) Kind(er)
chips Pommes Frites, Kartoffelchips
chocolate Schokolade, Praline
choice Wahl
to choose, (chose, chosen) (aus)wählen
Christmas Weihnachten
church Kirche
cigarette Zigarette
cinema Kino
city Stadt
class (Schul-)Klasse
classmate Klassenkamerad(in)
classroom Klassenzimmer
to clean; clean reinigen, putzen; sauber
to clear; clear säubern, räumen; klar
clever klug, schlau, clever
to climb klettern
clock (Wand-)Uhr
to close; close schließen; dicht, nahe
clothes Kleidung
cloud Wolke
coal Kohle
coast Küste
coat Mantel
coffee Kaffee
coin Münze
cold kalt
to collect sammeln, abholen
collection Sammlung
college (Fach-)Hochschule, College
colour Farbe
to comb; comb kämmen; Kamm
to come, (came, come) kommen
comfortable bequem
to communicate kommunizieren, übermitteln
communication Kommunikation, Übermittlung
company Gesellschaft, Firma
to compare vergleichen
competition Wettbewerb, Konkurrenz
competitor Konkurrent(in), Wettbewerbsteilnehmer(in)
to complete; complete fertigstellen, vervollständigen; vollständig
to connect verbinden
connection Verbindung, Zusammenhang
to contact; contact sich in Verbindung setzen mit; Verbindung, Kontakt
to contain enthalten
container Behälter
to continue fortsetzen, weitermachen, weitergehen
to cook; cook kochen; Koch, Köchin
cooker Herd
to cooperate zusammenarbeiten
cooperation Zusammenarbeit
to copy; copy kopieren, abschreiben; Kopie, Exemplar
corner Ecke
to correct; correct korrigieren, verbessern; korrekt, richtig
correction Verbesserung, Korrektur
to cost, (cost, cost); cost kosten; Kosten
cotton Baumwolle
to count zählen, ins Gewicht fallen
counter Ladentisch, Schalter
country Land
couple Ehepaar, Paar
course Kurs, Lauf, Gang, Strecke
to cover; cover (be)decken, besetzen; Abdeckung, Umschlag
cow Kuh
to cross überqueren
crossing Kreuzung
crowd (Menschen-)Menge
crowded dicht gedrängt, voll
to cry; cry schreien, weinen; Schrei
cup Tasse
curious neugierig, seltsam
curtain Vorhang
customer Kunde, Kundin
customs Zoll, Zoll-
to cut, (cut, cut); cut schneiden; Schnitt
to cycle Fahrrad fahren

D

daily täglich
to damage; damage beschädigen; Schaden
to dance; dance tanzen; Tanz
danger Gefahr
dangerous gefährlich
dark dunkel
darkness Dunkelheit
date Datum, Zeitpunkt, Verabredung
date of birth Geburtsdatum
daughter Tochter
day Tag
dead tot
to deal, (dealt, dealt) (in, with); deal handeln (mit, von); Geschäft
dear lieb
death Tod
to decide (sich) entscheiden
decision Entscheidung
deep tief
to deliver liefern, (Rede) halten
delivery Lieferung
department Abteilung
department store Kaufhaus
to depend (on) abhängen (von)
to describe beschreiben
description Beschreibung
to design; design entwerfen, konstruieren; Entwurf, Muster
desk Schreibtisch
to destroy zerstören
destruction Zerstörung
detail Einzelheit, Detail
to develop entwickeln
development Entwicklung
to dial (Telefon) wählen
to dictate diktieren
dictation Diktat
dictionary Wörterbuch
to die sterben
to differ (from) sich unterscheiden (von)
difference Unterschied
different verschieden, unterschiedlich
difficult schwierig, schwer
difficulty Schwierigkeit
dining room Esszimmer
dinner (Mittag-, Abend-)Essen
to direct (to); direct richten, lenken (auf); direkt
direction Richtung

dirty dreckig, schmutzig
disadvantage Nachteil
to disagree (with) anderer Meinung sein, nicht übereinstimmen (mit)
to discuss besprechen, diskutieren
discussion Gespräch, Diskussion
to dislike nicht mögen
distance Entfernung, Strecke, Abstand
doctor Arzt, Ärztin
dog Hund
door Tür
down hinunter, unten
downstairs die Treppe hinunter, unten, im Erdgeschoss
to draw, (drew, drawn) zeichnen, ziehen
drawing Zeichnung
to dream; dream träumen; Traum
to dress; dress (sich) anziehen; Kleid, Kleidung
to drink, (drank, drunk); drink trinken; Getränk
to drive, (drove, driven); drive fahren; Fahrt
driver Fahrer(in)
to dry; dry trocknen; trocken
during während
dustbin Mülltonne
duty Pflicht, Zoll

E

each jede(r, s)
each other einander, sich
ear Ohr
early früh
to earn verdienen
earth Erde
east Osten; östlich, Ost-, ostwärts
easy leicht
to eat, (ate, eaten) essen
economy Wirtschaft
edge Kante, Rand, Schneide
to educate erziehen
education Erziehung
to effect; effect durchführen, erzielen, leisten; Wirkung
egg Ei
either ... or entweder ... oder
to elect wählen
election Wahl
electric elektrisch
electricity Elektrizität
electronics Elektronik
else sonst
emergency Notfall
to employ beschäftigen, einstellen
employed beschäftigt
employee Angestellte(r), Arbeitnehmer(in)
employer Arbeitgeber(in)
employment Beschäftigung, Anstellung, Arbeit
empty leer
to end; end (be)enden; Ende, Schluss
energy Energie, Kraft
engine Motor, Triebwerk, Lokomotive
engineer Ingenieur(in), Techniker(in)
engineering Technik; technisch
to enjoy genießen, sich freuen an
enjoyable schön, angenehm, unterhaltsam
enough genug
to enquire (about) sich erkundigen (nach), fragen (nach)
enquiry Anfrage, Erkundigung, Untersuchung
to enter eintreten, eingeben
entrance Eintritt, Eingang
envelope Umschlag
environment Umwelt, Umgebung, Umfeld
equal gleich
equipment Ausrüstung, Ausstattung
especial besondere(r, s)
even eben, gleich; sogar, selbst
evening Abend
event Ereignis
ever je, jemals
every jede(r, s)
everybody jeder
everyone jeder
everything alles
everywhere überall
exact genau
exam(ination) Prüfung
example Beispiel
excellent ausgezeichnet, hervorragend
exciting aufregend
to excuse; excuse (sich) entschuldigen; Entschuldigung
exercise Übung
to exist existieren, bestehen
exit Ausgang, Ausfahrt
to expect erwarten
expensive teuer
experience Erfahrung
to explain erklären
explanation Erklärung
to export; export exportieren, ausführen; Ausfuhr, Export
to express; express ausdrücken, äußern; Schnellzug, als Eilsache
expression Ausdruck
extra besonders
eye Auge

F

to face; face (einer Sache) ins Auge sehen, gegenübertreten; Gesicht
fact Tatsache
factory Fabrik
fair Messe, Markt; gerecht, fair
to fall, (fell, fallen); fall fallen; Fallen, Sturz; *(AE)* Herbst
false falsch
family Familie
famous berühmt
far weit
fare Fahrpreis, Fahrgeld
farm Bauernhof, Farm
farmer Landwirt
farming Landwirtschaft
fast schnell
fat dick, fett
father Vater
favourite Lieblings-
to feed, (fed, fed) füttern
to feel, (felt, felt) fühlen
feeling Gefühl
few wenige
field Feld
to fight, (fought, fought); fight kämpfen; Kampf
to fill füllen
final Finale, Endrunde; letzte(r, s), endgültig
to find, (found, found) finden
fine Strafe; fein, schön, gut
to finish; finish beenden, abschließen, aufhören; Ziel, Vollendung
to fire; fire feuern; Feuer
firm Firma; fest, verbindlich
first erste(r, s), zuerst
first of all zuerst, vor allem
to fish; fish fischen; Fisch
to fit; fit (zusammen)passen, einbauen; gesund, in Form
to fix befestigen, reparieren, besorgen
flat Wohnung; flach
flight Flug
floor Boden, Stock, Etage
flower Blume
to fly, (flew, flown); fly fliegen; Fliege
to follow folgen
food Essen, Nahrung, Lebensmittel
foot, feet Fuß, Füße
football Fußball
for example zum Beispiel
foreign ausländisch, fremd
forever für immer
to forget, (forgot, forgotten) vergessen
fork Gabel
to form; form formen, gestalten; Form, Formular, Klasse
fortunate glücklich
forward(s) vorwärts
to free; free befreien; frei, kostenlos
freeway *(AE)* Autobahn
frequent häufig
fresh frisch
fridge Kühlschrank
friend Freund(in)
friendly freundlich
front Vorderseite
fruit Obst, Frucht, Früchte
full (of) voll (von, mit)
fun Spaß
furniture Möbel
further weiter
future Zukunft

G

game Spiel
garage Autowerkstatt, Garage
garden Garten
gate Tor

gentleman Herr
to get, (got, got) bekommen, erhalten, werden
to get married heiraten
to get up aufstehen
girl Mädchen
girlfriend Freundin
to give, (gave, given) geben
to give up aufgeben
glad froh
glass Glas
glasses Brille
glove Handschuh
to go, (went, gone) gehen, fahren
to go down untergehen, sinken, fallen
to go on weitergehen, weitermachen
to go shopping einkaufen gehen
to go up hinaufgehen, wachsen, steigen
good gut
goodbye auf Wiedersehen
goods Güter, Waren
to govern regieren
government Regierung
grandfather Großvater
grandmother Großmutter
grandparents Großeltern
grateful dankbar
great groß, großartig
green grün
to greet grüßen
grey grau
grocer Lebensmittelhändler(in)
ground Boden
group Gruppe
to grow, (grew, grown) wachsen
grown-up Erwachsene(r)
growth Wachstum
to guess (er)raten
guest Gast

H

hair Haar
half Hälfte; halb
hall Flur, Saal
ham Schinken
handbag Handtasche
handkerchief Taschentuch
to hang, (hung, hung) (auf)hängen
to happen geschehen, passieren
happy glücklich, heiter
harbour Hafen
hard hart, schwierig, anstrengend
hardly kaum
hat Hut
to hate; hate hassen; Hass
to have (got), (had, had) haben
to have to müssen
to head; head anführen, fahren nach; Kopf, Leiter
headache Kopfschmerz
headline Überschrift
health Gesundheit
healthy gesund
to hear, (heard, heard) hören
heart Herz
to heat; heat heizen; Hitze
heating Heizung
heavy schwer
height Höhe
hello hallo
to help; help helfen; Hilfe
helpful hilfreich
here hier
here you are bitte(schön)!
to hesitate zögern
to hide, (hid, hidden) (sich) verstecken
high hoch
high tech (high technology) Hochtechnologie
hill Hügel
history Geschichte
to hit, (hit, hit); hit schlagen; Schlag, Treffer, Erfolg
to hold, (held, held) halten
hole Loch
holiday Urlaub, Ferien, freier Tag, Feiertag
home Zuhause
homework Hausaufgaben
honest ehrlich
to hope; hope hoffen; Hoffnung
horse Pferd
hospital Krankenhaus
hot heiß, scharf
hour Stunde
house Haus
housewife Hausfrau
housework Hausarbeit
how wie
how are you? wie geht es Dir/Ihnen?
however jedoch
hundred Hundert
hungry hungrig
to hurry; hurry sich beeilen; Eile
to hurt, (hurt, hurt) verletzen
husband Ehemann

I

ice cream Eiskrem
idea Idee, Vorstellung
if wenn, falls, ob
ill krank
illness Krankheit
to imagine sich vorstellen
immediate unmittelbar, unverzüglich
immigrant Einwanderer, Einwanderin
to immigrate einwandern
to import; import einführen, importieren; Einfuhr, Import
importance Wichtigkeit
important wichtig
impossible unmöglich
to improve (sich) verbessern
in fact tatsächlich
in front of vor
in italics kursiv
in my opinion meiner Meinung nach
in time rechtzeitig
inch Zoll (Maßeinheit)
to include einschließen
income Einkommen
to increase zunehmen, steigen, erhöhen
indeed tatsächlich
industry Industrie
to inform informieren
inside in, innerhalb
instead (of) anstatt
to instruct unterrichten, anweisen
instruction Unterricht, Anweisung, (Gebrauchs-)Anleitung
insurance Versicherung
to intend beabsichtigen
interest Interesse, (Plural) Zinsen
interesting interessant
to introduce einführen, vorstellen
introduction Einführung, Vorstellung
to invent erfinden
invention Erfindung
to invest investieren
invitation Einladung
to invite einladen
island Insel
IT Informationstechnik

J

jacket Jacke
jam Marmelade
job Arbeit, Beruf, Job
to join (sich) anschließen, beitreten
journey Reise
juice Saft
to jump; jump springen; Sprung
just genau, soeben, nur

K

to keep, (kept, kept) (be)halten, aufbewahren
key Schlüssel
to kill töten
kilo(gram) Kilo(gramm)
kind Art, Sorte; freundlich
king König
to kiss; kiss küssen; Kuss
kitchen Küche
knee Knie
knife Messer
to knock klopfen
to know, (knew, known) wissen, kennen
knowledge Wissen

L

ladder Leiter
lady Dame
lake See
lamp Lampe
land Land
landlady Vermieterin, Wirtin
landlord Vermieter, Wirt
language Sprache
large weit, groß
to last; last dauern; letzte(r, s)
late spät
later on später
latest neueste(r, s)
to laugh lachen
laughter Gelächter

law Gesetz
to lay, (laid, laid) legen
lazy faul
to lead, (led, led) führen, leiten
leaflet (Hand-)Zettel, Flugblatt
to learn, (learnt, learnt) lernen
learner Lernende(r), Anfänger(in)
least wenigste(r, s), geringste(r, s)
to leave, (left, left) (ver)lassen, abfahren
left links; übrig
leg Bein
leisure Freizeit
lemon Zitrone
to lend, (lent, lent) verleihen
length Länge
less weniger
lesson Unterrichtsstunde
to let, (let, let) lassen
letter Brief, Buchstabe
to lie, (lied, lied) lügen
to lie, (lay, lain) liegen
life (lives) Leben
to lift; lift anheben, aufheben; Aufzug, Mitfahrgelegenheit
light Licht, Lampe; hell, leicht
to like; like mögen; wie
to limit; limit beschränken, begrenzen; Grenze, Beschränkung
line Linie, Zeile
lip Lippe
to list; list aufführen, auflisten; Liste
to listen (to) (zu)hören
little klein, wenig
to live; live leben, wohnen; direkt, live
living room Wohnzimmer
to load; load laden; Ladung
local lokal, ortsansässig, örtlich
long lang
to look schauen, (aus)sehen
to look after sich kümmern um
to look for suchen
to look forward to sich freuen auf
to look out aufpassen, hinaussehen
to look up nachschlagen, heraussuchen, aufblicken
lorry Lastwagen
to lose, (lost, lost) verlieren
loss Verlust
lot Menge, Los
lots of viel(e)
loud laut
to love; love lieben; Liebe
lovely hübsch
low niedrig
luck Glück, Schicksal
lucky glücklich (im Sinne von: Glück haben)
luggage Gepäck
lunch Mittagessen

M

machine Maschine, Gerät, Automat
mad verrückt
madam gnädige Frau
magazine Zeitschrift
mail Post
main Haupt-
mainly hauptsächlich
to make, (made, made) machen, herstellen
man (men) Mann (Männer), **Mensch**
to manage zu Stande bringen, schaffen, leiten, verwalten
management (Geschäfts-)Leitung, Verwaltung, Durchführung
many viele
map (Land-)Karte
market Markt
marmalade (Orangen-)Marmelade
married verheiratet
to marry heiraten
mass Masse
to match; match passen, zuordnen; Wettkampf, Streichholz
mathematics Mathematik
to matter; matter etwas ausmachen; Angelegenheit
may dürfen
maybe vielleicht
meal Mahlzeit
to mean, (meant, meant) bedeuten, meinen
meaning Bedeutung
(in the) meantime inzwischen
meanwhile inzwischen
meat Fleisch
mechanic Mechaniker(in)
media Medien
to meet, (met, met) (sich) treffen, kennenlernen
meeting Treffen
member Mitglied
to mend reparieren
to mention erwähnen
message Mitteilung, Nachricht
method Methode
metre Meter
microwave Mikrowelle
middle Mitte; mittlere(r, s)
midnight Mitternacht
might könnte(n); Gewalt, Macht
mile Meile
milk Milch
to mind; mind etwas ausmachen; Meinung, Gedanken, Verstand
mine Bergwerk
minute Minute
mirror Spiegel
Miss Fräulein
to miss vermissen, verfehlen, verpassen
mistake Fehler
to mix; mix mischen; Mischung
moment Augenblick
money Geld
month Monat
moon Mond
more mehr
morning Morgen
most meiste(r, s), die meisten
mother Mutter
mountain Berg
mouth Mund
to move bewegen, umziehen
movement Bewegung
Mr Herr (Anrede)
Mrs Frau (Anrede für eine verheiratete Frau)
Ms Frau (Anrede)
much viel
mum Mutter, Mama
music Musik
must müssen
must not nicht dürfen

N

to name; name benennen; Name
narrow eng
near nahe
nearby nahe gelegen
nearly fast, beinahe
necessary notwendig
to need; need brauchen, benötigen; Notwendigkeit
neighbour Nachbar(in)
neither ... nor weder ... noch
never nie(mals)
new neu
news Nachrichten, Neuigkeit
newspaper Zeitung
next nächste(r, s)
nice nett, schön, hübsch, gut
night Nacht
no kein(e); nein
no longer nicht mehr
no one niemand
nobody niemand
noise Lärm, Geräusch
noisy laut
noon Mittag
north Norden; nördlich, Nord-, nordwärts
nose Nase
not nicht
not either auch nicht
not even nicht einmal
not yet noch nicht
note Notiz
to note notieren
nothing nichts
to notice; notice bemerken; Aushang, Kenntnis, Beachtung
now jetzt
nowadays heutzutage
nowhere nirgendwo
number Zahl, Nummer, Anzahl
nurse Krankenschwester
nursery school teacher Erzieher(in)

O

o'clock Uhr (Zeitangabe)
ocean Meer, Ozean
of course natürlich
off von ... weg, aus, weg
to offer; offer anbieten; Angebot
office Büro, Amt
often oft, häufig

oil Öl
old alt
on time pünktlich
once einmal, einst
only nur, erst
to open; open öffnen; offen, geöffnet
opinion Meinung
opposite Gegensatz
or oder
to order; order bestellen, befehlen; Bestellung, Befehl, Reihenfolge
organization Organisation
to organize organisieren
other andere(r, s)
out of work arbeitslos
outside Außenseite; draußen, außerhalb
to own; own besitzen; eigene(r, s)
owner Eigentümer(in)

P

to pack; pack packen; Packung
packet Paket
page Seite
to paint; paint malen; Farbe
pair Paar
paper Papier
parent Elternteil
to park; park parken; Park
part Teil
to pass vorbeigehen, (Prüfung) bestehen, (ein Gesetz) verabschieden, zupassen
passenger Passagier(in), Fahrgast
passport Pass
past Vergangenheit
to pay, (paid, paid); pay (be)zahlen; Lohn, Bezahlung
peace Friede
pen Stift, Füller
pence Plural von Penny
pencil Bleistift
penny Penny (engl. Münze)
people Leute, Volk
per cent Prozent
perfect vollkommen, perfekt
perhaps vielleicht
period Periode, Zeitraum, Schulstunde
personal persönlich
petrol Benzin
to phone; phone anrufen, telefonieren; Telefon
photograph Foto
to pick pflücken, wählen
to pick up nehmen, aufheben
picture Bild
piece Stück
pipe Pfeife, Röhre
to place; place stellen, legen; Platz, Ort, Stelle
to plan; plan planen; Plan
plane Flugzeug
to plant; plant pflanzen; Pflanze, Fabrikanlage
plate Teller, Platte, Schild
platform Bahnsteig, Plattform
to play; play spielen; (Schau-)Spiel
player Spieler(in)
playground Spielplatz
please bitte
pleasure Vergnügen
pocket Tasche
to point; point zeigen; Punkt
police Polizei
policeman Polizist
policewoman Polizistin
political politisch
politician Politiker(in)
politics Politik
to pollute verschmutzen
polluted verschmutzt
pollution Umweltverschmutzung
poor arm
popular beliebt, populär
population Bevölkerung
port Hafen
possibility Möglichkeit
possible möglich
post office Post
postcard Postkarte
postman Briefträger, Postbote
pot Topf
potato Kartoffel
pound Pfund
power Kraft, Energie, Strom
power station Kraftwerk
practice Übung
to practise üben
to prefer vorziehen
to prepare vorbereiten
to present; present vorstellen; Geschenk, Gegenwart; anwesend, gegenwärtig
to press; press drücken, pressen; Presse
pretty hübsch, ziemlich
price Preis
pride Stolz
prize Preis, Gewinn
probable wahrscheinlich
to produce produzieren, herstellen
producer Hersteller(in), Produzent(in)
product Produkt
production Herstellung, Produktion
to profit; profit profitieren; Gewinn
profitable rentabel, einträglich, lohnend
programme Programm, Sendung
to promise; promise versprechen; Versprechen
to pronounce aussprechen
pronunciation Aussprache
to protect schützen
protection Schutz
proud stolz
pub Kneipe
public Öffentlichkeit; öffentlich
to pull ziehen
pupil Schüler(in)
purpose Zweck, Absicht
to push; push schieben, stoßen; Stoß
to put, (put, put) setzen, stellen, legen
to put on anziehen, auftragen, aufsetzen
to put up (Hand) heben, bauen, aufstellen

Q

quality Qualität
quantity Menge
quarter Viertel
queen Königin
question Frage
quick schnell
quiet ruhig
quite ganz, ziemlich

R

railway Eisenbahn
to rain; rain regnen; Regen
to raise (hoch)heben, erheben, großziehen
rather ziemlich
to reach erreichen
to read, (read, read) lesen
reader Leser(in)
ready fertig, bereit
real wirklich
reality Wirklichkeit
reason Grund
reasonable vernünftig, günstig
to receive erhalten, bekommen
recent jüngst, kürzlich
reception Empfang
receptionist im Empfang arbeitende Person
to record; record aufnehmen; Rekord, Aufnahme, Schallplatte
red rot
regular regelmäßig
relative Verwandte(r); relativ
to relax entspannen, sich erholen
to remain bleiben
to remember sich erinnern an, daran denken
to remind (of) erinnern an
to rent; rent mieten, vermieten; Miete
to repair; repair reparieren; Reparatur
to repeat; repeat wiederholen; Wiederholung
to replace ersetzen
to reply; reply antworten; Antwort
to report; report berichten; Bericht
reputation Ansehen, Ruf
to rescue; rescue retten; Rettung
to rest; rest ruhen; Rest, Ruhe
to result; result resultieren; Ergebnis
to return; return zurückkommen; Rückkehr, Rückgabe
rich reich
to ride, (rode, ridden); ride reiten, fahren; Ritt, Fahrt
right richtig, rechts
to ring, (rang, rung); ring klingeln, anrufen; Ring, Anruf
to rise, (rose, risen); rise (auf)steigen, zunehmen; Aufstieg, Zunahme
river Fluss
road Straße
roof Dach
room Zimmer, Raum, Platz
round rund, herum

rubber (Radier-)Gummi
rubbish Abfall, Müll
to rule; rule herrschen; Regel
to run, (ran, run) laufen, rennen

S

sad traurig
safe sicher
safety Sicherheit
sale (Schluss-)Verkauf
salesman/woman Verkäufer(in)
salt Salz
same der-/die-/dasselbe, gleiche(r, s)
to save retten, sparen
to say, (said, said) sagen
school Schule
sea Meer
seat Sitz
second Sekunde; zweite(r, s)
secret Geheimnis; geheim
secretary Sekretär(in)
to see, (saw, seen) sehen, verstehen
to seem (er)scheinen
to sell, (sold, sold) verkaufen
seller Verkäufer(in)
to send, (sent, sent) schicken, senden
to sentence; sentence verurteilen; Satz, Urteil
serious ernst
to serve (be)dienen, servieren
to service; service (Auto) warten; Dienst, Betrieb
to set, (set, set) setzen, stellen, legen
several mehrere
shall sollen
to share; share teilen; Anteil
sheet Blatt, Bogen
shelf Regal
to shine, (shone, shone) scheinen, leuchten
to ship; ship verschicken; Schiff
shirt Hemd
shoe Schuh
shop Geschäft, Laden
shop assistant Verkäufer(in)
short kurz
should sollte(n)
shoulder Schulter
to shout rufen
to show, (showed, shown); show zeigen; Ausstellung, Vorstellung, Show
to shut, (shut, shut) schließen
sick krank
side Seite
sight Sicht, Anblick, Sehenswürdigkeit
to sign; sign unterschreiben; Zeichen
simple einfach
since seit
since then seitdem
to sing, (sang, sung) singen
sir Herr (Anrede)
sister Schwester
to sit, (sat, sat) sitzen
to sit down sich hinsetzen
size Größe
skill Fertigkeit, Fähigkeit, Können
skirt Rock
sky Himmel
to sleep, (slept, slept); sleep schlafen; Schlaf
slim schlank
slow langsam
to slow down verlangsamen
small klein
to smell, (smelt, smelt); smell riechen; Geruch
to smile; smile lächeln; Lächeln
to smoke; smoke rauchen; Rauch
to snow; snow schneien; Schnee
so far bisher, bis jetzt
soap Seife
soccer Fußball
sock Socke
soft weich
solution Lösung
to solve lösen
some einige, etwas
somebody jemand
someone jemand
something etwas
sometimes manchmal
son Sohn
song Lied
soon bald
sorry betrübt, tut mir Leid!, Entschuldigung!
to sound; sound klingen; Geräusch, Klang
south Süden; südlich, Süd-, südwärts
space Raum, Platz, Weltraum
spare time Freizeit
to speak, (spoke, spoken) sprechen
speaker Sprecher(in)
special besondere(r, s), spezielle(r, s)
speech Rede
speech bubble Sprechblase
to speed; speed schnell fahren; Geschwindigkeit
to speed up beschleunigen
to spell, (spelt, spelt); spell buchstabieren; Zauber(spruch)
to spend, (spent, spent) ausgeben, verbringen
spoon Löffel
spring Frühling, Quelle, Brunnen
staff Belegschaft, Kollegium
stamp Briefmarke
to stand, (stood, stood) stehen
to start; start anfangen, beginnen; Anfang
to state; state erklären, darlegen; Staat, Zustand
station Bahnhof
to stay bleiben
still dennoch, noch
stone Stein
to stop; stop beenden, anhalten, aufhören; Halt
to store; store lagern, speichern; *(AE)* Laden, Kaufhaus, Lager
storm Sturm
story Geschichte
strange merkwürdig
street Straße
to strike; strike streiken, schlagen; Streik, Treffer, Schlag
strong stark
to study; study studieren; Studium, Studie
subject Fach, Thema
suburb Vorort
to succeed (in) Erfolg haben (in, bei)
success Erfolg
successful erfolgreich
such solche(r, s)
sudden plötzliche(r, s)
sugar Zucker
to suit; suit passen; Anzug
suitcase Koffer
sum Summe
summer Sommer
sun Sonne
sunshine Sonnenschein
supermarket Supermarkt
supper Abendessen
to suppose annehmen, vermuten
sure sicher
to surprise; surprise überraschen; Überraschung
surprised überrascht
survey Überblick, Umfrage
sweet süß
to swim, (swam, swum) schwimmen
to switch; switch schalten, wechseln; Schalter

T

table Tisch, Tabelle
to take, (took, taken) nehmen
to take part in teilnehmen an
to take place stattfinden
to talk; talk reden, sprechen; Gespräch, Unterhaltung, Vortrag
tall hoch(gewachsen), groß
to taste; taste schmecken, probieren; Geschmack
tasty lecker
tax Steuer
tea Tee
to teach, (taught, taught) lehren, unterrichten
teacher Lehrer(in)
team Team, Mannschaft
technical technisch
technology Technik, Technologie
(tele)phone Telefon
television (TV) Fernsehen
to tell, (told, told) erzählen
terrible schrecklich, furchtbar
to test; test testen, überprüfen, untersuchen; Klassenarbeit, Versuch
than als
to thank danken, sich bedanken
that dass; jene(r, s), welche(r, s)
then dann, damals

there dort, da
there is/are es gibt
therefore deshalb
these diese
these days heutzutage
thick dick
thin dünn
thing Ding, Sache
to think, (thought, thought) denken, glauben, meinen
thirsty durstig
this diese(r, s)
those diese, jene
though obwohl, trotzdem
thousand Tausend
through durch
to throw, (threw, thrown) werfen
thus so
ticket Fahr-, Eintrittskarte
tidy ordentlich, aufgeräumt
till bis
time Zeit, Zeitdauer, Uhrzeit
times Mal(e)
tired müde
tobacco Tabak
today heute
toe Zeh
together zusammen
toilet Toilette
tomato Tomate
tomorrow morgen
tongue Zunge
tonight heute Abend
too auch
tool Werkzeug
tooth, teeth Zahn, Zähne
top Spitze, Top, Oberteil
tour (Rund-)Reise, Tour
toward(s) in Richtung
tower Turm
town Stadt
toy Spielzeug
to trade (in); trade handeln (mit); Gewerbe, Handwerk, Handel
traditional traditionell, herkömmlich
traffic Verkehr
traffic light(s) Ampel
to train; train ausbilden, trainieren, eine Ausbildung machen; Zug
training Ausbildung, Training
to translate übersetzen
translation Übersetzung
to transport; transport transportieren; Transport
to travel reisen, fahren
tree Baum
trip (Kurz-)Reise
trouble Schwierigkeit(en)
trousers Hose
true wahr, richtig
truth Wahrheit
to try; try versuchen; Versuch
to turn (sich) drehen, wenden
to turn left/right links/rechts abbiegen
to turn on/off ein-/ausschalten
to turn over umdrehen, überschlagen
twice zweimal
type Art, Typ
typewriter Schreibmaschine
typical typisch
typist Schreibkraft

U

umbrella Schirm
uncle Onkel
to understand, (understood, understood) verstehen
unemployed arbeitslos
unemployment Arbeitslosigkeit
unfortunate unglücklich
unfortunately leider
unfriendly unfreundlich
unhappy unglücklich
university Universität
until (till) bis
upon auf
upstairs (nach) oben, im Obergeschoss
to use gebrauchen
used gebraucht, gewohnt
useful nützlich
useless nutzlos
usual gewöhnlich

V

vacation *(AE)* Ferien
van Lieferwagen
vegetable(s) Gemüse
vehicle Fahrzeug
very sehr
village Dorf
to visit; visit besuchen; Besuch
visitor Besucher(in)
vocabulary Wortschatz, Vokabelverzeichnis
voice Stimme
to vote; vote abstimmen, wählen; Abstimmung, Stimme

W

to wait warten
waiter Kellner
waitress Kellnerin
to wake, (woke, woken) (up) wecken, aufwachen
to walk; walk gehen; Spaziergang
wall Wand, Mauer
to want wollen
war Krieg
warehouse Lager
to warm; warm wärmen; warm
to warn warnen
to wash waschen
washing machine Waschmaschine
to waste; waste verschwenden; Abfall, Verschwendung
to watch; watch beobachten, sehen; Uhr
water Wasser
way Weg, Art und Weise
weak schwach
to wear, (wore, worn) (Kleidung) tragen
weather Wetter
week Woche
weekend Wochenende
weight Gewicht
to welcome; welcome willkommen heißen, begrüßen; Willkommen, Empfang
well gut, gesund; na ja …
well-known bekannt
west Westen, westlich, West-, westwärts
wet nass, feucht
what was
what about . . . was ist mit …
what else was noch
what . . . for wofür, wozu
wheel Rad
when wann
where wo
whether ob
which welche(r, s)
while während
white weiß
who wer
whole ganz
whom wem, wen
whose wessen
why warum
wide weit
wife (wives) Ehefrau(en)
will werden; Wille
to win, (won, won) gewinnen
window Fenster
wine Wein
to wish; wish wünschen; Wunsch
within innerhalb
without ohne
woman (women) Frau (Frauen)
wonderful wunderbar
wood Holz, Wald
wool Wolle
word Wort
to work; work arbeiten; Arbeit
worker Arbeiter(in)
world Welt
worse schlechter
worst am schlechtesten
worth wert
to write, (wrote, written) schreiben
writer Verfasser(in), Schriftsteller(in)
wrong falsch

Y

year Jahr
yellow gelb
yesterday gestern
yet jedoch, schon
you're welcome gern geschehen!
young jung
youth Jugend

Bildquellennachweis **4** iStockphoto (Andrey Tsidvintsev), Calgary, Alberta; **4** iStockphoto (Chris Schmidt), Calgary, Alberta; **4** Klett-Archiv, Stuttgart; **5** Fotolia LLC (Olga Khoroshunova), New York; **5** Fotolia LLC (Monkey Business), New York; **5** iStockphoto (Ana Abejon), Calgary, Alberta; **6** Fotolia LLC (Yuri Arcurs), New York; **6** Thinkstock (Digital Vision), München; **8** Fotolia LLC (Mark Stout), New York; **8** shutterstock (fotum), New York, NY; **8** iStockphoto (Rich Legg), Calgary, Alberta; **8** shutterstock (Yurchyks), New York, NY; **8** Dream Maker Software (RF), Colorado; **10** iStockphoto (René Mansi), Calgary, Alberta; **10** iStockphoto (Anastasia Pelikh), Calgary, Alberta; **10** JupiterImages photos.com (photos.com), Tucson, AZ; **10** iStockphoto (Anton Gvozdikov), Calgary, Alberta; **10** shutterstock (Lorraine Swanson), New York, NY; **10** iStockphoto (Chris Bernard), Calgary, Alberta; **11** iStockphoto (VMJones), Calgary, Alberta; **12** Fotosearch Stock Photography, Waukesha, WI; **12** iStockphoto (Mehmet Salih), Calgary, Alberta; **14** iStockphoto (Sean Locke), Calgary, Alberta; **14** iStockphoto (Oleg Prikhodko), Calgary, Alberta; **15** Dreamstime LLC (Gino Santa Maria), Brentwood, TN; **15** shutterstock (Andrejs Pidjass), New York, NY; **15** shutterstock (Tracy Whiteside), New York, NY; **15** iStockphoto (Jacob Wackerhausen), Calgary, Alberta; **15** shutterstock (zerra), New York, NY; **15** iStockphoto (Lise Gagne), Calgary, Alberta; **16** iStockphoto (Joris van Caspel), Calgary, Alberta; **16** shutterstock (Andy Lim), New York, NY; **16** Fotolia LLC (richard villalon), New York; **16** Fotolia LLC (endostock), New York; **16** shutterstock (Jason Stitt), New York, NY; **17** iStockphoto (Duncan Walker), Calgary, Alberta; **18** BigStockPhoto.com (starfotograf), Davis, CA; **20** Klett-Archiv (A. Raftaki), Stuttgart; **21** iStockphoto (Sean Locke), Calgary, Alberta; **22** iStockphoto (Jacob Wackerhausen), Calgary, Alberta; **22** Dreamstime LLC (Koh Sze Kiat), Brentwood, TN; **22** Fotolia LLC (AVAVA), New York; **22** shutterstock (Losevsky Pavel), New York, NY; **23** iStockphoto (nullplus), Calgary, Alberta; **23** iStockphoto (Neustockimages), Calgary, Alberta; **23** Avenue Images GmbH (Brand X pictures), Hamburg; **24** Fotolia LLC (Yuri Arcurs), New York; **24** Fotolia LLC (Sandor Jackal), New York; **24** iStockphoto (Zsolt Nyulaszi), Calgary, Alberta; **25** Avenue Images GmbH (Image Source), Hamburg; **27** iStockphoto (VanDenEsker), Calgary, Alberta; **28** Fotolia LLC (mangostock), New York; **29** iStockphoto (RF/Alex Brosa), Calgary, Alberta; **30** iStockphoto (Olivier Blondeau), Calgary, Alberta; **30** iStockphoto (Can Balcioglu), Calgary, Alberta; **30** iStockphoto (Oks_Mit), Calgary, Alberta; **30** shutterstock (Maksim Shmeljov), New York, NY; **30** shutterstock (JustASC), New York, NY; **31** Greenpeace, Hamburg; **33** Fotolia LLC (Joanna Zielinska), New York; **34** Thinkstock (iStockphoto), München; **35** Dreamstime LLC (Monkey Business Images), Brentwood, TN; **37** iStockphoto (Jeff McDonald), Calgary, Alberta; **37** iStockphoto (Jorge Delgado), Calgary, Alberta; **37** iStockphoto (Damir Karan), Calgary, Alberta; **37** Avenue Images GmbH (stock disc), Hamburg; **38** iStockphoto (Andrey Tsidvintsev), Calgary, Alberta; **39** www.cartoonstock.com (ahun20), Bath; **39** www.cartoonstock.com (Slane, Chris), Bath; **39** BigStockPhoto.com (PCUMMINGS), Davis, CA; **39** iStockphoto (RUDI TAPPER), Calgary, Alberta; **40** BigStockPhoto.com (lephotography), Davis, CA; **40** shutterstock (Khafizov Ivan Harisovich), New York, NY; **40** Interfoto (Archiv Friedrich), München; **40** iStockphoto (Wouter van Caspel), Calgary, Alberta; **42** Wikimedia Foundation Inc. (PD), St. Petersburg FL; **43** Corbis (Eric Robert/Sygma), Düsseldorf; **44** iStockphoto (Roberto A Sanchez), Calgary, Alberta; **45** iStockphoto (Carmen Martínez Banús), Calgary, Alberta; **45** iStockphoto (Greg Nicholas), Calgary, Alberta; **46** Cagle Cartoons (Dave Granlund), Santa Barbara, CA; **46** shutterstock (Monkey Business Images), New York, NY; **47** iStockphoto (Chris Schmidt), Calgary, Alberta; **48** www.cartoonstock.com (Hawkins, Len), Bath; **48** www.cartoonstock.com (Eales, Stan), Bath; **48** www.cartoonstock.com (Baldwin, Mike), Bath; **50** iStockphoto (JasonRWarren), Calgary, Alberta; **51** Fotolia LLC (Michal Adamczyk), New York; **52** iStockphoto (Dan Barnes), Calgary, Alberta; **52** iStockphoto (Joanna Pecha), Calgary, Alberta; **54** shutterstock (Losevsky Pavel), New York, NY; **55** iStockphoto (Sean Locke), Calgary, Alberta; **55** Fotolia LLC (Olga Khoroshunova), New York; **55** Klett-Archiv (Renate Weber), Stuttgart; **55** Fotolia LLC (BVDC), New York; **55** iStockphoto (Dan Chippendale), Calgary, Alberta; **56** iStockphoto (Hans F. Meier), Calgary, Alberta; **56** shutterstock (Colin Stitt), New York, NY; **56** shutterstock (ND Johnston), New York, NY; **56** Fotolia LLC (Otmar Smit), New York; **57** shutterstock (yvon52), New York, NY; **59** iStockphoto (Mostafa Hefni), Calgary, Alberta; **59** iStockphoto (Christopher O Driscoll), Calgary, Alberta; **62** Fotolia LLC (Rohit Seth), New York; **62** iStockphoto (Huchen Lu), Calgary, Alberta; **62** iStockphoto (VikramRaghuvanshi), Calgary, Alberta; **62** Fotolia LLC (Galina Barskaya), New York; **62** shutterstock (niderlander), New York, NY; **62** Dreamstime LLC (Nikhil Gangavane), Brentwood, TN; **62** Fotolia LLC (Lario Tus), New York; **63** Cagle Cartoons (John Darkow), Santa Barbara, CA; **64** shutterstock (John Hoffman), New York, NY; **64** laif (Sasse), Köln; **64** shutterstock (Fernando Rodrigues), New York, NY; **65** Fotolia LLC (pressmaster), New York; **66** Kessler-Medien, Saarbrücken; **66** Dreamstime LLC (Debra James), Brentwood, TN; **67** Fotolia LLC (Franz Pfluegl), New York; **68** shutterstock (Sharon K. Andrews), New York, NY; **68** Corbis (Pablo Corral V), Düsseldorf; **70** Fotolia LLC (Monkey Business), New York; **70** iStockphoto (RF/Celso Pupo Rodrigues), Calgary, Alberta; **72** shutterstock (Rafael Ramirez Lee), New York, NY; **72** iStockphoto (René Mansi), Calgary, Alberta; **72** shutterstock (Kevin Britland), New York, NY; **72** iStockphoto (Ana Abejon), Calgary, Alberta; **73** Dreamstime LLC (Nikhil Gangavane), Brentwood, TN; **73** iStockphoto (Miodrag Gajic), Calgary, Alberta; **73** Fotolia LLC (pressmaster), New York; **73** Fotolia LLC (kristian sekulic), New York; **74** iStockphoto (Andrew Rich), Calgary, Alberta; **75** shutterstock (Blazej Maksym), New York, NY; **75** iStockphoto (Jacom Stephens), Calgary, Alberta; **76** Dreamstime LLC (Zdravko Bajazek), Brentwood, TN; **76** Fotolia LLC (CROSS DESIGN), New York; **78** shutterstock (photo25th), New York, NY; **78** iStockphoto (Jessica Liu), Calgary, Alberta; **78** Picture-Alliance (dpa), Frankfurt; **78** TransFair e.V., Köln; **78** www.cartoonstock.com (Lynch, Mark), Bath; **79** Fotolia LLC (Andre Bonn), New York; **79** shutterstock (Olga Lyubkina), New York, NY; **79** iStockphoto (Dušan Zidar), Calgary, Alberta; **80** United Nations Photo Library, New York; **81** Geoatlas, Hendaye; **82** iStockphoto (Duncan Walker), Calgary, Alberta; **82** Fotolia LLC (Loic LE BRUSQ), New York; **83** Dreamstime LLC (Darren Robertson), Brentwood, TN; **83** shutterstock (Estelle), New York, NY; **84** iStockphoto (Joseph C. Justice Jr.), Calgary, Alberta; **84** Corbis (Patsy Lynch/Retna Ltd.), Düsseldorf; **84** iStockphoto (Lisa F. Young), Calgary, Alberta; **86** www.cartoonstock.com (RGJ -Richard Jolley), Bath; **87** Photographic service of the Council of the EU © European Communities; **88** iStockphoto (Martin McCarthy), Calgary, Alberta; **88** iStockphoto (Kimberly Cubero), Calgary, Alberta; **88** iStockphoto (Frances Twitty), Calgary, Alberta; **88** iStockphoto (Oleg Prikhodko), Calgary, Alberta; **88** iStockphoto (Julie Ridge), Calgary, Alberta; **88** Thinkstock (Digital Vision), München; **90** iStockphoto (Charlotte Allen), Calgary, Alberta; **90** iStockphoto (Dori OConnell), Calgary, Alberta; **90** iStockphoto (MARIA TOUTOUDAKI), Calgary, Alberta; **90** iStockphoto (Adam Kazmierski), Calgary, Alberta; **91** iStockphoto (Dmitriy Shironosov), Calgary, Alberta; **92** Fotolia LLC (pressmaster), New York; **92** iStockphoto (Jacom Stephens), Calgary, Alberta; **95** Thinkstock (Digital Vision), München; **96** shutterstock (Marcel Mooij), New York, NY; **96** shutterstock (Andresr), New York, NY; **97** iStockphoto (Olga Utlyakova), Calgary, Alberta; **97** iStockphoto (tracy lorna), Calgary, Alberta; **97** iStockphoto (mark wragg), Calgary, Alberta; **97** iStockphoto (dobri dobrinov), Calgary, Alberta; **98** iStockphoto (Timothy Large), Calgary, Alberta; **98** shutterstock (Vibrant Image Studio), New York, NY; **98** Dreamstime LLC (Kasiden), Brentwood, TN; **99** Fotosearch Stock Photography (Banana Stock), Waukesha, WI; **99** Thinkstock (Rayes), München; **100** Fotolia LLC (Jan Rose), New York; **100** iStockphoto (Angus Forbes), Calgary, Alberta; **100** iStockphoto (Marcus Lindström), Calgary, Alberta; **100** iStockphoto (Jan Rose), Calgary, Alberta; **101** iStockphoto (ene), Calgary, Alberta; **101** iStockphoto (JohnnyGreig), Calgary, Alberta; **101** Fotolia LLC (Christelle), New York; **104** BigStockPhoto.com (stvan4245), Davis, CA; **106** shutterstock (Mikhail Olykainen), New York, NY; **107** www.cartoonstock.com (Mosedale, Mike), Bath; **108** Corbis (James Leynse), Düsseldorf; **110** Fotolia LLC (Rob), New York; **111** www.cartoonstock.com (Bacall, Aaron), Bath; **112** iStockphoto (mandygodbehear), Calgary, Alberta; **114** iStockphoto (Piotr Marcinski), Calgary, Alberta; **115** www.cartoonstock.com (Fischer, Ed), Bath; **116** Dreamstime LLC (Paul Hakimata), Brentwood, TN; **118** shutterstock (Tim Jenner), New York, NY; **119** www.cartoonstock.com (Martin, John), Bath; **119** www.flaggen-server.de; **120** Thinkstock (Jupiterimages), München; **123** www.cartoonstock.com (Stik -Bill Greenhead), Bath; **124** iStockphoto (Cliff Parnell), Calgary, Alberta; **126** iStockphoto (rollover), Calgary, Alberta; **127** www.cartoonstock.com (Greenberg, Steve), Bath; **128** Klett-Archiv, Stuttgart; **128** BBC Information and archives, London; **129** BBC Information and archives, London; **130** BBC Information and archives, London; **131** Klett-Archiv, Stuttgart; **131** BBC Information and archives, London; **136** Avenue Images GmbH (Fancy), Hamburg; **136** Thinkstock (James Woodson), München; **136** Thinkstock (George Doyle), München; **137** Dreamstime LLC (Jeremyrichards), Brentwood, TN; **137** Thinkstock (Digital Vision), München; **139** iStockphoto (René Mansi), Calgary, Alberta; **141** iStockphoto (kzenon), Calgary, Alberta; **141** Thinkstock (Digital Vision), München; **143** iStockphoto (Justin Horrocks), Calgary, Alberta; **143** Thinkstock (iStockphoto), München; **145** Thinkstock (Jupiterimages, Brand X Pictures), München; **147** Thinkstock (Jupiterimages), München; **147** Avenue Images GmbH (Fancy), Hamburg; **150** iStockphoto (Nigel Carse), Calgary, Alberta; **152** Thinkstock (iStockphoto), München; **154** iStockphoto (Aleksandar Nakic), Calgary, Alberta; **158** BigStockPhoto.com (Yuri_Arcurs), Davis, CA; **161** iStockphoto (blackred), Calgary, Alberta; **170** shutterstock (Jason Stitt), New York, NY; **172** iStockphoto (Rich Legg), Calgary, Alberta; **174** iStockphoto (lana13r), Calgary, Alberta; **176** Fotolia LLC (Robert Cocquyt), New York; **179** iStockphoto (Chris Schmidt), Calgary, Alberta; **181** Avenue Images GmbH (Fancy), Hamburg; **183** iStockphoto (Chris Schmidt), Calgary, Alberta; **185** Thinkstock (iStockphoto), München; **207** Klett-Archiv, Stuttgart; **COVER** Corbis (Bilderbuch/Design Pics), Düsseldorf; **COVER** DHBW, Stuttgart

Sollte es in einem Einzelfall nicht gelungen sein, den korrekten Rechteinhaber ausfindig zu machen, so werden berechtigte Ansprüche selbstverständlich im Rahmen der üblichen Regelungen abgegolten.